COMMUNAL SOLIDARITY

STUDIES IN IMMIGRATION AND CULTURE

ISSN 1914-1459

ROYDEN LOEWEN, SERIES EDITOR

16 *Communal Solidarity: Immigration, Settlement, and Social Welfare in Winnipeg's Jewish Community, 1882–1930*, by Arthur Ross
15 *Czech Refugees in Cold War Canada: 1945–1989*, by Jan Raska
14 *Holocaust Survivors in Canada: Exclusion, Inclusion, Transformation, 1947–1955*, by Adara Goldberg
13 *Transnational Radicals: Italian Anarchists in Canada and the U.S., 1915–1940*, by Travis Tomchuk
12 *Invisible Immigrants: The English in Canada since 1945*, by Marilyn Barber and Murray Watson
11 *The Showman and the Ukrainian Cause: Folk Dance, Film, and the Life of Vasile Avramenko*, by Orest T. Martynowych
10 *Young, Well-Educated, and Adaptable: Chilean Exiles in Ontario and Quebec, 1973–2010*, by Francis Peddie
9 *The Search for a Socialist El Dorado: Finnish Immigration to Soviet Karelia from the United States and Canada in the 1930s*, by Alexey Golubev and Irina Takala
8 *Rewriting the Break Event: Mennonites and Migration in Canadian Literature*, by Robert Zacharias
7 *Ethnic Elites and Canadian Identity: Japanese, Ukrainians, and Scots, 1919–1971*, by Aya Fujiwara
6 *Community and Frontier: A Ukrainian Settlement in the Canadian Parkland*, by John C. Lehr
5 *Storied Landscapes: Ethno-Religious Identity and the Canadian Prairies*, by Frances Swyripa
4 *Families, Lovers, and Their Letters: Italian Postwar Migration to Canada*, by Sonia Cancian
3 *Sounds of Ethnicity: Listening to German North America, 1850–1914*, by Barbara Lorenzkowski
2 *Mennonite Women in Canada: A History*, by Marlene Epp
1 *Imagined Homes: Soviet German Immigrants in Two Cities*, by Hans Werner

COMMUNAL SOLIDARITY

Immigration, Settlement, and Social Welfare in Winnipeg's Jewish Community, 1882–1930

ARTHUR ROSS

Communal Solidarity: Immigration, Settlement, and Social Welfare in
Winnipeg's Jewish Community, 1882–1930

23 22 21 20 19 1 2 3 4 5

University of Manitoba Press
Winnipeg, Manitoba, Canada
Treaty 1 Territory
uofmpress.ca

Cataloguing data available from Library and Archives Canada
Studies in Immigration and Culture, ISSN ISSN 1914-1459; 16
ISBN 978-0-88755-837-5 (PAPER)
ISBN 978-0-88755-577-0 (PDF)
ISBN 978-0-88755-575-6 (EPUB)

Cover images: Courtesy of Author
Cover design John van der Woude
Interior design by Karen Armstrong

Printed in Canada

The University of Manitoba Press acknowledges the financial support for its publication program provided by the Government of Canada through the Canada Book Fund, the Canada Council for the Arts, the Manitoba Department of Sport, Culture, and Heritage, the Manitoba Arts Council, and the Manitoba Book Publishing Tax Credit.

Funded by the Government of Canada | Canadä

To Kathy

CONTENTS

INTRODUCTION

Between 1882 and 1914, approximately 7,300 Jewish immigrants from the Pale of Settlement in Tsarist Russia settled in Winnipeg. Their decision to travel across an unfamiliar continent, embark on a difficult and lengthy transatlantic journey, and finally make their way to an unknown city thousands of kilometres from their port of entry was motivated by harsh necessity. Fleeing destitution, state persecution, and sporadic but increasingly murderous pogroms, emigration was a calculated risk. However, the estimated 2 million Jews who left the Pale of Settlement for the United States or Canada between 1882 and 1914 understood that, if they remained in Tsarist Russia, they had little prospect of improving their lives and would continue to endure unremitting hardship.[1] They also knew that the traditional leaders of Jewish communities in the Pale of Settlement were incapable of either protecting them from oppressive state policies or alleviating their poverty. For those who made the difficult decision to emigrate, hopelessness outweighed the uncertainties of migration. After they arrived in Winnipeg, their previous experiences shaped their settlement, the process of finding a means of earning a living, and their founding of new Jewish communal institutions in an alien urban society. Freed from the social, economic, and legal constraints that had impoverished them and thwarted their ambitions, they were determined to earn a living either by finding the same type of work or by reinventing themselves, embracing new skills or occupations to take advantage of the diverse employment and business opportunities offered by Winnipeg's burgeoning market economy. Similarly, no longer bound by the constraints of traditional Jewish communal authority, having been exposed in Tsarist Russia to the diverse social and political manifestations of a growing debate on Jewish emancipation, they were predisposed to take advantage of Canada's liberal democratic freedoms to establish new forms of communal governance.

In *Canada's Jews: A People's Journey*, Gerald Tulchinsky writes that the history of Canadian Jewish life contains elements of continuity and change.[2] In 1902, two decades after the arrival of approximately 360 Jewish refugees from Tsarist Russia (the beginning of an influx of Jews from the Pale of Settlement that laid the demographic foundation of Winnipeg's Jewish community), 182 Jewish immigrants arrived in the city and exited the Canadian Pacific Railway station to begin their new lives in Canada. The vast majority gravitated to the North End, the district where close to 89 percent of Winnipeg's Jews lived. After an arduous journey and the confusion and frustration of having to deal with railway, steamship, and government officials who gave instructions or interrogated them in languages that they did not understand, they were relieved to find themselves once again in familiar surroundings, an ethnic enclave of 1,157 Jews who conversed in their own language, Yiddish.[3]

The immigrants quickly discovered that, much like the *shtetlekh*, the small Jewish villages and towns that they had left behind, life in Winnipeg's small Jewish community revolved around religious observance. By 1902, the community supported three synagogues. They provided Jewish immigrants not only with the comfort of a spiritual home, a place of worship where they could once again recite the familiar prayers and observe the religious holidays that had been an integral part of their communal life in the Pale of Settlement, but also membership in a congregation enabled them to make new friends and participate in social events such as weddings and celebrations of Jewish festivals such as Purim and Hanukkah. For the Jewish immigrants who established Winnipeg's first synagogues, religious observance provided spiritual sustenance and an institutional base that enabled them to maintain their identities and adapt to an alien and often hostile society. In addition, as the only major institutions that had been established in the Jewish community, synagogues became forums for discussing communal affairs and safeguarding the welfare of its most vulnerable members. Throughout the early history of this community, synagogues provided an organizational platform to establish charities that dispensed assistance to destitute members of the community.

But reminiscent of the religious disputes that had disrupted Jewish communities throughout the Pale of Settlement, beginning in 1883 the synagogue congregations of Winnipeg's Jewish community engaged in a series of bitter disagreements that divided the community, drained its financial resources, and undermined its capacity to raise money to protect its vulnerable members. As the leaders of the community—men whose wealth enabled them to make substantial donations to synagogue building funds—organized factions that competed with one another to promote the legitimacy of one form of religious observance at the expense of all others, their quarrelsome behaviour was an unwelcome reminder for many immigrants of how the rabbinate and men of wealth and privilege had dominated communal governance in the Pale of Settlement. Beginning in 1903, Jewish newcomers resolved to separate the provision of social welfare from religious adherence. Rejecting the prevailing synagogue-based practice of dispensing charity, a form of social welfare that divided members of the Jewish community into donors who made decisions about who was deserving and what they were entitled to receive and powerless supplicants who depended on their benevolence, these new immigrants began to establish mutual aid societies, organizations based upon egalitarian principles of communal solidarity. Implementing principles of self-help and reciprocal responsibility, mutual aid societies dealt with the pervasive problem of economic insecurity by providing financial benefits to their members free of the stigma of charity.

The organization of mutual aid societies accelerated the development of a vibrant public sphere in Winnipeg's Jewish community in which decisions about the provision of social welfare were made democratically based upon the authority and participation of the people. As Tulchinsky notes, the adoption of democratic forms of communal governance by mutual aid societies led to the birth of a "new Jewish society" in Winnipeg. Referring to the "chaotically democratic meetings, fraught with pressing needs," held by mutual aid societies, he states that "from this convocation of old East European communities there emerged a Winnipeg Jewry, schooled in communal governance and experienced in the practicalities of self-help."[4] Supported by the waves of Jewish immigrants who settled in Winnipeg after 1900, part of a generation of Jews who had come of age during the modernization of Jewish communal governance in the Pale of Settlement, communal debates on and discussions of issues and problems of concern to the Jewish community quickly shifted from religious congregations to the public sphere, the common ground of public meetings and gatherings of members of mutual aid societies.

By the 1920s, the adoption of a secular, democratic form of communal governance had transformed Winnipeg's Jewish community. Building upon the democratic practices adopted by mutual aid societies, beginning in 1911 the public sphere became a forum for debates on, and ratification and implementation of, a series of secular initiatives to establish a system of social welfare for vulnerable members of the community. The successful launch of each initiative depended on securing a public mandate, a resolution approved by an open assembly of members of the Jewish community granting its supporters the authority to establish an institution or organization. Within four years, destitute Jews could turn to a communal charity for assistance, an orphanage that provided care for dependent children, and a home that housed the elderly. As the number of Jewish immigrants arriving in Winnipeg steadily increased, in 1912 communal activists expanded the scope of social welfare services by organizing an immigrant aid society. Until the First World War brought transatlantic immigration to Canada to an end, this society assisted immigrants by providing inexpensive meals for them, helping them to find employment and accommodation, and holding English-language classes.

As the First World War engulfed their former homes in the Pale of Settlement, Winnipeg's Jews became aware that hundreds of thousands of Jews, including many friends and members of their families, had become civilian casualties of war or victims of forced displacements, homelessness, epidemics, and hunger. In 1914, the leaders of the North End Relief Society, the Jewish community's largest communal charity, held a fundraising drive to assist Jews living in the Eastern European war zone. This effort culminated in the formation of an aid organization that became part of an international effort to alleviate the suffering of Eastern European Jews. By raising money to assist war victims in Eastern Europe, communal activists added an international dimension to the Winnipeg Jewish community's system of social welfare. These activists expected that the Canadian government would once again adopt an "open door" policy on immigration after the war, and when it became increasingly difficult to distribute aid to war victims they shifted their attention to assisting immigrants, helping family members and relatives who had been prevented from emigrating because of the war to come to Canada, and rescuing refugees from the former Russian Empire stranded in Europe. In 1920, members of Winnipeg's Jewish community enthusiastically supported the transformation of the immigrant aid society into the Winnipeg branch of a new national organization, the Jewish Immigrant Aid Society of Canada. Once again Winnipeg's Jewish community became part of an international effort to assist Eastern European Jews by resettling as many as possible in Canada.

The establishment of an institution that provided free medical care completed the development of the Winnipeg Jewish community's system of social welfare. Established in 1926, the Mount Carmel Clinic was founded upon the principle, first established by mutual aid societies that provided medical benefits, and after 1915 developed by the Winnipeg Hebrew Free Dispensary, that access to physicians' services and medication should be based upon medical need rather than the ability to pay. The clinic, which provided by 1927 medical care to approximately 20 percent of Winnipeg's Jewish community, exemplified the essential features of communal solidarity. Managed by a large board of directors elected by and accountable to its 2,000 members, and supported by twelve affiliated mutual aid societies, the clinic was staffed by twenty physicians and dentists who donated their time and expertise.[5] Both the construction of the clinic and the annual operating budget were funded by membership dues and fundraising campaigns that solicited thousands of donations throughout the Jewish community. The volunteers who served on the clinic's board of directors, its medical staff, and the hundreds of members who solicited donations in annual fundraising drives believed that Winnipeg's Jewish community had a collective responsibility to provide the best possible health-care services to its members. If these services were available to those who could pay for them, then they should be available to all; collective action could overcome income-based inequalities that determined who could or could not afford to see a physician or purchase medicine and ensure that no one was denied medical treatment because he or she could not afford to pay for it.

This study of the formation of Winnipeg's Jewish community examines the achievements of a remarkable generation of immigrants. In addition to documenting the organizational histories of the societies, institutions, and organizations that they created, the study explores how their beliefs about communal solidarity shaped both their understanding of community life and their decisions about their collective future. This book is also a testimonial to the determination of innumerable communal activists—since so many records, particularly of mutual aid societies, have been lost, too few of them could be identified—to build a Jewish community that not only assumed collective responsibility for the welfare of each member but also contributed to international efforts to aid Jews in Eastern Europe. Their debates on who had the authority to act in the name of the Jewish community—networks of Jewish notables or democratically elected communal activists—and how they resolved conflicts over communal governance provide insights into the complex dynamics of the settlement and integration of Jewish immigrants in Canada's third largest city at the time. Above all, this study seeks to honour the dedication, resourcefulness, and organizational enterprise of the Jewish immigrants who self-confidently carved out a public sphere in an alien and often hostile British Canadian society to create the better world that they dreamed of when they made the momentous decision to emigrate from the Pale of Settlement in Tsarist Russia and other countries in Eastern Europe.

CHAPTER 1

Jewish Life in the Pale of Settlement

A majority of the Jewish immigrants who settled in Winnipeg before the First World War emigrated from the southern and southwestern provinces of the Pale of Settlement of Tsarist Russia.[1] Established in 1835, the Pale of Settlement was a vast region of fifteen *gubernii* or "provinces" comprising the western borderlands of the Russian Empire (parts of the Baltic region, Lithuania, Belorussia, Ukraine, Bessarabia, and "New Russia," the three southern provinces of Kherson, Ekaterinoslav, and Taurida). In 1881, when Jews living in the Pale became the targets of widespread outbreaks of violence, the pogroms that precipitated the emigration of the first contingent of Russian Jews who settled in Winnipeg, an estimated 2.9 million Jews or 94.6 percent of the total Jewish population of the Russian Empire (excluding the Kingdom of Poland), lived in the fifteen provinces of the Pale.[2]

As the Russian state pursued its goal of modernizing and industrializing the Russian economy, it subjected Jews confined in the Pale to a "program of social engineering," a series of laws, proclamations, and administrative rulings designed to segregate Russian Jews from the Christian majority, regulate and limit their role in the economy, and prevent them from migrating to centres of economic growth.[3] Successive tsars and state officials perceived the presence of a large Jewish community within the Russian Empire that stubbornly adhered to its "alien" religious beliefs and traditions as a threat to Russian society. Judeophobia, the identification and treatment of Jews as the alien "other," a community based upon religious beliefs that were an affront to Christianity and whose members exploited the Russian people, permeated the Russian state, church hierarchy, and general population. By 1881, only a few Jews, approximately 53,000 or 1.7 percent of the Jewish population of European Russia, were able to live in the thirty-five *gubernii* outside the Pale.[4] Coveted residence permits were granted to a select number of economically productive or useful Jews—wealthy merchants, members of tightly regulated artisan guilds, and university-educated professionals—as well as retired soldiers who, having completed their compulsory military service, had demonstrated their loyalty to the tsar.

With the exception of this small, carefully regulated minority, the Jewish population of European Russia was compelled by law to endure economic segregation and marginalization within the Pale of Settlement, where they shared a "single caste-like status."[5] According to one estimate of the occupational profiles of the Jewish community within the Pale, 16,847 Jews could be considered members of the bourgeoisie, and approximately 40,000 were factory workers, emerging class formations characteristic of a nineteenth-century European society undergoing industrialization.[6] With the exception of this small working class, and by 1900, 97,000 Jewish agriculturalists, the overwhelming majority of economically active Jews were engaged in pre-industrial artisan production or the provision of services and unskilled labour, or they were petty traders and small merchants.[7] The success of these economic pursuits, and therefore the viability of Jewish communities in cities and small towns and villages or *shtetlekh* where most Jews resided, ultimately depended on the purchasing power of rural peasants and trade with larger urban centres in the Pale.[8]

However, neither local nor regional markets generated sufficient incomes; although the agricultural sector employed over half of the Russian workforce, low productivity and surplus agricultural labour depressed incomes and impoverished peasants, and small-scale, labour-intensive, craft-based manufacturers struggled to compete with factories outside the Pale that benefited from the introduction of technologies of mass production and an emerging railway network that distributed low-cost consumer goods. Confined in hundreds of small communities throughout the Pale in a stagnating, highly regulated regional economy, Jews were forced to engage in injurious competition either to sell goods in local markets at modest profit margins or to sell goods, labour, or services within their communities to equally impecunious Jews.

Competition to earn a living was exacerbated by demographic pressures. Between 1825 and 1880, the Jewish population of the Pale grew by nearly 150 percent, increasing from approximately 1.2 million to nearly 3 million, compared with an 87 percent increase in the total population.[9] This dramatic natural increase was the result of early marriages, relatively high birth rates, and declining death rates, particularly infant and child mortality, almost 50 percent lower than the overall rate in European Russia.[10] A distinctive feature of the growth of the Jewish community was the high proportion of children: approximately half of the Jewish population was under the age of nineteen.[11] Such a large proportion of dependent children severely strained limited family resources and increased the pressure on women and youth to augment family incomes. High rates of female participation in the labour force and a constant stream of young people attempting to contribute to family incomes intensified competition to earn a livelihood and further undermined the economic viability of marginal Jewish communities struggling to survive in the stagnating economy of the Pale.[12]

By the second half of the nineteenth century, Jewish communities in the Pale of Settlement experienced widespread underemployment and unemployment. Estimates suggest that the survival of nearly 40 percent of Jewish families depended on the inadequate earnings of unskilled workers without an occupation or capital who relied on irregular employment.[13] Statistical evidence is fragmentary, but the chronic destitution of the Jewish community in the second half of the nineteenth century was evident in contemporary studies by both Russian and foreign observers.[14] Approximately one-third of the Jewish population lived in abject poverty with inadequate food, shelter, and clothing, and the remainder struggled to maintain modest and insecure incomes in an economy beset by periodic and lengthy depressions that increased unemployment.[15]

The Jewish community's marginal and precarious existence in the Pale of Settlement was further jeopardized by the Russian state's reaction to the outbreak in 1881 of anti-Jewish pogroms following the assassination of Tsar Alexander II. Between April 1881 and June 1884, three waves of riotous assaults on Jewish communities in 259 cities, towns, and villages resulted in widespread injuries, deaths, and the destruction of hundreds of millions of rubles of property.[16] Tsar Alexander III and his advisors concluded that the most effective way to deal with social unrest and restore public order was to blame the victims of the pogroms. The new tsar chose Nikolai Ignatiev to devise and implement a strategy to restore and aggressively expand autocratic authority to contain social changes that had created unrest among the Russian masses and threatened to undermine the state. Appointed minister of the interior and head of the Council of Ministers in May 1881, Ignatiev acted decisively to attribute the violence and instability to the Jews' exploitation of the Russian people.[17]

In 1882, Ignatiev's ministry implemented the "May Laws," a sustained legal assault on a traumatized Jewish community that continued until the overthrow of the tsar in 1917. Expanded by subsequent revisions and additions and subject to arbitrary enforcement, the May Laws intensified the legal encirclement and economic marginalization of Russia's Jewish community. In the following decade, tens of thousands of Jews were expelled from major centres of economic growth such as Moscow, Saint Petersburg, Kharkov, and Kiev; retired soldiers were no longer allowed to live outside the Pale of Settlement; residency restrictions were vigorously enforced throughout the Pale; and the government targeted "some 580,000" Jews for expulsion from the countryside, forcing them to live in small towns and villages, an edict that limited their mobility and economic opportunities.[18] Police harassment, periodic roundups of illegal residents, expulsion orders, and arrests for violations of laws governing travel and residence permits became permanent features of government policy, making earning an adequate income even more precarious and causing widespread personal hardship as families were summarily displaced and divided.[19]

Additional state measures restricted access to secondary and postsecondary education, which offered small numbers of Jewish youth an avenue of occupational mobility and an opportunity to secure residence rights outside the Pale of Settlement. In 1887, the government established a *numerus clausus* for secondary schools and universities.[20] Jewish student enrolment in universities, which had increased from 129 in 1865 to 1,856 in 1886, declined dramatically; between 1886 and 1902, it decreased by half.[21] After 1889, restrictions on the admission of Jews to the bar resulted in dramatic reductions in the number of Jewish lawyers, and a quota of 5 percent was imposed on the number of Jewish physicians appointed to state hospitals or serving as army doctors.[22]

No such restrictions applied to military service. Following the implementation of revised legislation on military service in 1874, conscription for the first time accorded Jewish youth legal status equal to that of other Russian subjects; both were now obliged to serve for five years in the armed forces. However, Jewish youth were selected in a separate draft lottery, had recourse to fewer exemptions, and were punished by a fine of 300 rubles if they evaded the draft; these measures were designed to ensure that the Jewish community contributed a proportional number of conscripts.[23] The measures proved to be effective; the 1897 census revealed that the proportion of Jews serving in the armed forces "exceeded their population ratio by nearly 40 percent."[24] For countless Jewish families, this disproportionate level of military conscription meant the loss of an indispensable income earner and a greater risk of destitution. The cumulative effect of the May Laws and the subsequent legal measures that intensified the economic marginalization of the Jewish community was to exacerbate the poverty of Russian Jews. Throughout the 1890s, the increasing impoverishment of Jewish communities in the Pale of Settlement was evidenced by the increasing dependence on social welfare organizations. Between 1894 and 1898, the number of Jewish families dependent on welfare assistance increased by 26 percent in northwestern *gubernii* and, significantly, by 40 percent in the southern provinces of the Pale, where Jewish migrants attracted by higher rates of economic growth had moved to seek employment.[25] Thus, internal migration, the mass movement of an estimated one-third of the Jewish population, from economically marginal *shtetlekh* to urban centres of economic growth, from the overpopulated *gubernii* of the northern and northwestern Pale to the relatively underpopulated southern Pale, that was experiencing economic growth, did not substantially alter the marginal existence of Russia's Jewish community or alleviate its deepening poverty.[26]

By the end of the nineteenth century, the Jewish community in the Pale of Settlement was at an impasse; for the vast majority of Russian Jews, the future appeared to be bleak and unalterable. Jewish families and communities throughout the Pale became increasingly embroiled in intense discussions about the future. One option was to join the growing number of Jews who decided to leave Russia in search of better lives elsewhere. Choosing to join the mass emigration from Russia precipitated by the pogroms of 1881 was based upon a calculation of risks, the well-known disadvantages and perils of remaining in Russia versus an imagined but uncertain future in a new country.

Another option was to remain in Russia in the hope that their lives would improve. However, Jewish communities throughout the Pale of Settlement lacked leaders or governing institutions with the legitimacy or capacity to cope effectively with economic marginalization or the Russian state's increasingly oppressive policy on Jews. Like the *kahal* (traditional Jewish governing councils) that preceded them, communal governing councils were composed of wealthy members of the community who assumed responsibility for organizing the collection of taxes, running the election of crown rabbis, and supervising charitable institutions, so they were preoccupied with dealing with local administrative matters and fulfilling their responsibilities to the state bureaucracy.[27] Content to supervise the provision of charitable assistance to the poor (often viewed as an unwelcome and unaffordable burden on limited communal revenues), these secular leaders were not willing to jeopardize their wealth or authority by challenging the May Laws or other restrictive measures that contributed to widespread underemployment, unemployment, and poverty.

The rabbinate, both Orthodox and Hasidic, was fixated on the strict observance of religious laws and practices. Rabbis accepted the inevitability of suffering; it was God's punishment for Jews' lack of piety and failure to study the Torah. Redemption, they proclaimed, was possible only through prayer, not improvement in worldly life.[28] Fearful of even the appearance of challenging the state, religious leaders advocated acceptance and restraint, appeasement rather than confrontation. Both secular and religious leaders counselled that the survival of the Jewish community depended on cooperation with the Russian state. They made no attempt to establish forums either at the local level or throughout the Pale of Settlement to engage Jews in collective deliberations about alleviating their distress or shaping their future in Russia. This leadership and institutional vacuum set the stage for a conflict between defenders of the traditional authority of secular and religious communal leaders and advocates of more modern forms of authority and governance.

The Transformation of Communal Politics

The emergence of modern forms of Jewish politics and communal governance in the Pale of Settlement was a response to two interrelated questions. What could be done to protect the Jewish community from state oppression? And what could bring about its regeneration? The solution was mobilization of the Jewish "masses" so that they could free themselves from the outdated ideas, institutions, and loyalties that perpetuated their poverty and subjugation and, through self-determination, lay the foundation for a rebirth of the Jewish community. On this rebirth both individual Jews dissatisfied with their lives and future prospects as well as those with broader concerns about the plight of the Jewish community in Tsarist Russia could agree. But differences over the meanings and goals of self-determination and ultimately emancipation in the second half of the nineteenth century and the early twentieth century led to the formation of communal organizations and political movements with different political principles, strategies, and prescriptions for the future. As they competed for the loyalty and support of the Jewish masses, their ideas and activities transformed communal governance.

Influenced by the scepticism and rationalism of the European Enlightenment, *maskilim* ("supporters") of the *Haskalah* ("enlightenment") movement believed that the uncritical acceptance of Jewish religious and traditional communal authority explained Jews' inability to adapt to changes in Russian society, their limited opportunities, and their chronic poverty.[29] The solution, they argued, was individual self-determination, or self-improvement through secular education, which would lead to productive employment. By becoming economically productive members of Russian society, *maskilim* believed, Jews could gradually shed their image as the tradition-bound alien "other" and be accepted as useful citizens who would be gradually granted full civil rights. Beginning in the 1840s, the *Haskalah* movement's advocacy of secular education, which emphasized vocational training and advanced studies at the secondary and university level, was aligned with the Russian government's policy of promoting the assimilation of Jews by encouraging their enrolment in state schools to learn Russian and be exposed to Christianity, the preconditions of assimilation.

In their appeals to the "people," the great majority of Russian Jews confined in the Pale of Settlement, *maskilim* asserted that the regeneration of communal life and the emancipation of the Jewish people depended on the development of a new Jewish identity and civic consciousness. Self-development through secular education would enable Jews to escape from chronic underemployment and unemployment. It would also, they argued, free Jews from the outdated beliefs that perpetuated the authority of religious and traditional secular leaders incapable of responding to the deepening crisis of the Jewish community and lead to the creation of new institutions of communal governance more responsive to the "will of the people."

Organizations such as the Society for the Promotion of Culture among the Jews of Russia (ORPE), established in 1863 by wealthy members of Saint Petersburg's Jewish community, encouraged Jewish youth to study Russian, enrol in secular schools, and aspire to become merchants, tradespeople, agriculturalists, or university-educated professionals.[30] By striving to become skilled workers and agriculturalists, leaders of the *Haskalah* movement believed, Jews could escape from the stifling confines of traditional communities in which their prospects of employment were bleak and demonstrate that they were economically productive members of Russian society. This transformation would gradually break down the stereotypes that sustained Judeophobia, and like their co-religionists in Western Europe, Russian Jews would gain both acceptance and increased civil rights.

However, the outbreak of pogroms in 1881 followed by the repressive May Laws shattered the credibility of the *Haskalah* movement. Not only did the May Laws abruptly reverse education reforms, tighten residence restrictions, and introduce new measures that intensified the economic marginalization of Jews in the Pale of Settlement, but also the Russian government as well as Russian-language newspapers and writers adopted a crude discourse of anti-Semitism. They increasingly demonized the Jewish community, arguing that because of their immutable racial characteristics Jews were the alien "other" who could never be integrated into Russian society. Faced with an unprecedented crisis, the *Haskalah* movement was powerless, incapable of mobilizing the Jewish community in support of a viable political strategy to defend itself from waves of armed assaults on Jewish communities, mounting anti-Semitism, and increased state oppression. Nor were its leaders able to persuade the Russian government to protect Jews from mob violence or to deviate from its response to the pogroms, the May Laws, which laid the foundation for a policy of debilitating legal restrictions on the Jewish community. Ultimately, the *Haskalah* movement did not transform the worldviews or improve the living conditions of the majority of Russian Jews.

The failure of the *Haskalah* movement's strategy of tacit collaboration with the Russian state to promote individual rights and opportunities was a turning point in the political development of Russia's Jewish community. The fear and insecurity that pervaded the community following the pogroms, the sudden emigration of many Jews (a manifestation of the seriousness of the crisis engulfing the community), and disillusionment with the *Haskalah* movement among the Jewish intelligentsia created widespread anxiety and a growing sense of urgency.[31] But the *Haskalah* movement had posed fundamental questions about Jewish emancipation and, through its promotion of modern, secular education, contributed to the formation of a new generation of Jewish intellectuals impatient for change and determined to take up the cause of "the people."[32]

Territorialists, Zionists, and Socialists

Two forms of political activity, each with the goal of auto-emancipation, dominated the post-1881 political development of Russia's Jewish community and shaped Jewish emigrants' views and experiences of communal governance: territorialists, who believed that the solution to the crisis engulfing the Jews was national autonomy, and the General Jewish Workers' Party of Lithuania, Poland, and Russia, universally known as the Bund, which was committed to organizing Jewish workers into an autonomous socialist movement. The territorialists included "autonomists" such as Simon Dubnow, who advocated secular Jewish communal governance by a democratically elected national council; Leon Pinsker and Asher Ginsberg, who assumed leadership roles in Hibbat Zion (Love of Zion), the precursor of the Russian branch of the World

Zionist Organization; and supporters of Poale Zion (Workers of Zion), who agreed that Jews did not have a future in Russia but argued that national-cultural renewal and self-determination could be achieved only by establishing a Jewish homeland in Palestine based upon socialist principles.[33] Inspired by the revolutionary potential of Marxist thought, the Bund attempted to reconcile the universal working-class struggle to defend economic interests and demand political rights with the recognition of Jewish national-cultural identity, ultimately adopting a program asserting that the emancipation of the Jewish proletariat was inextricably linked to national autonomy.[34]

By creating new political movements to give expression to the "people's will" autonomists, proto-Zionists and socialists transformed the organizational life of the Jewish community. As they competed for the allegiance and support of "the people," they developed tactics of political mobilization that focused on expanding their influence by enrolling members in a network of local organizations to promote debate and activism in as many communities as possible throughout the Pale of Settlement.

The appeal of political movements that advocated collective Jewish self-determination and emancipation was the result of the convergence of many factors: unrelenting poverty, state oppression, a crisis of confidence in both traditional religious and communal leaders, disillusionment with the *Haskalah* movement's promise of liberal reforms, and mass anxiety caused by the death and destruction resulting from renewed outbreaks of pogroms in 1903–04 and again in 1905–06. But the success of the leaders of these competing political movements, members of the Jewish intelligentsia and activists alike, in establishing organizations and attracting tens of thousands of supporters throughout the Pale of Settlement was only possible because of the ascendancy in the late nineteenth century and the early twentieth century of Yiddish as a language of popular culture, political communication, and organizational life.[35]

The Ascendancy of Yiddish in Jewish Communal Life

In the nineteenth century, Yiddish was the language of daily life in communities throughout the Pale of Settlement. But it was overshadowed by Hebrew, the scholarly language of revered religious texts, the Torah and the Talmud together with its commentaries, as well as the language of prayer and daily religious rituals. Proficiency in Hebrew conferred social status, commanded respect, and, within communal decision-making bodies, was instrumental in the exercise of power. As the authoritative language of Jewish religious law, Hebrew was commonly used to encode the constitutions and bylaws, as well as to record the proceedings, of the *kahal*, the traditional institution of communal governance, as well as the *hevrot*, "voluntary associations" such as burial and charitable societies. The names of *hevrot* incorporated the term *kaddisha* ("sacred"), establishing their legitimacy by emphasizing their religious character.[36] Consequently, though the vast majority of Jews used Yiddish in the home and their daily interactions in public life, it was primarily a spoken language; proficiency in written Hebrew was a prerequisite for leadership selection and effective participation in communal deliberations. For those with the advantage of a traditional education based upon advanced Torah and Talmudic studies, their authoritative interpretations of legal texts and records written in Hebrew provided a means of dominating communal decision making.[37]

The status of Hebrew was reinforced by the *Haskalah* movement. *Maskilim* regarded Yiddish as a "corrupt German-Jewish jargon," the language of the poor, superstitious, and uneducated: it lacked consistent grammar and cultural legitimacy and was therefore considered unsuitable for literary or scholarly writing.[38] Despite its criticism of traditional religious and communal leaders, the *Haskalah* movement emphasized Hebrew as the language of Jewish cultural renewal and the study of Russian as a vehicle for social integration into Russian society. By the middle of the nineteenth century, an emergent Jewish intelligentsia promoted Hebrew, the immemorial language of Jewish scholarship and learning, as an authentic and legitimate medium to bring about a rebirth of the Jewish community. Through literature, newspapers, and books on philosophy, history, and science written to modernize Jewish education and encourage independent thought, Jewish intellectuals expressed their vision of modern, emancipated Jews freed from the debilitating constraints of traditional beliefs and practices that condemned them to endure segregated lives of poverty and limited opportunity.[39]

But the dissemination of Hebrew publications and the attempts of the *Haskalah* movement to extend its influence beyond urban centres of intellectual life to reach "the people" living in *shtetlekh* throughout the Pale of Settlement were thwarted by a persistent barrier: Yiddish remained the dominant functional language of almost all the Russian Jews who lived in the Pale. In 1869, Menashe Morgulis, an ORPE leader, had presciently argued that there was "no reader among the masses and absolutely no book market for Hebrew."[40] Thirty years later, despite the efforts of The Society for Handicraft and Agricultural Work among the Jews of Russia (ORT) and other supporters of the *Haskalah* movement to promote the use of Hebrew, the 1897 Russian census revealed that Yiddish remained the "mother tongue" of 97 percent of Jews in the Russian Empire.[41]

By the 1860s, aspiring Jewish writers and publishers became aware of a potential mass market for Yiddish-language publications. Despite government restrictions on licences to print newspapers in Yiddish, growing awareness of a mass market for Yiddish-language literary works, as well as the proliferation of articles written in Yiddish on social problems and current affairs, led to the publication in Russia of a series of Yiddish newspapers.[42] *Kol mevaser* (the Heralding Voice, 1862–72), published in Odessa, became an outlet for emerging writers and published articles on social problems that broadened its appeal to women, as did its publication of the writing of female authors. Through extensive discussion of linguistic problems, the weekly also contributed to the standardization of the Yiddish language based upon a dialect (Volhyn) accessible to both male and female readers in the Pale of Settlement. *Kol mevaser* pioneered a format that subsequently characterized the Yiddish press.[43] The weekly attempted to broaden its readers' knowledge of the modern world; each issue included biographies of historical figures and articles on "science, technology, medicine and health."[44] In addition to international and Russian news and information on events in Jewish communities outside Russia, reports from self-appointed correspondents throughout the Pale informed readers about "Jewish communal conflicts and the shortcomings of local institutions and leaders."[45] Publishing articles that criticized traditional beliefs and practices, the Yiddish press provided members of Jewish communities throughout the Pale with unprecedented opportunities to learn about and reflect on shared experiences of communal politics. The editors of mass-circulation newspapers competed for readers by publishing controversial articles on topical social issues and featured columnists who engaged in territorialist-Zionist debates. A more radical perspective on communal politics and broader questions concerning the politics of Jewish self-determination was provided by explicitly socialist Yiddish publications. Following its formation in 1897, the Bund published an underground Yiddish-language newspaper, *Di arbayter shtime* (the Workers' Voice, 1897–1905). And, with the relaxation of censorship in 1905, the Bund published two legal dailies, *Der veker* (the Awakener, 1905–07) and *Folkstsaytung* (People's Press, 1905–07), and the Zionist Socialist Workers' Party published *Der nayer veg* (the New Way, 1906–07).[46]

By the early 1900s, the gradual increase throughout the 1880s and 1890s in the publication and consumption of Yiddish-language literature, newspapers, and journals had established the linguistic foundation for a dramatic upsurge in cultural activity. In 1888, when Sholem Aleichem published his first volume of *Di yidishe folks-bibliotek* (The Jewish People's Library), he included a list of the titles of seventy-eight Jewish books printed in the Russian Empire; by 1912, the number had increased to 407, including 236 works of Yiddish literature, translations of European novels, and books on science, history, and philosophy.[47] In 1888, only one Yiddish periodical was published in the Russian Empire, but by 1912 there were thirty-three.[48] In the 1880s, the editor of the only Yiddish-language newspaper published in the Russian Empire, the weekly *Dos yudishes folk-blat* (Jewish People's Newspaper), estimated that its circulation peaked at 7,000 copies.[49] Established in January 1903, the Yiddish daily *Der fraynd* (The Friend) developed a network of distribution agents in "dozens" of cities throughout the Pale of Settlement and Congress Poland.[50] It had a circulation of 15,000 in its first month; by 1905, its circulation was 50,000; within a few years, its circulation nearly doubled.[51] Between 1906 and 1913, the total circulation of Yiddish newspapers published in Warsaw and distributed throughout the Pale increased from 96,000 to 190,000.[52] Since copies of newspapers distributed throughout the Pale were shared by a number of readers or read aloud in informal groups, the extent of the readership of Yiddish-language newspapers was considerably larger than these figures suggest.[53]

The ascendancy of Yiddish publications linked even the smallest Jewish communities in the Pale of Settlement to Jewish intellectuals in urban centres. Yiddish became the foundation of a communication network that rapidly diminished the historical isolation of Jewish communities and promoted national integration. The energetic efforts of a Jewish intelligentsia anxious to communicate with the "masses" gave Jews throughout the Pale both access to timely information on events and personalities and exposure to debates and controversies arising from the political and cultural ferment of the late nineteenth century and early twentieth century. Together with the formation of political movements and parties committed to Jewish emancipation, the rapid development of a Yiddish-language culture that asserted a secular national identity and consciousness altered the daily lives of Jews and redefined communal relationships throughout the Pale. Both the politics of Jewish emancipation and cultural production extended the scope and influence of a public sphere that fostered debate, organizational activity, and the establishment of Jewish communal institutions that promoted Yiddish culture outside the confines of traditional Jewish life.

In addition to transforming Jewish reading habits, Yiddish publications provided alternative modes of learning. Before the advent of Yiddish-language newspapers, novels, and periodicals, for the vast majority of Jews, reading and learning were limited to prescribed religious books. Although subscriptions, mail orders, and growing numbers of bookstores and itinerant booksellers created a mass market for Yiddish publications, they were often unaffordable, especially for Jewish youth. The solution was informal reading groups that frequently evolved into book clubs or reading circles. Members shared the cost of purchasing books and periodicals and met for public readings and discussions.[54] Although many reading circles were formed spontaneously, primarily by Jewish youth seeking access to Yiddish-language publications, they became the focus of political mobilization. By the mid-1890s, Jewish social democrats began distributing Yiddish-language socialist pamphlets to Jewish workers' circles in Vilna, Minsk, Vitebsk, and other urban centres.[55] Beginning in 1887, organizers of the Bund travelled throughout the Pale of Settlement to distribute pamphlets on economics, the history of socialism, politics, as well as revolutionary poetry and literature to existing reading circles or to establish new ones as part of their drive to recruit members and establish a network of clandestine cells.[56] For the Bund, political education and agitation were not restricted to discussions and lectures dealing with topical issues and events related to the Jewish socialist movement in Russia and abroad. Bundist cells held literary evenings that featured discussions of short stories written by Dovid Pinsky, Avrom Reyzen, and I.L. Peretz that captured working-class struggles and aspirations. The recitation or communal singing of popular revolutionary poems was a common feature of Bundist meetings and public demonstrations, transforming popular culture into an emotional instrument of political mobilization.[57]

The success of reading circles led to widespread interest in establishing public lending libraries, institutions that would pool resources to provide a public space where all members of the community had access to permanent collections of books and periodicals.[58] But Jewish proponents of public libraries were often thwarted by the Russian government's policy of strictly regulating, with the exception of religious observance, all forms of voluntary association, and only books approved by the censor could be included in library collections.[59] Nevertheless, public enthusiasm for secular libraries overcame legal restrictions and the opposition of traditional leaders. In the *shtetl* of Zastavye, pious Jews who had gathered in the *bet midrash* (house for Torah study) reacted to the establishment of a library with alarm, denouncing those who spread heretical views in their midst, and parents tried to convince their children not to use the library. But "the word 'library' was like a magical incantation, a siren that enticed people there and no force in the world could keep them back."[60] The library became a popular meeting place for Zastavye's Jewish youth, who "threw themselves in to the books with life and soul and . . . devoured them just like hotcakes. Every book went from hand to hand."[61]

By 1905, there were 100 Jewish libraries registered in the Russian Empire, the majority (eighty-four) located in the Pale of Settlement.[62] Many libraries, such as the Odessa Jewish Clerks' Library, were established by mutual aid societies, secular organizations formed to assume collective responsibility for the financial well-being of their members. Establishing libraries of Yiddish-language publications also became part of the Bund's strategy of political mobilization. In 1895, Jewish socialists in Vilna established a "jargon" committee to make Jewish publications available to workers. For three years, the committee translated fiction as well as books on science and politics into Yiddish. Building upon the model of a Yiddish library established in 1893 for workers in Vilna, by 1895 the committee had established libraries in Minsk and Bialystok. After the formation of the Bund in 1897, these libraries formed the foundation for the development of its extensive network of clandestine libraries.[63] The Bund supported the conversion of reading circles into libraries and developed an elaborate administrative apparatus to purchase books and distribute them to its own libraries, which in many communities constituted local Bundist cells, or libraries established by *kassy*, "craft-based" mutual aid societies. In addition to lending books and organizing group discussions, libraries became centres of social activity, hosting lectures and celebrations, complete with speeches and fundraising.[64]

By 1910, there were 229 Jewish libraries in the Pale of Settlement, compared with eighty-four in 1905, one library for every 15,000 Jews.[65] For Jewish youth—three-quarters of library members were usually under the age of thirty—the rapid development of a network of Jewish libraries in the Pale not only increased access to books and encouraged secular learning but also created unprecedented public spaces for social interactions and the exchange of ideas.[66] Libraries became community centres where both men and women could mingle and join social networks free from the scrutiny of parents and religious authorities. For young Jewish women excluded from Jewish schools, and therefore denied a basic education, library collections of Yiddish-language publications gave them an opportunity to broaden their horizons through independent study and exposure to modern perspectives on gender roles, a common theme of popular novels.[67] Unencumbered by the hermetical pedagogy of a religious education, young women were particularly open to secular Yiddish culture and ideas. Libraries also offered public spaces to establish identities and share ideas outside the rigidly constructed gender hierarchy of traditional Jewish society. Bundist libraries that exposed women to socialist principles and the possibility of transforming a society that limited their freedoms and opportunities undoubtedly contributed to the large number of female members, "nearly a third of the total membership," and their prominence in leadership positions of the Bund.[68]

In conjunction with libraries, widespread public participation in events that featured prominent literary figures contributed to a major expansion of the public sphere. Following the relaxation of restrictions on public gatherings in 1906, lecture tours by literary celebrities such as I.L. Peretz, Sholem Asch, and Sholem Aleichem became popular highlights of Jewish cultural life.[69] By the 1880s, theatrical performances engaged countless numbers of Jews in the secular Jewish public sphere. The Yiddish theatre challenged orthodox religious beliefs by defying conventions that limited theatrical performances to the celebration of religious rites such as marriage ceremonies or skits that dramatized themes of the holiday of Purim.[70] The intermingling of the sexes both on the stage and in the audience also challenged social conventions rooted in rabbinic law, which prescribed the strict separation of men and women. But it was the Yiddish theatre's contribution to expanding the secular public sphere, its creation of a site outside the synagogue where Jews could express spiritual longing, explore the meaning of social change, and nurture the emergence of a national Jewish consciousness that posed the greatest challenge to traditional religious definitions of Jewish authority and identity.[71]

The works of popular playwrights such as Jacob Gordin, I.L. Peretz, Dovid Pinski, Sholem Aleichem, and Sholem Asch often dramatized family disputes to portray the conflicts between an older generation immersed in tradition and the aspirations of modern youth grappling with contemporary moral dilemmas and political choices, experiences familiar to a new generation of theatre audiences.[72] Touring Yiddish theatrical companies captured the imagination of Jewish youth seeking an outlet for modern cultural expression. In many Jewish communities, they formed amateur theatre troupes that staged independent productions or performed plays as parts of cultural events sponsored by Jewish literary societies, and together with lectures and discussions these plays became a means of propagating the goals of Bundist and Zionist organizations.[73] Amateur theatrics, which offered Jewish youth the freedom to express their aspirations on a public stage, had an irresistible appeal for many young Jewish women. Yiddish plays frequently dealt with themes that resonated with women, such as the choice between an arranged marriage and romantic love or the obligations of traditional Jewish family life versus a secular education and an opportunity for independence. Professional theatre troupes included young women who performed strong female parts and often became influential role models for female theatregoers.[74] Membership in an amateur theatrical troupe also provided young women with a social circle of like-minded men and women grappling with modern dilemmas, and acting in the roles of the female characters frequently prominent in Yiddish plays they could express their aspirations for a life free from the constraints of parental authority and rigid social conventions defined by religion.

The ascendancy in the late nineteenth century and early twentieth century of Yiddish as a language of political mobilization, new forms of cultural expression and learning, and the organization and operation of secular institutions and associations was central to the formation of a secular Jewish public sphere. The dominance of Yiddish in the home and on the street, its rapid transformation from a jargon into a modern language of mass media, Jewish culture, intellectual inquiry, politics, and organizational life had provided, in effect, the linguistic foundation for widespread public engagement in the restructuring of a dimension of communal governance—social welfare—vital to Jews throughout the Pale of Settlement.

CHAPTER 2

Social Welfare and Communal Governance

For Jews living in the Pale of Settlement, the obligation to provide for the poor and vulnerable was a fundamental component of traditional Jewish communal governance. For Talmudic scholars, "public charity" or *tzedakah* "was an act of piety that no religious Jew could ignore," and they defined in considerable detail the obligation to give, the forms of charity, and the entitlement of recipients.[1] Charity was intended not to narrow or minimize social and economic inequality but to provide basic forms of assistance to alleviate the abject poverty of destitute members of the community and, to a lesser extent, the distress of strangers, itinerant paupers, and refugees. The provision of charity varied in different Jewish communities, but by the middle of the nineteenth century communal responsibility for the poor and vulnerable took the form of charitable institutions funded by taxation, services and financial aid provided by *hevrot* (self-governing "voluntary associations"), and individual acts of benevolence.

Most Jewish communities had a central institution, a "great charitable *kassa*" (*tzedakah ha-gedolah*), funded by the *korobka*, a tax primarily levied on ritually slaughtered meat but also on other consumer goods such as candles.[2] It provided various forms of assistance such as weekly allowances to the poor, free food and in larger communities soup kitchens, dowries for brides from impoverished families, burials for paupers, and additional aid to enable the poor to observe the Sabbath, Rosh Hashana, Yom Kippur, and Passover.[3] Orphaned boys were clothed and educated in a Talmud Torah, a school established to provide them with a religious education until they were old enough to work.

The central charity also paid a subsidy to families willing to provide homes for orphaned girls. In exchange for food and lodging, they performed household chores considered suitable vocational training to prepare for marriage or employment as servants. In many communities, communal taxation also funded a *hekdesh*, an institution that functioned as a "poor house" for poor widows, itinerant paupers, and the disabled, as well as a home for the elderly and orphaned boys who could not be placed with families. The *hekdesh* also served as a primitive hospital, though its primary purpose was to quarantine the sick rather than provide medical care for them.[4] As an alternative to institutional care, vouchers were issued by some *hekdesh* supervisors that entitled an applicant to assistance for room and board in a private home. In addition to a central charitable institution, *hevrot* provided specific forms of charitable assistance such as visiting the sick or financial aid to particular categories of the deserving poor such as mothers.[5]

Individual benevolence was a vital part of communal charity. Providing assistance to the poor and disadvantaged was a collective responsibility, but paying taxes to support a central charitable institution was not a substitute for individual acts of charity. When the poor went door to door before Hanukkah and Purim to solicit contributions to enable them to celebrate the holidays, or ate a "paupers' meal" as guests at family dinners, wedding celebrations, or *hevrot* social events, both donors and recipients understood that providing assistance was a binding religious obligation.[6] Similarly, the practice of making regular donations to a *pushke*, a "charity box" placed in a home or synagogue to provide additional revenue for central charitable institutions and funding for *hevrot*, was deeply embedded in communal life. *Hevrot* also often benefited from the support of wealthy donors or were the beneficiaries of bequests.[7] Since rabbinic teaching emphasized that all wealth is created by and belongs to God, it was imperative that individuals who had accumulated wealth fulfill their religious obligation to share it with the less fortunate.[8] For the wealthy, fulfillment of this obligation was a public measure of their virtue and legitimized their privileged position in the community. Philanthropy also provided a means of supplementing communal resources when they were insufficient to deal with an emergency such as a famine or assisting the victims of pogroms. In addition, large donations were essential to enable communities to fund the construction of major communal institutions such as synagogues.

Rabbinic teaching and Talmudic law emphasized that the poor were entitled to assistance and must be treated with dignity and respect and protected from experiencing shame or degradation.[9] However, since the social distinctions based upon learning and wealth not only determined who held decision-making positions in communal governance but also permeated all aspects of Jewish life, including hierarchical seating arrangements in synagogues, the identities of donors to and recipients of charity were public knowledge. Officers of *hevrot* and affluent donors were honoured for their contributions to the community, whereas beneficiaries of communal charity, however legitimate their needs, were treated as supplicants whose claims for assistance were subject to close public scrutiny. For example, officials of central charitable institutions used regular needs tests to determine if applicants were eligible for weekly allowances, and providing dowries to poor brides was conditional upon investigations of families' financial circumstances.[10] Recipients were also subject to social regulation; eligibility for communal charity depended on conforming to community standards of religious observance and moral behaviour.

When dispensing charity, the distinctions that officials made between genuine need and dependence on charity, regarded as shameful, were often based upon the constraints of limited budgets rather than the imperatives of *tzedakah*. Although Jewish communities in large urban centres had access to more tax revenue and greater numbers of affluent donors compared with *shtetlekh* that invariably struggled to fund communal charitable institutions, the dismal state of institutions such as the *hekdesh* and Talmud Torah throughout the Pale of Settlement suggests that the harsh treatment and precarious lives of orphans, widows, the disabled, and other vulnerable members of the Jewish community reflected their marginal status and powerlessness rather than the amount of tax revenue or sizes of donations.[11]

An alternative form of traditional communal charity that protected the dignity of recipients and reinforced self-reliance was the interest-free loan. Rabbinic teaching emphasized that, since there was no shame in borrowing and repaying money, the highest order of *tzedakah* was to give loans so that recipients could help themselves and not become dependent on communal charitable assistance.[12] Based upon the principle that those who contributed to a pool of capital would be entitled to loans without paying interest, *gemilut hasadim* or "free-loan societies" institutionalized a form of reciprocal communal self-help or mutual aid. In return for annual membership fees, members could borrow small sums to deal with financial emergencies or take advantage of business opportunities; loans would be repaid in weekly instalments. Since members could only afford to pay modest membership fees, free-loan societies often raised additional capital through communal fundraising campaigns or depended on donations from wealthy patrons.[13]

But traditional forms of Jewish communal charity were increasingly unable to fulfill the obligations of *tzedakah*. Throughout the second half of the nineteenth century, chronic underemployment and unemployment together with increases in the number of family dependants contributed to the progressive impoverishment of Jewish communities in the Pale of Settlement. By 1900, approximately a third of the Jewish population, and in some communities 40–50 percent, were destitute and dependent on charity, and the remainder (70 percent) were among the ranks of the working poor; only a small fraction (1.3 percent) could be considered affluent.[14] Urbanization, together with migration and emigration, also altered the structure of the Jewish family, contributing to growing numbers of abandoned or orphaned children and dependent elderly people who could no longer turn to extended family members for care or support.[15] Increasingly, the demand for charitable assistance exceeded communal financial resources. The overwhelming majority of Jews were poor and could contribute only small amounts to charity, and since few affluent Jews lived outside major urban centres, most small Jewish communities did not benefit from philanthropy. Consequently, funding traditional forms of charitable assistance depended on the *korobka*, the primary source of communal tax revenue.

The *korobka* was primarily a consumption tax levied on kosher meat. It was a regressive tax, since it did not take into consideration the income or ability of the consumer to pay it. Although the *korobka* placed a disproportionate tax burden on the poor and raised the cost of meat, the most expensive food staple, the only way for communal authorities to raise additional revenue was to increase the tax rate. In addition, university graduates and members of merchant guilds were exempt from taxation, and non-observant Jews who did not purchase kosher meat escaped the tax. Thus, the tax rate, and consequently the tax burden on the poor, were often increased to compensate for rebates and tax avoidance as well as the practice in most communities of leasing the right to collect the *korobka* to a tax collector who retained a portion of tax revenues as payment for his services.[16]

By the 1860s, the increasing impoverishment of Jewish communities in the Pale of Settlement prompted critics of traditional authority to call for a restructuring of the communal governance of charity. They advocated a shift from traditional authority to new organizations that would be more representative of and responsive to the needs of the people. For *maskilim*, the inequities of taxation and the failure of traditional forms of charity to provide adequate assistance to poor and vulnerable members of the Jewish community illustrated the need to modernize an outdated system of communal governance paralyzed by a crisis of leadership. They argued that the rabbinate, preoccupied with the strict observance of religious laws and practices and fearful that reforms of communal governance would undermine their religious authority, was incapable of providing leadership. Similarly, little could be expected from traditional secular leaders; they jealously guarded their status and power and were not willing to cede authority to new organizations to make decisions about communal charity or philanthropy.[17] *Maskilim* were divided on which elements of the Jewish community could create a new civic consciousness that would lead to the reform of communal charity. Pragmatists debated whether enlightened rabbis could persuade the rabbinate to become leaders of a reform movement or whether Saint Petersburg Jewish notables were better qualified for the task.[18] But critics of both the rabbinate and Saint Petersburg notables argued that they were insurmountable obstacles to reform; only the consent and participation of "the people" would build a legitimate foundation for the reform of communal charity.[19]

The Modernization of Jewish Social Welfare

By the late 1850s, the emergence of a secular Jewish public sphere provided a forum in which Jewish notables who had bolstered their prestige and authority by donating or bequeathing their wealth to synagogues and prayer houses laid claim to communal leadership by supporting the establishment of modern social welfare institutions. Their paternalistic philanthropy was informed by Western European examples of Jewish social welfare institutions governed by secular boards and run by staff with the professional training and administrative skills to provide rational, scientific forms of charity, or modern forms of social welfare, that efficiently offered high-quality care to the elderly, the orphaned, and the sick and reduced the dependence of the poor on scarce communal resources by making them self-sufficient.[20] For wealthy Jewish philanthropists, modern social welfare institutions would alleviate the widespread destitution that reinforced the pervasive opinion of tsarist officials that Jews tarnished the image of Russian society. Training for a new generation of Jewish artisans, domestic servants, and agriculturalists would demonstrate that, like themselves, all Jews could become economically productive citizens. Donating large sums to finance the construction of modern buildings to house social welfare institutions also provided tangible evidence of their generosity and confirmed their status as leaders of the Jewish community and contributing members of Russian society.[21]

The development of modern social welfare institutions in the Pale of Settlement depended on the local initiatives of wealthy philanthropists. Their donations, often supplemented by subsidies from the *korobka* and public fund-raising, provided the money to construct and operate institutions that replaced traditional forms of communal charity. In 1864, the first Jewish home for the aged in the Pale was established in Vilna. It provided a home for homeless elderly Jews who had been housed in a two-room *hekdesh*. Under the direction of its board of directors, it expanded by 1917 from about thirty residents to a four-storey building with accommodation for "some four hundred."[22] Between the 1860s and the First World War, sixteen old-age homes were established.[23] Unlike the *hekdesh*, small buildings providing primitive and often unsanitary housing for the elderly, travellers, orphans, the ill, and the disabled, old-age homes were built exclusively for the elderly. They had furnished rooms for residents, dining halls, examination rooms for medical care, synagogues, and some had gardens.[24] Similarly, growing concern about the failure of the *hekdesh* to provide adequate housing and care for orphaned boys and the limitations of a Talmud Torah education, as well as communal neglect of the welfare of orphaned girls, led to the founding of orphanages, modern child welfare institutions that offered hygienic accommodations, nutritious meals, proper clothes, medical supervision, and access to vocational training to equip orphans with marketable skills.[25] With advances in medical science and increasing numbers of Jewish physicians, philanthropists began to devote their wealth to modernizing communal health care, funding hospitals and outpatient clinics to provide professional medical treatment as an alternative to the basic nursing care that members of *bikkur holim* ("visiting the sick") societies provided to the poor in their homes.[26]

The establishment of modern Jewish social welfare institutions to replace or supplement traditional forms of communal charity not only changed how *tzedakah*, the obligation to care for the poor and vulnerable, was fulfilled but also transformed communal governance. Together with Jewish libraries and branches of the Jewish Literary Society and the Society for the Promotion of Culture among the Jews of Russia, old-age homes, orphanages, and hospitals extended public participation in communal decision making.[27] In contrast to traditional forms of communal governance based upon religious authority and personal networks of power and influence, cultural associations and social welfare institutions adopted a model of governance based upon principles of civic membership and democratic decision making. The principle that the membership constituted the legal and democratic foundations of Jewish charitable associations was formally recognized by the Russian government's decision in 1897 to introduce model charters allowing Jews to apply for legal permission to engage in voluntary charitable activities.[28] The model charters required that voluntary charitable associations enrol members, collect membership dues, and register constitutions that identified executive officers and procedures for their election.[29] By the turn of the century, secular Jewish social welfare institutions increasingly exhibited the characteristics of modern organizations: membership bodies, constitutions, bylaws, annual budgets, and elected boards of directors that hired staff with professional or administrative skills.[30]

Because large donations were often the catalysts for the establishment of social welfare institutions, the possession of wealth often determined who was elected to or recruited to be a member of a board of directors. Such donations enabled women with wealthy husbands and affluent widows concerned about social problems to have roles in communal decision making. Excluded from traditional forms of communal governance, female philanthropists participated by making donations to existing social welfare institutions or founded their own organizations to expand the scope of communal charity.[31] But in most Jewish communities social welfare institutions were funded by a combination of large donations to construct buildings and small donations, membership dues, fundraising drives, and a share of the *korobka* to cover operating expenses.[32] Consequently, though philanthropists commanded great respect, the composition of boards of directors and the management of Jewish social welfare institutions were subject to constant public scrutiny that often led to conflict over institutional decision making or, in the case of Kiev, fundamental questions of communal governance.

For over three decades, a small group of philanthropists in Kiev had used their wealth to establish and monopolize control of the Jewish community's major social welfare institutions. Under the authority of the Jewish Welfare Committee and subsequently the Representation for Jewish Welfare, governance bodies whose members were self-appointed from among Kiev's wealthy Jewish elite, philanthropists controlled the expenditure of revenue from the *korobka* on social welfare. In the period 1896–1902, the Representation allocated the largest portion of the *korobka*—almost four times the amount to assist the poor, unemployed, and orphans—to one institution, the Jewish hospital.[33] In newspaper editorials, reports, and letters, critics of the Representation claimed that Kiev's communal leaders were indifferent to the plight of the majority of Kiev's Jewish community and that they were sacrificing the welfare of those who bore the burden of taxation to provide preferential funding to an institution that they had established and continued to expand with great public fanfare as a prominent symbol of their status and benevolence.[34]

In 1890, Kiev's artisan leaders petitioned the provincial governor complaining that their taxes were controlled by an unelected body neither accountable for its decisions nor responsive to the Jewish community.[35] They requested control of one-quarter of the revenue of the *korobka* to assist poor artisans.[36] They were influenced by the upsurge in political participation during the 1905 revolution, and their persistent complaints about the Representation for Jewish Welfare culminated in demands for the democratization of Jewish communal governance in Kiev. In 1906, the nine self-appointed members of the Representation were replaced by members selected by a two-tier electoral process: members of Kiev's communal institutions campaigned to be elected one of among approximately 100 electors who in turn elected the twenty-four members of the Representation. However, not only did this system of electing board members fall short of the civic equality and democratic practices that had been adopted by Jewish political and cultural organizations, but also critics continued to complain that the Representation persisted in funding institutions favoured by wealthy philanthropists and remained insensitive to the needs of the poor.[37]

The tenacious control by Kiev's wealthy philanthropists of the Jewish community's social welfare expenditures was exceptional, but providing financial support to establish and operate institutions that cared for orphans, the elderly, and the sick while neglecting the working poor and unemployed was widespread throughout the Pale of Settlement. Orphans, the elderly, and the sick, without question, were deserving recipients of communal charity, and the modern social welfare institutions that cared for them were acclaimed as a credit to the community. However, providing assistance to the working poor and unemployed was controversial, particularly for Jewish employers beset by growing agitation for higher wages, shorter hours, and improved working conditions.[38] Advocates of modern forms of social welfare not only argued that alleviating the poverty of the large number of Jewish poor would impose an unaffordable burden on communal resources but also asserted that providing financial assistance to the poor fostered dependence; therefore, communal resources should be devoted to training workers who could be economically productive and self-sufficient. Those in dire need had recourse to traditional forms of charity such as distributions of free food and soup kitchens. However, as orphanages, homes for the aged, and hospitals became the foci of philanthropic donations, fundraising, and the expenditure of tax revenues, assistance to the working poor and unemployed continued to be inadequate, an underfunded component of communal social welfare.[39]

Mutual Aid and Self-Help

The marginalization of the welfare of the working poor and unemployed demonstrated the limits of both working-class participation in communal governance and communal solidarity and led to the creation of an alternative type of social welfare. Influenced by nationalist and socialist political movements that advocated collective action to achieve self-determination, Jewish workers sought emancipation from their dependence on traditional forms of communal charity, which subjected recipients to the humiliation of providing evidence that they were deserving but provided only minimal assistance to those successful in doing so. They established independent, egalitarian, and democratic self-help organizations founded upon the principles of mutual aid established by *gemilut hasadim*, traditional free-loan societies. Secular rather than religious, and financed exclusively by equal membership dues rather than philanthropic charitable donations and fundraising campaigns, modern self-help organizations established by Jewish workers were based upon the conviction that their individual welfare depended on class solidarity and autonomy.

The primary function of Jewish self-help organizations was to provide members with a measure of social security. Mutual aid societies levied membership fees and weekly dues to amass and sustain a fund to provide financial assistance to members and their families who experienced a loss of income because of illness, unemployment, or death. Similarly, free-loan societies, often in exchange for a pledge or with the assurance of a guarantor, offered their members interest-free loans to cope with a loss of income, invest in a business, or purchase household goods. Interest-free loans were particularly beneficial for artisans, who used them to purchase essential tools and materials, freeing them from paying the usurious interest rates charged by a *vokher* or community "money lender."[40]

In the late 1880s, Jewish workers in Vilna, Minsk, and other urban centres formed *kassy*, or "self-help societies," that a decade later provided the organizational foundation for trade unions organized by the Bund.[41] The newly formed trade unions aggressively pursued better wages and working conditions, adding strike pay to the list of self-help benefits. Conflicts over wages and working conditions also led to tensions within artisan guilds, the traditional *hevrot* that bound masters, journeymen, and apprentices to an occupational hierarchy with unequal earnings sanctified by religious obligations.

As industrial forms of production made the guild system of producer cartels obsolete, masters became employers, and artisans were increasingly united by their common interests as skilled workers. The "brotherhood" of the guilds dissolved as artisans established independent self-help societies that often evolved into trade unions.[42] New categories of workers who had not been part of the guild system, such as clerks employed in administrative positions and shop assistants, formed their own secular mutual aid and free-loan societies.

Self-help societies also offered women a unique form of social security. Throughout the nineteenth century, married women participated in the public sphere as merchants and traders, and by the end of the century single women whose employment had been mainly restricted to domestic service worked as shop assistants; artisans manufacturing gloves, stockings, and clothes; and labourers in factories producing cigarettes and matches.[43] For married women, self-help societies provided financial assistance in the event of loss of income because of illness or the death of a spouse. In addition to a measure of income security, *kassy*—which provided forums for lectures and discussions, organized cultural events, and gave members access to libraries—became centres of political education.[44] They provided widowed, divorced, and single women with a secular social network and a substantial amount of independence from the restrictions of traditional communal authority.[45] Since membership responsibilities included participation in regular meetings to discuss benefits and trade union issues, as well as to elect *kassy* officers, women acquired experience in democratic decision making, financial management, and leadership.[46] For many young Jewish women, membership in *kassy* led to participation in the Bund and immersion in its clandestine labour union and political agitation.[47]

The organization of modern mutual aid and free-loan societies was impeded by government restrictions on establishing secular voluntary associations. Unlike *gemilut hasadim* societies, which escaped government scrutiny because of their association with religious observance, secular mutual aid and free-loan societies, like all forms of voluntary activity that contributed to the formation of civil society, were considered by the Russian government a potential threat to the state. Government officials were particularly suspicious of working-class associations, which forced most *kassy* to function secretly. Nevertheless, provincial government officials approved some petitions to establish mutual aid societies. In 1863, clerks and other white-collar workers seeking independence from a synagogue's *gemilut hasadim* founded the Odessa Jewish Clerk's Mutual Aid Society, and by 1889 Jewish shop assistants in Bialystok and Vilna had formed legal self-help societies.[48] A survey conducted by the Jewish Colonization Society in 1898 identified more than 350 self-help societies.[49]

The growing demand for access to credit led to the application of the principles of self-help and mutual aid to the establishment of savings and loan cooperatives. In 1896, the Russian government approved a petition to establish the first legal credit cooperative, the Savings and Loan Fund, in Paritchi, a *shtetl* in Minsk *gubernia*.[50] And in 1898, a year after the Russian government announced model charters that allowed Jews to submit applications for legal permission to establish voluntary organizations, the Savings and Loan Society for Artisans and Merchants was established in Vilna.[51] By 1902, there were fifty savings and loan cooperatives in the Pale of Settlement, and with the liberalization of legislation in 1904 their number had increased by 1913 to 680, with a total membership of 450,000.[52] The success of savings and loan cooperatives was a result of their capacity to provide the credit needed by artisans as well as merchants and petty traders. Unlike free-loan societies, they accumulated large pools of capital and consequently could issue substantial loans. For example, between 1897 and 1902, the average loan of the Krasnopolie Free Loan Society, whose members paid dues of between fifty kopecks and two rubles a year and had an annual capital fund of approximately 1,200 rubles, was close to eleven rubles.[53] By 1913, savings and loan cooperatives, which required that each member deposit between ten and fifteen rubles, which could be paid in instalments, and offered savings accounts, had on average approximately 58,800 rubles in capital.[54] Loans averaged sixty rubles, though lending limits ranged from 100 to 300 rubles.[55]

Since Jewish artisans, merchants, and traders rarely had access to a bank or qualified for bank loans, they were often forced to borrow from money lenders, who charged ruinous interest rates of 100 percent or more.[56] Consequently, they enthusiastically supported savings and loan cooperatives, which charged more affordable interest rates of 10–12 percent.[57] Loans provided artisans with working capital to remain competitive by purchasing tools and materials or with a source of income in periods of low demand for their goods. Many cooperatives also acted as purchasing agents for artisans, who benefited from lower costs of materials, and sellers of the goods that artisans produced, giving them access to new markets. Similarly, merchants used loans to purchase inventory, and traders used them to finance transactions. Although most of the members of the cooperatives were artisans, merchants, and traders, membership was open to professionals and other members of the community.[58]

The savings and loan cooperatives were owned and controlled by their members. Constitutions established the rights of members to participate in the governance of the cooperatives as well as the number and responsibilities of elected board members. The board hired administrative staff to manage daily operations and issued annual reports and financial statements that enabled members to monitor the cooperative's finances and hold its elected officers accountable for the performance of their duties. Consequently, in addition to assisting members to earn livelihoods and expanding collective responsibility for social welfare, savings and loan cooperatives increased the scope of democratic decision making in communal governance.

Politics and Communal Governance

Increasingly, the coexistence of traditional forms of communal authority and a burgeoning secular public sphere raised questions about the foundation and structure of communal governance. In most Jewish communities in the Pale of Settlement, the successors of the *kahal*, cliques comprised of wealthy individuals and religious leaders, continued to have quasi-legal responsibility for communal governance and dealing with the tax revenue and administrative claims of the Russian government. However, with the proliferation of libraries, cultural societies, social welfare institutions, self-help societies, and savings and loan cooperatives, communal leadership and decision making shifted from the synagogue and *hevrot* to the public sphere, from traditional authority to the "will of the people" embodied in constitutions which provided for the election of leaders. As secular leaders laid claim to revenue from the *korobka* to help fund cultural societies and social welfare institutions, the issue of control of communal taxation led to disputes about the right of traditional leaders to speak or act for the Jewish community.

In some communities, secular organizations succeeded in negotiating agreements with traditional leaders for a share of *korobka* revenues, but little was accomplished to reform communal governance. The Russian government was opposed to granting Jews any form of communal autonomy, and Jewish political activists were divided: socialists were committed to a revolutionary transformation of the Russian state, Zionists were preoccupied with establishing a Jewish homeland, and liberals supported ORPE programs that assisted Jewish youth to become economically productive members of Russian society. The proclamation of the 1905 October Manifesto, which granted basic civil liberties and promised an elected parliament (Duma), raised hopes that the establishment of a constitutional democracy would lead to the emancipation of the Jews.

Socialists distrusted Tsar Nicholas II's commitment to constitutional reforms but took advantage of the new political freedoms to mobilize support for the revolutionary cause. Faced with police harassment and voting restrictions that disenfranchised nearly all workers in the Pale of Settlement, the four socialist parties decided to boycott the 1906 election of the first Duma.[59] Zionists and liberals, comparatively free of police harassment, joined forces to contest the election under the banner of the Union for Attainment of the Full Equal Rights of the Jewish People and succeeded in electing 12 of the 478 deputies.

Jewish deputies accomplished little to advance Jewish rights in the short life of the first Duma.[60] Despite their disappointment with the first Duma, Zionists and Jewish liberals remained optimistic that parliamentary government would force the tsar and his Council of Ministers to repeal anti-Jewish legislation and ultimately accept full Jewish civic equality. Together with the Bund and other socialist parties that abandoned their boycott, Zionists and liberals contested the 1907 election of the second Duma. The Bund supported candidates of the Jewish People's Group, an offshoot of the Union for Attainment of the Full Equal Rights of the Jewish People, but only four Jewish deputies were elected, two representing the Jewish People's Group, one Zionist, and one Social Democrat.[61]

In June 1907, after a five-month session that also failed to pass legislation to address Jewish civil rights, Tsar Nicholas II dissolved the second Duma. With increasing state repression, widespread anti-Jewish violence, and changes to the electoral law that favoured conservative Russian voters and discouraged Jews from voting, disillusioned liberal and socialist activists lost confidence in parliamentary democracy.[62] For socialists, the revolutionary change that appeared imminent in 1905 was increasingly unattainable; membership in the four Jewish socialist parties—the Bund, Jewish Social Democratic Workers' Party, Jewish Socialist Workers' Party, and Zionist Socialist Workers' Party—rapidly declined, as did the circulation of socialist newspapers.[63] Recognizing the limitations of electoral politics, socialist leaders attempted to revive activist support for political mobilization of the "masses" to advance the interests of workers by shifting the focus of political activity from revolutionary change to involvement in voluntary associations and agitation for the democratization of communal governance.[64] As Bund leader Vladimir Medem recalled, "we had to plunge into the thick of *kehilla* affairs, seeking to fight the patrician leadership in the area of the practical, daily concerns of Jewish life. To do this we ourselves had to become distinctly knowledgeable about such concerns, and also enlighten the working masses about them."[65]

In 1909, representatives of the Bund and the Jewish Socialist Workers' Party were among 120 delegates from forty-six cities inside and outside the Pale of Settlement who attended a conference of community activists in Kovno organized by the Jewish People's Group.[66] The conference was widely criticized as being unrepresentative of the entire Jewish community—delegates were invited by the Jewish People's Group rather than elected—but it attracted a diverse cross-section of Jewish leaders to discuss the modernization of communal governance.[67] In addition to socialists and liberals, delegates included Simon Dobnow of the Folkspartey (autonomists), M. Ussishkin (Zionists), and a number of prominent rabbis. The conference dealt with three major issues: qualification for membership in the Jewish community, communal taxation, and modernization of the structure of communal decision making.

Differences emerged in heated debates between traditionalists who wanted to restrict membership in the community and the right to vote to adherents of Judaism and secularists who argued that all Jews, whether religious or not, were entitled to full membership and a vote. Traditionalists also defended the *korobka*, primarily applied to kosher meat, because it was universal and reinforced the religious foundation of the Jewish community. The views of the traditionalists reflected the concerns of the Orthodox rabbinate that was determined to perpetuate a religious definition of Jewish identity and communal membership in order to bolster its authority.[68] Critics argued that the *korobka* was a regressive tax on the poor and called for its replacement with a progressive income tax with exemptions for low-income earners. As the conference proceeded, lines were drawn between defenders of traditional authority and supporters of secular, democratic, communal governance. Ultimately, the reformers prevailed, and the delegates approved resolutions calling for the election by universal franchise of a communal council that would elect an executive composed of between seven and ten members empowered to implement a progressive income tax administered by a committee accountable to the communal council and to make decisions on expenditures. At the conclusion of the conference, delegates elected a forty-one-member executive to advise the two Jewish People's Group deputies in the Duma on the legislative changes needed to enable Jews to establish communal councils and mobilize support in the Jewish community for the reform of communal governance.[69]

The Kovno conference led to renewed interest in communal organizations. After the conference, socialist parties resolved to participate in the democratization of communal governance; however, faced with a rapid decline in membership support and dwindling organizational resources, they struggled to prevent the collapse of trade unions and maintain their influence in cultural and educational organizations.[70] Generating popular interest in reforming communal governance proved to be impossible, and many socialists joined existing organizations that had been established by Jewish liberals to promote social integration and benefited from the stable financial support of wealthy patrons. Both the ORPE, which supported the modernization of Jewish education, and the Society for Handicraft and Agricultural Work among the Jews of Russia, which provided Jewish artisans with occupational training, attracted new members.[71] Socialists and other communal activists also devoted their energy to establishing libraries and savings and loan cooperatives.

Ultimately, the democratization of communal governance depended on the enactment of legislation removing anti-Jewish restrictions, establishing the civic equality of Jews, and reforming municipal governments to recognize the rights of national minorities. However, the tsar, his Council of Ministers, and a majority of deputies in the Duma (1907–12) were opposed to recognizing Jewish rights, and legislative debates mirrored the growing anti-Semitism of Russian newspapers and reactionary political parties such as the Union of the Russian People (the Black Hundreds).[72] In February 1911, after three years of lobbying by its two Jewish deputies, the first major bill dealing with Jewish legal rights was finally introduced in the third Duma. But the bill, which would have abolished the Pale of Settlement, thereby eliminating residence restrictions, did not come to a final vote. It was referred to a committee for further study, and a hostile majority of deputies ensured that it remained there, in effect ending the third Duma's consideration of Jewish rights.

But the very introduction of the bill provoked a campaign against Jewish rights in nationalist newspapers, and the Russian government implemented additional anti-Jewish measures. It increased expulsions of Jews living illegally outside the Pale of Settlement, imposed additional restrictions on Jewish enrolment at universities, and abruptly closed the Jewish Literary Society.[73] In March 1911, the Union of the Russian People claimed that the death of a twelve-year-old boy in Kiev was a Jewish ritual murder, and this claim led to the arrest of Mendel Beilis. Publicity about his imprisonment and trial generated venomous attacks on Jews in the Russian press, a crusade against the Jewish predatory enemy within that overshadowed the 1912 election of the fourth Duma. Three Jewish deputies were elected, but the issue of Jewish rights became "hopeless."[74]

The close to 7,300 Jewish immigrants from the Pale of Settlement who settled in Winnipeg between 1882 and 1914 emigrated to escape poverty, oppression, and anti-Jewish violence. Although early immigrants had little prior knowledge about life in Canada, they hoped that emigration would give them an opportunity to enjoy freedom from persecution and a measure of prosperity. Their goal was to re-establish their lives in a new land, first to find a means of earning a livelihood and then, as their numbers increased, to create a new kind of Jewish community. The community that they established incorporated elements of continuity and change: Winnipeg's Jewish immigrants established numerous synagogues as well as secular institutions, societies, and organizations. Their collective consciousness had been defined by religious faith and observance and the emergence of a secular public sphere, by autocratic religious authority and modern forms of social organization, political participation, and communal governance.[75] Freed from the constraints of their former communities, the traditional institutions, hierarchical relationships, and loyalties that determined social status and who wielded power, these immigrants resolved the conflict between tradition and modernity by establishing a community in Winnipeg constituted on the basis of the separation of religious authority and communal governance. The rabbinate remained the custodian of deeply rooted religious values and beliefs. Rabbis continued to provide religious leadership and guidance for members of synagogues, officiated at weddings and funerals, and supervised the enforcement of the community's dietary laws. However, as the following chapters demonstrate, Jewish immigrants who had experienced the upsurge of organizational activity in the Pale of Settlement embraced democratic practices and took advantage of permissive Canadian laws to establish a vibrant public sphere in which communal governance was based upon the authority, support, and participation of the people.

CHAPTER 3

Jewish Immigration and Settlement in Winnipeg

On 3 July 1912, fifteen days after departing from Antwerp, Belgium, the Canadian Pacific steamship *Lake Michigan* docked in Quebec City. The steamship's manifest classified 1,017 of its 1,131passengers, including 157 Jews, as immigrants subject to inspection to determine their admissibility under the Immigration Act. Miriam Epstein, aged twenty-three, accompanied by her twenty-one-year-old brother-in-law Leib and her two children, Israel (one and a half) and Feige (three months), informed immigration officers that they were joining her husband, Moishe, who had immigrated to Canada in June 1911 and settled in Winnipeg.[1]

Between 1881 and 1914, more than 2 million Jews emigrated from Russia.[2] The majority of them travelled to Western European and British ports, where they embarked on ships destined for North America; more than 1.5 million settled in the United States, and close to 84,100 settled in Canada.[3] Between 1882 and 1914, approximately 9,000 Jewish immigrants settled in Winnipeg. Like the Epstein family, 81 percent of them came from the Pale of Settlement, 7 percent from Romania, 4 percent from England, 2 percent from Austria-Hungary, and 1 percent from Poland.[4] This wave of immigration laid the demographic foundation of a Jewish community in Winnipeg that by 1914 was the third largest in Canada.

The first Jewish immigrants settled in Winnipeg in the late 1870s.[5] In 1881, on the eve of the mass migration of Jews from the Pale of Settlement in Russia, only twenty-six Jews resided in Winnipeg.[6] However, outbreaks of pogroms in the Pale in 1881 precipitated a mass exodus of Jewish refugees, which led to a dramatic increase in Winnipeg's Jewish population. In 1882, approximately 360 Jewish refugees arrived in Winnipeg, a small contingent of the more than 20,000 Jews who had fled Russia.[7] Jewish immigration to Winnipeg continued throughout the next decade but at a much slower pace. Between 1883 and 1891, only 212 Jewish immigrants settled in Winnipeg.[8] However, supplemented by the arrival of Jewish migrants from Quebec and the birth of seventy-six children, by 1891 Winnipeg's Jewish population totalled 645.[9] With the arrival of 436 Jewish immigrants in the next decade and the birth of 301 children, by 1901 Winnipeg's Jewish population had increased to 1,156.[10] However, two decades of steady but modest increases were only the prelude to a period of remarkable growth. Consistent with the upsurge in Jewish emigration from Russia after 1900, Jewish immigration to Canada, and in turn to Winnipeg, increased significantly.[11] Between 1902 and 1916, 8,058 Jewish immigrants settled in Winnipeg.[12] High levels of immigration plus the birth of 4,457 children contributed to dramatic population growth; by 1916, Winnipeg's Jewish community numbered 13,473.[13]

Canada's Immigration Policy

Between 1882 and 1914, Jewish immigrants from the Pale of Settlement seeking admission into Canada faced few government restrictions. They were required to pass a medical examination, take a literacy test, and demonstrate that they were not "paupers" "likely to become a public charge."[14] Beginning in 1908, admission into Canada was conditional on producing a sum of cash or landing fee, typically $25 for adults and $12.50 for children between the ages of five and eighteen, plus railway tickets to their final destinations or their cash equivalents. However, immigration officers were authorized to waive the landing fee in cases of family reunification, such as a wife and children joining a husband/father resident in Canada, a brother or sister reuniting with a brother, a minor who was the responsibility of an adult sister, or a parent invited to live with a son or daughter.[15] The Canadian government's flexible approach to family reunification facilitated chain migration: after establishing a residence in Canada, Jewish immigrants could "sponsor" the immigration of both immediate and extended family members. Chain migration explains why so many of the Jewish immigrants who settled in Winnipeg came from the southern and southwestern provinces of the Pale of Settlement.

Moreover, prior to 1914, Jewish immigrants from the Pale and their dependants immigrating to Canada were not impeded by occupational restrictions. Large-scale immigration was a central component of the Canadian government's economic development strategy. Using aggressive advertising campaigns, the inducement of 160 acres of free land, bonuses paid to shipping agents to recruit immigrants, and reduced transatlantic and railway fares, immigration policy focused on attracting agriculturalists to settle in western Canada. With the exception of some areas of the Pale—primarily the provinces of Kherson, Kiev, Minsk, and Mogilev—Russian laws prevented Jews from owning agricultural land, so few Jewish immigrants could provide convincing evidence that they qualified as "bona fide" agriculturalists.[16] However, immigration legislation did not specify a preference for agriculturalists or prohibit the admission of immigrants with other occupations.[17] Despite official government pronouncements and instructions to immigration agents in Great Britain and Europe to recruit experienced agriculturalists, in practice Jewish immigrants seeking admission into Canada benefited from the persistent demand for skilled and unskilled labour created by the rapid expansion of railway construction as well as the industrial, service, and natural resource sectors of the economy.

Employers continuously lobbied the government to ensure that immigration policy did not impede a steady flow of cheap labour. In addition, railway and steamship companies, which not only profited from the transportation of immigrants but also depended on Canada's population growth to increase the domestic and international freight traffic essential for their future profitability and expansion, aggressively promoted an open immigration policy.[18] In their public pronouncements, instructions to immigration department officials, and allocations of departmental expenditures between 1896 and 1914, successive cabinet ministers responsible for immigration repeatedly emphasized that the recruitment of agriculturalists was the primary goal of immigration policy. In practice, though, under both Liberal and Conservative governments, immigration agents at Canada's ports of entry continued to admit skilled and unskilled workers. In 1913–14, when close to 400,000 immigrants entered Canada, only 24.5 percent of men admitted were agriculturalists; the remainder were classified as general labourers, mechanics, clerks and traders, and miners.[19] Consequently, Jewish immigrants and their dependants travelling independently to Canada did not face occupational restrictions; immigration officers who interviewed them on arrival at Canadian ports of entry to determine their eligibility for admission readily accepted the validity of their stated work experience.[20]

Similarly, between 1882 and 1914, despite growing anxiety about changes in the racial composition of Canada and pervasive anti-Semitism, Jewish immigrants from the Pale of Settlement benefited from the Canadian government's expansion of immigrant recruitment in Europe.[21] Immigration officials judged the suitability of prospective immigrants based upon their ethnoracial identities, the extent to which they shared the same racial characteristics, language, values, and religious beliefs as British Canadians and therefore could be readily assimilated into English-speaking Canadian society. To promote British Canadian conformity as the foundation of Canada's social development, Canadian immigration policy admitted or excluded immigrants according to a hierarchy of preference. Preferred immigrants, the most desirable, came from the "mother country," Great Britain, followed by immigrants from the United States and, though they did not speak English, Northern and Western European countries whose people exhibited racial characteristics similar to those of Anglo-Saxons. Less preferred, but admitted to achieve the government's goal of populating western Canada, were immigrants from Central and Eastern Europe.[22] All other immigrants, in particular those from India, China, and Japan, were considered racially "inferior" because they posed a threat to Canada's "political, moral, social and economic development."[23] Between 1885 and 1914, successive Canadian governments enacted legislation and implemented regulations to limit or bar the admission of immigrants deemed racially inferior.[24]

According to W.D. Scott, who served as superintendent of immigration from 1903 to 1919, Jews were not preferred immigrants: "No effort is or has ever been made by the government of Canada to induce Jewish immigrants to come to the Dominion." However, despite his concerns that Jewish immigrants contributed to urban congestion and established sweatshops that he associated with the "ghettos and slums of New York," under his direction Canada's immigration policy did not exclude or restrict the admission of Jewish immigrants or their dependants.[25]

Pre–First World War Jewish immigration from Eastern Europe peaked in 1913–14. Although transatlantic passenger ships continued to transport a limited number of Eastern European immigrants to Canada throughout the war, most immigrants came from Great Britain. By the end of 1914, the Eastern Front, the theatre of war between Germany and its ally the Austro-Hungarian Empire and Russia, extended from the Baltic Sea to the Black Sea, making travel from the Pale of Settlement to a Western European port virtually impossible. Jewish immigration to Canada, which reached 11,252 in 1913–14, dropped to 3,107 in 1914–15 and to only sixty-five in 1915–16.[26]

Jewish immigration from Eastern Europe resumed in 1920, but because of restrictions on the admission of Jews into Canada it did not reach prewar levels.[27] Between 1920 and 1931, when the depression and rising unemployment induced the government to severely limit immigration, Canada admitted 41,800 Jews, approximately 63 percent of the number who arrived between 1904 and 1915.[28] By 1921, births increased Winnipeg's Jewish population from 13,355 in 1916 to 14,449 or 8 percent of the city's residents, and with the resumption of immigration and additional births it reached 17,236 or 7.9 percent of the total population of the city in 1931.[29] The modest growth of Winnipeg's Jewish community between 1921 and 1931 was partly a result of the decline in Jewish immigration to Canada. However, between 1921 and 1931, Jewish immigrants arriving in Canada increasingly gravitated to Montreal and Toronto. Winnipeg's Jewish population increased by 19 percent between 1921 and 1931, but Toronto's increased by 26.6 percent and Montreal's by 34.5 percent.[30] Consequently, it was the approximately 9,000 Jewish immigrants who arrived between 1882 and 1914 together with their children born in Canada who established the demographic, organizational, and institutional foundation of Winnipeg's Jewish community.

Winnipeg: A Booming British Canadian Metropolis

On 22 May 1905, the first passengers began to arrive and depart through the Canadian Pacific Railway's new Winnipeg station.[31] To design the new station, which included railway administrative offices, the CPR had commissioned the Montreal firm of Edward and W.S. Maxwell, prominent practitioners of the Beaux-Arts classical style of architecture. The massive station, with its grandiose front entrance framed by limestone columns, majestic raised rotunda with marble terrazzo floor illuminated by an arch of amber glass, together with ornate carved stone cornices and the lavish use of marble, brass, and wood panelling, provided ample evidence of both the CPR's pre-eminent role in Winnipeg's development as the gateway to western Canada and the railway company's enormous wealth.[32] Similarly, with its immense rotunda, grand staircase, and amenities—which included a banquet hall and two ballrooms—the 350-room Royal Alexandra Hotel that opened the following year adjacent to the station was designed to acclaim Winnipeg's emerging status as the third largest city in Canada. Named after Alexandra, the wife of King Edward VII, the luxury hotel's vice-regal suite—complete with a salon, waiting room, private dining room, and bedrooms—assured the city's politicians,

1. Canadian Pacific Railway Station and Royal Alexandra Hotel, 1911.

businessmen, and socialites that Winnipeg not only ranked among the great cities of Canada but also could proudly accommodate visiting royalty, which for many of Winnipeg's British Canadian elite was the ultimate benediction.[33]

But not all passengers arriving in Winnipeg on CPR trains experienced the grandeur of the new railway station. The thousands of Jewish immigrants who arrived in Winnipeg between 1905 and 1914 had a very different introduction to the city and their new lives in Canada. When CPR trains arrived from eastern Canada, passengers travelling in first- and second-class cars stepped onto a platform facing the rear entrance of the station. Conductors and station staff directed passengers to the station's spacious arrivals hall, and baggage porters were available to assist them with their luggage. From the arrivals hall, where they could be greeted by friends or relatives, they entered the station's expansive rotunda, which provided access to a ladies' waiting room, a men's smoking room, a café, and a dining room. Leaving the railway station, passengers could either walk through an interior passageway to the Royal Alexandra Hotel or exit the station through its front doors, which led to a driveway bordering a small park facing one of Winnipeg's major thoroughfares. Immigrants, however, who typically travelled third class in rudimentary colonist cars that comprised the rear section of the train, entered Winnipeg through an austere Canadian government portal. After gathering their belongings, immigrants detrained

2. Dominion Immigration Building, 83 Maple Street, with CPR tracks in the foreground, 1970.

onto a separate platform in front of the immigration hall, where they were met by uniformed immigration officers who escorted them inside.

Beginning in 1872, the Canadian government constructed a series of immigration halls in Winnipeg to receive immigrants and, if required, provide them with temporary accommodations.[34] Following completion of the CPR passenger network from eastern ports to Winnipeg in 1886, the flow of immigrants to Winnipeg steadily increased, and the government's immigration hall was frequently overcrowded, forcing immigration officials to search for temporary accommodations elsewhere. Under pressure from the City of Winnipeg, whose officials were concerned that immigrants living in congested quarters with rudimentary sanitation posed a threat to public health, the federal government assembled land in 1887 for the construction of a larger immigration hall, completed in 1900. But the three-storey Dominion Government Immigration Hall proved to be inadequate as soon as it opened, forcing Winnipeg's commissioner of immigration to secure additional facilities to accommodate immigrants arriving in the summer months.[35] In 1904, as the CPR began construction of its new passenger and hotel complex, the federal cabinet approved a contract to build a second immigration hall located adjacent to the new railway station facing the railway tracks. Constructed of stone and brick, the new four-storey immigration hall was completed in 1906. The main floor of the new building, named the Dominion Immigration Building, was devoted to offices for the commissioner of immigration for western Canada and his staff. Upon entering the hall, each immigrant was processed a second time by immigration officers, creating a registry containing most of the same information entered in ships' landing records at ports of entry: name, age, nationality, name of the steamship that brought the person to Canada, date of arrival, and final destination.[36]

The Dominion Immigration Building offered accommodations for up to 500 immigrants; each of the building's three upper floors had separate rooms for families, a dormitory for single men, communal kitchens, a dining room, and washrooms with baths. However, this modern building, which became known as Immigration Hall No. 1, was reserved for the exclusive use of "preferred" immigrants, English-speaking migrants from the "mother country," Great Britain. Once interviewed, "foreign" immigrants, including Jews from Eastern Europe, were taken to Immigration Hall No. 2, located next to the new building. Immigration Hall No. 2, an antiquated wooden structure built in 1890, was one-third the size of Immigration Hall No. 1.[37] Although the sleeping, dining, and sanitary facilities in Immigration Hall No. 2 were cramped and overcrowded, they were deemed suitable for "foreigners" considered a "poorer class" of immigrants.[38] Upon arrival, therefore, Jewish immigrants were immediately introduced to the distinctions and disparities based upon social class, ethnoracial identity, and place of residence that would define their settlement and future lives in Winnipeg.

Jewish immigrants leaving the immigration hall entered a city far different from the small towns and *shtetlekh* of the Pale of Settlement, where a majority of them had lived. Whereas Russia's nascent economic modernization had scarcely improved life in Jewish communities—Russian laws and regulations had been systematically crafted to perpetuate the segregation and economic marginalization of Jews in the Pale—between 1882 and 1914 Winnipeg emerged as a dynamic metropolis, the epicentre of unrestrained and rapid economic development in western Canada. In 1871, Winnipeg was a village at the confluence of the Red and Assiniboine Rivers with a population of 241 that served as the commercial centre of the fur trade and the more populous Red River agricultural colony.[39] However, as the frontier of agricultural settlement expanded to southern and southwestern Manitoba, creating a growing market for the city's manufacturing, wholesale, and retail businesses, the population of the newly incorporated City of Winnipeg surged to 3,700 in 1874 and to 7,744 in 1881.[40] Beginning in 1881, the rapid expansion of the CPR's railway network from Winnipeg to western Manitoba, Saskatchewan, and Alberta accelerated agricultural settlement and led to the establishment of a growing number of villages, towns, and ultimately cities. Between 1881 and 1921, the population of Manitoba, Saskatchewan, and Alberta increased from approximately 119,000 to 1.96 million, creating a vast hinterland market for goods and services provided by western Canada's gateway city.[41]

Enriched by the growing demand for vast quantities of agricultural implements, hardware, construction materials, clothing, and household goods, Winnipeg's wholesale and distribution businesses made an enduring contribution to the city's economic development. However, Winnipeg's entrepreneurs quickly branched into retail sales, manufacturing, metal foundries and fabrication, brewing, flour mills, and meat packing.[42] By the 1880s, Winnipeg had emerged as the headquarters of the western grain trade. As wheat production on the prairies rapidly increased—from 1.1 million bushels in 1880 to 293 million bushels in 1921—financing the grain trade contributed to the expansion of Winnipeg's banks, which in conjunction with real estate, insurance, trust, and mortgage companies quickly established the city as the financial centre of western Canada.[43] Between the 1880s and 1914, Winnipeg's rapid economic development stimulated a building boom and with it a growing number of contractors and building supplies companies.[44] The proliferation of Winnipeg businesses led to the construction of factories, warehouses, hotels, office blocks, retail stores, and financial institutions. Public investments included federal, provincial, and municipal buildings, public utilities and infrastructure, as well as thirty-eight hospitals and schools.[45] The CPR, Great Northern, and Pacific Grand Trunk railway companies built administrative and maintenance facilities, extensive marshalling yards, two railway stations, and two luxury hotels. In addition, residential construction to house Winnipeg's growing population contributed to the building boom.[46]

Between 1881 and 1921, Winnipeg's population increased from 7,985 to 179,087, a rate of growth that surpassed those of Montreal and Toronto.[47] Ranked seventeenth in population in 1881, by 1906 Winnipeg was Canada's third largest city.[48] Between 1890 and 1914, approximately 84 percent of Winnipeg's population growth was the result of migration.[49] Offering seemingly limitless investment and employment opportunities, Winnipeg attracted a growing stream of migrants. Before 1881, most migrants came from eastern Canada, primarily Ontario. However, once completion of the CPR linked Winnipeg to ocean ports, the city emerged as a major destination for transatlantic immigrants. By 1891, immigrants from Great Britain and Europe together with increasing numbers from the United States accounted for a larger share of Winnipeg's population growth than migrants from other provinces.

Despite a growing influx of immigrants from Europe—the proportion of European-born residents increased from 8.2 percent in 1891 to 17.2 percent in 1916—the vast majority of the people of Winnipeg either migrated from or were the children of migrants from Ontario or immigrants from Great Britain.[50] Winnipeg's population was not only predominantly British Canadian but also overwhelmingly Protestant. In 1916, slightly more than 71 percent of the residents of Winnipeg stated that they were Anglican, Methodist, Presbyterian, Lutheran, Baptist, or other Protestant denominations.[51] Winnipeg's British Canadian residents not only shared a common religion, language, and ethnoracial identity but also harboured an ingrained distrust and suspicion of foreign "races." For "foreign-born" immigrants from Europe, particularly Jews, whose language, culture, and religious beliefs were considered by the British Canadian majority to be "alien" and therefore inferior, their conspicuous ethnoracial identity impeded their integration into Winnipeg's economic, social, and political spheres.

The ascendancy of an "optimistic, expansionist, and aggressive" British Canadian business elite was central to British Canadian domination of Winnipeg's economic and social development.[52] Composed of wholesalers, merchants, manufacturers, financiers, dealers in real estate, contractors, and grain merchants, Winnipeg's business elite was exclusively of British origin and Protestant. Attracted by Winnipeg's potential to emulate Chicago's growth and wealth, almost all of the entrepreneurs who became leaders of Winnipeg's business community migrated from Ontario and Great Britain.[53] Realizing their ambition, the acquisition of wealth, was both a measure of individual achievement and the standard by which the advancement of society was judged. Although most members of Winnipeg's business elite came from relatively affluent or even wealthy families, and enjoyed advantages such as access to capital, business connections, or a superior level of education, invariably they believed that their success was solely the result of individual enterprise and self-reliance.[54] Nevertheless, they were conscious of the benefit of harnessing the resources of the government to promote their business interests and aggressively enlisted its support.

Members of the business elite not only used business organizations such as the Winnipeg Board of Trade to lobby Winnipeg City Council but they also controlled it. Between 1874 and 1914, the business elite succeeded in electing one of their own—a merchant, financier, real estate agent, manufacturer, or contractor—as mayor in all but four years.[55] Similarly, in the same period, members of Winnipeg's business elite accounted for 81 percent of the elected representatives on City Council and 91 percent of the positions on the Board of Control, the council's powerful executive committee.[56] Whether debating measures such as spending public funds to promote immigration and attract industries, or incurring a $3.23 million debt for a hydroelectric project so that Winnipeg manufacturers had access to low-cost electricity, members of City Council invariably determined that public expenditures that benefited the business elite were justified because they stimulated the economic development and growth of the entire community and therefore served the public interest.[57] However, when considering public expenditures to deal with pressing problems of urban growth, such as public health, poverty, or inadequate housing, members of the business elite serving on City Council were reluctant to expand their definition of the public interest to include social welfare. Even when confronted with typhoid and other epidemics and high infant mortality rates, members of City Council were slow to concede that increasing expenditures on public health measures was justified. In part, their reluctance to approve expenditures on public health and other social welfare measures was related to the fact that the incidence of disease and the risk of death were much higher in neighbourhoods where foreign-born immigrants rather than British Canadians lived, and their first impulse was to assume that threats to public health persisted because of immigrants' "ignorance, laziness and immorality."[58] However, for city councillors, social welfare expenditures were simply, in economic terms, an unproductive use of the city's resources.

Members of the business elite were equally aggressive in their pursuit of political influence on provincial and federal governments. Provincially, the business elite focused on limiting government expenditures as well as on policies to promote agricultural settlement, the construction of railways, and lower railway tariffs. Each new farm increased wheat production and the consumption of goods and services, and the expansion of railway networks through the construction of branch lines provided greater access to consumers and consolidated Winnipeg's dominance of the grain trade by efficiently transporting wheat from producers to international markets. Expanding railway networks to compete with the CPR also promised to increase competition and lower the cost of transportation. Winnipeg's business elite was primarily concerned with lowering the cost of shipping goods to consumers but also recognized that lower tariffs on the transportation of grain would increase farmers' incomes and consequently their purchasing power. Thus, they supported the Manitoba government's efforts to challenge the CPR monopoly by asserting its constitutional authority to grant a legislative charter to a railway company. Once the federal government acknowledged the province's right to charter a railway, the provincial government entered into negotiations with railway promoters that resulted in the establishment of the Northern Pacific and Manitoba and Canadian Northern Railway Companies, which supported the expansion of agricultural settlement in southern and northwestern Manitoba, undermined the CPR's monopoly on the shipment of grain, and by 1903 resulted in lower freight rates.[59]

Because Winnipeg was underrepresented in Manitoba's Legislative Assembly—the city's share of seats, which ranged from 8 percent in 1871 to 18 percent in 1921, continuously lagged behind increases in its share of the provincial population—members of the business elite could not hope to enjoy the same amount of provincial as municipal political influence.[60] Nevertheless, business elites were active in both political parties and successfully contested elections as Liberal or Conservative candidates in Winnipeg constituencies. Of the twenty-seven members of the Legislative Assembly elected in Winnipeg constituencies between 1871 and 1920, twelve were members of the business elite, and eight were corporate lawyers.[61] Although Winnipeg's elected representatives comprised a small minority in the Legislative Assembly, both Liberal and Conservative premiers recognized the importance of including a member of Winnipeg's business elites in cabinet. Their large campaign contributions, dominant role in Winnipeg's business community, and personal relationships with leaders of federal political parties made them an indispensable political asset.

For example, in 1889, Thomas Greenway, the Liberal premier of Manitoba, appointed Daniel McMillan as provincial treasurer, a position that he held until 1900. McMillan was a former vice-president of the Liberal Party and the owner of the grain brokerage firm D.H. McMillan and Company. His prominence in the grain trade led to his election in 1888 as the first president of the Winnipeg Grain Exchange. During his term as provincial treasurer, McMillan continued to pursue his business interests. Consistent with the prevailing ethos of holding public office, he did not believe that taking advantage of business opportunities was incompatible with being a cabinet minister. Indeed, since the primary responsibility of the provincial government was to promote economic development by supporting private enterprise, business acumen was considered a prerequisite for making informed public policy decisions. In 1891, together with fourteen other investors, McMillan established the Great-West

Life Assurance Company and remained a director of it throughout his term of office.[62]

The career of Rodmond Roblin, the Conservative leader whose party governed Manitoba between 1900 and 1915, also illustrated the fluid interchange between business and political life. Before he became a member of the Legislative Assembly in 1888, his business career as a general merchant, mortgage lender, and grain buyer culminated in membership in the Winnipeg Grain Exchange and, in 1887, his appointment as president of the Dominion Elevator Company. When his political career came to an end in 1915, Roblin resumed his position as president of the company.[63] Upon assuming office, he appointed as attorney general Colin Campbell, a corporate lawyer and wealthy investor who had briefly served as a City of Winnipeg councillor, and as minister of public works Robert Rogers, who had amassed a large fortune in the grain trade, speculation in real estate, and mining.[64] Rogers, responsible for dispensing the patronage that transformed the Conservative Party into a formidable political machine, along with Campbell, became Roblin's closest collaborators. Despite the underrepresentation of Winnipeg in the Legislative Assembly, between 1900 and 1911 members of the city's economic elite held a third of the cabinet posts in the Roblin government.[65]

Members of the business elite in Winnipeg were similarly active in federal politics. Through the Board of Trade, they successfully lobbied the federal government for reductions in freight rates that protected Winnipeg shippers from competition from both eastern and western Canadian rivals, secured funding for the construction of locks to improve navigation on the Red River, and supported the efforts of the Western Canadian Immigration Association to secure funding for its activities promoting agricultural settlement.[66] They also contested federal elections; four of the twelve members of Parliament elected in Winnipeg constituencies between 1882 and 1921 were members of the business elite, and three were corporate lawyers.[67]

Despite their political differences, members of the business elite who supported the Liberals or Conservatives mingled in the same social sphere. By the mid-1890s, many members of the elite lived in large Victorian houses in a neighbourhood adjacent to the legislative building. However, by the early 1900s, Winnipeg's wealthiest families began to gravitate to Armstrong's Point, Crescentwood, and Roslyn Road. Property developers in these fashionable residential enclaves offered large lots governed by restrictive covenants ensuring that only the wealthy could afford to build houses there.[68] Conscious of their status, members of the business elite commissioned architects to build palatial houses whose size, grandeur, and distinctive designs provided suitable evidence not only of their wealth and prominence but also of their sophistication and good taste.[69] Members of the elite lived close to one another and belonged to the same social and recreational clubs whose restrictive admission procedures and high initiation fees ensured that membership was limited to wealthy men who enjoyed the confidence and respect of their peers.[70] Premier Roblin as well as more than 40 percent of the MLAs and MPs elected in Winnipeg constituencies between 1874 and 1920 belonged to the prestigious Manitoba Club, 21 percent belonged to the Carleton Club, and 38 percent belonged to the St. Charles Country Club.[71] In addition to providing venues for members to socialize over dinner or drinks, exclusive clubs became private forums where Winnipeg's business and political leaders exchanged information and made many of the decisions that charted the city's future.[72] Together with membership in music and art clubs; innumerable social events attended by members of the wealthy families who presided over "Winnipeg Society"; worship at prestigious Presbyterian, Methodist, and Anglican churches; and the education of their daughters at Havergal Ladies College and their sons at St. John's College School or Tuckell's Boy's School for Boys, private clubs solidified the social networks that joined members of the business elite in their collective enterprise, the domination of Winnipeg's economic development and political life.[73]

Although their wealth, status, and political influence gave members of the elite every reason to be confident about the future, they were troubled by immigration. They welcomed immigrants because their labour and consumption of goods and services contributed to economic growth and the business elite's accumulation of wealth. However, as dramatic increases in immigration swelled Winnipeg's population, the business elite became more and more concerned that immigrants threatened to undermine British Canadian values, beliefs, and institutions, the very foundation of the social consensus that enabled them to maintain their power and privilege. Since most members of the business elite were the sons of immigrants from Great Britain, they welcomed an infusion of "our blood," English-speaking Protestants who would quickly integrate and become "Canadian."[74] Although the business elite had reservations about the class of British immigrants arriving in Winnipeg—too many of them proved to be unreliable workers, especially the unemployed from the slums of London or Manchester who had been assisted by emigration societies to seek opportunities in Canada—they were encouraged by the proliferation of religious and secular organizations that assisted immigrants to integrate into

British Canadian society. Protestant churches that followed liturgies familiar to British immigrants preached a gospel steeped in imperial traditions and images. Sermons invariably included references to imperial ideals of duty and loyalty, and prayers of thanksgiving acknowledged and celebrated the blessings of living under the British crown.

As British immigrants flocked to the growing number of Anglican, Presbyterian, and Methodist churches, clergy not only provided them with emotional support and moral guidance but also organized "women's auxiliaries, musical societies, athletic clubs and youth organizations."[75] In addition to promoting fellowship, fraternal organizations such as the Masons, Sons of England Benefit Society, and St. Andrew's Society formed a social network in which established immigrants provided new arrivals with advice and assistance finding employment. By 1920, over half of Winnipeg's fraternal societies offered life insurance and sickness benefits, binding old and new members in a relationship of shared responsibility for their collective welfare. British immigrant women, excluded from membership in fraternal organizations, were encouraged to join the Imperial Order of Daughters of the Empire or women's organizations affiliated with the Local Council of Women of Winnipeg.[76] For British immigrants, attending a Protestant church or joining a secular organization provided more than fellowship and practical assistance. As these immigrants attempted to overcome the dislocation and confusion of migration and establish new lives in Winnipeg, these churches and organizations affirmed their identity and defined their place as British Canadians.

Nevertheless, despite the success of Protestant churches and secular organizations in integrating British immigrants, the business elite was forced to contend with rising labour militancy. Beginning in the 1880s, British immigrants, including many who had participated in the trade union movement before emigrating, concluded that collective action was essential to increase wages, reduce hours of work, and improve working conditions. Despite bitter opposition from Winnipeg employers, British immigrants began to form craft unions and engaged in strikes to press their demands for union recognition and the right to negotiate contracts.[77] In 1894, ten unions formed the Winnipeg Trades and Labour Council, which by 1914 represented over 8,000 workers organized in more than sixty-two union locals.[78] The growth in union membership, the annual Labour Day parade, union-sponsored social and sporting events, the publication of a labour newspaper (the *Voice*), and the formation of the Labour Party, Socialist Party of Canada, and Social Democratic Party of Canada to contest municipal and provincial elections provided ample evidence that a substantial portion of British immigrants rejected the business elite's domination of Winnipeg's economic and political life.[79] By the early 1900s, a series of bitter strikes highlighted Winnipeg's class divisions and polarized public opinion. Employers were adamant that they had an absolute right to unilaterally fix wages and working conditions. They fired union leaders, hired strike breakers, and appealed to the courts and municipal authorities to authorize the police to protect their property and disperse strikers.[80] But British immigrant workers were equally resolute in their determination to exercise their right to negotiate with employers. The measures that employers used to frustrate union demands for collective bargaining confirmed that, though the business elite welcomed their integration into Winnipeg's British Canadian community, they refused to accept British immigrant workers' right to participate in decisions affecting the management of businesses or their entitlement to a reasonable standard of living.

By the early 1900s, members of Winnipeg's largely Ontario-born business elite became aware that immigration had irrevocably altered the scope of their sphere of influence. Although the business elite continued to amass wealth and enjoy undiminished political power, as Winnipeg's population increased, the proportion of residents who belonged to their social network of private clubs, exclusive social circles, and prestigious churches steadily declined. The growth of a militant labour movement confirmed that increasing numbers of British immigrants were prepared to challenge their authority in the workplace and politics. For the most part, Winnipeg's growing middle class of professionals, managers, clergy, public servants, and businessmen identified with the values and aspirations of the business elite and supported their pre-eminent role in politics and authoritarian view of labour relations, but relatively few were considered suitable candidates for membership in a private club or invited to exclusive social events. They were welcome, however, to join fraternal societies such as the Independent Order of Odd Fellows, but few members of the middle class needed the benefits that they provided or wanted to socialize with the workers and small-business owners who belonged to them.[81] As conflicts over wages and working conditions escalated, and as increasing numbers of British immigrants joined unions, Winnipeg's business elite helped to establish an organization to engage the middle class in promoting a "national sentiment" that would transcend class divisions.[82]

In 1904, twenty-eight charter members, a group that included prominent members of the business elite, founded the Canadian Club of Winnipeg.[83] Its stated purpose was to "develop and maintain a greater love for our country and devotion to the Imperial ideal."[84] Resolutely committed to the "British connection," they expressed devotion to the British crown and the values, beliefs, and institutions that they believed constituted the British Empire's contribution to the worldwide advance of civilization. Their primary responsibility, as the club's constitution declared, was to "foster patriotism" and "unite Canadians" to work for the "welfare and progress of the Dominion."[85] However, uniting Canadians did not mean extending membership in the club to all residents of Winnipeg. Charter members of the club were determined to recruit British Canadian, middle-class men, who—because of their positions in business, public service, or the professions—could effectively promote its ideals. To ensure that prospective members had the necessary qualifications, membership was restricted to applicants who had the support of two members, and each application had to be approved by a 90 percent vote.[86] The club also adopted the practice of holding lunchtime meetings at a downtown hotel; only those with occupations that allowed considerable autonomy could attend them.

The Canadian Club was immediately successful. Shortly after it was established, it could proudly proclaim that "the audiences that assemble at the luncheons are thoroughly representative of the best type of Winnipeg's business and professional classes."[87] In 1907, inspired by Rudyard Kipling, who predicted in an address to the club that Winnipeg was on the "threshold of an unbelievable future," a group of women established a "sister club," the Women's Canadian Club of Winnipeg, to provide a similar forum for middle-class women.[88] By 1909, when membership in the Canadian Club increased to 1,100, audiences of 800–900 members heard lectures delivered by Canadian and British dignitaries on topics such as "The New National Spirit," "The Empire and the Development of Western Canada," "Relations of Canada to the Mother Country," and "The Imperial Navy."[89] The club's program communicated an unmistakable message: promoting the realization of a Canadian national identity was inextricably linked to strengthening the British Empire and, in doing so, participating in the global expansion of an Anglo-Saxon, Christian civilization that embodied the world's most advanced ethical and political principles.

Despite a steady increase in the number of European-born immigrants settling in Winnipeg, the Canadian Club's mission of uniting Canadians did not include admitting "foreigners" as members. Although the club's constitution stated that all British subjects whether by birth or by naturalization could join, its membership rules effectively excluded European immigrants judged doubly undesirable: they were working class, and because they did not share British "blood" they were considered racially inferior and incapable of understanding or promoting national ideals. Nevertheless, the club's success suggested that under its leadership the "best type of Winnipeg's business and professional classes" could effectively promote a "national sentiment" that would mould the city's British Canadian majority into a cohesive bulwark against foreign influences. However, as immigration from Europe grew, Winnipeg's religious, business, and political leaders became increasingly alarmed about the "foreign problem": immigrants with little understanding of British traditions, questionable loyalty, and possible anarchistic or socialist tendencies whose resistance to assimilation threatened to undermine British Canadian values, beliefs, and institutions, and whose high birth rates raised the spectre that "we will no longer be British, probably no longer Anglo-Saxon."[90]

The Perceived Threat of "Foreign" Immigration

European immigrants were "strangers within our gates": they did not speak English, dressed differently, had unfamiliar customs and questionable morals, and practised forms of Christianity that did not adhere to British Canadian Protestant theology or religious rites or, in the case of Jews, espoused a religion that rejected the fundamental precept of Christian belief. Having chosen to settle in Winnipeg, European immigrants were expected to assimilate quickly, to embrace the opportunity to become "British subjects" by eradicating all vestiges of their pre-immigration lives and integrating into the dominant British Canadian community. Not to assimilate, or not to accept their responsibility to make every effort to do so, constituted a willful rejection of deeply held British Canadian values and beliefs and a declaration that they were determined to remain foreigners rather than become Canadians. According to J.W. Dafoe, the influential editor of the *Manitoba Free Press*, if every immigrant was not prepared to be a Canadian first, "he should pack his trunk and go back home where he belongs. He is not wanted here."[91]

Some European immigrants, "the best foreigners," confirmed expectations that Winnipeg could become a "melting pot," that through assimilation, a "fusion of races," the British Canadian majority could successfully transform strangers into loyal Canadians.[92] Applying prevailing racial stereotypes based upon a combination of national characteristics and innate traits, contemporary observers such as J.S. Woodsworth concluded that Northern Europeans, immigrants from Iceland, Scandinavia, and Germany, were similar to Anglo-Saxons and predisposed to assimilate; they would become "excellent citizens."[93] However, a majority of immigrants arriving from Europe came from the Austro-Hungarian and Russian Empires; Slavs and Jews outnumbered Northern Europeans three to one.[94] Products of "centuries of poverty and oppression," Galicians, whose racial characteristics, according to Woodsworth, applied to Ukrainian, Polish, and Russian immigrants, were hard working but illiterate, ignorant, and inclined to commit crimes.[95] They were also dominated by religious leaders who encouraged them to forge a hybrid Ukrainian Canadian identity, a concept abhorrent to Canadian nationalists such as Dafoe who believed that "hyphens should be left at the port of embarkation."[96] Nevertheless, as members of Ukrainian Catholic or Orthodox congregations, they offered some assurance that, though they adhered to religious rites steeped in superstition and autocracy, they shared many religious beliefs with the British Canadian majority, and in time this would provide a foundation for assimilation.

Jews, however, with their long history as a people apart in Europe, were less likely to assimilate. According to Woodsworth, the most important Jewish characteristic was the ability to thrive: "They come here wretchedly poor, and yet in some way they exist and make money."[97] He praised their natural qualities—"religious, temperate, home-loving, intelligent, industrious and ambitious, the Jew is bound to succeed"—as well as their generosity in caring for "their poor through their own charitable organizations."[98] However, "the majority are disinclined to do hard physical labour" and prefer to engage in business; they share the same "keen business instincts" of the "money barons who control the world's finances."[99] This business acumen together with a tendency to "be miserly" explained their success.[100] If the phrase "determination to save" was substituted for the term "miserly," then this description could have been applied to J.H. Ashdown, Alexander Brown, John McKechnie, or Elisha Hutchings, members of the British Canadian business elite who worked at skilled trades until they accumulated sufficient capital to establish successful businesses.[101] The accomplishments of these self-made men whose "business instincts" had contributed to Winnipeg's growth and prosperity were widely celebrated. Certainly, they were never publicly criticized for their desire to become businessmen instead of working at "physical labour"; their success in business and great wealth were considered evidence of their ambition and character. In contrast to the public acclaim of the economic contributions of members of the business elite as well as countless enterprising British Canadian small-business owners, Woodsworth declared that Jews were "largely non-producers."[102] Although he conceded that they were "by no means parasites," his assessment of their role in Winnipeg's economic life was similar to the Russian government's depiction of Jews in the Pale of Settlement: they might thrive, but their success was suspect because they were not economically productive members of society.[103]

Nevertheless, Woodsworth was impressed with one characteristic of the Jews: "No people more highly value an education."[104] Accomplished linguists, Jews quickly learned English and were "omnivorous readers" who "plunge[d] into all kinds of intellectual activities."[105] However, they practised a religion that separated them from the British Canadian majority. Despite encouraging signs that under the influence of Christian churches Judaism was becoming more liberal—Woodsworth believed that by rejecting orthodox religious beliefs Jews would become more independent thinkers and therefore more susceptible to assimilation—he was concerned that by continuing to practise their religion Jews would remain a people apart, immune from the influence of Protestant churches that Woodsworth regarded as the most effective means of instilling the Anglo-Saxon values and beliefs that formed the foundation of a modern, civilized society.

Winnipeg's North End

Although debates continued about the desirability of European immigrants and which racial characteristics inhibited or facilitated assimilation, British Canadian anxiety about the foreign problem increasingly focused on the concentration of Jewish and other Eastern European immigrants in Winnipeg's North End, its infamous "foreign quarter." The construction of the CPR transformed the North End from a residential annex of Winnipeg's central business area into a separate district. The railway's main line and extensive network of marshalling yards, locomotive shops, and storage facilities, which extended from the Red River in the east to the city boundary in the west, divided Winnipeg, creating a physical barrier that limited access from the North End to the business and administrative centre. As a result, the North End's boundaries became the CPR tracks to the south, the city boundaries to the west and north, and the Red River to the east. The construction of the CPR, which also led to the construction of factories, saw mills, and other industries adjacent to the railway line, transformed the North End's residential character and shaped its future development.

Prior to the construction of the CPR, Point Douglas, the historical centre of the North End, was Winnipeg's most prestigious residential neighbourhood, home to Premier John Norquay, MP John Schultz, and prominent merchant J.H. Ashdown. However, when Point Douglas became isolated from the city centre and plagued by noise and pollution, property values there dropped. As its affluent residents relocated to more desirable neighbourhoods in Central Winnipeg, they were replaced by immigrants attracted by the older and therefore more affordable housing stock of Point Douglas as well as its proximity to the CPR and other employers of skilled and unskilled labour. As increasing numbers of immigrants arrived in Winnipeg, the demand for housing created a property boom. Real estate speculators purchased lots and large tracts of undeveloped land north of the CPR yards west of Main Street for residential construction. To maximize profits, contractors constructed cheaply built, wood-frame houses or multi-family dwellings on narrow lots twenty-five to thirty-two feet wide, creating a residential district deemed suitable for working-class immigrants; densely populated, it had limited access to the city's water supply, substandard sewer facilities, and few parks or public spaces for sports or other recreational activities.[106]

Between 1886 and 1916, the population of the North End increased from 7,372 to 69,616.[107] Immigration from Eastern Europe transformed the ethnoracial composition of the district. In the 1880s, the vast majority (89 percent) of the residents were British Canadian.[108] By 1901, however, the proportion of British Canadian residents (65 percent) declined: European immigrants—primarily German (1,360), Jewish (1,023), Scandinavian (832), Austro-Hungarian (950), and Russian (472)—made up 35 percent of the population.[109] In 1916, when less than 39 percent of its residents claimed to be of British origin, the North End was home to 11,746 Jews, 87 percent of Winnipeg's entire Jewish community (the settlement of Jews in Central and South Winnipeg is discussed below).[110] Jews constituted the largest ethnoracial minority (19.3 percent), followed by Ukrainians (11.2 percent), Poles (8 percent), Austrians (7 percent), Germans (6.4 percent), and Russians (3.5 percent).[111] Because of the North End's large Eastern European population, British Canadians adopted the term "foreign quarter" both to describe and to stigmatize the district, but this characterization ignored the high degree of ethnoracial residential segregation within it.

By 1901, all of the 1,023 Jews residing in the North End lived in a distinct Jewish enclave in Ward Five, the southern half of the district.[112] Ward Five included Point Douglas and a section of the district delineated by the CPR rail yards in the south, Flora Avenue in the north, Main Street in the east, and the city boundary in the west. A small number of European immigrants, primarily from Germany, settled in Ward Six, the section of the North End north of Flora Avenue, but it was overwhelmingly (85.4 percent) British Canadian.[113] Between 1901 and 1911, Jewish immigration extended the northern boundary of the North End's Jewish enclave to Burrows Avenue in Ward Six. However, with the exception of a few families who lived north of Burrows Avenue or west of McKenzie Street, almost all of the approximately 7,700 Jews residing in the North End lived either in the western half of Point Douglas or in a neighbourhood seven by nine square blocks north of the CPR marshalling yards, south of Alfred Avenue and west of Main Street.[114]

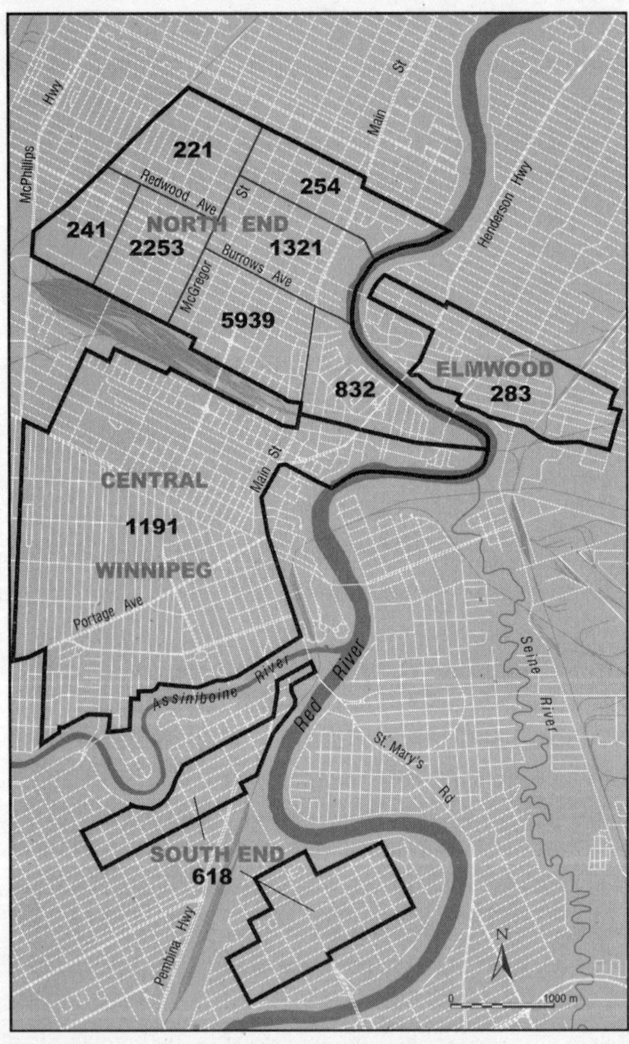

3. The distribution of Winnipeg's Jewish population in 1916. The population count for the North End, which is based on a calculation of Jewish residents listed on census enumeration forms, differs slightly from the figure given in the 1916 census.

Between 1911 and 1916, the Jewish population of the North End grew by 3,700, increasing the density of Jews residing within the 1911 borders of the enclave and enlarging it. Jewish immigrants settled west of McKenzie Street, extending the western boundary of the section of the enclave between the CPR rail yards and Aberdeen Avenue to Sinclair Street. They also migrated north to newer and less congested residential neighbourhoods, extending the northern boundary of the enclave six streets north to St. John's Avenue.[115] This Jewish enclave was not homogeneous—Jews lived side by side with other European immigrants and British Canadians—but they comprised 52.2 percent of the population.[116] On some streets, notably Lorne Avenue in Point Douglas (70 percent), Flora Avenue (63 percent), Selkirk Avenue (87.5 percent), and Manitoba Avenue (58.6 percent), Jews comprised a large majority of the residents.[117] Complete with synagogues, Jewish schools, a Yiddish-language newspaper, social welfare institutions, mutual aid societies, a Yiddish theatre, a farmers' market, and a shopping precinct on Selkirk Avenue, with the exception of employment, the enclave was home to a self-contained Jewish community. Surrounded by an almost homogeneous British Canadian neighbourhood to the north and a mixed Ukrainian, Polish, and German neighbourhood to the west, Jewish immigrants established a "New Jerusalem," an ethnoracial enclave that became home to the vast majority of Jewish immigrants who settled in Winnipeg until immigration to Canada virtually ended in 1931.[118]

Although the vast majority of Jewish immigrants settled in the North End, 1,753 Jews (13 percent of Winnipeg's Jewish population) lived in Central and South Winnipeg by 1916.[119] Jewish immigrants settled in Central Winnipeg—a district bounded by the CPR tracks in the north, Portage Avenue in the south, the Red River in the east, and the city boundary in the west—because of its proximity to the CPR station and Main Street. As immigrants streamed into Winnipeg in the 1880s and 1890s, employment agencies, clothing stores, hardware merchants, grocers, and hotels transformed the section of Main Street south of the CPR station into a thriving hub of commercial activity. The CPR and the many industries located in Central Winnipeg provided employment, and Jewish entrepreneurs took advantage of opportunities to establish businesses. By 1891, 135 Jews lived in Central Winnipeg (21 percenof the city's Jewish population).[120] Over the next twenty-five years, the Jewish population of Central Winnipeg continued to increase; by 1916, 1,191 Jews lived in the district. However, once they exited the immigration hall, most Jews bypassed Central Winnipeg and settled in the North End. Central Winnipeg's share of the city's Jewish population declined from 21.6

percent to 8.6 percent, and unlike in the North End, where Jews constituted the largest ethnoracial minority, they comprised only 1.8 percent of Central Winnipeg's residents.[121]

Jews constituted an even smaller minority in South Winnipeg (1.3 percent), a district bounded by the Red River to the east, Portage Avenue to the north, and the city boundaries to the west and south.[122] Census records indicate that four Jews lived in the South End in 1891 but none in 1901.[123] However, by 1916, 618 Jews, 4.5 percent of Winnipeg's Jewish population, lived in the South End.[124] Most of the Jews who lived in the South End had originally settled in the North End or Central Winnipeg. Having accumulated sufficient wealth, they migrated south to more prestigious neighbourhoods. Approximately 46 percent resided in spacious middle-class homes located between Portage Avenue and the Assiniboine River, and 34 percent lived in two of Winnipeg's wealthiest neighbourhoods, Crescentwood and the Roslyn Road area.[125] Unlike the densely populated enclave in the North End, with the exception of Jewish-owned businesses on Main Street and a synagogue, Jews living in Central and South Winnipeg were less visible. As small minorities living in predominantly British Canadian districts, their presence was overshadowed by the 87 percent of Winnipeg's Jewish community who lived in the North End, which became the primary focus of public concern about the "foreign problem."

For Winnipeg's business elite, the geographic segregation and perceived social isolation of Jewish and other Eastern European immigrants in the North End were not simply obstacles to their assimilation into the dominant British Canadian community. Anxiety about unassimilated ethnoracial minorities who either rejected or were considered to be indifferent to British Canadian values and beliefs that were the very foundation of civilized society merged with unease that the development of a district simultaneously foreign and working class would exacerbate class divisions in Winnipeg. Although they were frustrated by increasing labour militancy among British immigrant workers, Winnipeg's employers were confident that the leaders of the union movement were basically concerned about exercising their right to collective bargaining to improve wages and working conditions. As loyal British subjects, they respected democratic practices and parliamentary institutions; their political objectives were limited to legislative reforms to protect working-class interests and attempts to secure the election of labour candidates.[126] Although employers were dismayed that prominent Methodists such as Salem Bland espoused a social gospel that linked Christianity to social justice, they were confident that Christian leaders would temper the radical impulses of the labour movement.

The same could not be said of working-class Eastern European immigrants. For example, Galician immigrants were accused of debasing democracy. Having no experience with elections, they were misled or bribed by political party "agents and heelers" who manipulated their votes for partisan advantage.[127] According to Woodsworth, allowing Galicians to vote was "absurd as well as dangerous": "Accustomed to despotism, untrained in the principle of representative government, without patriotism—such people are utterly unfit to be trusted with the ballot."[128]

Of even greater concern was the emergence in the North End of political organizations committed to the transformation of capitalism and state institutions. In 1905, three immigrants from the Russian Empire—Herman (Chaim) Saltzman, Jacob Penner, and Peter Ternenko—formed a branch of the Socialist Party of Canada. Members of the Socialist Party were organized into "language locals"; the Ukrainian branch was the largest, followed by Jewish, Polish, and other language branches. Support for the Marxist party in the North End's Jewish and Ukrainian communities confirmed suspicions that immigrants in the "foreign quarter" were importing revolutionary ideas from Eastern Europe that posed a threat to private property, the foundation of the business elite's wealth, and the British institutions of government that they revered. In 1910, 200 disaffected supporters of the Socialist Party of Canada frustrated with its gradualism, an emphasis on educating the working class rather than organizing direct political action, formed the more militant Marxist Social Democratic Party of Canada. Adopting the term "social democratic," the hallmark of Marxist parties in Germany and the Russian Empire, reinforced the widely held perception that immigrant communities harboured dangerous radicals influenced by alien ideologies. Within four years, Social Democratic Party branches in Winnipeg had close to 700 members.[129]

Most supporters of the Social Democratic Party lived in the North End. The Jewish branch held study sessions, sponsored public lectures, organized the unemployed, and supported the election of working-class candidates. The activities of the Jewish and other North End branches of the Social Democratic Party were widely publicized. In 1915, a series of fifteen lectures attracted an average audience of 400.[130] In April 1915, the Social Democratic Party organized a march of 15,000 to demand that the provincial government take action to alleviate unemployment. Two weeks later, on the eve of the annual May Day parade, the *Israelite Press* announced that the parade was a "workers' demonstration opposing the existence of the capitalist system with an expression of international workers' solidarity."[131] In the parade, party organizers led a Jewish contingent that marched behind the banner "Proletarians of the World Unite." The parade culminated in a rally at Market Square in Central Winnipeg, where speakers addressed a crowd of thousands of workers in English, Ukrainian, German, Yiddish, Polish, and Russian.[132] For Woodsworth, support for the Socialist and Social Democratic Parties in the North End's Jewish enclave confirmed that for many Jews "socialism has come as a gospel, [and] they have welcomed it with almost religious devotion."[133]

Emma Goldman's 1907 visit to Winnipeg to deliver a series of lectures provided more alarming evidence that Winnipeg's immigrant communities harboured dangerous radicals influenced by alien ideologies. Invited by the Free Society, an organization of Jewish anarchists, Goldman delivered five lectures in April 1907 to capacity audiences at the Trades Hall. Her reputation as an anarchist, an exponent of revolutionary ideas frequently linked to assassinations and acts of violence, preceded her. Nevertheless, though a majority of her audiences were "plainly of foreign origin," members of the business elite who worried that they might be the targets of anarchist activities had reason to be reassured by newspaper assessments of her lectures.[134] In response to her first lecture, entitled "Misconceptions about Anarchism," the *Winnipeg Telegram* editorialized that "Emma Goldman, as long as she promotes her work in English-speaking countries, is sowing on barren ground. Where British institutions flourish the weeds of anarchism have little chance to grow."[135] Similarly, an editorial in the *Voice*, the official publication of the Winnipeg Labour Council, stated that Goldman's lectures "did not make a single convert to her doctrine."[136] However, Mayor J.H. Ashdown was not reassured. When Goldman returned to Winnipeg at the invitation of the Free Society to deliver a second series of five lectures a year later, he wrote to Minister of the Interior Frank Oliver requesting that she be denied entry into Canada.

Ashdown might have been alarmed by newspaper reports two days before Goldman's arrival in Winnipeg that an anarchist, Selig Cohen (Silverstein), had detonated a bomb in New York City. Ashdown's letter to Oliver emphasized that Winnipeg's "foreign population"—"15,000 Galicians, 11,000 Germans, 10,000 Jews, 2000 Hungarians and 5000 Russians and other Slavs and Bohemians"—was receptive to radical and dangerous ideas: "They are just the crowd for Goldman or persons of her character to sow seeds which are bound to cause the most undesirable growths in the future."[137] On the advice of the minister of justice, Oliver concluded that the Immigration Act did not provide grounds to exclude "professional agitators," but the federal government shared Ashdown's view that anarchism was particularly dangerous. In

1910, it amended the Immigration Act to prohibit the entry of "persons who believe in or advocate the overthrow by force or violence of the Government of Canada . . . or who disbelieve in or are opposed to organized government, or who advocate the assassination of public officials, or who advocate or teach the unlawful destruction of property."[138] Insulating Winnipeg's ethnoracial minorities from radical and dangerous ideas by barring the admission of well-known anarchists might have alleviated the business elite's anxiety that their inflammatory rhetoric would exacerbate class divisions and lead to violence, but it did not address the underlying problem of how to assimilate ethnoracial minorities who did not share British Canadian values and beliefs. By 1908, J.S. Woodsworth, J.H. Ashdown, G.F. Chipman, J.W. Dafoe, and other advocates of British Canadian conformity concerned about the geographic segregation and perceived social isolation of Jewish and other Eastern European immigrants in the "foreign quarter" concluded that the solution was to marshal the resources of the church and public education system to "Canadianize" immigrant children and through them their parents.

Close to half of Winnipeg's Protestants belonged to Methodist or Presbyterian churches. Their national leaders believed that the "Anglo-Saxon race had developed the highest form of Christianity and civilization" and that Canada's British heritage had to be protected because it was the foundation of national identity.[139] Confronted with "foreign" immigration that threatened to undermine Canada's British heritage and jeopardize its future, church leaders responded by arguing that, as part of their worldwide mission to spread the gospel of Christian civilization, Methodists and Presbyterians had a responsibility to assimilate immigrants throughout western Canada to ensure "that they be Canadianized and Christianized."[140] In 1907, Reverend James Woodsworth was appointed superintendent of All People's Mission. The mission consisted of the Maple Street Congregational Church located close to the CPR station, which served British immigrants, and the Bethlehem Slavic Mission, situated in the heart of the "foreign quarter" on Stella Avenue. In the next two years, Woodsworth supervised the construction of two institutional buildings equipped with reading rooms, swimming pools, and gymnasiums—the first on Sutherland Avenue in Point Douglas (1908) to provide additional services to European immigrants and the second (1909) to replace the Bethlehem Slavic Mission on Stella Avenue—and bought a church on Burrows Avenue to provide additional programs.

Under the direction of his predecessor, Reverend Hamilton Wigle, in addition to religious services, All People's Mission provided night classes for adults in English, a kindergarten, a sewing school for girls seven to twelve, a club for girls twelve to fourteen, mothers' meetings, and charity in the form of clothing, food, and fuel.[141] As Wigle reported, "this children's work means the Protestantizing and Canadianizing of 215 mothers and homes in the near future."[142] J.V. Kovar, the minister in charge of the Stella Avenue mission, was particularly pleased that "a number of Jewish girls" attended kindergarten classes.[143] With the financial support of national Methodist missionary societies, donations from the congregations of local Methodist churches, and a grant of $1,000 from the City of Winnipeg, Woodsworth, assisted by thirteen staff and "over one hundred volunteer workers," continued Wigle's strategy of offering children's programs to reach immigrant homes.[144] He added cooking classes for girls, a choir and band, boys' clubs that focused on sports and recreation, and a system of home visits by deaconesses. In 1909, he reported that 909 children, including 109 Jewish children, participated in kindergarten and other programs.[145] Woodsworth believed that kindergartens were the "best means" of establishing a relationship with "foreign peoples": "Already the children call themselves Canadians," he enthusiastically reported, "and look at us as their friends and allies."[146]

Ashdown, who served on the mission's advisory committee and hosted meetings to discuss the goals and management of the mission at his home, was one of Woodsworth's strongest supporters. He regarded Winnipeg's perceived immigrant problem as an "extreme case" and argued that the Methodist Church should redirect some of the money that it spent on foreign missions to construct five more buildings to replicate the work of the Stella Avenue mission: "If the heathen or the non-civilized are worth looking after in their own countries, surely the same must be true of them when they come to our own land where their presence may have such a corrupting influence."[147] Chipman, who described assimilation as "the refining process," shared Ashdown's view that domestic missions deserved more support: "Why search the foreign fields for missionary work when there is such an abundant opportunity so convenient and waiting?"[148]

Leaders of the Presbyterian Church also believed that Christians faced a momentous choice. According to S.C. Murray, the superintendent of Presbyterian Home Missions in Manitoba, the values and beliefs of new Canadians "differ vastly from our own": "If we teach them in the spirit of Christ they will become a magnificent asset to our Canadian civilization. If we fail, they will become a menace to our best institutions."[149] In 1911, with the support of the Woman's Home Mission Society and subscriptions from

Winnipeg congregations, the Presbyterian Church built a settlement house on Burrows Avenue, the Robertson Memorial Institute.[150] In addition to a Sunday school and religious services, the institute (with a staff of five supplemented by volunteers) ran recreational and social clubs for children and mothers and a kindergarten. The institute primarily served British immigrants but also attempted to attract Ukrainians, part of the Presbyterian Church's plan to Canadianize the Ukrainian community by supporting the Independent Greek Church, a Protestant alternative to the Greek Catholic and Greek Orthodox Churches.[151] However, the Jewish community was the main focus of the Presbyterian Church's missionary work in the North End.

Surveying the history of the Jewish people and their immigration to Canada, Reverend S.B. Rohold concluded that Jews "are growing in numbers and wealth and thus in strength and influence and are bound to become an important factor in the moulding of the life and character of Canadians."[152] Rohold, who administered the Presbyterian Church's Mission to the Jews, believed that they had "special claims upon the Christian Church."[153] Having persecuted Jews in the past, "the Christians of to-day must make some reparation for the sins of their forefathers."[154] In 1911, Rohold supervised the opening of a branch of the Mission to the Jews in the heart of Winnipeg's Jewish enclave staffed by two evangelists, converts from Judaism who had worked at the London City Mission in England, and a nurse. In addition to religious services and Bible classes, to "reach effectively the home and life of the whole Jewish family," the mission offered a reading room and night school classes for adults, sewing classes for women and girls, a Boy Scout troop and manual training for boys, a nursery, and twice a week a free dispensary.[155]

The Jewish and other Eastern European immigrant families who took advantage of the programs and services provided by the Methodist and Presbyterian missions undoubtedly had reservations about exposing their children to evangelical zealots, but no other institutions in the North End provided free kindergarten, instruction in practical skills, or music and recreational programs for children. However, despite enthusiastic reports that many "foreign" children who participated in various mission programs also attended Sunday school, their parents were not easily converted; religious services were "chiefly" attended by British immigrants.[156] The All People's Mission also had limited success Christianizing the North End's foreign population, and in 1908–09 the 900 children and approximately 170 adults who participated in the classes and programs represented no more than 6 percent of the district's Eastern European immigrant population.[157] Thousands more children attended classes offered by schools established by Jewish, Ukrainian, and Polish religious institutions.[158] Similarly, comparatively few adults attended the missions' evening classes to learn English compared with the vast majority who continued to converse in Yiddish, Ukrainian, Polish, or German on a daily basis. The North End's Eastern European immigrants lived in self-contained communities in which they read newspapers published in their native languages and participated in religious services, cultural events, political gatherings, social activities, and meetings of mutual aid societies at which English was rarely used. Despite his enthusiastic advocacy of mission work, Woodsworth recognized its limitations; he concluded that public schools were the only institutions that could effectively assimilate immigrant children and had the staff and facilities to offer evening classes for adults.

Between 1882 and 1914, the Winnipeg School Board established nine schools in the North End. As the school-age population soared, board officials were frequently forced to build additions to newly constructed schools to provide additional classrooms, and teachers were confronted with classes of fifty students. However, though all children between the ages of five and sixteen had the right to attend school, attendance was not compulsory. To the dismay of Woodsworth, Dafoe, and other proponents of assimilation, in 1907 an estimated one-third of children did not attend school and were illiterate.[159] Woodsworth was convinced of the need for compulsory education. When a motion in support of compulsory primary education was defeated in the legislature, Dafoe launched a campaign in the *Manitoba Free Press*, publishing a constant stream of articles and editorials advocating legislation to force children to attend school.[160] The demand for a compulsory education system resonated with the business elite. In 1909, two former mayors, J.H. Ashdown and Thomas Ryan, attended a citizens' meeting that called for the immediate passage of legislation making education compulsory, a measure that the Canadian Club also supported.[161] Addressing the Canadian Club, Reverend D.M. Gordon emphasized that school attendance was essential to Canadianize "foreigners": "Of all the agencies that we have to deal with the foreign element the public school is the one upon which we must most firmly rely. It is the mill that gathers all into its hopper, and turns them out with the stamp of the king and of the maple leaf."[162]

Woodsworth and Ashdown also recognized that schools in Winnipeg were underutilized and that they could be open in the evenings to offer English-language classes. During his term as mayor, Ashdown persuaded the Winnipeg School Board to establish a system of evening classes for immigrants. In 1907, the board ran ten classes, and six more were added the following year. Twelve of the classes, advertised in foreign-language newspapers and handbills printed in five languages, were offered in North End schools.[163] Praising "foreign pupils" for their ambition to "improve their qualifications," Chipman noted that most of the students attending evening classes were Jews ranging in age from the young "up to the grey-haired."[164] To encourage enrolment in evening classes, the Canadian Club allocated $100 each year to award prizes to "non-English students" for "marked progress" in learning the English language.[165]

Jewish immigrants settling in Winnipeg therefore encountered a city dominated by a British Canadian business elite that was segregated on the basis of social class, ethnoracial identity, and place of residence.[166] Jewish immigrants also faced prejudice and discrimination. Unlike migrants from Ontario or British immigrants, Jews were "foreigners" whose distinctive ethnoracial identity and determination to maintain their religious traditions posed a threat to dominant British Canadian values and beliefs. British Canadian attitudes toward Jews ranged from reluctant acceptance (in part because residential segregation meant that the Jewish community was largely contained in the North End), to suspicion and distrust because of their perceived failure to unreservedly embrace assimilation, to overt anti-Semitism.[167] Ultimately, British Canadian businessmen had little interest in modifying their commercial practices or employment policies to accommodate the needs or aspirations of "foreigners." Consequently, to secure a means of earning an income, Jewish immigrants had to overcome numerous obstacles.

Finding Employment

In Winnipeg, English was the universal language of finance, commerce, manufacturing, and public administration. With the exception of a small minority of Jews who spoke English when they arrived in Winnipeg—in 1916, approximately 9 percent identified Great Britain, the United States, or another Canadian province as their place of birth—immigration rendered a majority of Jewish immigrants functionally illiterate.[168] They were fluent in Yiddish, and many could converse in Russian, Ukrainian, or Romanian; however, unlike their children who were either born in Winnipeg or came to Canada at a very young age and therefore attended public school, most adult Jews did not have the time or opportunity to become proficient in English. Having arrived in Canada with small amounts of money, typically from twenty-five to thirty dollars, they were compelled to earn an income as soon as possible.[169] For the majority of Jewish immigrants, this meant finding employment in a labour market dominated by British Canadian employers.

Despite periodic recessions—notably in the early 1890s, 1907–08, and 1913–15—that generated high rates of unemployment, Winnipeg's rapid economic development created a growing labour market dependent on immigrant labour.[170] However, Jewish immigrants seeking employment were in direct competition with immigrants from Great Britain, who had many advantages. No matter how limited their formal education, most British immigrants could read and write in English; they were able to take direction from supervisors, communicate with fellow workers, and deal directly with the public. Given the similarities between British and Canadian workplace cultures and practices, they also understood employers' expectations. Prior to emigration, many British immigrants had worked in modern factories or as clerks in large businesses and upon arrival in Winnipeg often required little training to fulfill their responsibilities on the shop floor or in stores and offices. In contrast, the vast majority of Jewish immigrants were unable to speak, read, or write English and were poorly educated. Prior to emigrating, most Jewish boys attended a *heder*—girls were not admitted—that focused on religious studies. Very few attended Russian "state schools" (*gymnasia*), which taught science and mathematics, or had access to vocational training. Having lived in the Pale of Settlement, a region with a precarious, pre-industrial economy, most Jewish immigrants had little exposure to modern forms of factory production or opportunities to work in clerical or administrative positions in large business enterprises. Compared with their British competitors, therefore, Jewish immigrants seeking employment had a limited range of work experience: in the Pale, the overwhelming majority of economically active Jewish men either worked as unskilled labourers and independent artisans or earned modest incomes as petty traders and small merchants. Similarly, unmarried women who worked outside the home were typically tailors or dressmakers; after marriage, women contributed to the family income by assisting their husbands to produce artisanal goods or running small businesses.[171] Consequently, Jewish immigrants were not considered qualified for many skilled factory jobs, public or private sector clerical or administrative positions, or work in retail stores that served English-speaking British Canadian customers.[172]

Jews also had to overcome preferential and overtly discriminatory hiring practices. British Canadian employers who welcomed an infusion of "our blood," English-speaking Protestants who would easily integrate, believed that they had an obligation to hire immigrants who would reinforce Canada's British heritage. In addition, they assumed that by choosing to live in Canada every European immigrant had a responsibility to quickly learn to read and write English, and they had little tolerance for job applicants not proficient in English. Moreover, unlike British immigrants, Jews did not have access to British Canadian social networks that linked immigrants seeking employment with supervisors, foremen, and employers who made hiring decisions. For example, the Sons of England and other fraternal organizations established by British immigrants provided advice and assisted new arrivals to find jobs in the public sector as police constables and with the City of Winnipeg or major private employers such as Ashdown's warehouse and retail store, the Winnipeg Street Railway Company, T. Eaton Company, Canadian Northern Railway, and Canadian Pacific Railway. Eaton's and the CPR not only systematically discriminated in favour of British immigrants applying for employment but also recruited skilled workers in Great Britain.[173] Winnipeg employers' preference for British workers even extended to using public funds to assist "worthy British workmen to bring their families to Winnipeg."[174] In 1911, the Winnipeg Development and Industrial Bureau, run by members of the business elite, who used their influence on Winnipeg City Council to get close to 70 percent of its funding, launched the Imperial Home Reunion Association.[175] The goal of the association was to reunite British immigrants working in Winnipeg with their families. Over a two-year period, the association provided British immigrants with loans that enabled a total of 2,427 wives and children to travel to Winnipeg.[176]

Despite the obstacles that they faced, most Jewish immigrants and their children living in the North End succeeded in finding a means of earning an income. In 1916, census enumerators who surveyed residences in the North End recorded the occupations of 2,842 Jewish men fifteen years and older.[177] A total of 2,571 had an occupation that generated an income, thirty were retired, twenty-three were serving in the armed forces, and thirteen were students (enumerators used the term "none" to identify 181 Jewish men who did not have an occupation, and they did not record any information for sixty men).[178] Approximately two-thirds (67.5 percent) of the 2,571 Jewish men with occupations were wage earners or earned an income by providing services. Skilled workers—including tailors (203), carpenters (91), painters (60), tinsmiths (58), butchers (56), teachers (50), printers (48), barbers (45), shoemakers (41), blacksmiths (29), plumbers (19), machinists (19), musicians (18), bakers (17), furriers (14), jewellers (13), and watchmakers (13)—comprised the largest category (51.7 percent), followed by semi-skilled workers (34 percent), including clerks (197), drivers/teamsters (147), salesmen (128), and factory workers (78), and finally unskilled workers (14.2 percent), mostly labourers (217).[179]

Although many of Winnipeg's major British Canadian employers were reluctant to hire Jewish immigrants, labour shortages, particularly of skilled workers, forced them to set aside their preference for British immigrants or overcome their prejudice. For example, the Kemp Manufacturing Company, which fabricated stoves, hired Jewish tinsmiths, the CPR hired Jewish machinists and carpenters, and Jewish tailors worked for the Scotland Woolen Mills Company and the city's major department stores.[180] Winnipeg's major meat-packing plants—Gordon, Ironside, and Fares Company; Gallagher, Holman Company; and Western Packing Company—hired Jewish butchers and labourers. Jewish labourers also found employment with the Canadian Pacific Railway, Canadian National Railway, and Grand Trunk Pacific Railway. In addition to labourers, the City of Winnipeg employed Jewish teamsters.[181] However, access to many premium jobs depended on having either skills in demand or the advantage of growing up in Winnipeg. For example, most of the Jewish immigrants employed by Winnipeg's largest employer, the CPR, worked as labourers earning approximately $600 a year.[182] Jews employed as skilled workers earning $800 to $850 a year were either immigrants who had acquired their skills before coming to Canada or youths educated in Winnipeg and proficient in English and therefore considered suitable candidates for apprenticeships. For instance, in 1916, the CPR employed ten Jewish carpenters: eight who immigrated as adults, one who came to Canada at the age of fifteen, and one born in Winnipeg. Similarly, the CPR employed eleven Jewish machinists: eight were adults when they came to Canada, two immigrated at young ages (five and fifteen), and one was born in Winnipeg.

Thus, the CPR hired qualified machinists, carpenters, tinsmiths, blacksmiths, upholsters, and other skilled workers, a policy that benefited Russian immigrants with previous work experience who could demonstrate that they had the required skills. If enough qualified skilled workers were not available, the company was prepared to hire apprentices but only youths proficient in English. Consequently, a small number of Jewish youths, those who had been born in Winnipeg and attended school or had immigrated at an age that enabled them to become proficient in English, completed apprenticeships and became skilled workers. So, unskilled Jewish workers who immigrated to Canada as adults had limited labour mobility; the CPR was willing to hire them for poorly paid labour jobs but not willing to train them for higher-paying skilled jobs.

Given Winnipeg employers' preference for British immigrants, a small number of Jewish immigrants from Great Britain undoubtedly benefited from a British accent or an English name. For example, Jack Blumberg, who emigrated from England at the age of nineteen, was hired by Winnipeg Street Railway Company as a motorman, earning approximately $900 a year. Similarly, Nate Goldstone, who left England at the age of seventeen, was employed by the Post Office as a letter carrier, a position that paid $720 a year. Mark Harris, a Jewish immigrant from England, was the only Jew employed by the CPR as a train engineer. Earning approximately $2,000 a year, Harris held the highest-paid operations job on the railway. An English name was also an advantage for Jewish immigrants from the Russian Empire. William Nelson, a Jewish immigrant who arrived in Canada in 1905 from Russia at the age of fourteen, worked for the City of Winnipeg as a chemist. An English name likely gave another Jewish immigrant from Russia, Henry Miller, who immigrated to Canada at the age of forty-two, a competitive advantage. For the CPR, which tended to hire workers in their twenties, Miller was an older and therefore less desirable worker.[183] Nevertheless, the company hired him as a carpenter.

Far fewer female Jewish immigrants participated in the labour market. Only 530 of 2,325 (23 percent) Jewish women fifteen years of age and older living in the North End worked outside the family home, and with few exceptions all of them were under the age of twenty-three.[184] Most Jewish women married at an early age and were responsible for all domestic work: cooking, cleaning, and caring for children. Since Jewish families tended to be large—fewer than four children was unusual, four or five was the norm, and many couples had six or more—virtually all married women worked in the home throughout their productive years. They continued to work in the home after their children were grown rather than seeking the restricted employment opportunities that might have been available to an older female worker with a limited command of English. Almost all of the Jewish women who worked were unmarried and living with their parents or an adult brother or sister who had assisted them to immigrate to Canada. Since many Jewish families could not survive on the income earned by the male head of the family, children fifteen years of age and older living at home were expected to work and help support their parents and siblings. However, though young Jewish men invariably left school to work, fewer than one in four young Jewish women worked outside the home before marriage, and those who were employed stopped working by the age of twenty-two to marry. Slightly more than half (52.5

percent) of the Jewish women who worked outside the home were employed as skilled workers, including dressmakers (154), stenographers (83), teachers (7), hairdressers (4), and midwives (3). Approximately 44 percent were semi-skilled; they included factory workers (103), clerks (81), and saleswomen (40). The remainder (4 percent) were mostly domestics (15) and labourers (6) who worked in unskilled jobs.[185]

Typically, women earned lower wages than men. For example, female dressmakers in a shop averaged sixteen cents an hour, whereas male tailors in the same age group earned between twenty-one and twenty-six cents an hour. Similarly, saleswomen were paid less than their male counterparts, earning about thirteen cents as opposed to twenty-one cents an hour. Gender-based wage differentials were even greater in factories. Women making clothing earned from ten to twelve cents an hour, whereas the hourly wage for men ranged from twenty to twenty-six cents. Female cigar makers working in factories were also paid less. Gender-based disparities in wages earned are illustrated by the earnings of the Hoffman siblings. Both Isidor, aged twenty-two, and his sister Ethel, aged eighteen, worked a sixty-hour week in a factory making cigars. Ethel earned slightly more than thirteen cents an hour, whereas Isidor was paid twenty-three cents an hour. Their two younger sisters, Rachel (aged sixteen) and Hattie (aged fifteen), also worked sixty hours a week, but for four cents an hour, presumably a rate of pay that reflected their status as apprentices.[186] Whatever their occupation, the skills of female Jewish workers were devalued; the highest-paid female Jewish worker consistently earned considerably less than the lowest-paid male Jewish labourer.

As Winnipeg's Jewish community grew, Jewish workers became less dependent on British Canadian employers. By 1916, the ranks of Jewish entrepreneurs included 499 merchants, a category that included small neighbourhood grocery stores, clothing stores, bakeries, butcher and tailor shops, as well as large wholesale distributors, twenty-one manufacturers, twenty-one contractors, and six hotel owners. Most of the Jewish businesses were small family-run stores that hired at most a few Jewish clerks or salesmen. However, by 1910, Winnipeg had a number of large and medium-sized Jewish-owned businesses. For example, the Western Shirt and Overall Company, Jacob and Crowley, and Monarch Overall Company employed Jewish garment workers, shippers, and sales representatives, and Weidman Brothers, a wholesale grocery business, employed Jewish clerks, shippers, and teamsters.[187] Numerous Jewish contractors hired carpenters, plumbers, painters, and electricians, and Jewish-owned metal shops hired tinsmiths. In addition, numerous small factories, such as the

Orpheum Cigar Company, which had thirty employees, and the L. Galpern Candy Company, which had about twenty workers, provided employment to Jewish immigrants.

Of course, entrepreneurship did more than provide Jewish immigrants with additional employment opportunities; it also offered them an alternative means of earning an income, a way of bypassing a labour market that penalized immigrant job seekers who did not have marketable skills, were considered too old by employers, or were not fluent in English. It also offered Jewish immigrants a measure of independence as opposed to submission to the authority of an employer and freedom from the discipline of the workplace. Most importantly, entrepreneurship offered Jewish immigrants the possibility of enjoying higher incomes than wage labour could provide. Approximately 30 percent of the 2,571 Jewish men with occupations living in the North End owned businesses; they included merchants (371), peddlers (189), dealers (165), contractors (21), manufacturers (13), real estate brokers (12), insurance agents (7), auctioneers (3), a cinema owner, and the proprietor of a hotel. A small number of women also owned businesses (16 merchants and 2 peddlers). Almost all of the women who owned businesses were widows. Since they were virtually unemployable, owning businesses that they had likely inherited from their husbands provided incomes that enabled them to be self-sufficient or at least reduced their dependence on adult children.[188]

Little information on business income is available; enumerators who recorded personal data for the 1911 census were only authorized to collect data on wages. However, they occasionally listed the incomes of business owners, and census data suggest that the incomes of many peddlers, small merchants who operated grocery stores and dealers, were similar to those of well-paid workers earning $800 to $1,000 a year. However, a number of merchants had incomes that ranged between $1,500 and $4,000 per year, and it is reasonable to assume that other business owners, such as manufacturers and real estate brokers, did as well. One measure of comparative affluence is whether a family could afford to employ a domestic servant. Since domestic servants were paid $225 to $300 a year, they were an unaffordable luxury for working-class families. Not surprisingly, the heads of almost all (90 percent) of the forty-two Jewish families who employed servants were either merchants (36) or manufacturers (2).[189] Together with thirty-two professionals, including rabbis (15), barristers (5), pharmacists (4), and dentists (2), plus managers/foremen (9), affluent business owners constituted a small middle class. It consisted of approximately 248 (9.5 percent) of the 2,571 men and 530 women with occupations living in the North End who had annual incomes in excess of $1,200.[190]

The high proportion (90.5 percent) of Jewish immigrants who were either working-class earners or low-income small-business owners was a defining characteristic of the North End Jewish community. Fewer Jewish workers lived in Central Winnipeg (43 percent of all Jews employed) or the South End (39 percent) compared with the North End (67 percent). In addition, a higher proportion of male Jews living in Central Winnipeg (24.6 percent) and the South End (42 percent) had middle-class or higher incomes than those in the North End (9.5 percent).[191] Also, far fewer women worked—15.6 percent in Central Winnipeg and 10.5 percent in the South End compared with 23 percent in the North End—suggesting that fewer Jewish families in Central and South Winnipeg needed additional income. Certainly, the South End was home to most of Winnipeg's most affluent Jews. Most of them were entrepreneurs who had immigrated in the 1880s or early 1890s, established successful businesses, and accumulated sufficient wealth to move from the North End or Central Winnipeg to the South End. They either purchased homes in middle-class neighbourhoods between Portage Avenue and the Assiniboine River or built luxurious residences in Crescentwood and the Roslyn Road area. Twenty-six Jewish families in the South End employed servants; one for every twenty-four Jewish residences compared with one for every 279 in the North End. Based upon the value of their homes and the limited census information available on their incomes, at least twenty to twenty-five Jewish residents of the South End could have been considered comparatively wealthy.[192]

Compared with the Pale of Settlement, Winnipeg offered Jewish immigrants a wide variety of employment and business opportunities. Although they had to overcome numerous barriers—their inability to speak fluent English, employers who did not recognize or value their pre-emigration work experience, exclusion from British Canadian social networks that linked job seekers with business owners and supervisors who made hiring decisions, and discrimination in employment and business dealings—unlike the Russian Empire the Canadian state did not legislate the economic exclusion of Jews by restricting their access to employment or their right to own property. Measured by their economic integration, the settlement of Jewish immigrants can be considered a success. The vast majority of male Jews had employment or business income—relatively few (approximately 6 percent) did not have an occupation—and, though the range of jobs open to women was much more limited, young female Jews were successful in finding employment.[193] However, the incomes earned by the great majority of Jewish immigrants were inadequate, forcing families to adopt various strategies to maintain a comfortable standard of living and establish a modest measure of financial security.

In 1911, the minimum cost of food, shelter, and clothing for a family of five was approximately $918 a year. Including twenty-five dollars a year for public transportation and the same amount for household furnishings, a family of five needed an annual income of at least $968 to afford the necessities of life.[194] However, the average annual income of male Jewish workers between the ages of twenty-one and sixty-five was $778.[195] Only 11 percent of male Jewish workers in this age group earned more than $968 a year (their average income was approximately $1,100), and a majority of small-business owners earned about $1,000 a year.[196] Consequently, out of necessity, Jewish immigrant families adopted a variety of strategies to augment their incomes or reduce household expenditures. The most common strategy was to encourage children to leave school and seek employment. For Jewish youths, entering the workforce at an early age was common; in 1916, only fifteen young Jewish men fifteen years of age or older were enrolled in school or university. At best, they left school after grade eight and completed their education working as labourers and clerks or apprentices learning how to be a tailor, tinsmith, or printer. The employment income of young people made a significant contribution to improving a family's standard of living. For example, in addition to the $600 a year that their father earned as a carpenter, the Bergal brothers, aged eighteen and nineteen, employed as "drivers," contributed an additional $1,250 to their family's income. Although fewer young women than young men between the ages of fifteen and eighteen joined the workforce, the $350 to $400 that they earned as factory workers, dressmakers, or stenographers added to or became a crucial component of family income. In the case of the Rabinowitch family, the incomes of Alice (age seventeen), who worked in an overall factory, and her two brothers, Hymie (age sixteen), an office boy, and Harry (age nineteen), a salesman, supported their widowed mother and eight siblings.[197]

However, since Jewish immigrants tended to be young—the average age of an adult Jewish immigrant arriving in Canada was thirty-one—not all families included children old enough to work.[198] For example, Albert Altman, age twenty-eight, a harness maker, supported his wife, daughter, and mother-in-law on a salary of $780 a year; Nathan Friedman, age thirty-five, a driver, supported his wife and four young children on an income of $700 a year. To supplement employment income, families with only one wage earner frequently rented rooms to boarders. With a wife and six young children to support, Israel Merson, who earned $780 a year working as a driver for a bakery, augmented his family's income by renting rooms to three boarders. Similarly, the income from three boarders assisted Henry Fruitlander, who earned $700 a year working as a barber, to support his wife and two children. Since rent was the largest component of a family's household expenditures, another strategy that Jewish immigrants employed was to share a house. The Ackerman family—consisting of Harry, Rebecca, their three children, and Rebecca's mother—shared a house with the Dorfman family, which included Charles, Rebecca, their four children, and Rebecca's mother. Although the house was very crowded, for Harry, who earned $600 a year as a clerk, and Charles, who worked as a presser earning $900 a year, sharing the cost of rent as well as fuel and electricity substantially reduced their household expenditures.

Despite these strategies, 90.5 percent of Jewish families in the North End (85 percent of all Jewish families in Winnipeg) had at best a modest and precarious standard of living. Many families were poor, barely subsisting on an annual income of $600 to $900, the minimum amount needed to afford the necessities of life. Accumulating savings to protect the family from an interruption or loss of income was almost impossible, an illness or disability that prevented a wage earner from working could plunge a family into debt, and even short-term or seasonal unemployment could have catastrophic consequences. Certainly, saving for retirement or setting aside a modest amount to pay for a dignified burial was beyond their means. To varying degrees, families with incomes above $900 enjoyed a higher—albeit modest by prevailing middle-class standards—level of material comfort. Many had enough disposable income to save the $300 to $400 needed to make a down payment on a house. However, though investing in a house provided a measure of financial security, monthly payments and property taxes were fixed costs that increased a family's expenditures and inhibited savings. Consequently, even Jewish families with higher annual incomes were not necessarily able to save enough money to cope with an interruption or loss of income.

However, inadequate incomes not only compromised the well-being of Jewish immigrants but also had far-reaching consequences for their children who were forced to leave school and find employment. Young Jewish men hired as "learners" or apprentices were fortunate. After acquiring four or five years of experience, they were considered qualified tailors, tinsmiths, or printers. Consequently, their wages almost doubled, increasing in the case of tinsmiths, for example, from $400–$450 to $850 a year. However, young Jewish men who entered the workforce as labourers or factory workers had limited occupational mobility. After four or five years of work experience, they were still considered unskilled and paid considerably less, earning approximately $580 a year. Vocational training was also advantageous for young women. Both the Success Business College and the Winnipeg Business College offered day and evening classes in subjects such as bookkeeping, commercial correspondence, shorthand, and typing. Young Jewish women who worked as bookkeepers or stenographers earned between $450 and $600 a year compared with factory workers (approximately $330) or saleswomen (approximately $400), and they enjoyed the advantage of working fewer hours each week.

No private institution offered vocational training to young men. However, by 1910, the Winnipeg School Board recognized that students needed practical skills to succeed in the workforce. By providing vocational training in high school, students who typically left school by grade eight would have an incentive to continue their studies. The board built two technical high schools, St. John's in the North End and Kelvin in the South End. St. John's, which opened in 1912, offered boys who completed grade eight a program of studies that incorporated training in machining, woodworking, electrical work, mechanical drawing, and plumbing.[199] Girls were given an opportunity to take commercial courses and learn how to type. However, financial pressures continued to take precedence over opportunities to complete high school; few families could afford basic household expenses without the additional income that children provided. With few exceptions, the sons and daughters of Jewish immigrants continued to begin their working lives at age fifteen. Before the 1920s, only a small number of Jewish students graduated from high school with the academic credits needed to apply to a university, and graduating from university was an unaffordable and therefore impossible dream.[200]

Despite the hardships of immigration and adapting to a new way of life, Jewish immigrants who settled in Winnipeg between 1882 and 1914 had many reasons to feel vindicated. On balance, their belief, whether based upon desperation, confidence, or hope, that the advantages of emigration far outweighed the risks had been justified. Little could alleviate the pain of separation from parents and siblings left behind, but unlike in the Pale of Settlement, where Jews continued to endure government persecution, economic segregation, and the threat of pogroms, Jewish immigrants in Canada enjoyed individual freedoms, unregulated access to employment and business opportunities, and personal security. Furthermore, though few Jewish immigrants achieved the often mythologized prosperity of the New World, compared with their grinding poverty in the Pale, they achieved a substantial measure of material well-being. Nevertheless, the vast majority shared a common problem: the inability to save enough money to protect their families from a loss of income because of calamities such as unemployment, illness, or the death of a wage earner. The solution was to draw on their experience of organizational activity in the Pale and establish through collective action what was beyond the means of an individual or family: financial security.

CHAPTER 4

Government Charitable Assistance and the Emergence of Jewish Social Welfare

In December 1910, the business manager of the Winnipeg General Hospital informed the Immigration Branch of the Department of the Interior that a destitute immigrant had been admitted for treatment. In his reply, W.D. Scott, the superintendent of immigration, advised the hospital's business manager that, if the immigrant required treatment for "more than one month," the patient's name should be sent to Winnipeg's commissioner of immigration "with a view to deportation."[1] Based upon amendments to the Immigration Act enacted in 1906 and 1910, Scott was acting on his legal authority to instruct his officials to identify, detain, and deport any person who, "within three years after landing in Canada," became a public charge or an inmate of a "hospital, insane asylum or public charitable institution."[2] A deportation order applied not only to an adult but also to a dependent spouse and children. The federal government's deportation powers reinforced the fundamental premise of Canada's immigration policy. Immigrants were expected to be self-supporting, and those who failed to do so and became public charges (whether dependent on charitable assistance because of illness or unemployment, an indigent patient in a hospital, or an inmate in an asylum for the mentally ill) were characterized as unfit to be permanent residents of Canada. Their speedy deportation was essential to ensure that they were unable to accumulate the three years of residency required to qualify for naturalization.[3] Once immigrants became citizens, the government no longer had the legal authority to enforce self-reliance by deporting those who violated the terms of their admission into Canada by failing to become self-supporting and turning to the government for assistance.

Amendments to the Immigration Act codified hegemonic beliefs about individual responsibility and self-reliance disseminated by politicians, newspapers, and the clergy.[4] According to the doctrine of individual responsibility and self-reliance, securing the necessities of life—food, shelter, clothing, and medical care—depended on hard work, thrift, and savings to offer some protection from the calamities of life, such as temporary interruptions in income because of illness or unemployment, the death of a family's main income earner, and the inevitable time when old age made paid work impossible. Since Canada was believed to be a country that offered ample opportunities to industrious immigrants determined to succeed, the only plausible explanation for an immigrant's failure to become self-reliant was that some individuals inevitably exercised poor judgement or, worse, were morally flawed.

According to J. Howard Falk, the general secretary of the Associated Charities, the agency that the City of Winnipeg established in 1908 to investigate all applications for assistance on behalf of its Relief Department, "the large majority of applications for relief are caused by thriftlessness, mismanagement, unemployment due to incompetence, intemperance, immorality, desertion of the family and domestic quarrels."[5] Although Falk conceded that "relief is always necessary for the sake of the children," it was essential to ensure that the "giving of it does not simply make it easier for the parents to shirk their responsibilities or lead a dissolute life."[6] This contradicted his own research, which confirmed that the main causes of destitution were unemployment, disability, and widowhood rather than "character failing" and that for wage earners "the margin between dependence and independence is a very narrow one."[7] However, his public statements alleging that applicants for assistance were responsible for their own misfortune undoubtedly reassured members of the business elite who dominated the governing council of the Associated Charities and contributed most of the donations that it received to provide assistance to the destitute.[8] According to members of Winnipeg's business elite, the destitute were not the victims of low wages or circumstances beyond their control, such as illness or cyclical unemployment; rather, poverty was self-inflicted. Ultimately, the members of the governing council were adamant that the poor were responsible for their predicament, not the employers or adverse economic conditions.

Nevertheless, if interviews and home visits confirmed that families and homeless women were truly deserving of assistance, they received money for groceries, clothing, rent, and fuel. In exchange, employable married men were expected to look for work and while doing so perform unpaid labour for three days a week for the City of Winnipeg maintaining roads. Employable single women were required to register for employment with the Women's Free Casual Employment Bureau. In return for room and board, able-bodied single men had to work in the city's wood yard until the Men's Employment Bureau could find them a job working in a lumber camp or for a farmer or railway contractor.[9] The policy of the Associated Charities was unambiguous: charitable assistance was intended to provide recipients with an opportunity for redemption. It was a measure intended to provide the poor with the basic necessities of life temporarily. Unless ill or a widow, applicants had to demonstrate their commitment to individual responsibility, self-sufficiency, and the work ethic; male recipients had to earn their assistance, and all able-bodied men and women were expected to accept any form of employment that the Employment Bureau found for them.[10] If an applicant refused to perform unpaid labour or accept work, the Associated Charities withheld assistance. However, many applicants who were not Canadian citizens were denied opportunities for redemption, and the Associated Charities recommended their deportation to the Winnipeg office of the immigration commissioner. As Frank Kerr, the City of Winnipeg relief officer, bluntly stated, "it is cheaper in the end. It doesn't take many groceries and cords of wood to eat up the price of a [steamship] ticket."[11]

The immigration commissioner was not predisposed to give immigrants labelled public charges a sympathetic hearing. For example, when Mary Evans, president of the Women's Canadian Club, asked Immigration Commissioner Bruce Walker why a "fine, intelligent-looking man" who had been referred by the Associated Charities was being deported because he was deaf, when "$20 or so spent on some autophone appliance would probably make him hear, and make him a valuable citizen," Walker replied that he could do nothing for him.[12] Immigrants referred by the association were swiftly deported.[13]

Of course, a destitute immigrant could avoid the risk of deportation by finding any means to survive rather than becoming a public charge.[14] However, many immigrants who were injured or became seriously ill and needed medical treatment in a hospital could not help but become public charges. The Winnipeg General Hospital charged $1.50 a day for treatment in a public ward, approximately a day's wages for a labourer. A lengthy stay in the hospital could quickly deplete a worker's savings, and if a relative or friend did not assume responsibility for paying for treatment an immigrant could quickly become a public charge. If the patient recovered and was discharged within a month, the Department of the Interior paid the hospital fifty cents a day for the treatment provided.[15] But immigrants who did not recover within a month were deemed incapable of becoming self-reliant and deported.

Immigrants who contracted tuberculosis were not given a period of grace. The treatment of tuberculosis involved a lengthy period of rest in a sanatorium, and the prognosis was often poor. Unless immigrants could afford to pay for their treatment, admission to the Ninette Sanatorium immediately became grounds for deportation.[16] Similarly, immigrants who suffered from a mental illness were not only unlikely to recover and therefore were considered incapable of ever being self-reliant but also viewed as a threat to the health and safety of society. Given the fear that the mentally unfit contributed to "racial degeneration," simultaneously the greatest threat to the vitality of the Anglo-Saxon race and the source of a variety of social problems that plagued Canada, immigrants admitted to either the Brandon or the Selkirk Hospital for the Insane were speedily deported.[17]

Falk and administrators of the Winnipeg General Hospital or the Ninette Sanatorium were not under any legal obligation to report immigrants who applied for relief or were admitted to a hospital. To implement the federal government's deportation policy, Winnipeg's immigration commissioner depended on them to voluntarily provide information about the immigration status of beneficiaries of charitable assistance. Since charities and hospitals were under provincial jurisdiction, the federal government did not have the legislative authority to compel administrators of hospitals or municipal relief workers to comply with its request to identify candidates for deportation, but both the Province of Manitoba and the City of Winnipeg had financial incentives to do so: the deportation of immigrants decreased public expenditures on social welfare.

The politicians who governed Manitoba and dominated Winnipeg City Council believed that the government had minimal responsibility for the welfare of the residents of Winnipeg. The primary purpose of the government was to promote private enterprise; dispensing relief to the poor and building and operating hospitals or institutions for orphans and the elderly were essentially private rather than government responsibilities. Taxation, viewed as a drain on the economy because it inhibited both investment and consumption, was grudgingly accepted as a necessary evil when tax revenues were used to fund government expenditures on infrastructure such as roads and railways, investments that stimulated economic development.[18] However, taxation for the purpose of expanding the role of the government to make welfare a social rather than a private responsibility was strongly resisted because it threatened to undermine self-sufficiency. If individuals and families were unable to assume responsibility for their own welfare, then private charity was the preferred solution, not government-funded programs or services.

The Manitoba government adopted two strategies to minimize its responsibility for the welfare of the residents of Winnipeg. The first strategy, with the exception of five institutions that the provincial government deemed to be in the public interest (two hospitals for the mentally ill, a home for incurables, a reformatory for delinquent boys, and a school for the deaf), was to make hospitals, orphanages, children's aid societies, and institutions for the elderly dependent on the willingness of a group of sponsors to raise money to build them and assume responsibility for their ongoing operation. If a group of sponsors petitioned the provincial government, then the Provincial Secretary, on behalf of the executive, would introduce a bill of incorporation in the legislature, in effect granting the sponsors the legal authority to establish and manage an institution, agency, or organization under the direction of a board of directors.

For example, in 1875, a group of fifteen prominent residents of Winnipeg petitioned the provincial government to incorporate the Winnipeg General Hospital. The hospital's act of incorporation referred to possible "grants, gifts and bequests" from the federal government, the Province of Manitoba, and the City of Winnipeg.[19] However, donations from life members and annual membership dues were the only specific sources of revenue identified in the act. In fact, it emphasized that only members of the corporation who had made sizable donations to the hospital could be elected to the board of directors.[20] In 1875, the board authorized the construction of a new hospital. Located on land donated by two wealthy benefactors, the new hospital was financed by public subscription. Once the hospital was built, the provincial government and the City of Winnipeg provided annual operating grants, and the federal government paid a subsidy for the treatment of immigrants. However, half of the hospital's operating revenue came from fees paid by private patients and public appeals for donations.[21] As Winnipeg's population rapidly increased, the board of directors was confronted with the need to build a larger facility. It authorized the construction of a new hospital complex, completed in 1883. However, because of an economic recession, public donations were insufficient to finance the project, and the members of the board were forced to sign personal bonds of indemnity to guarantee the hospital's debt. Finally, after three years of lobbying, the board persuaded the provincial government and the City of Winnipeg to make capital grants that, together with public donations, provided enough money to pay off the hospital's debt.[22]

Funding of the establishment, expansion, and operation of the Winnipeg General Hospital exemplified the division of responsibility between governments and private entities for social welfare. The government of Manitoba provided modest operating grants and, if lobbied successfully, contributed capital or building grants. However, most of the hospital's revenue came from private sources, fees paid by patients who could afford the daily charge for treatment, and donations from the public. For example, in 1913, the Winnipeg General Hospital received $613,181.27 in revenue. The Province of Manitoba provided $25,000 for "building purposes," and based upon a per diem of twenty-five cents for each patient treated in public wards the hospital received an operating subsidy of $11,846.75.[23] Income from "pay patients" totalled $112,493.84, and the hospital received $83,572 in general donations, bequests, fees, and withdrawals from its equipment and building funds.[24] The hospital also received $4,499 from the federal government, $44,706 from the City of Winnipeg, and $9,937 from other municipalities to pay for the treatment of indigent patients in public wards.[25] Nevertheless, this income was insufficient; the hospital relied on an overdraft of $242,104 to balance its budget. Since neither the Department of the Interior nor the City of Winnipeg was prepared to pay its share of the cost of treating indigent immigrants resident in Canada for less than three years, given the fiscal situation of the hospital, its business manager had compelling financial reasons to refer them to Winnipeg's superintendent of immigration for deportation.

The subsidy that the Winnipeg General Hospital received from the City of Winnipeg and other municipalities—four times the amount received from the province—illustrates the second strategy that the Province of Manitoba adopted to minimize its financial responsibility for the welfare of the residents of Winnipeg. By statute, the provincial government assigned responsibility for "aiding charitable institutions" to the City of Winnipeg. In effect, under the terms of its 1873 act of incorporation, and subsequently the Charitable Aid Act and the Children's Act, by 1913 the City of Winnipeg had extensive responsibility for the funding of social welfare services.[26] It was solely responsible for providing relief and paying annual grants to the city's charities. In addition, it paid per diem subsidies to hospitals for the treatment of indigent patients in public wards and contributed to the cost of maintaining children who were wards of the Children's Aid Society or living in orphanages. The

City of Winnipeg was also responsible for residents of the city admitted as indigent patients to both the Ninette Sanatorium and the Portage la Prairie Home for Incurables.[27]

The success of the Manitoba government's strategy to minimize its responsibility for social welfare can be measured by its public expenditures. In the 1915 fiscal year, the provincial government's net expenditures on social welfare amounted to $444,272, which represented 7.8 percent of its total spending.[28] Approximately 20 percent of this amount, $89,238, consisted of grants to social welfare institutions and agencies located in Winnipeg. This was a small fraction of the amount spent by the City of Winnipeg. In the 1914–15 fiscal year, Winnipeg's expenditures on social welfare amounted to $393,047: $282,766 on hospitals, $69,975 on subsidies paid to the Home for Incurables and other institutions, $14,400 to the Associated Charities for relief, and $18,905 in grants to fourteen charities, including the Children's Aid Society, the Old People's Home, and the Victorian Order of Nurses.[29]

Although the City of Winnipeg's expenditures on social welfare comprised only 7.64 percent of annual expenditures, members of the business elite who served on Winnipeg City Council were concerned about increases in what they considered to be an unproductive use of the city's financial resources.[30] Between 1912 and 1915, the city's total expenditures increased by 46 percent, but spending on social welfare increased by 132 percent.[31] City councillors were averse to raising property taxes, the source of 90 percent of the municipality's revenue. Not only were property taxes unpopular, but also city councillors questioned the morality of taxing the provident to assist the improvident. To minimize increases in property taxes, they attempted to limit the city's liability for providing assistance to the indigent.

Under the Charity Act, the City of Winnipeg had the legal authority to attempt to recover the costs of its subsidies for the treatment of indigent patients by garnishing their wages, seizing and disposing of their property, or making claims on their estates. However, a majority of those treated in public wards had neither wages nor assets.[32] In 1915, revenue from "hospital collections" totalled $13,821.75, a small fraction (5 percent) of the subsidies paid to city hospitals.[33] The City of Winnipeg could not control who was admitted to hospital, but it could limit eligibility for relief. City councillors not only reduced its liability for the cost of relief by joining with members of the business elite to establish the Associated Charities but also gave the businessmen who dominated its governing council the authority to establish policies that determined who was eligible for relief.

Under the direction of J. Howard Falk, the Associated Charities recruited thirty-three volunteers who served as investigators. Almost all of these volunteers were married British Canadian women.[34] They were given the responsibility of interviewing married couples, widows, widowers, women who were separated or had been deserted, and single women who applied for assistance to determine if they were deserving of relief. Given that approximately 40 percent of applicants were immigrants from Europe, language barriers undoubtedly made it difficult for the investigators to fully understand applicants' circumstances. Furthermore, given prevailing views of "foreigners," the investigators were undoubtedly less than sympathetic to the plight of immigrants from Eastern Europe. Nevertheless, the reports that the investigators submitted to the four family relief agents of the Associated Charities determined whether applicants received "material charitable relief" or simply "friendship, advice, reproof, [or] encouragement" when the investigators decided that this was "all they really needed."[35] In 1911–12, only 232 of the 878 family and single female applicants who requested assistance were judged deserving.[36] Similarly, the Associated Charities found work for only 223 of the 636 single men who applied for assistance.[37] Aside from those deported or refused assistance, many applicants "disappeared," possibly because they did not want to leave Winnipeg or were unwilling to accept work on farms for little or no pay.

Despite the use of volunteers, in 1911–12 the Associated Charities spent $11,124 on administration compared with $18,903 on material relief—$7,940 from its own budget and $10,963 allocated by the City of Winnipeg for relief of the poor.[38] Acknowledging criticism of the high cost of administration in relation to the amount of relief distributed, J.H. Ashdown, treasurer of the Associated Charities, pointed out that "it is not primarily a Society for giving material relief" but an administrative agent for the City of Winnipeg that fulfilled its mandate by not giving assistance to "more than half the cases it deals with."[39] Distinguishing the deserving from the undeserving poor was expensive, but the damage to self-sufficiency caused by providing assistance to the improvident more than justified the cost. Since the Associated Charities had a deficit, Ashdown emphasized that "the number of contributors should increase," but his appeal for more donations referenced the need to regulate the poor rather than assist them.[40]

To augment its income, the Associated Charities sold the wood that single men were required to cut to earn the assistance that they received. The Associated Charities made a profit of only $170 operating its wood yard, but its primary purpose was not to generate revenue but to reinforce the work ethic and deter shirkers.[41] As Falk noted in his report, "there are scores of men who would rather be in jail with food, clothes, warmth and shelter provided, rather than work steadily to supply them for themselves and their families."[42] The Associated Charities also attempted to recover the cost of providing assistance by pursuing legal claims, targeting the assets of recipients, or seeking out family members who could be held responsible for the relief that claimants received. Although the amount recovered was small, the $939 in relief payments "refunded" by families and homeless single men made a clear statement: charitable assistance was intended for the destitute, applicants should not apply unless they had exhausted all of their resources, and the Associated Charities was prepared to use legal remedies to pursue recipients who it discovered did not truly deserve assistance.[43]

Between 1910 and 1916, the provincial government implemented legislation recognizing that, under certain circumstances, individuals should not be held responsible for their failure to be self-sufficient. Even though opposed by members of the business elite in 1910, after three years of lobbying by the Winnipeg Labour Council, the provincial legislature passed legislation to provide compensation to workers injured or killed because of workplace accidents.[44] As a result, injured workers or the families of those who had died no longer had to sue employers for damages, a costly and often futile remedy since employers frequently persuaded judges that accidents were caused by workers' own negligence or that workers understood and accepted the risks when they accepted offers of employment. However, workers' compensation was limited to 50 percent of wages to a maximum of ten dollars a week, and both weekly payments and death benefits could not exceed $1,500.[45] Although benefit levels were increased in 1916 and 1920, with the possible exception of permanently disabled skilled workers, the income that individuals and families dependent on workers' compensation received was lower than the annual earnings of a poorly paid labourer.[46] Nevertheless, workers' compensation was a legislated entitlement, which meant that injured workers, their families, and the spouses and children of workers killed at the workplace were no longer forced to apply for relief and spared the indignity both of satisfying investigators that they were deserving and of trying to survive on the meagre and precarious assistance that the Associated Charities dispensed.

In 1916, the Legislative Assembly passed An Act to Provide Allowances for Mothers.[47] Supported by feminists such as Nellie McClung, the Social Workers Club, campaigners for votes for women, and social reformers, the act established a legislated entitlement to mothers' allowances for women with dependent children who were either widowed or whose husbands were unable to support their families because they were disabled, inmates of a prison, or committed to an insane asylum.[48] Although the stated objective of the act was to assist destitute mothers, its real goal was to provide vulnerable children with stable homes. In effect, mothers were a means to an end, a mothers' allowance would enable them to care for their children, thereby reducing the incidence of neglect, truancy, and delinquency. Assisting destitute mothers was also cost effective: more than 1,000 children in Manitoba were placed in orphanages because their sole-support mothers could not survive on relief, and unless they had relatives or friends who could provide child care they could not work.[49] Not only was institutional care considered a poor substitute for maternal care, but also the average cost of maintaining a child in an orphanage was 9.4 percent higher than the average cost per child of the mothers' allowance.[50]

Unlike the twenty-five-page Workmen's Compensation Act, which detailed the terms and conditions of those entitled to compensation and the amounts that they would receive, the Mothers' Allowance Act was only one page in length. Other than establishing that widows and women whose husbands were unable to support their families because of a disability or because they were inmates of a prison or an insane asylum were entitled to "support or partial support," the act established a commission empowered by orders-in-council to "prescribe rules and regulations" governing all expenditures.[51] To reduce the province's liability for the costs of the allowances, the legislature imposed a levy on municipalities that made them responsible for 50 percent of all expenditures.

Although the wording of the Mothers' Allowance Act suggested that all mothers in financial need because of the reasons prescribed were entitled to assistance, the Mothers' Allowances Commission adopted a strict set of criteria for assessing which mothers were deserving that limited its application. The commission had three main objectives: restriction of immigrants' access to the allowance, moral regulation of mothers, and promotion of self-sufficiency. In addition to demonstrating financial need, applicants were required to submit certificates of marriage, birth, death, and citizenship.[52] Immigrants who could not produce naturalization certificates, either because their husbands had not fulfilled the five-year residency requirement or because they had not applied for citizenship, were disqualified.[53] However, even if they possessed naturalization certificates, few Jews or other immigrants from the Russian Empire had government-issued documents verifying marriages or births.

The Mothers' Allowance Commission was determined to uphold the sanctity of marriage and reinforce married women's obligation to be dutiful wives. Only applicants judged to be "fit and proper person[s]" were eligible. This definition automatically disqualified women in common law relationships, women whose husbands had deserted them, or divorcees. Divorced women were assumed to be recipients of alimony and, if responsible for the breakup of the marriage, not considered a morally "fit and proper person" to care for children.[54] To determine if technically eligible applicants were indeed fit mothers who could be trusted to preserve the "sacredness of the home" and care for their children, the commission employed three "visitors" who inspected their homes and evaluated their characters.[55] Once their applications were approved, the commission's visitors were responsible for inspecting recipients' homes at least twice a year to ensure that mothers spent their allowances responsibly, sent their children to school, and provided them with appropriate maternal care.[56]

Although the stated purpose of the Mothers' Allowance was to provide "adequate means to properly care" for dependent children, the commission established regulations to minimize public expenditures and promote self-sufficiency.[57] To reduce expenditures, cabinet issued regulations to limit eligibility to widows and wives of patients in mental asylums. Although these regulations contravened the wording of the act, the wives of prisoners and the disabled were excluded. In addition, the commission's budget was based upon a predetermined appropriation and did not take into consideration the number of eligible applicants. As a result, allowances could not be provided for "many most deserving and otherwise eligible cases."[58] The regulations also incorporated a narrow definition of the welfare of dependent children and the benefits of maternal care. Based upon the problematic assumption that mothers with one child could both work and find care for their children, they were not eligible for allowances. Furthermore, the eligibility of mothers with two or more children and the amounts that they received depended on their children's ages.[59] Once a child reached fifteen years of age, the family's allowance was reduced. Children fifteen and older were considered employable and capable of contributing to the family's income. If a mother had two or more children fourteen years of age or younger, she would continue to receive a reduced allowance, but a mother with one child under the age of fifteen was no longer eligible since she was expected to find employment. Thus, according to the commission's application of the Mothers' Allowance Act, once women fulfilled their maternal responsibilities by providing for the well-being of their young children, they had served their purpose; they were then expected, with the financial assistance of their children forced to leave school and find work, to become self-sufficient.

Charity, Mutual Aid, and Communal Solidarity in the Jewish Community

The vast majority of Jewish immigrants who settled in Winnipeg proved to be resourceful and resilient. Having experienced poverty in the Pale of Settlement, they were determined to take advantage of any employment or business opportunity in Winnipeg's burgeoning economy. Despite language barriers, competition from the British Canadian workers preferred by Winnipeg's major employers, scepticism and distrust of their qualifications, periodic recessions, and pervasive discrimination against "foreigners," few Jewish workers were unemployed.[60] Similarly, drawing on their pre-immigration business experience or motivated by a desire to avoid the uncertainties of the labour market and be self-employed, approximately one-third of Jewish male immigrants became entrepreneurs. For the most part, they established small owner-operated businesses. However, 85 percent of Jewish families in Winnipeg had at best a modest standard of living. Many families were poor, barely subsisting on an annual income of $600 to $900, the minimum amount that a family needed to afford the necessities of life. For poor families, accumulating savings to protect themselves from a temporary loss of income because of illness, unemployment, or adverse business conditions was almost impossible. A long-term illness or disability that prevented a wage earner from working or an entrepreneur from running a business could plunge a family into debt, and, unless a family included employable children who could contribute to household expenses, the death of a primary income earner could have catastrophic financial consequences. Although families with incomes above $900 enjoyed a higher, albeit still modest, standard of living, they also found it difficult to save enough money to deal with decreases or temporary interruptions in income, and the long-term disability or death of a primary income earner could be equally calamitous. Certainly, for most Jewish workers and small-business owners, unexpected medical and hospital bills were constant worries, and saving for retirement or accumulating a modest amount to pay for a dignified burial was often beyond their means.

For the vast majority of Jewish immigrants, neither relief nor the Mothers' Allowance provided a feasible means of coping with a loss of income because of unemployment, illness, disability, or the death of a wage earner.[61] The threat of deportation—a far greater calamity than destitution—deterred Jewish immigrants ineligible for citizenship from applying for assistance. Those who did apply for it faced a gauntlet of regulations designed to restrict eligibility: interviews, investigations, and home inspections administered by British Canadians with little understanding of or sympathy for the plight of "foreigners." Their destitution—often attributed to racial traits—confirmed that they were incapable of self-sufficiency and should never have been allowed to immigrate to Canada.[62] Instead of providing Jewish immigrants with the means to cope with a crisis and marshal their resources to provide for themselves once again, charitable assistance was likely considered to promote dependency, so it was not redemptive but self-defeating and a waste of scarce financial resources.

Consequently, based upon *tzedakah*, the religious obligation of Jews to make contributions to provide charitable assistance to alleviate the distress of poverty-stricken members of the community, when the first wave of Jewish immigrants arrived in Winnipeg, its Jewish residents attempted to provide assistance to them. However, the arrival in May and June 1882 of approximately 360 Jewish refugees fleeing from pogroms in the Pale of Settlement overwhelmed Winnipeg's small Jewish community. Composed of immigrants from England, Germany, and the Pale of Settlement, this community had only twenty-six members. Most of Winnipeg's first Jewish residents had spent a number of years in Great Britain or the United States before immigrating to Canada in search of business opportunities. They spoke English fluently, they had years of experience living in Western societies, and other than their names little distinguished them from other residents of Winnipeg. Although they were alarmed by the rapid influx of such a large number of refugees, when they arrived in Winnipeg members of the Jewish community escorted them to their temporary accommodations in the government's immigration sheds, organized welcome dinners, and distributed donated clothing.[63] They also organized a relief committee—which quickly raised $360 from Jewish donors—to assist the destitute refugees. A Jewish delegation met with the bishop of Rupert's Land, who donated $100, and two Winnipeg businesses donated mattresses and pillows.[64] In addition, the federal government provided the relief committee with food (1,000 pounds of flour, 200 pounds of oats, ten pounds of tea, and two kegs of syrup), thirty tents, and a subsidy—based upon the submission of receipts for eligible expenditures—of five dollars per adult.[65]

Despite limited employment opportunities (Winnipeg was still recovering from the devastation caused when the Red River flooded sections of the city and from the collapse of the 1881–82 real estate boom in the spring of 1882 that led to restrictions on credit, bankruptcies, and unemployment), with the assistance of seven men from the Jewish community who volunteered to act as interpreters, many of the male refugees found jobs in Winnipeg as manual labourers, carpenters, and tinsmiths, and the Canadian Pacific Railway hired about 150 to lay tracks across the prairies.[66] By the end of the summer construction season, most of the refugees had found accommodations in Winnipeg and had either found permanent employment or saved enough money to establish small businesses. However, in November 1882, more than two dozen destitute families were still living either in the immigration shed, which having been built for summer use was not considered habitable in the winter months, or in an adjacent shantytown of shacks and tents. Suffering from the cold and a lack of food, the plight of the Jewish refugees was vividly described in an article published in the *Manitoba Free Press* on 8 January 1883.[67]

In an accompanying editorial, W.F. Luxton emphasized that "this is no place for paupers who have been schooled in dependence and beggary," but he called on Winnipeg City Council and "all good people" to ensure that the refugees did not "freeze or starve to death."[68] That evening City Council authorized $100 for relief, and the next day the three leaders of the Jewish relief committee (Philip Brown, Louis Wertheim, and Victor Victorson), together with a group of prominent Winnipeggers (including Professor George Bryce, Reverend D.M. Gordon, Isaac Pitblado, lawyer C.E. Hamilton, and Councillor Thomas McCrossan), attended a public meeting to organize relief efforts.[69] Speaking on behalf of the Jewish community's relief committee, Philip Brown reported that, in addition to the $360 raised in May 1882, it had collected over $840 in the previous seven months. In total, Brown stated, the committee had spent $1,180 on food, medicine, and railway fares to enable Jewish refugees to take advantage of employment opportunities outside Winnipeg.[70]

However, Winnipeg's small Jewish community had reached the limit of its resources, and the assembly decided to form a new organization, the Citizens' Relief Committee, to launch a broad public appeal to assist the refugees. Its executive, composed of C.E. Hamilton (elected chair), Thomas McCrossan, and Victor Victorson, established a depot at which the public could donate money, food, and clothing. Members of the executive immediately began visiting the immigration shed to distribute relief, and within a week Hamilton reported that, in addition to donated food and clothing, the executive had spent eighty-eight dollars on flour, firewood, groceries, fish, and clothing.[71] In addition to coordinating the committee's relief efforts, Hamilton attempted to find employment for the refugees. In February 1883, Mark Samuel, chairman of the Toronto branch of the Anglo-Jewish Association, sent $250, the proceeds of its appeal for donations to assist the refugees, to support the work of the committee.[72] By the summer of 1883, the crisis was over; almost all of the destitute Jewish refugees had found employment, and the Citizens' Relief Committee disbanded.[73]

Following the sudden influx of refugees in 1882, Jewish immigration to Winnipeg decreased dramatically. The Jewish community grew slowly, increasing from approximately 380 members in 1882 to 510 in 1885 and 645 in 1891.[74] Although the community remained small, immigration from the Pale of Settlement added enough members to support the creation of communal institutions. Having come of age in the middle of the nineteenth century, when Jewish life was defined by religious faith and observance, both the pre-1882 immigrants and the refugees from the Pale first sought to establish a synagogue. In August 1883, a meeting of Winnipeg Jews elected a committee to launch a fundraising drive to build a synagogue in Central Winnipeg.[75] Once the campaign was under way, the committee invited J. Friedman, a rabbi from Montreal, to serve as the religious leader of the new congregation. In what was planned to be a religious gathering that united the community, the new rabbi led prayers in a rented room celebrating Rosh Hashanah, the Jewish new year. Once the holiday services were over, a meeting of congregants was held to elect an executive committee to complete plans to begin construction of a synagogue before the end of the year.[76]

Although the executive included representatives of both the pre-1882 Jewish community and the recently arrived refugees, it was unable to bridge what proved to be irreconcilable differences regarding religious observance. Instead of bringing the Jewish community together, the services to celebrate the Jewish new year, a time of introspection and reconciliation, launched a series of conflicts that embroiled executive members in divisive and costly religious controversies. A majority of the eight-member executive, including the president, vice-president, and secretary-treasurer, were drawn from the pre-1882 Jewish community. They were determined to establish a Reform synagogue. Influenced by liberal trends in Judaism that had originated in Germany and spread to Great Britain and the United States, they wanted—contrary to the wishes of the majority of the Jewish community, who envisioned a traditional Orthodox synagogue modelled on those in the Pale of Settlement—to build a modern place of worship, a synagogue with religious practices that reflected the status and aspirations of Western, acculturated Jews. As the Jewish community quickly divided into opposing factions, fundraising faltered, and plans to build a new synagogue were suspended.

To preserve what it considered the only authentic and therefore legitimate form of Judaism, the Orthodox faction in turn recruited Rabbi Krasel Feigeson from the United States and established its own congregation, the Sons of Israel. In October 1883, three weeks after members of the Jewish community had gathered to celebrate the new year together, the Sons of Israel congregation, which adhered to traditional Hebrew prayers, religious rituals, and liturgical music, conducted its inaugural service.[77] In May 1884, the Reform faction established the Montefiore Hebrew Benevolent Society. Named after Moses Montefiore, an eminent English Jewish philanthropist, the society was mandated to establish a "Jewish reformed temple" and "assist deserving objects of charity."[78] Adopting the name Beth El, the society founded a new congregation that held its first service in July 1884 in a rented room. Led by Rabbi Friedman, the service confirmed the worst fears of Winnipeg's Orthodox Jews. Organ music, which Eastern European Jews associated with Christian churches, accompanied the procession carrying the sacred Torah scrolls, Rabbi Friedman delivered his sermon in English rather than the traditional Hebrew, and men and women sat together, an affront to Orthodox religious practice.

For the next three years, religious differences continued to divide the Jewish community. The Sons of Israel and Beth El congregations competed to attract new members at the other's expense, additional members whose financial contributions would make it possible to raise enough money to build a synagogue. However, neither congregation succeeded; blocks apart, both the Sons of Israel and Beth El continued to hold services in rented rooms. The prospect of a successful fundraising campaign became more elusive when, in September 1885, an additional religious division emerged in the Jewish community: a small group of dissidents left the Sons of Israel to form a separate congregation. Finally recognizing that the Jewish community had reached an impasse that jeopardized any hope of building a synagogue or organizing a Jewish education program for children, officers of the Beth El congregation attempted to negotiate a merger with the Sons of Israel. Their efforts failed, but in August 1887 they did succeed in persuading some of the members of the Sons of Israel to join them in forming a new Reform congregation, Beth El of Israel.[79] Winnipeg now had three congregations: Beth El of Israel, the Sons of Israel, and the "German" congregation made up of former members of the Sons of Israel. By 1889, the Beth El of Israel congregation had attracted enough congregants to launch a fundraising drive to build Winnipeg's first synagogue.

At a public meeting held in August 1889, supporters of the Beth El of Israel congregation elected a building committee composed of many of the Jewish community's most successful businessmen.[80] To attract support from members of the Sons of Israel congregation and other Orthodox Jews, the building committee made a commitment that the new synagogue, the Shaarey Zedek, would accommodate adherents of both religious traditions, Reform and Orthodox. Based upon this understanding, the Sons of Israel congregation contributed $400, a building lot, and "furniture and paraphanalias [*sic*]" with a value of $1,500.[81] However, when the Winnipeg Jewish community's first synagogue opened in March 1890, it became apparent that accommodation did not mean that the two factions had equal status. Although the minority, the Orthodox members of the congregation, had the right to elect their own officers, the Shaarey Zedek Board of Officers, controlled by the majority Reform faction, made the final decisions on all "rules and regulations."[82] In addition, whereas the main hall was reserved for Reform services, the Orthodox members of the congregation were relegated to a small adjoining chapel for their services. Further, though Orthodox members of the congregation were unable to worship in the main hall, they were still required to pay full synagogue membership fees plus an amount to pay for the maintenance of their chapel and the cost of their own rabbi. Not surprisingly, believing that they had donated money to construct a synagogue in good faith and been deceived, the Orthodox members of the congregation complained bitterly about their subordinate status. In response, two weeks after its dedication, the Shaarey Zedek Board of Officers terminated Orthodox services, and for the second time in a decade an attempt to forge religious unity ended in conflict, bitterness, and schism.[83]

In April 1890, with the support of disaffected members of the Shaarey Zedek synagogue, members of the Sons of Israel congregation bought a small wooden building in Central Winnipeg to serve as an Orthodox synagogue, which they named Beth Israel. According to members of the Shaarey Zedek Board of Officers, establishing a second synagogue was "most disgraceful to Judaism and to the Jewish community."[84] The sole purpose of Beth Israel, the board concluded, was "to injure the welfare of this congregation."[85] The board not only refused to send a representative to attend the Beth Israel synagogue dedication ceremony but also threatened to punish any member of the Shaarey Zedek congregation who did so by excluding him or her from full participation in services for one year.[86]

When the wooden structure was destroyed in a fire in December 1892, the Beth Israel congregation bought a lot two blocks from the Shaarey Zedek synagogue and built a new synagogue. Named Rosh Pina, it opened in August 1893. It offered Jewish immigrants from the Pale of Settlement a place of worship that faithfully followed Orthodox religious rituals, and a succession of cantors attracted worshipers for whom musical chants and melodies were indispensable parts of prayer. With three congregations—Shaarey Zedek, Rosh Pina–Sons of Israel (Schford [*sic*]), and Sons of Israel (Asknas Schford [*sic*])—by 1894 Winnipeg's small Jewish community was even more deeply divided over religious differences.[87] Competing for the loyalty and financial support of the community's observant Jews, congregations, which had as few as forty members, struggled financially and in some instances had difficulty assembling a *minyan*, the ten men needed to hold a service.[88]

The rivalry between the Shaarey Zedek congregation and its Orthodox counterparts became an ongoing source of acrimony and conflict. Shortly after Rosh Pina was established, the Shaarey Zedek Board of Officers attempted to undermine the legitimacy and viability of its competitors. In January 1894, the board petitioned the Legislative Assembly to amend the Marriage Act so that Jewish marriages could only be performed by a person "ordained by at least twenty members" of an incorporated congregation or synagogue.[89] Since Shaarey Zedek was the only incorporated synagogue, this amendment would have given it complete control over the performance of marriages in the Jewish community. This was a direct threat to the viability of other congregations: losing the right to perform an important religious function threatened to undermine their legitimacy and deprive their members of a venue in which to celebrate one of the most important events in Jewish family life. Losing the right to solemnize marriages also had significant financial consequences for congregations, particularly those with small memberships. For example, a portion of the Rosh Pina rabbi's salary was dependent on the fees that the rabbi received for performing marriage ceremonies.[90] Representatives of the two Sons of Israel and Rosh Pina synagogues met with the Provincial Secretary and persuaded him to modify the amendment so that all Jewish congregations were granted the authority to perform marriage ceremonies, but the widely publicized dispute exacerbated tensions between adherents of Reform and Orthodox Judaism.[91]

Disputes between factions within congregations also divided members of the Jewish community. As the congregation of Rosh Pina grew, new members began to resent the "iron-fisted rule" of the clique that had founded the synagogue.[92] Similarly, shortly after the founding of Shaarey Zedek, a group of congregants began to demand that the synagogue modernize its religious service and adopt more progressive practices. Concerned that the synagogue was not meeting the needs of their children, they demanded sermons in English and changes in decorum to attract a younger generation of members.[93] When, after nearly a decade, the synagogue's board steadfastly refused to modernize services, in 1903 the dissidents appointed a committee that called a public meeting to discuss a proposal to hold English-language religious services "that would be conducted in a manner as shall be understood and appreciated by young people of both sexes."[94]

Despite widespread support for English-language services, the Shaarey Zedek Board of Officers refused to adopt their proposal, and by January 1904 the dissidents launched a fundraising drive to build Holy Blossom synagogue to provide a spiritual home for a new Reform congregation. However, they failed to attract enough members to raise the money needed to build a new synagogue. Concluding that the congregation's Reform rabbi, recruited because of his progressive views, was perceived as too radical, the leaders of the congregation quickly decided to revert to more traditional religious practices. Although the congregation continued to hold Friday-night services in English, in 1905, in a public declaration that it had moderated its progressive views, the congregation recruited a less liberal rabbi from Montreal and dropped the name Holy Blossom in favour of the more traditional Shaarey Shomayim. Although in September 1907 the new congregation succeeded in raising enough money to build a 520-seat synagogue on a site in Central Winnipeg, attendance at regular services was low.[95] Recognizing that both the Shaarey Shomayim and the Shaarey Zedek congregations were plagued by poor attendance and financial problems, in 1913 the leaders of the two synagogues negotiated a merger. Healing a nine-year rift, a joint board of synagogue officials—including many of the same individuals party to the dispute that culminated in the 1903 split that divided Shaarey Zedek—decided to form a new congregation. In a spirit of compromise, since the larger Shaarey Shomayim synagogue became the home of the united congregation, the joint board decided that it would continue to use the name Shaarey Zedek.[96]

However, by 1903, the religious disputes and rivalries that had preoccupied the leaders of the Rosh Pina and Shaarey Zedek congregations were overtaken by demographic changes. Between 1891 and 1901, as the Jewish population of Winnipeg increased from 546 to 1,156, the geographic centre of the Jewish community shifted away from Central Winnipeg to a growing district north of the CPR railway. By the late 1890s, bolstered by an influx of *fusgeyers* ("wayfarers") from Romania, Jewish immigrants arriving in the city from the Pale of Settlement bypassed Central Winnipeg and settled in the North End.[97] Scrupulously Orthodox, they viewed their predecessors' attempts to liberalize Judaism with distrust, confirmation of the repeated warnings that they had heard from rabbis in Eastern Europe that emigration would imperil their faith and destroy the continuity of Jewish life. Determined to establish a congregation that would provide a traditional spiritual home in the centre of the North End's growing Jewish community, they built a small wooden synagogue on Schultz Street in 1903. Within a year, supporters of the new congregation, named Beth Jacob, had raised enough money to build Winnipeg's largest synagogue. Built at a cost of $7,000, Beth Jacob could accommodate 700 worshipers. However, within two years, it could no longer meet the increasingly diverse spiritual needs of the North End's growing Jewish community. In 1906, two groups of Orthodox believers established new congregations, B'nai Zion and Chevra Mishnayes. Animated by a disagreement over religious practices, wishing to belong to a congregation composed of immigrants who came from the same town or district in the Pale of Settlement or Romania, or wanting a place of worship within walking distance of their homes, the North End's Jewish community continued to fragment on the basis of religious affiliation, and by 1930 the district had fourteen more synagogues.[98]

Since synagogues emerged as the first and for close to twenty years the only communal institutions, they provided the organizational foundation for offering charitable assistance. However, instead of uniting Winnipeg's small Jewish community, religion became a source of ongoing disagreements and conflicts. Beginning in 1884, when eighteen charter members established theMontefiore Hebrew Benefit Society, the Jewish community's first charitable organization, differences over religious observance and building synagogues inevitably undermined the Jewish community's efforts to mobilize resources either to assist newly arrived immigrants to settle in a new and often inhospitable city or to provide relief to destitute Jews.[99] Although the society had a mandate to provide charitable assistance to "deserving" Jews, its primary purpose was to raise money to build a Reform synagogue. This alienated Orthodox Russian Jews who were members of the Sons of Israel congregation. Determined to raise money to build their own synagogue, they shunned the society, believing that any money that they donated was self-defeating: it would be used not to assist the poor but to help their rivals, the "German Jews," to build a synagogue that was an affront to their religious beliefs.[100] They also had reason to be concerned that the leaders of the Hebrew Benevolent Society were more interested in seeking public recognition and acceptance than assisting destitute Jews. In March 1887, members of the society decided to donate $100 to the

Winnipeg General Hospital in the name of their president, Louis Vineberg, an amount that would entitle him to become a life governor of the hospital.[101]

To broaden the appeal of the society, in 1887 the name Montefiore, not well known to Eastern European Jews, was dropped, and the society became the Hebrew Benevolent Society (Ezras Achim). However, it remained under the control of members of the newly formed Reform congregation, Beth El of Israel, and by 1889 its seventy-one members became affiliated with the Shaarey Zedek synagogue.[102] The leaders of the Hebrew Benevolent Society, the only Jewish charitable organization, continued to attempt to enlist the support of all members of the community. However, the controversy generated by the formation and then acrimonious split of the Shaarey Zedek congregation, which led to the establishment of the Rosh Pina–Sons of Israel synagogue, and the public dispute over the solemnization of marriage so embittered relationships between supporters of the rival synagogues that the society was unable to raise enough money to assist the poor. Claiming that Winnipeg's Jewish community was "too poor" to support "indigent people," in November 1891 the society attempted to send a destitute Jewish family to the United States, "where they would find a haven among the wealthier" Jewish communities.[103] In part, the society's isolation and declining membership—by 1894 its membership had dropped to forty-five—contributed to its failure to assist destitute members of the Jewish community, but religious rivalries had also imposed a substantial financial burden on its members.[104] Between 1884 and 1894, the proliferation of rival congregations resulted in substantial expenditures on salaries for rabbis, Torah scrolls, payments for rented rooms to hold services, and major investments in the construction and furnishing of synagogues. These expenditures, which totalled more than $19,000, consumed most of the financial resources of Winnipeg's small Jewish community.[105]

The Hebrew Benevolent Society asserted that it was assisting newly arrived Jewish immigrants from Russia by finding employment for them on Mennonite farms during the harvest season. Claiming that the 120 men whom it had sent to southern Manitoba in the fall of 1891 returned to Winnipeg with between eighty and ninety dollars, its treasurer was confident that such "good workers" would have "no difficulty securing employment during the winter."[106] However, many of the recently arrived Jewish immigrants were not convinced that the leaders of the Hebrew Benevolent Society could be relied on to assist them. In January 1892, a "large" number of Russian Jews attended a meeting to appoint an "agent" to seek financial assistance from Baron de Hirsch to establish farms in Manitoba.[107] Instead of in a synagogue, they chose to hold the meeting in the dominion immigration hall. Bypassing the leaders of the Hebrew Benevolent Society, they invited William Fonseca, a prominent Winnipeg businessman, to attend the meeting, and by a unanimous vote they selected him to represent them.[108] Ten days later they held another meeting in the immigration hall to organize their own society, which they named Agudas Achim, or Society of Brothers, to assist Jewish immigrants arriving from Russia.[109]

In 1897, the leaders of the Hebrew Benevolent Society further complicated its attempts to broaden its membership by merging with the Hebrew Independent Political Club. In the June 1896 federal election, members of the club had campaigned in support of a Conservative candidate, alienating many Jewish voters. To its critics, the merger confirmed their suspicions that the leaders of the society were not genuinely committed to assisting immigrants and destitute Jews but were using it to promote their political ambitions.[110] Although the leaders of the Hebrew Benevolent Society continued to raise money to fulfill what they believed to be their responsibility to provide charity to members of the Jewish community, by 1897 the society no longer monopolized the provision of charitable assistance.

The establishment in 1893 of the Rosh Pina synagogue provided a second organizational base for charitable activities. The first benevolent society established by and for members of the Rosh Pina congregation in 1896 departed from the charitable practices of the Hebrew Benevolent Society. Instead of dispensing charitable donations to deserving supplicants, the Hebrew Sick Relief Society operated on principles of self-help and mutual aid. The society collected monthly contributions of twenty-five cents from its members; in return, the society helped members who became ill to pay for a physician and medicine and, when needed, sent a representative to provide nursing care.[111] By 1898, the Hebrew Sick Relief Society had 125 members, a large enough base to expand its self-help and mutual aid activities. It decided to raise $200 to establish a fund to provide interest-free loans. In return for a monthly contribution of twenty-five cents to increase and sustain the society's pool of capital, members who needed temporary financial assistance were entitled to receive an interest-free loan, sparing them the indignity of asking for charity.[112] Unlike the Hebrew Benevolent Society, governed by donors who decided how charity would be dispensed and who was deserving of it, the Hebrew Sick Relief Society was egalitarian: its members and the executives whom they elected were simultaneously both contributors and potential recipients bound by reciprocal obligations of mutual aid.

With the establishment of the Hebrew Sick Relief Society, dispensing charity became the responsibility of the Rosh Pina Ladies' Aid Society. Although Rosh Pina was an Orthodox synagogue that adhered to traditional religious practices—women were segregated in an upstairs gallery, more as observers of than participants in religious services, and could not vote or serve on the executive of the congregation—in 1896 female members of the congregation established a charitable organization, the Ladies' Aid Society, to assist the deserving poor.[113] Autonomous and governed by an all-female executive elected by its members, the Ladies' Aid Society became a vehicle for Jewish women to enter the public sphere, where they organized concerts and other social activities to raise money to support recent immigrants and destitute Jews.[114] Similarly, in 1898, women who belonged to the Shaarey Zedek synagogue established a Ladies' Aid Society to support the "Jewish poor."[115]

The Rosh Pina and Shaarey Zedek Ladies' Aid Societies increased the scope of voluntary activity to raise money and provide assistance to immigrants and destitute Jews. However, the Jewish community's charitable activities remained fragmented. These two societies and the Hebrew Benevolent Society were extensions of two rival congregations. Their supporters inhabited different social circles; the annual balls and concerts that each society held to raise money for its charitable work were major social events that reinforced social relationships that divided rather than united the Jewish community. Instead of cooperating to coordinate their activities, each society raised money independently and followed its own procedures for identifying and assisting recipients.[116]

The arrival in August 1900 of seventy-nine destitute Romanian Jewish refugees revealed the weakness of the Jewish community's fragmented system of providing charitable assistance. To assist the refugees, the Baron de Hirsch Institute in Montreal authorized Rabbi A.M. Ashinsky to go to Winnipeg and spend \$100 to help them find employment and sent \$450 to M. Vineberg, president of the Hebrew Sick Relief Society, to pay for food and clothing.[117] However, the latter amount was sufficient to meet the needs of only forty-five of the refugees. Since the Jewish community's charitable societies were unable to assist the refugees, Vineberg formed an immigration committee to make a public appeal for donations.[118] On 12 August 1900, the committee held a public meeting that raised an additional \$250 and made plans to find employment for the refugees on farms. Although fewer in number, another group of Jewish refugees from Romania arrived the following summer, prompting the secretary of the Hebrew Sick Relief Society to send a request to the Baron de Hirsch

Institute for funds to assist them.[119] In an acknowledgement that Winnipeg's Jewish community was not able to assist groups of destitute Jewish immigrants who arrived in the city, the secretary also requested that the "Society should be made a branch of the Baron de Hirsch Institute."[120]

The Hebrew Benevolent Society and the Rosh Pina and Shaarey Zedek Ladies' Aid Societies continued to function, but the focus of organizational activity increasingly shifted away from synagogues to the public sphere. In May 1903, when news of the Kishinev pogroms reached Winnipeg, it was the Winnipeg Zionist Society rather than a synagogue that organized a public meeting to protest the failure of the tsar to protect Russian Jews.[121] Attended by over 300 Jews, the gathering raised $100 to send to Russia to assist victims of the pogroms and appointed two committees to solicit additional donations from members of Winnipeg's Jewish community.[122]

The shift of organizational activity from synagogues to the public sphere was not confined to communal responses to international events. In July 1903, a group of Romanian Jews established the Dr. Gaster Benevolent Society.[123] Although conflicts between rabbis who opposed the ideas of *maskilim* and secular Jewish leaders in Romania between 1895 and 1905 prevented the establishment of new charitable and self-help organizations, having lived close to the border between Romania and Russia, Jewish immigrants from Romania were familiar with the savings and loan cooperatives that had been established in the Pale of Settlement.[124] The founders of the society wanted to establish a *landsmanshaft*, an organization that would provide a forum for social activities among Jews from the same country who shared similar pre-emigration experiences and provide them with charitable assistance. However, though the society continued to distribute charitable assistance to newly arrived immigrants, sick benefits quickly became a priority. Within months, the society became a mutual aid society; in 1904, it established a sick benefit fund, which—in exchange for weekly contributions—offered its members replacement income when illness prevented them from working. In 1903, the society distributed $816.50 in charity, but by 1904 it had paid $1,165 in sick benefits, and charitable benefits had declined to $300. Attracted by the sick benefit fund, Jewish immigrants from Russia and the Austro-Hungarian Empire soon became members of the society.[125] By 1904, it had displaced the Rosh Pina's Hebrew Sick Relief Society, which ceased operations.[126] The following year sick benefit payments increased to $1,345.80, and charitable distributions amounted to $365. By 1907, buoyed by the society's success, the executive confidently announced plans to raise $40,000 to construct a building to house a school where children could learn Hebrew, a night school to teach immigrants English, and a shelter for the homeless.[127]

By 1905, the organizational landscape of Winnipeg's Jewish community had changed. Synagogues coexisted with secular organizations that attracted members from across the Jewish community. The emergence of a public sphere for Jewish communal activity enabled members of disparate congregations to join together to support mutual aid organizations such as the Dr. Gaster Benevolent Society or, as in 1903, to cooperate with secular organizations to mobilize the resources of the entire community to deal with a crisis such as a large influx of refugees.

Government repression of Jewish political movements in the Pale of Settlement following the Russian Revolution and an epidemic of pogroms in 1905–06 dramatically increased the flow of refugees to Winnipeg: 500 Jews arrived there from Russia in 1904, 469 in 1905, and 748 in 1906.[128] Events in the Pale galvanized the Jewish community, and representatives of the Hebrew Relief Society and the Dr. Gaster Benevolent Society formed a committee to assist the refugees. In April 1905, the committee opened a dining room that offered the refugees three meals a day.[129] By November, the number of refugees arriving in Winnipeg was so great that the committee established a dormitory in the hall of worship of Beth Jacob synagogue. When the hall was full, the committee raised $400 to pay refugees to expand the synagogue's basement to accommodate an additional dormitory and purchase beds and blankets.[130] To help the refugees find employment, the committee also established a free night school that offered English lessons.[131] In response to an appeal for donations launched by the New York–based National Committee for the Relief of Sufferers of Russian Massacres organized by Jacob H. Schiff, the committee held a series of public meetings in November and December 1905 to raise money so that Jews in Russia could either be "supplied with arms to defend themselves or with food with which to sustain life" or be "transported from Russia to another country."[132] Over a three-week period, the Jewish community raised close to $3,000; in addition to the $400 spent to transform the Beth Jacob synagogue's basement into a dormitory, the committee sent $2,500 directly to Russia and $1,000 to the National Committee for the Relief of Sufferers of Russian Massacres.[133]

Between 1882 and 1903, religious affiliation defined the associational life of most of the members of Winnipeg's Jewish community. They devoted their time, energy, and money to establishing congregations, building synagogues, and engaging in interminable disputes about religious observance. Synagogues were both places of worship and centres of social and organizational life. They not only provided Jewish immigrants with a spiritual home but also offered them a place of refuge in an alien society, a sense of community and belonging. However, synagogues also created divisions in the Jewish community that undermined its capacity to mobilize its limited financial resources to assist arriving immigrants or support the destitute; synagogue-based charitable assistance was inadequate and unreliable. In 1900, the collective failure of synagogue-based charitable organizations—the Hebrew Benevolent Society, the Rosh Pina Ladies' Aid Society, and the Shaarey Zedek Ladies' Aid Society—to assist Romanian Jewish refugees forced the Jewish community to depend on funds provided by the Baron de Hirsch Institute. When the funds provided by the institute were exhausted, instead of turning to the Jewish community's charities for assistance, a hastily formed immigration committee organized a public meeting in August 1900 to appeal for donations to assist the refugees. The need to organize a public meeting in effect confirmed that Winnipeg's synagogue-based charities were unable to act independently or to cooperate to pool their resources to assist the refugees; fostering communal solidarity to mobilize the resources of the Jewish community to deal with a crisis depended on engaging its members in the public sphere.

This lesson shaped the Jewish community's responses to the pogroms that began in Kishinev in 1903 and the political repression and widespread pogroms that accompanied the Russian Revolution in 1905. In both of those years, public meetings became community forums that solicited donations and elected committees to organize the provision of assistance to refugees. Community forums not only demonstrated that they were an effective means of superseding parochial loyalties and interests to mobilize the resources of the Jewish community but also confirmed that the public sphere provided common ground on which Jews could set aside their religious differences and synagogue affiliations and work together to achieve their goals or find collective solutions to their problems.

Certainly, based upon their experience as destitute immigrants, the Romanian Jews who established the Dr. Gaster Benevolent Society, the Jewish community's first secular mutual aid society, were well aware of the limitations of synagogue-based charitable organizations and the importance of the public sphere; it was the Baron de Hirsch Institute together with an immigration committee that made a public appeal for donations that had provided the assistance that they desperately needed. Although many of the Romanian Jews belonged to synagogues, they rejected the practice of basing the organization of charitable assistance on membership in a congregation. When a small group of Romanian Jews decided to form a benevolent society, they launched their new organization by holding a public meeting to elect officers who would recruit additional members. Their mandate was to establish a secular organization that operated in the public sphere and accepted members based solely upon their commitment to the principles of self-help and mutual aid. Despite its origin and name, the Dr. Gaster Benevolent Society quickly expanded to include Jews from Russia and the Austro-Hungarian Empire.

The emergence of the public sphere between 1900 and 1905 transformed communal governance. Observant Jewish immigrants continued to join established synagogues or, increasingly after 1905, establish new ones. However, though synagogues remained a vital part of Jewish life, they no longer served as the only organizational platforms for the provision of assistance to newly arrived immigrants or destitute Jews. Unlike Winnipeg's first Jewish residents, who arrived before 1882, or the immigrants who arrived in the 1880s and 1890s (Jews who came of age in an era when synagogues were both places of worship and centres of communal governance), the waves of Jewish immigrants who settled in Winnipeg after 1900 had experienced the modernization of Jewish communal governance in the Pale of Settlement. Not only did they import new ideas and beliefs about the role of secular rather than religious organizations in the provision of social welfare, but also by 1905 they comprised a majority of the members of the Jewish community. Mirroring challenges to traditional forms of authority and communal governance taking place in Jewish communities in the Pale, the Jews who settled in Winnipeg after 1900 enthusiastically embraced opportunities to establish a vibrant public sphere in which decisions about the provision of social welfare were based upon the authority and participation of the people.

CHAPTER 5

Communal Charity, Mutual Aid, and International Relief

In 1932, Winnipeg's Yiddish-language newspaper, the *Israelite Press*, published a "100th Anniversary Souvenir," a tribute to a century of Jewish settlement and progress in Canada.[1] The tribute included an essay written by the newspaper's editor, H.E. Wilder, outlining the fifty-year history of Winnipeg's Jewish community. Referring to the impact of the "third immigration stream," the arrival of Jewish refugees who had "stood in the front ranks of the radical circles in Russia" and come to Canada to "escape the persecution that followed the suppression of the abortive revolution of 1905," Wilder stated that the "period between 1905 and 1908 was one of the most crucial in the life of the Jewish community."[2] This influx was not only the "largest numerically," Wilder noted, but also the "most pregnant with future possibilities."[3]

Demographically, the surge of Jewish immigrants fleeing the series of pogroms that began in Kishinev in 1903 together with the influx of refugees following the Russian Revolution in 1905 was the first of several dramatic increases in the size of Winnipeg's Jewish community. In 1901, 1,156 Jews lived in Winnipeg. In 1902, 112 Russian Jews arrived followed by 201 in 1903 and 500 in 1904. Between 1905 and 1908, 1,926 Russian Jews arrived. Together with 213 Jews from Romania and 230 from other countries, this "third" stream increased Winnipeg's Jewish population to close to 5,000. The total number of Jewish immigrants settling in Winnipeg declined briefly—from 409 in 1908 to 366 in 1909—but beginning in 1910 it began to increase steadily, peaking at 1,254 in 1913.[4] By 1911, Winnipeg's Jewish population was 9,023, and in 1916 it totalled 13,555. However, the arrival of more than 12,250 Jewish immigrants between 1903 and 1916 did not simply increase the size of Winnipeg's Jewish community, it also transformed communal decision making and governance.

By 1905, the approximately 1,300 Jews who settled in Winnipeg between 1882 and 1902 had become a minority within the Jewish community. Although many of the men and women who had become prominent members of the community, including the officers of the Shaarey Zedek and Rosh Pina congregations and their associated charitable organizations, continued to have influential roles in communal decision making, they were eclipsed by a new generation of leaders. Most of the thousands of Jewish immigrants who arrived in Winnipeg after 1903 had come of age—their average age on arrival in Canada was thirty-one—in the Pale of Settlement in an era when modern forms of social organization and communal governance had displaced traditional authority.[5] Some of the Jewish refugees who had fled pogroms had witnessed the failure of traditional leaders to defend their communities. Many had survived pogroms because members of newly formed Jewish political organizations, the Bund and Poale Zion, had established armed self-defence forces that had saved lives by confronting the pogromists and forcing them to withdraw from Jewish communities. Others had been Marxist socialists, "autonomists," or Socialist Zionists, members of the Bund, Poale Zion, Zionist Socialist Workers' Party, Jewish Social Democratic Workers' Party, or Jewish Socialist Party, organizations committed to social and political emancipation from both traditional forms of communal authority and Russian state oppression. Those who had not been political activists had been exposed to the flowering of Yiddish-language literature, newspapers, journals, and theatre, the assertion of a secular Jewish identity and consciousness in an expanding, vibrant public sphere, or had been members of the secular self-help societies that had proliferated throughout the Pale.

The Transformation of Winnipeg's Jewish Community

The Jewish immigrants who settled in Winnipeg after 1903 transformed the cultural, political, and organizational landscape of the Jewish community. Drawing on their pre-immigration experiences, they took advantage of the opportunities provided by an evolving diasporic community to continue the activities that had invigorated Jewish life in the Pale of Settlement. In 1904, a protégé of the playwright and theatre director Avrom Goldfadn, the impresario who organized the first modern Yiddish theatre troupe in Eastern Europe, established the Jewish Operatic Company in Winnipeg. Supported by a large troupe of amateur actors, the company performed Goldfadn's *Bar Kokhba* and *Sacrifice of Isaac*, plays that had galvanized Jewish audiences in the Pale of Settlement. They also performed Jacob Gordin's *The Jewish King Lear*, an adaptation of Shakespeare's play that incorporated themes that resonated with Jewish immigrants.[6] A second theatre troupe, established in 1905, the Yiddish Dramatic Club, performed plays by the literary icon Sholem Aleichem as well as the work of emerging New York–based Jewish playwrights such as Dovid Pinsky and Leon Korbin, who dramatized the dilemmas of modern Jewish life experienced by immigrants.[7] The purchase, in 1907, of a church on Selkirk Avenue and its conversion into the Queen's Theatre provided a permanent venue for local theatrical productions as well as plays starring celebrated Russian-born actors such as Jacob Adler and Keni Liptzin, who had contributed to the rise of Yiddish-language theatre in New York.

By 1910, Yiddish became a means of mass communication as well as cultural expression. Published weekly, the *Canadian Israelite* (*Der Kanader Yid*)—in 1915 its name changed to the *Israelite Press* (*Dos Yiddishe Vort*)—provided its readers with extensive coverage of local events together with reports on Jewish life in the United States and Europe. Forceful editorials encouraged members of the Jewish community to support initiatives to build communal institutions and exercise their political rights to secure representation of their interests at all levels of government. The newspaper also supported the cultural life of the Jewish community by publicizing theatrical and musical events. It kept its readers up to date with literary trends by publishing stories and poems by Jewish literary notables and encouraged local writers to submit their work for publication. It also provided detailed summaries of public lectures by prominent exponents of Yiddish cultural expression. Large, enthusiastic audiences who welcomed Yiddish-speaking luminaries such as the popular author and playwright Sholem Asch, the dramatist Peretz Hirschbein, and the proponent of a secular Jewish identity, Dr. Chaim Zhitlovsky, made Winnipeg a frequent destination on North American lecture tours.[8]

Although its editors were committed to promoting the use of Yiddish as a vibrant language of contemporary culture as well as a means of engaging members of the Jewish community in discussions about communal issues, the *Israelite Press* supported all initiatives to establish Jewish schools. It published articles written by Hebraists, advocates of a traditional Hebrew-based religious education, as well as the views of Yiddishists, who believed that instruction in Yiddish was central to a modern, progressive Jewish education.[9] In 1912, an editorial urged the newspaper's readers to support a fundraising drive to build the Talmud Torah, a Hebrew-language school, and in 1914 an equally enthusiastic editorial appeared supporting the efforts of the Yiddisher Yugend Farein, a literary and cultural organization, to open the National Radical School, a Yiddish-language institution.[10] The editor of the *Israelite Press* had a policy of supporting all community initiatives, but he also recognized that, whether parents chose to supplement their children's public school education with instruction in Hebrew or Yiddish, the fact that the debate over the future of Jewish education took place in the pages of *Israelite Press* confirmed the status of Yiddish as the dominant language of Winnipeg's Jewish community.

No longer content with simply voting, by the late 1880s Jewish immigrants began to join and become active members of Liberal Party and Conservative Party constituency organizations.[11] Eager to exercise political influence and benefit from government patronage, Jewish political activists organized election meetings to support Liberal and Conservative candidates contesting federal, provincial, and municipal elections.[12] Despite partisan differences, Jewish Liberals and Conservatives joined forces in 1904 to campaign for a candidate to represent the North End on Winnipeg City Council. Taking advantage of a concentration of Jewish voters in Ward Five, they succeeded in electing Moses Finkelstein, who appealed to Jewish voters by promising to advocate for more spending on sewers, sidewalks, and other neglected public works in the North End as well as building a second bridge to span the CPR tracks to reduce the district's isolation from the rest of the city.[13] The election clearly demonstrated the advantages of political cooperation, but the lessons of Finkelstein's victory were not applied to provincial and federal politics, in which partisanship continued to divide the Jewish vote. However, in 1910, when the Liberals nominated a Jewish candidate, S. Hart Green, to run in the constituency of North Winnipeg, the prospect of electing a Jew to the Legislative Assembly trumped partisan loyalties, and he was elected with a substantial majority.[14]

The election of Finkelstein and Green confirmed that Jewish voters recognized the importance of electing candidates who truly represented their community, Jews who not only understood the difficulties experienced by recent immigrants but also shared and could articulate their aspirations for the future. Nonetheless, beginning in 1904, Jewish immigrants who had received their political education in the Pale of Settlement challenged the claims of either Liberals or Conservatives to represent the interests of the Jewish community. Schooled in the politics of Jewish emancipation, they quickly established organizations that replicated the competing ideologies of the political movements that had captured their imaginations and won their allegiance before they were forced to immigrate to Canada. By 1907, a variety of Jewish political organizations—Branch No. 169 of the Arbeiter Ring (Marxist), Branch No. 506 of the Arbeiter Ring (Socialist Zionist–Poale Zion), and the "Free Society" (anarchist)—developed social, educational, and cultural programs to propagate their communitarian visions of how Jews could free themselves from oppression and achieve social justice.[15]

Whereas the two branches of the Arbeiter Ring and the members of the "Free Society" focused on education programs, discussion groups, and public debates on whether Marxism, Socialist Zionism, or anarchism offered the most viable prospect for Jewish emancipation, other radicals recognized that electoral politics provided an opportunity to promote workers' interests. In 1905, a group of Jewish Marxists formed a local unit of the Socialist Party of Canada. However, frustrated with its leaders' lack of commitment to a fundamental principle of Marxist theory and practice, the revolutionary mission of the working class, and their inability to recognize the importance of operating in Yiddish or other languages spoken by workers in the North End to expand the party's membership, Jewish members of the party left it and in 1910 formed a branch of the newly organized Social Democratic Party of Canada. The party's platform, which called for the eradication of capitalism, combined electoral politics to achieve reforms with support for unions and the unemployed.[16] Members of the Jewish branch of the Social Democratic Party failed to elect any of their stalwarts; however, between 1913 and 1919, their support contributed to the electoral success of four labour councillors (Richard Rigg, John Queen, A.A. Heaps, and John Blumberg), a labour member of the provincial legislature (Richard Rigg), as well as the election of a school trustee, Rose Alcin, a member of Poale Zion.

By stimulating public debates on and discussions of Marxism, socialism, the possibility of a Jewish homeland in Palestine, secularism, anti-Semitism, Yiddish literature, international politics, union rights, and unemployment, members of the Social Democratic Party and the three branches of Arbeiter Ring helped to shape the intellectual life of the Jewish community. As Marxists, Socialist Zionists, and anarchists, they had endless disagreements over the politics of social class, Jewish identity, and individual freedom, but they all believed in the importance of collective action to achieve equality and social justice. Collectively, they disseminated secular communitarian ideals throughout the Jewish community, nurturing the development of a new generation of modern communal social welfare organizations.

Communal Solidarity and Mutual Aid

The Jewish immigrants who settled in Winnipeg after 1903 faced the same challenges as their predecessors: finding employment or establishing a business that provided sufficient income to enable them to afford the cost of food, shelter, clothing, and medical services and, hopefully, accumulate savings. However, employment was often insecure, layoffs or dismissals meant immediate loss of income, and businesses were vulnerable to variable profits and often failed. Moreover, in an era when employers had little interest in workplace safety, work-related injuries frequently occurred, and illness, particularly in the North End, was a constant threat.[17] Injury and illness not only meant lost income but also additional expenditures for medicine, physicians' fees, and hospital bills. Savings were essential to cope with interruptions in income, pay for medical care, and ultimately ensure that money was available for funeral and burial expenses. However, accumulating savings was extremely difficult for workers and small-business owners, and immigrants lived in chronic insecurity.

To protect themselves from becoming dependent on public charity, which was inadequate and could result in deportation, or being forced to endure the shame of accepting assistance from Jewish charitable organizations, post-1903 Jewish immigrants chose to achieve collectively what an individual immigrant or family had difficulty achieving alone: a measure of economic security. They rejected the prevailing belief that cautiously dispensing charity to the deserving poor, dividing the Jewish community into donors and supplicants, was the only way that Jews could assist one another. The synagogue-based charitable organizations established by their predecessors reminded Jewish immigrants of the hierarchical institutions, paternalism, and social distinctions that afflicted Jewish life in the Pale of Settlement. Drawing on their pre-immigration experience or knowledge of secular *kassy* ("self-help societies") and savings and loan cooperatives, they embraced an egalitarian model of social assistance based upon principles of self-help and reciprocal responsibility.[18] Inspired by the success of the founders of the Dr. Gaster Benevolent Society in 1905, Jewish immigrants began transforming the organizational foundation of their community by establishing fifty-six mutual aid associations.

Such associations were typically formed by a small group of Jewish immigrants who assumed collective responsibility for ensuring that, in exchange for paying dues, members had a right to specific benefits. Once a mutual aid association was organized, its founders applied for incorporation under the Charitable Associations Act, which granted them legal authority to promote "their mutual protection by means of contributions, subscriptions, donations

4. Board of Directors, Hebrew Sick Benefit Association.

and assessments against all casualties caused by disease, unavoidable accident or death" as well as to "assist any individual members of the association . . . financially, by means of donations or loans."[19] Although the act specified that as few as ten people "holding together not less than one hundred dollars" were entitled to apply for incorporation, the success of a mutual aid association depended on attracting enough members to generate sufficient revenue to pay for the benefits that it provided.[20]

The benefits provided by mutual aid societies varied. By 1913, Winnipeg's Jewish community had three types of these societies. The first provided a sick benefit, income assistance for members unable to work because of illness, and a cash payment when a member died. Founded in October 1906 by three brothers from the Pale of Settlement, the Hebrew Sick Benefit Association (HSBA) had enrolled by January 1907 twenty-four members, who petitioned the Provincial Secretary for letters patent under the Charitable Associations Act.[21] Initially, the HSBA focused on providing a sickness benefit of six dollars per week and a death benefit of $300.[22] However, as its membership increased—close to 500 by 1925—it provided additional benefits. In 1910, the HSBA opened a cemetery and began to offer members and their wives free burial plots and tombstones. It also paid members a benefit when they were observing *shiva*, the seven-day period of mourning. In addition, the HSBA provided a range of health benefits, including free care by a physician whose fee was paid by the association, up to five dollars to subsidize the cost of

5. Banquet celebrating the twentieth anniversary of the Hebrew Sick Benefit Association, 2 May 1926.

consulting a specialist, and free medicine that could be obtained at one of two pharmacies affiliated with the association. In exceptional circumstances, the HSBA also assumed responsibility for members in financial need. Members no longer entitled to sickness benefits could apply for interest-free loans repayable only if the borrower could afford to make payments.[23] The range of benefits provided by the HSBA was exceptional; most of the mutual aid associations subsequently established to provide cash benefits focused on replacing income for injured members or those too sick to work and providing a lump sum payment when a member died.[24]

The second type of mutual aid association was established to provide its members with interest-free loans. For example, the Kiev Free Loan Association was founded in 1914 by nine charter members, and in January 1916 twenty-nine petitioners received letters patent for it.[25] Credit was a chronic problem for immigrants since financial institutions were unwilling to lend money to borrowers who could not provide substantial collateral to guarantee loans, and

high interest rates made the cost of borrowing prohibitive. Joining a free-loan association gave members access to loans up to $100 with a manageable weekly repayment schedule. Borrowers invariably made their payments on time, for failing to make a payment not only imposed a burden on fellow members and jeopardized the possibility of future loans but also was a breach of trust. When members joined a free-loan association, they promised to fulfill their obligations to it and simultaneously made commitments to each other. Nevertheless, no penalty applied if the borrower missed a payment, and in some instances loans were forgiven. Jewish immigrants used interest-free loans as personal sources of credit to pay unexpected hospital bills or make major purchases such as furniture or appliances. Interest-free loans also enabled recently arrived immigrants to expedite family reunifications. Instead of waiting years to save the hundreds of dollars needed to purchase steamship tickets, members of free-loan associations could borrow money to bring first their wives and children and then their parents, sisters, and brothers to Canada. Access to interest-free loans became an important component of Jewish immigrants' financial planning. They provided the financial security that many Jewish immigrants needed to allocate fixed parts of their incomes to mortgage payments, assisting them to buy homes.

Access to credit was particularly important to merchants and other small-business owners. Jewish immigrants established the Commercial, Merchants, Second Hand Dealers, and other free-loan associations to provide business loans. Since small profit margins made it difficult for many Jewish businessmen to build the capital reserves that they needed to purchase goods, cope with recessions, or expand their businesses, access to credit was essential. Whether their enterprises were secure or precarious, interest-free loans lowered the cost of doing business. For many small-business owners, membership in a free-loan association provided a competitive advantage, whereas for others it was essential to survive.

A third type of mutual aid association provided benefits as well as interest-free loans. For example, members of the Kiev Free Loan and Aid Association, Pavolotch Loan and Aid Association, and Zion Loan and Benevolent Association had the advantage of belonging to organizations that offered both income security and access to credit.

No matter what form of financial assistance they provided, all three types of mutual aid associations adhered to a fundamental principle, that the cost of membership—both becoming a member and paying monthly membership dues—be kept as low as possible. Upon joining an association, each member made a cash contribution, typically ten dollars, to an operating fund and paid monthly dues.[26] To be financially viable, mutual aid societies had to recruit enough members to be self-sustaining. The operating fund, augmented by revenue from monthly dues, was used to pay for benefits or provide interest-free loans until the association recruited enough members to generate sufficient revenue from dues to meet its expenses. The operating fund then became a reserve fund replenished from monthly revenues and then increased to an amount that members determined would enable the association to deal with unexpected expenses, subsidize social events, or make contributions to support communal institutions or activities.[27]

Mutual aid associations that provided sickness and death benefits considered two factors when they assessed dues: the cost of providing benefits—for example, the amount and number of weeks of sickness benefits that members were entitled to receive and the amount of the death benefit—and a determination of possible financial liabilities, based upon the number of members likely to apply for benefits.[28] Since expenditures, particularly on sickness benefits, were difficult to predict, the assessment of dues also took into consideration how much revenue was needed to maintain a reserve fund. Although associations did not need large memberships to be financially viable—a stable membership that provided a predictable revenue stream was more important than its size—recruiting new members generated more revenue, which could be used to provide additional benefits. For example, in 1906, when the HSBA was founded, its members paid monthly dues of sixty-five cents, which entitled them to sickness benefits and a modest death benefit. In 1925, with close to 500 members, the association could afford to provide additional benefits, such as free medical services, a death benefit of $500, a free burial, and replacement income while in mourning, all for monthly dues of one dollar.[29]

Similarly, free-loan associations initially relied on membership contributions and monthly dues to establish a fund that could be used to provide loans. As an association's membership increased, it used additional membership contributions and monthly dues to replenish and then increase the size of its loan fund. The size of the fund determined the maximum amount and the number of loans that the association could afford to provide. Typically, as a free-loan society grew, its members had access to larger loans.[30] Since these societies could rely on a steady stream of weekly revenue in the form of loan payments, they could preserve their capital and consequently afford to impose membership dues as low as twenty-five cents a month.[31] Like mutual aid associations that provided benefits, free-loan associations cautiously reserved parts of their loan funds for contingencies such as members who found themselves in dire straits and missed payments or defaulted on their loans.[32] Once they were well established, free-loan societies also used reserve funds to make financial contributions to communal institutions and causes.

The vast majority of mutual aid associations were founded by men.[33] Since married men were the primary income earners in families, by providing them with a measure of financial security mutual aid associations protected all of their dependants. Unmarried adult men also had an incentive to become members; completely self-supporting, they were particularly vulnerable to a loss of income because of illness or injury. Women, however, were rarely financially independent. Almost no married women worked outside the home, less than a quarter of unmarried women worked, and those who did work lived with their parents or married siblings until marriage, which invariably took place before the age of twenty-three.[34] Nevertheless, in 1906, a small group of young unmarried Jewish women held a public meeting to discuss establishing a free-loan society. They formed the Girls' Benevolent Loan Society to provide interest-free loans to "girls under twenty years of age."[35] The primary purpose of the society was to assist young women affected by seasonal unemployment. To establish a loan fund, they sold honorary memberships and raised money by holding annual dances. In exchange for monthly dues of twenty-five cents, members were entitled to borrow up to twenty dollars. By 1913, the society had fifty members and outstanding loans totalling almost $600.[36]

Since the overwhelming majority of married women did not earn an income, making a contribution to join a mutual aid association and paying monthly dues did not make economic sense, for they would not be entitled to sickness benefits or free loans. Recognizing that the economic security of their families depended on their husbands' earnings, married women understood the importance of belonging to a mutual aid association and viewed membership as a family responsibility. However, many women were not content to be dependent members; those who wanted to have a voice in running the mutual aid associations that their husbands joined formed ladies' auxiliaries, parallel associations composed of women that organized social and cultural events and raised money for Jewish communal institutions. Nevertheless, in an exceptional assertion of financial independence, in 1917 ten married women formed the Hebrew Ladies' Free Loan Association of Elmwood.[37]

Although legally identified as an association, a mutual aid association was invariably called "the society" by its members. These associations were primarily established to provide Jewish immigrants with financial assistance, but they were also societies, groups of people bound together by the need for companionship. By joining mutual aid societies, Jewish immigrants formed lasting social networks. As immigrants, they had experienced the dislocation of leaving their homes and families and the difficulties of establishing new lives in an unfamiliar city. At least ten of the mutual aid associations established by Jewish immigrants in Winnipeg were *landsmanshaftn*, societies composed of *landsleyt*, Jews from the same *shtetl*, city, or province in the Pale of Settlement. Drawn to each other by relationships formed before emigration and shared memories of their former lives, they founded mutual aid associations that both maintained links to the past and helped them to plan for the future. Former residents of Propoisk (Mogilev *gubernia*) founded the Propoisker Hebrew Society, and Jews from Samhorodok and other Jewish communities in Kiev *gubernia* established the Kiev Free Loan and Aid Association.[38] Similarly, Jews from other parts of Eastern Europe founded the Austrian Hebrew Association, the Roumanian [*sic*] Hebrew Sick Benefit Society, and the Russian Polish Jewish Association.

Pre-immigration political allegiances and experiences led to the formation of two mutual aid associations. In 1907, a group of Marxists founded Branch No. 169 of the Arbeiter Ring. Pledged to the eradication of capitalism, they combined their determination to raise the political consciousness of the Jewish working class with a commitment to mutual aid. Also that year twenty members of the branch established the Arbeiter Ring Sick Benefit Association.[39] Similarly, in 1915, a group of anarchists who formerly belonged to the "Free Society" concluded that forming a branch of the Arbeiter Ring was consistent with their belief in free association and would enable them to assist each other financially. Despite their hostility to the authority of the state in 1915, ten members of Branch No. 564 applied for letters patent to establish the Arbeiter Ring Free Loan Association.[40]

However, membership in most of Winnipeg's Jewish mutual aid associations was open to anyone committed to the principles of mutual aid. Since

6. Founding members of the Kiev Free Loan Association, 1914.

7. Banquet celebrating the tenth anniversary of the Achdus Free Loan Association, 4 November 1924.

the success of each association depended on recruiting enough dues-paying members to make mutual aid financially viable, every member had an incentive to induce relatives, friends, and acquaintances to join it. Whatever the intentions of their founders, once established many *landsmanshaftn* adopted a flexible membership policy, recognizing that adhering to a narrow definition of who qualified as a *landsleyt* could be self-defeating. Whatever the composition of their memberships, all mutual aid associations assisted Jewish immigrants to adjust to their new lives. They provided the immigrants with a welcome remedy for loneliness and isolation, a social forum in which they could share their problems and aspirations as well as celebrate their achievements. Regular meetings and social events such as dinners, picnics, and holiday celebrations attended by members' wives promoted friendships and enriched their lives. Every gathering of members inevitably sparked informal discussions of communal issues and current events. For a *griner*, a "newcomer," membership in a mutual aid association provided an opportunity to acquire a circle of friends, to have a social life, and to meet established immigrants who could offer advice on

finding better jobs, dealing with business setbacks, or financing the purchase of steamship tickets to bring their families to Winnipeg.

By the mid-1920s, Winnipeg's Jewish mutual aid associations had over 3,800 members, including approximately 80 percent of the Jewish men in the city.[41] Membership in these associations provided them with a practical education in communal governance. Egalitarian and democratic, they engaged members in the elections of officers, deliberations about sickness benefits and loans, and discussions of financial statements. Members acquired an understanding of constitutions, democratic practices, rules of procedure, and how to manage the financial affairs of a voluntary organization. Mutual aid associations functioned in Yiddish, the language that all Jews understood and used in their daily lives; constitutions were drafted, meetings were conducted, and minutes and annual financial statements were written in Yiddish. Through mass membership in mutual aid associations, Yiddish continued to evolve, becoming a language of communal governance. For many Jewish immigrants, membership in a mutual aid association transformed their perceptions of authority and participation in communal decision making and gave them the confidence and skills to participate in the governance of other organizations and institutions in the Jewish community.

Communal Charity

Although mutual aid associations provided the vast majority of Jewish immigrant families with a substantial measure of financial security, they did not eliminate the need for charity. The associations could only afford to pay sickness benefits for short periods, loans were repayable on a weekly basis, and once funeral expenses had been paid very little of the death benefit would be left for living expenses. Consequently, even with the protection provided by membership in a mutual aid association, unless children were old enough to work, a disability or chronic illness that prevented a family's primary income earner from working or his death could lead to destitution. Jewish immigrant families also faced the risk of unemployment, particularly during the recessions of 1907–08 and 1913–14, both periods of peak immigration.

Rather than risk deportation or submit to the humiliating practices of the Associated Charities, the City of Winnipeg's relief agency, most destitute Jewish families turned to either the Hebrew Benevolent Association or the Rosh Pina Ladies' Aid Association. However, as Winnipeg's Jewish population increased, neither organization could cope with the demand for charitable assistance. The Hebrew Benevolent Association had not changed in the preceding fifteen years. In 1908, it remained an insular organization, controlled by businessmen who were prominent members of the Shaarey Zedek synagogue (three of the association's leaders, Hiram Weidman, Ben Zimmerman, and Abraham Lechtzier, had served on its executive in 1892).[42] To raise money, the association relied on soliciting donations from members of the Shaarey Zedek congregation. However, by 1909, the association was forced to admit publicly that the "burden was too heavy."[43] Appearing before Winnipeg City Council's Board of Control in January 1909, a delegation from the association stated that in the past they "had taken care of their own poor" but could no longer do so without assistance from the city.[44] The delegation's request for a grant was refused. However, under increasing pressure to provide charitable assistance, the following January another delegation appeared before the Board of Control with a request for a grant of $500. The delegation stated that in 1909 the association had spent $1,727 providing charitable assistance, leaving a year-end balance of $5.61.[45] Although the city controller acknowledged that $500 was not an excessive amount, he stated that the Board of Control was not authorized to make grants, and to do so would establish a precedent that would encourage other charitable organizations to request money.[46] Advising the association of the board's decision, the mayor stated that he would instruct the city's relief department to cooperate with the Hebrew Benevolent Association, assuring its president that the "feelings of the Jewish people would be respected in every possible way."[47]

Although the Rosh Pina Ladies' Aid Association also assisted destitute Jews, its financial resources were limited. Following the practice of Jewish women in Montreal, Ottawa, Windsor, and numerous cities in the United States, members of the association decided in 1908 to downplay its relationship with the Rosh Pina synagogue and enter the public sphere. Pursuing a measure of personal and collective autonomy, they renamed the association the Winnipeg Hebrew Ladies' Aid Society.[48] By 1913, the society had 200 members, but as married women few of them had independent sources of income, limiting the amount that they could raise by soliciting donations. Their main source of revenue was an annual charity ball; in 1912, ticket sales funded half of their annual expenditure of $800.[49] Combined with the efforts of the Hebrew Benevolent Association, charitable assistance dispensed by the Hebrew Ladies' Aid Society helped to alleviate the distress of some of the Jewish community's "sick, old and needy,"[50] but by 1911 it became apparent that the Jewish community's system of providing charitable assistance was in crisis.

In January 1911, one of the leaders of the Hebrew Benevolent Association, Hiram Weidman, and J.K. Levin, the rabbi of Shaarey Shomayim synagogue, held a meeting attended by members of the B'nai B'rith Lodge to discuss the formation of a new charitable organization to replace the ineffective Hebrew Benevolent Association.[51] Enlisting the support of Israel Kahanovitch, the rabbi of Beth Jacob synagogue and the chief rabbi of western Canada, Rabbi Levin established a committee to plan a public meeting to establish the United Hebrew Charities. Members of the Shaarey Shomayim and B'nai B'rith dominated the committee. In addition to Rabbi Kahanovitch, the committee was composed of Rabbi Levin as well as A.H. Aronovitch and H.A. Isaacs, both members of the board of the Shaarey Shomayim congregation. Aronovitch and Isaacs, together with two other members of the committee, H.E. Wilder and Moses Finkelstein, were founding members of Winnipeg's B'nai B'rith Lodge. In 1911, Aronovitch served as president of the lodge, and Finkelstein was a member of the executive of the Hebrew Benevolent Association.

Chaired by Aronovitch, the meeting, held on 26 February 1911 in the Colonial Theatre in Central Winnipeg, was carefully managed. Following speeches by Rabbi Kahanovitch, Rabbi Levin, and Finkelstein, Isaacs presented the committee's report, which called for the formation of a new charitable organization, the United Hebrew Charities, to replace the Hebrew Benevolent Association. After circulating pledge cards, Aronovitch revealed the names and generous amounts pledged by thirteen donors.[52] Announcing their names not only clearly established that these donors were able to make large donations but also suggested that, given their wealth and commitment, they should play prominent roles in the new charity. After the announcement, Aronovitch proceeded to the next item of business, the selection of a subscription committee to solicit donations from the Jewish community. Ignoring nominations from the audience, he appointed three of the donors—Benjamin Shragge, Moses Finkelstein, and David Balcovske—to form a subscription committee to canvass the community for additional donations.[53]

Selection of members of the subscription committee was guided by two goals. The first goal was to appoint members who belonged to the Shaarey Shomayim and Shaarey Zedek congregations and the B'nai B'rith, wealthy businessmen who could approach fellow congregants, lodge brothers, and business associates to solicit substantial donations.[54] Schragge, Finkelstein, and Balcovske self-confidently assumed that they had the authority to appoint members who, like themselves, were proven leaders of the Jewish community, notables such as Finkelstein himself, who had been a city councillor, a leader of the Hebrew Benevolent Association, a president of the Shaarey Zedek congregation, and a founder of B'nai B'rith Lodge No. 650. The second goal was to appoint members who belonged to the Beth Israel congregation, the largest synagogue in the North End, where 85 percent of Winnipeg's Jews lived, but Schragge, Finkelstein, and Balcovske were determined to dominate the committee.

Ultimately, twelve of the twenty members whom they appointed to the subscription committee lived in Central Winnipeg and the South End. By "unanimous consent," Schragge and Finkelstein, who lived in Central Winnipeg, and Balcovske, who resided in the South End, were also (self-) appointed to the committee, reducing the proportion of representatives of the North End on the twenty-three-member committee to approximately 32 percent. Thus, the committee was dominated by members of the Shaarey Shomayim and Shaarey Zedek congregations, five of whom belonged to B'nai B'rith.

The meeting concluded with an agreement that donors who responded to the subscription committee's appeal for donations and pledges of financial support for the United Hebrew Charities would meet in the near future to elect a board of directors. At the meeting, held two weeks later on 12 March 1911 in the Colonial Theatre, the donors elected a twenty-member board and made Rabbi Kahanovitch and Rabbi Levin ex-officio members. A total of ten members of the subscription committee were elected to the board. Nine of the members elected to the board were from the North End, nine from Central Winnipeg, and two from the South End. Thus, the North End, home to 7,700 Jews, was underrepresented on the board (it had one representative for every 855 Jewish residents), and Central and South Winnipeg, where 1,023 Jews lived, were vastly overrepresented (the two districts had one representative for every ninety-three residents).[55] The board of directors was also unrepresentative of the social composition of the Jewish community. Although the vast majority of Winnipeg's Jews, particularly those who lived in the North End, were working class or owned small businesses, over half of the board of directors, most of them residents of Central and South Winnipeg, were affluent or wealthy businessmen.[56]

Establishment of the United Hebrew Charities triggered strong opposition within the Jewish community. The same afternoon that donors gathered to elect a board of directors to manage the new charity a coalition of nine "different charitable and religious organizations" held a meeting at the Queen's Theatre in the North End.[57] Over three hours, the estimated 400–500 people present heard numerous speakers forcefully state that a "major portion of the Jewish community of this city did not approve of the action[s] of certain individuals who had organized themselves into a charitable body and were calling themselves 'The United Hebrew Charities'" because they did not first hold a mass meeting of "Jewish citizens."[58] The meeting concluded by passing a unanimous resolution that expressed non-confidence in the "so-called United Hebrew Charities," "denying the right of the said individuals to act on behalf of the whole Jewish community."[59]

This public declaration that the United Hebrew Charities was not a legitimate charity was based upon more than a belief that its founders had violated the democratic right of all members of the Jewish community to participate in decisions about the establishment and governance of a communal charitable organization. It was an assertion of the principle that affluence or wealth did not give a small group of individuals the authority to speak for or act on behalf of the Jewish community. It was also an expression of dissatisfaction with the Hebrew Benevolent Association, which had been controlled by a small group of wealthy donors. To its critics, there was little to distinguish the United Hebrew

Charities from the Hebrew Benevolent Association; destitute Jews who lived in the North End would continue to be powerless supplicants whose fate would be decided by a charitable organization controlled by a small unrepresentative group of donors who resided in a different district, led privileged lives, and belonged to social circles far removed from the experiences of the average member of the Jewish community.[60]

Determined to ensure that those who decided who was entitled to charitable assistance were democratically elected, critics of the United Hebrew Charities decided to establish a second charitable organization governed by residents of the North End, recent immigrants who had experienced the difficulties of earning a living and understood the plight of potential recipients. Within months, they established the North End Relief Society of Winnipeg. Both charitable organizations proceeded to solicit donations and dispense charitable aid, creating some confusion among both donors and recipients. In March 1911, a group of B'nai B'rith leaders convened a meeting to persuade representatives of the North End Relief Society to merge their organization with the United Hebrew Charities. They invited J. Howard Falk, general secretary of the Associated Charities, to address the meeting.

The organizers of the meeting considered Falk an authority on charitable assistance given his four years of experience managing the city's relief agency. In his address, Falk emphasized the advantages of having only one charitable organization raise money on behalf of the Jewish community.[61] Inviting him to address the meeting illustrated substantial differences in how the prosperous businessmen who belonged to B'nai B'rith and the recent immigrants who had become the leaders of the North End Relief Society viewed charitable assistance. To the former, Falk was a city official, a professional administrator with expertise managing a charitable agency who had established a reputation for probity and efficiency. To the latter, Falk symbolized the practice of the Associated Charities of using interviews, investigations, and home inspections to restrict eligibility for charitable assistance, the anti-foreigner prejudices of its staff, and its policy of reporting applicants who were not citizens to immigration officials, which resulted in their deportation. They had every reason to view Falk and his ideas with suspicion.

Ultimately, the meeting and subsequent negotiations failed to bring about a merger. Abandoning its attempts to create a single Jewish charitable organization, the executive of the United Hebrew Charities applied in March 1914 for letters patent.[62] Six months later the North End Relief Society followed suit, defiantly declaring the breadth of its support by submitting a petition with an

The poor are hit hardest!

The severe weather of the past few days is working extreme hardship with our unfortunate poor. The United Hebrew Relief is taking care of

50 Jewish Families

They must have your help at once.

They need food—The United Hebrew Relief must give it to them.

They need clothing, fuel and shelter and they turn to us for aid.

Mail That Cheque Today

UNITED HEBREW RELIEF

A. Slobinsky, President.
S. Cossoy, Chairman Campaign Com.

8. Appeal for donations, *Jewish Post*, 21 January 1927.

unprecedented sixty names.[63] However, within a year, it became apparent that the competition for donations between the two charitable organizations was alienating donors and dividing the community. In October 1915, the United Hebrew Charities and the North End Relief Society held a joint meeting that authorized a merger to form the United Hebrew Relief. To promote reconciliation between supporters of the United Hebrew Charities and the North End Relief Society, and to ensure that the new charity would have the broadest possible support, the inaugural board of the United Hebrew Relief had thirty-five members: ten from the United Hebrew Charities, ten from the North End Relief Society, ten from the newly established Ladies' Auxiliary, and five unaffiliated representatives of the Jewish community.[64]

In March 1916, the United Hebrew Relief submitted a petition to the Legislative Assembly applying for incorporation.[65] In addition to granting the organization legal authority to receive, own, and dispose of property and donations, incorporation enabled it to make bylaws "for the government" of the charity.[66] The bylaws resolved many of the problems that had led to the formation of two competing charitable organizations. By clearly codifying membership, voting rights, and rules governing annual meetings and the election of directors and officers, the bylaws established that the charity was created by and accountable to all members of the Jewish community who donated sums, whether large or small, in support of its stated goal—"through personal service, relief of material needs, and the cooperation of community resources and efforts to serve and develop normal family life in the Jewish community."[67]

Following the merger, the United Hebrew Relief opened an office in the Talmud Torah school in the North End and appointed a secretary who received and investigated applications for assistance. Since the secretary was familiar with the financial difficulties of North End Jews, they perceived his decisions on who was deserving of charitable assistance to be free from the ingrained prejudices displayed by officials of the city's Associated Charities. With the support of the Ladies' Auxiliary, which within a year had increased its members from 100 to 260, the United Hebrew Relief was able to distribute between $150 and $200 a week to assist Jewish families.[68] Fundraising for the charity became part of the fabric of Jewish life. In addition to door-to-door canvassing and fundraising events such as concerts and bazaars, making a donation to the United Hebrew Relief became a part of celebrating marriages and wedding anniversaries.[69] By 1926, the charity was able to raise $9,089 to provide food, fuel, and clothing to destitute Jews.[70]

International Relief

In 1914, the Jewish community's collective responsibility for the well-being of destitute Jews expanded to include providing assistance to Jewish victims of war in Eastern Europe. Shortly after the outbreak of the First World War, the Russian army adopted a policy of using mass expulsions and deportations to remove Jews from provinces in the Pale of Settlement near the front lines.[71] Targeted as "unreliable" and a threat to military security, hundreds of thousands of Jews became homeless, destitute refugees. Between April and October 1915, widespread looting and seizure of property led to a wave of over fifty pogroms, many of them in areas where Winnipeg Jews had lived.[72] Reports that the Pale had become a war zone alarmed members of Winnipeg's Jewish community. A majority of them had parents, siblings, close relatives, and friends at risk, and their immediate impulse was to send money to assist them.

Many members of Winnipeg's Jewish community had experience raising money to support relief efforts in Eastern Europe. In 1903 and 1905, public meetings launched fundraising drives to assist the victims of pogroms in

Russia. Similarly, in 1907, when reports of an outbreak of anti-Jewish violence in Romania reached Winnipeg, Leon Abramovitch, one of the Romanian Jews who had founded the Dr. Gaster Benevolent Society, called a public meeting that appointed a committee to raise money to assist the victims.[73] Following a precedent established in 1905, when the Jewish community's fundraising efforts became part of an international campaign to assist the victims of pogroms in Russia, the committee forwarded the more than $1,300 it raised to the Romanian Central Relief Committee in New York, which planned to raise $500,000 to send to Romania.[74]

Within months of the beginning of the First World War, reports from Eastern Europe confirmed that only a major and sustained relief effort would benefit destitute Russian Jews. In September 1914, the North End Relief Society issued a public appeal to all organizations in Winnipeg's Jewish community to send representatives to attend a public meeting. Attended by over 1,000 people, the meeting, held on 5 October 1914, yielded $500 in donations and a large number of pledges to make monthly contributions to a war relief fund.[75] The assembly also elected a ten-member committee to organize a fundraising campaign.[76] However, the conflict between members of the United Hebrew Charity and the North End Relief Society undermined efforts to mobilize the support of the whole Jewish community. A report of the proceedings of the meeting published in the *Israelite Press* noted that "the Big Ones . . . with their thick pocket books are missing."[77] A second meeting was held in November 1914 to consolidate the fundraising drive, but once again the affluent and wealthy South End Jews who held leadership positions in the Rosh Pina and Shaarey Zedek synagogues as well as the United Hebrew Charities did not attend. The *Israelite Press*, which for weeks had issued editorials about the need to assist Jewish war victims, appealed to them to participate in the fundraising campaign. Unwilling to participate in a campaign initiated by the North End Relief Society, they set up a separate committee that worked in tandem with B'nai B'rith to solicit donations from affluent and wealthy Jews who lived in Central and South Winnipeg.[78]

The Winnipeg Jewish community's international relief efforts coincided with the organization in New York of the Joint Distribution Committee of (the American) Funds for Jewish War Sufferers (JDC). Founded in November 1914, the JDC was created by two organizations established the previous month: the American Jewish Relief Committee, led by wealthy Reform Jews such as Jacob Schiff, who in 1905 had been treasurer of the fundraising campaign to aid the victims of pogroms, and the Central Relief Committee,

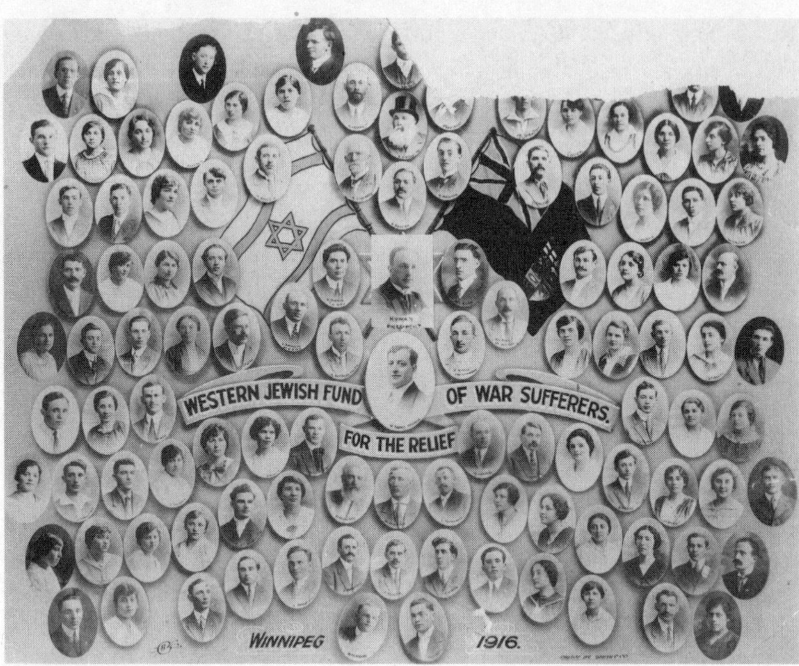

9. Board of Directors, Western Jewish Fund for the Relief of War Sufferers, 1916.

composed of Orthodox Jews from Eastern Europe. The primary purpose of the JDC was to distribute funds to Jewish aid agencies operating in Eastern Europe.[79] In August 1915, Jewish socialists and representatives of the labour movement established the New York–based People's Relief Committee, which became a member of the JDC.

The formation of the JDC and the establishment of relief committees in Montreal and Toronto spurred the leaders of Winnipeg's fundraising campaign to establish a permanent organization to coordinate the Jewish community's efforts to assist war victims. In August 1915, they invited representatives of forty-one Jewish mutual aid associations, synagogues, and organizations to a conference that established the Winnipeg Jewish Fund for the Relief of War Sufferers. In an attempt to win the support of South End Jews, the convention elected Herbert J. Samuel, the rabbi of Shaarey Zedek synagogue, as chairman of the new organization. However, the election of three socialists—Chaim Saltzman, Louis Gutkin, and Morris A. Gray—to the five-member executive signalled that the same radicals who criticized the disproportionate influence of a small minority of affluent and wealthy Jews on the Jewish community were now in control.[80] Moreover, the decision of the executive of the fund to send the donations that it collected to the People's Relief Committee, led by Meyer London, a labour activist and founding member of the Socialist Party of America, only increased the scepticism of South End Jews. When the fund renewed its fundraising campaign, they remained aloof, prompting the editor of the *Israelite Press* to warn of the consequences of breaching communal solidarity: "Jews from the south side of the subway, you must open your hearts and your pocketbooks for your unfortunate brothers and sisters if you do not want your names to remain blackened with shame."[81]

As fundraising progressed, the leaders of the Winnipeg Jewish Fund for the Relief of War Sufferers concluded that the success of their efforts to assist Eastern European Jews depended on soliciting donations from the entire Jewish community. If affluent and wealthy Jews were reluctant to make large donations, then the fund's goals could be achieved only by soliciting thousands of small donations. Consequently, the fund focused on building an inclusive organization that could enlist the support of an extensive network of volunteers. Annual meetings of the fund elected large executive committees—ranging from 159 in 1916 (112 men and forty-seven women) to twenty-five in 1921—that in turn appointed a committee of "captains" who supervised volunteer fundraisers.[82] Dividing the city into districts, each captain organized teams of two volunteers who went door to door on Sundays asking for donations.[83] In addition, the fund raised money by holding concerts, selling donated goods at bazaars, organizing an annual tag day to solicit donations from the public, and requesting contributions from the provincial and municipal governments.[84]

Despite paying for an office, a secretary, printing, postage, and other expenses, the fund was very efficient: expenditures on administration amounted to 4 percent of donations.[85] In addition to its fundraising activities, the fund became a conduit for sending remittances to relatives and friends in Eastern Europe. By 1920, remittances totalled nearly $18,000.[86] To maintain support for its activities, the fund held frequent general meetings to make fundraising decisions and used the *Israelite Press* to publicize its activities. Providing information on relief work in Eastern Europe became essential to reassure donors that their money was assisting Jewish war victims. The fund circulated pamphlets and

10. Emblem of the People's Relief Committee, New York.

annual reports published by the People's Relief Committee in New York. It also mailed copies of the People's Relief Fund newsletter, *Hilf* (Aid), as well as letters written by Baruch Zuckerman, its general manager, including an eyewitness account from Pinsk, to every Jewish residence in Winnipeg.[87]

By 1915, Jewish communities in Saskatoon, Saskatchewan, and Rumsey, Alberta, had established relief organizations that raised money to send to the People's Relief Committee. The Winnipeg office of the fund quickly became an intermediary for frequent letters to and from Zuckerman about the progress and problems of local fundraising activities. As the volume of letters increased, the executive of the fund decided that its office could maximize the effectiveness of fundraising throughout the prairies by coordinating and supporting local initiatives. Changing its name to Western Canada's Jewish Fund for the Relief of War Sufferers, the executive established a committee to liaise with the leaders of fundraising campaigns being established in Jewish communities in rural Manitoba and across Saskatchewan and Alberta. In 1918, the executive invited each relief organization to send delegates to a conference in Winnipeg to discuss fundraising and a proposal to create a regional organization. To emphasize the importance of the event and impress on delegates that their efforts were making a substantial contribution to alleviating the distress of Jews in Eastern Europe, the executive of the fund invited Zuckerman to attend the convention. Following Zuckerman's address on "Constructive Relief," the delegates agreed to establish twenty-four local branches of Western Canada's Jewish Fund for the Relief of War Sufferers: two in Manitoba, eighteen in Saskatchewan, and four in Alberta.[88] With the addition of branches in Vancouver and Fort William, as well as new branches in Saskatchewan and Alberta, by 1921 the fund's fundraising campaigns involved thirty-six Jewish communities.[89] However, as the war continued, the fund went through periodic lulls in fundraising. Despite the efforts of its leaders, the resolve of volunteers flagged, and they encountered donor fatigue. Nevertheless, between late 1914 and 1918, the fund raised an average of $4,000 to $5,000 a month.[90]

On 3 March 1918, the Central Powers and Russia signed the Treaty of Brest Litovsk, ending the war on the eastern front. Despite the treaty, fighting continued throughout the central and southern provinces of the Pale of Settlement as counterrevolutionary armies attempted to overthrow the Bolshevik government, which had seized power in 1917. The Russian Civil War raged until 1920, and, adding to the turmoil and devastation of the region, a war erupted between Poland and Russia (February 1919–March 1921). These post–First World War conflicts together with an epidemic of pogroms created hundreds of thousands of additional Jewish refugees who desperately needed food, clothing, shelter, and medical care.[91] Responding to urgent appeals for more money from the People's Relief Committee, the leaders of the fund resolved to intensify their fundraising activities.

However, the Spanish influenza epidemic that hit Winnipeg in the fall of 1918 forced the fund to suspend its activities for six months.[92] In April 1919, the executive of the fund made plans to revive fundraising, but a month later the Winnipeg General Strike paralyzed the city. The fund suspended door-to-door canvassing for the duration of the strike and, because of the interruption of mail delivery, was unable to communicate with its branch representatives.[93] When the six-week strike ended on 26 June 1919, the fund resumed fundraising, but prevailing economic conditions—a combination of widespread unemployment and high inflation—significantly reduced donations.[94] However, given the urgency of conditions in Eastern Europe, when the fund held its annual convention in October 1919, delegates decided to raise $100,000, double the amount raised in previous years. In conjunction with the Ukrainian Verband, the fund also began to organize a campaign to solicit donations of food, medicine, and clothing to ship to Eastern Europe.[95]

On 16 December 1919, the fund held a "mass" meeting to launch its $100,000 campaign. To publicize the event, the executive distributed a campaign bulletin with a message from Baruch Zuckerman, whom the fund's executive had invited to address the meeting. Based upon past experience, the executive hoped that his first-hand account of how effectively the JDC's relief work was alleviating the suffering of Jews in Eastern Europe would boost the morale of campaign workers and motivate donors. Motivating donors was a major concern. Given economic conditions in Winnipeg, the executive was worried that the fund might not reach its ambitious goal by appealing to its traditional donor base of small contributors. The solution was to find a means of enlisting the support of large donors, wealthier members of Winnipeg's Jewish community who had not been willing to participate in the fund's fundraising activities. In an appeal to Abraham Zucker, secretary of the People's Relief Committee, the fund's secretary, Max Mains, complained that "we are doing our utmost here but cannot succeed in getting the richer class of people to contribute to our work."[96] "If you have any special method or special literature which would be of assistance to us in this work," Mains inquired, "it would be to our mutual advantage."[97]

The leaders of the fund were unable to persuade prominent members of the Jewish community's "richer class of people" to join the executive or agree to form a separate "brigade" to canvass for donations. However, they came under increasing pressure to participate from another source. In February 1919, Lyon Cohen, one of the leaders of a Montreal-based relief organization, the Canadian Jewish Committee, convened a meeting of representatives of Jewish relief organizations from across Canada. Cohen, a member of a committee created to organize a founding convention to establish a Canadian Jewish Congress, encouraged the assembly to act on a major priority of the burgeoning congress movement, the formation of a national organization to coordinate fundraising for the relief of Jewish war victims. In his address to the meeting, Cohen emphasized that "our relief work has been weakened by division within our ranks. Better results and greater benefits would be obtained through united efforts."[98] The assembly, which established the Associated Jewish War Relief Societies of Canada, selected Cohen as its first president and elected Marcus Hyman, chairman of Western Canada's Jewish Fund for the Relief of War Sufferers, as vice-president. In addition, the assembly elected J.A. Cherniack, Jacob Chmelnitsky, and Max Mains, all past or current members of the executive of the fund, to serve as members of the executive of the new national organization.[99]

The assembly elected an additional representative from Winnipeg, Max Steinkopf, to serve on the executive. His election was an anomaly. A lawyer, wealthy businessman, and pillar of Shaarey Zedek synagogue, Steinkopf was not an active supporter of Western Canada's Jewish Fund for the Relief of War Sufferers. He was an ardent Zionist, however, who believed that establishing the Canadian Jewish Congress would help to achieve the goal of the Federation of Zionist Societies of Canada, the creation of a Jewish homeland in Palestine.[100] On 2 March 1919, Steinkopf and fellow Zionists M.J. Finkelstein and Hiram Weidman were among the twenty delegates elected at a meeting in Winnipeg to attend the founding convention of the Canadian Jewish Congress.[101] In a public endorsement of their contribution to Western Canada's Jewish Fund for the Relief of War Sufferers, six of the delegates elected, including Marcus Hyman, were serving members of the fund's executive, and four others had been members.[102] At the founding convention, held in Montreal two weeks later, delegates from across Canada elected a national executive structured to include representatives of Jewish communities in Montreal, Toronto, and Winnipeg. Two delegates who had prominent roles during the proceedings of the convention were elected to the executive: M.J. Finkelstein became the vice-president and Ben Sheps the secretary.[103]

Despite the spirit of unity that animated the formation of the Canadian Jewish Congress, his position on the national executive of the Associated Jewish

War Relief Societies of Canada, and overtures from Mains, Steinkopf was unwilling to join with fellow delegates to the convention and support the fund. His reluctance to cooperate turned to hostility as a result of the Winnipeg General Strike. A prominent Conservative, Steinkopf supported the Citizens Committee of 1,000, which hired "special constables" to break the strike. Steinkopf, Finkelstein, and Weidman were bitterly opposed to the "socialists" who, they believed, had fomented class warfare and embroiled Jewish workers in a conflict with constituted authority. Included among the socialists whom they reviled was Hyman, chairman of the fund, who had defended labour leaders arrested during the strike, as well as fund board members such as J.A. Cherniack and Sam Green, who belonged to Poale Zion, which supported the strikers, and Shloime Almasoff (Almazoff), imprisoned during the strike for alleged revolutionary activity. Although Cherniack, Green, and Almazoff were prominent supporters of the Canadian Jewish Congress, Steinkopf, Finkelstein, and Weidman considered them to be dangerous radicals who had exposed the Jewish community to anti-alien sentiment.[104]

However, by late 1919, a decision by the Associated Jewish War Relief Societies of Canada to launch a national campaign to raise $1 million created a dilemma for Steinkopf, Finkelstein, and Weidman. The national relief organization was determined to make the campaign a demonstration of the strength and resolve of the newly formed Canadian Jewish Congress, its capacity to unite and mobilize Jews from across Canada in support of its goals. For Lyon Cohen, president of both the Canadian Jewish Congress and the Associated Jewish War Relief Societies of Canada, all Jews who wanted the congress to succeed had a responsibility to support the $1 million campaign. Consequently, as the members of the executive of Western Canada's Jewish Fund for the Relief of War Sufferers made preparations to launch its $100,000 fundraising campaign, Hyman and Cherniack persuaded them to affiliate with the Associated Jewish War Relief Societies of Canada.[105]

On 2 December 1919, an estimated 10,000 Winnipeg Jews, "every man, woman and child," marched in a public demonstration of solidarity with the victims of pogroms in Ukraine.[106] When the fund announced a 16 December meeting to launch its $100,000 campaign, Steinkopf, Finkelstein, and Weidman were forced to demonstrate their support. Not to do so would have raised questions about their commitment to the Canadian Jewish Congress and jeopardized their standing in the Jewish community. However, unable to overcome their hostility to the leaders of the fund, they refused to participate in its fundraising campaign. They formed a committee to establish a separate relief organization, which they imperiously named Central Relief for European Jews.[107] Chaired by Max Steinkopf, almost all of the eighteen members of the committee were "South Enders" who belonged to Shaarey Zedek synagogue.[108] On 1 January 1920, Steinkopf chaired a meeting of the committee at the synagogue to launch their fundraising campaign. The committee based its campaign upon the fund's fundraising strategy. As chairman of the committee, he mailed a letter to members of the Jewish community appealing for donations. The letter, which announced that "we will call upon you in the next few days," appeared to be directed at affluent Jews rather than the small contributors who were the mainstay of the fund's campaigns: "We who live in luxury and ease," it stated, "must make our greatest sacrifice."[109] Having alerted potential donors, nine teams, each composed of two members of the committee, visited Jewish homes throughout January to collect pledges. When the committee finished its fundraising at the end of January, it made a $15,000 contribution to the fund's $100,000 campaign.[110]

On 15 February 1920, Western Canada's Jewish Fund for the Relief of War Sufferers held a convention in Winnipeg to discuss the progress of the campaign and make plans for future fundraising activities. The fund had raised close to $85,000, and based upon the contribution of $15,000 from Central Relief for European Jews its secretary was confident that the campaign would reach its $100,000 goal. Conducting two separate fundraising campaigns resulted in duplication and confused donors, but Steinkopf's committee had made a substantial contribution to the success of the fund's campaign. Two issues dominated the convention: the establishment of the Central Relief for European Jews and the fund's relationship with the People's Relief Committee in New York.[111] It emerged that Steinkopf and other members of his committee were prepared to support the fund's future fundraising campaigns but in return demanded a commitment that all of the money raised would be sent to the Associated Jewish War Relief Societies of Canada. Doing so would simultaneously bolster the newly formed Canadian Jewish Congress and sever the fund's long-standing relationship with the People's Relief Committee in New York, an organization that Steinkopf and many other supporters of Central Relief for European Jews believed was led by radicals.

Most of the delegates to the fund's convention supported the Canadian Jewish Congress. However, despite the $15,000 boost that supporters of Central Relief for European Jews had given to the fund's campaign, the delegates resented making a concession to a small group of wealthy Jews who had refused for five years to embrace a cause that had been of such importance

11. Simon Belkin, representing the Canadian Alliance of Ukrainian Jews (second from the left), and Salmon Koldovsky (far right), representing the American Jewish Joint Distribution Committee meet with members of the Presidium of the Moscow Central Relief Committee, 1920.

to the Jewish community. Ultimately, since the Associated Jewish War Relief Societies of Canada in Montreal sent almost all of the money raised by affiliated relief organizations to the JDC, the delegates approved a compromise: the fund would send the proceeds of its fundraising campaigns to Montreal with the stipulation that, when the money was forwarded to New York, half would be assigned to the Central Relief Committee and half to the People's Relief Committee.[112] In return, Steinkopf, who agreed to serve as chair, and three other members of Central Relief for European Jews (M. Tessler, Max Mitchell, and Morris Haid) joined the fund's ten-member campaign committee.[113] Having succeeded after a "great deal of hardship" in "uniting all forces together," the convention decided to launch a campaign to raise $250,000 in 1920 plus collect $50,000 in clothing, shoes, and tools and $50,000 in medical supplies to send to Ukraine.[114]

By October 1920, Steinkopf's commitment to the fund was based upon more than a desire to support the Canadian Jewish Congress. In July, Elias Heifetz, chairman of the All-Ukrainian Relief Committee for the Victims of Pogroms based in Kiev, met with leaders of relief organizations in Montreal. Heifetz reported that tens of thousands of homeless Jewish orphans were suffering from malnutrition and disease. He urged the leaders of the relief organizations to provide aid to the orphans and undertake to rescue as many as possible by bringing them to Canada.[115] On 11 July 1920 Lyon Cohen invited representatives of Montreal-based relief organizations to attend a meeting to discuss Heifetz's proposal. They decided that a new national relief organization was needed to aid the orphans and that Lillian Freiman was ideally suited to lead it.

Freiman, an Ottawa philanthropist and civic leader, was the interim leader of Hadassah, a national Jewish women's organization devoted to Zionist projects in Palestine.[116] Her husband, A.J. Freiman, a prominent Conservative Party supporter, was chairman of the Zionist Organization of Canada.[117] Through her involvement in the Red Cross, the Ottawa Women's Canadian Club, and organizing a poppy campaign to assist war veterans, she became acquainted with Isabel Meighen, the wife of Arthur Meighen, minister of the interior in the Unionist government.[118] Shortly after Meighen's appointment as prime minister, the Freimans used their influence to secure an appointment with Frederick Blair, secretary of the Department of Immigration and Colonization.[119] When Lillian Freiman met with Blair, she requested permission to bring 1,000 orphans to Canada. Following the meeting, Blair sent a letter to Freiman stating that the department would approve the admission of 200 orphans provided that arrangements were made for their care and adoption prior to their arrival and that the children passed the department's medical examination. Blair suggested that the department would consider giving permission to admit additional children if the plan to bring 200 orphans to Canada succeeded.[120]

To build support in western Canada for a fundraising campaign to assist Jewish orphans, Freiman contacted Marcus Hyman, chairman of Western Canada's Jewish Fund for the Relief of War Sufferers, to arrange a speaking tour for Elias Heifetz to provide Jewish audiences with a first-hand account of the suffering of Jewish children orphaned by war and pogroms. Addressing a "mass meeting" in Winnipeg on 17 August 1920 chaired by Hyman, Heifetz estimated that pogroms alone had created 125,000–150,000 orphans and that hundreds of them were dying of disease, malnutrition, and lack of shelter.[121] On 29 August, the fund held a two-day convention in Saskatoon to plan a fundraising campaign to raise $200,000 in western Canada to sponsor the orphans. Following an address by Heifetz, the delegates established a campaign committee composed of representatives from the four western provinces.[122]

Drawing on her nation-wide network of Hadassah activists, her husband's contacts in the Zionist Organization of Canada, a list of leaders of relief organizations in Montreal and Toronto provided by Lyon Cohen, and her connection with Marcus Hyman, Freiman organized a conference in Ottawa in October 1920 to establish a national organization committed to raising money to assist Jewish orphans in the Ukraine. J.A. Cherniack, Max Mains, and Max Steinkopf went to the conference as representatives of Western Canada's Jewish Fund for the Relief of War Sufferers. The delegates carefully elected an executive to draw on the organizational resources of relief funds as well as the support of the growing numbers of Zionists joining local chapters of Hadassah and branches of the Zionist Organization of Canada, organizations whose focus had been raising money for projects in Palestine rather than providing aid to Jews in Eastern Europe.[123]

Lillian Freiman was elected dominion chairman of the new relief organization, named the Canadian-Jewish-European Orphans Committee, and A.J. Freiman became executive chairman. Max Steinkopf was elected vice-chairman, and Max Mains accepted the position of honorary secretary. Winnipeg was also represented by J.A. Cherniack and Max Mitchell, who became members of the executive.[124] To enhance the public profile of the committee, Lillian Freiman persuaded Isabel Meighen to serve as honorary president.[125] Since the committee was formed to raise money for the victims of war in Eastern Europe, Mains and Cherniack viewed serving on the executive of the committee as a natural extension of their commitment to Western Canada's Jewish Fund for the Relief of War Sufferers. However, Steinkopf, who had only recently agreed to serve on the fund's campaign committee, was motivated to join the executive because of his close relationship with the Freimans and his support for the Zionist movement.

In October 1920, the committee opened an office in Ottawa to coordinate a national campaign to raise money to assist the orphans. Initially, the committee focused on raising money to buy clothing and supplies to ship to the Ukraine. However, despite widespread public sympathy in Jewish communities throughout western Canada, by October donations were far below the goal of raising $200,000 established at the Saskatoon convention. Shortly after the Ottawa conference, Steinkopf decided to bolster his commitment to Western Canada's Jewish Fund for the Relief of War Sufferers. At the conference, Freiman had announced plans for a speaking tour of western Canada and an ambitious national fundraising campaign. With both the Freimans' reputations and that of the Zionist movement tied to the committee's success, in November Steinkopf stood for election as vice-chairman at the fund's annual convention and became the chair of the "orphan committee," the body responsible for coordinating fundraising throughout western Canada.[126]

Speaking in Winnipeg on 11 November 1920, Freiman began her tour by announcing that on 27 November the Canadian-Jewish-European Orphans Committee planned to launch a national $1 million campaign in the city.[127] As Freiman toured western Canada to raise money, Steinkopf persuaded the executive of the fund to establish a separate account to ensure that the proceeds of the campaign were used "for Orphans only" and not "general relief work."[128] As the Canadian-Jewish-European Orphans Committee's fundraising campaign proceeded, the national office distributed application forms to adopt Jewish orphans and made preparations for a "unit" to travel to Eastern Europe to select 200 orphans and arrange for their transportation to Canada.[129]

After numerous delays, the unit departed on 5 February 1921, and on 12 March it arrived in Warsaw. Since the unit was unable to travel to areas of Ukraine under Soviet control, in early April it went to Rivne, near the newly established Polish-Ukraine border, where the JDC had established temporary shelters for thousands of Jewish orphans.[130] Because of their poor physical condition, selecting children who could pass the immigration department's medical examination proved to be a lengthy process. Having been told that the orphans would arrive in Canada before the end of December 1920, donors and campaign workers began to question the committee's repeated explanations for the delay.[131] Under pressure to expedite the arrival of the orphans in Canada, on 20 May 1921 A.J. Freiman instructed the unit to reduce the number of children selected from 200 to 150. Ultimately, by early June, after examining over 8,000 children, the unit's physician selected 146 of them.[132] A group of 102 children finally arrived in Quebec City on 20 August, and four days later twelve of them were entrusted to the care of the Winnipeg Jewish Orphanage, which cared for them until they could be placed with their adoptive parents. By January 1923, the remaining forty-four orphans finally arrived in Canada.

From the inception of the Canadian-Jewish-European Orphans Committee, the executive of Western Canada's Jewish Fund for the Relief of War Sufferers had been committed to raising money to bring Jewish orphans to Canada. Commenting on Dr. Elias Heifetz's visit to Winnipeg in August 1920, Max Mains wrote that "we are undertaking this work, and some of us plan that this should be our main work, if not the entire work."[133] Although Mains was concerned that the plan to bring Jewish orphans to Canada was not generating the interest that he expected—"the fact that we have only two hundred children does not inspire anyone yet"—in September the executive

12. Jewish orphans from Ukraine on the steps of the Winnipeg Jewish Orphanage, 1921.

began preparations to launch its $200,000 campaign.[134] And on 31 October, after hearing a report on the Ottawa conference that established the Canadian-Jewish-European Orphans Committee, delegates attending a conference held by the fund formally endorsed its plan to make arrangements for Jewish families to adopt the orphans.[135] Throughout November, fund volunteers collected and shipped to Montreal bundles of clothing for the orphans. Informed that the unit would be leaving on 24 November, the "orphan committee" voted to send $5,000 to the committee to purchase shoes and any additional clothing needed to take to the Ukraine to distribute to the children.[136]

However, as the unit's departure date drew near, the executive of the fund became increasingly concerned that it had not been informed about who would be going to the Ukraine or given details about their route and budget.[137] Instead of responding to the executive's inquiries, the secretary of the committee only referred to a "number" of unexpected "details" that had repeatedly forced the unit to postpone its departure.[138] Having received numerous requests for information about the departure of the unit, in late December 1920 the executive of the fund was relieved to learn that the unit was scheduled to leave for Europe on 14 January 1921.[139] However, the executive was "aggravated" when informed that Heifetz, who had its "full confidence," was no longer director of the unit. On 20 December 1920, the Freimans had appointed Gregory Sanders to replace Heifetz, Harry Hershman as assistant director, Dr. Joseph Leavitt as medical director, and William Farrar as transportation director.[140] With the exception of Farrar, who lived in Hamilton, all of the members of the unit were from Montreal.

The exclusion of Heifetz, elected general director of the committee when it had been founded, and the unilateral appointment of the members of the unit outraged members of the fund's executive. Not only were the appointments made "without even consulting the Vice-president [*sic*] and members of the Dominion Executive," but also Sam Berger had failed to provide a "satisfactory reply" to the executive's request to Lillian Freiman that one of its members, Chaim Saltzman, in Reval (Tallinn), Estonia, either be appointed to replace Harry Hershman or be added as a fifth member of the unit.[141] Unless the executive received a "proper explanation" and an "immediate solution," it threatened to withdraw its support for the committee's campaign. The Freimans' autocratic behaviour was only one of the executive's concerns. Repeated delays in the departure of the unit and Berger's inability or unwillingness to answer questions about the unit's budget and travel plans had undermined the executive's confidence in the leadership of the committee. When Berger suggested that the unit might not be able to enter the Ukraine, and that if it failed to do so it would contact the committee's Ottawa office for instructions, it appeared that, despite his claims that travel plans were being finalized, the unit might fail to achieve its goal of rescuing Jewish orphans from Ukraine and that "an enormous sum of money and energy will be spent in vain." After a "long and heated discussion," the executive of the fund decided by a unanimous vote to withdraw its support for the committee's campaign. Some of the members of the executive suggested that the "west work alone" and give Saltzman instructions to undertake bringing the orphans to Canada.[142]

The Freimans attempted to placate the executive of the fund by extending an invitation to send a delegate to a 1 February 1921 meeting in Montreal to "give us an opportunity to clear up many of these apparent misunderstandings . . . which prevent us from doing constructive work."[143] At the meeting, the Freimans reported that it was impossible to travel to Soviet Ukraine, but they had made an arrangement with the JDC for the unit to use its personnel, equipment, and facilities in Poland to interview and select Jewish orphans in the western part of the Ukraine, now Polish territory. They also announced that the unit would leave for Europe on 5 February. The executive of the fund was somewhat reassured when Marcus Hyman, its delegate to the meeting, reported that the unit was finally leaving and would travel to western Ukraine, but the Freimans remained insensitive to its concerns. When Gregory Sanders was forced to withdraw from the unit, they appointed Harry Hershman to replace him as director, but instead of appointing Chaim Saltzman to fill the position of assistant director they left it vacant.[144]

Despite its frustration with the committee, the executive of the fund reconsidered its decision to withdraw its support and continued to raise money to bring the orphans to Canada. However, by late March 1921, reports that the unit had been in Warsaw for two weeks but had not yet visited the JDC's shelters in Rivne precipitated another crisis of confidence in the committee. It had pledged that the orphans would be in Canada by the end of December 1920, but three months later the unit was still in Warsaw conferring with government officials. Members of the executive complained that the committee "has shown great weakness" in raising money (most of its revenue came from western Canada), its expenses were "running as high as 25% of income," and it had failed to achieve its goal of bringing the orphans to Canada.[145] The money being raised to pay for the unit's expenses, they argued, should immediately be spent in the Ukraine on hospitals, clothing, food, and medicine to assist the orphans directly. However, the committee had its defenders. Arguing that all of the money raised for the orphans should be sent to the committee, a group "calling themselves the '400'" expressed full confidence in the plan to bring the orphans to Canada.[146]

When disagreement among supporters of the fund reached the point that it threatened to disrupt its activities, the executive decided to hold a conference in Winnipeg to establish a definitive policy on its relationship with the committee. Normally fifty to sixty Jewish organizations responded to an invitation to send representatives to attend conferences organized by the fund, but it had "such important matters to decide" that 214 delegates representing "107 societies" attended the conference.[147] It was held on three consecutive Sundays beginning on 27 March and concluding on 10 April 1921. The first item on the convention's agenda dealt with the fund's relationship with the committee. The delegates voted in favour of a resolution stating that the fund should work "*independently*" rather than "*under*" the committee but agreed to continue to cooperate with it.[148] The second item on the agenda dealt with how to dispose of $44,000: a fund of $24,000 collected for the orphans "with the assistance of a few 'gentlemen of the 400'" and $20,000 in donations contributed as part of the fund's general relief campaign.[149] Arguments were presented in favour of spending the money to provide direct aid to all orphans in Ukraine, whereas the "gentlemen" "insisted that we should bring [the] orphans no matter what cost it may incur."[150] The delegates settled on a compromise, authorizing the executive to poll donors to ask how the $24,000 fund should be spent. If the donors did not respond within two weeks, then the balance of the $24,000 would be divided in two: half would be allocated to general relief work and half sent to the committee. The delegates also decided that $15,000 of the $20,000 donated for general relief work would be sent to Ukraine to provide aid to Jewish orphans and that the balance would be sent to the People's Relief Committee to support its campaign to buy tools for Jewish workers in the Ukraine.[151]

Elections for the executive took place on 10 April 1921, the last day of the conference and one week after the unit had arrived in Rivne. Dissatisfied with the compromises reached by the delegates, Max Steinkopf and other members of the "400" refused to do "their duty" and stand for election, leading the secretary of the fund, Isadore Hurwitz, to conclude bitterly "that while they are always on the spot at a time of *disposition of funds* ... they are conspicuous by *their absence* for 'raising' funds."[152] However, he was relieved that Marcus Hyman was re-elected as chairman, as was the "greater majority" of the fund's thirty-two-member executive. Having settled the issue of the fund's relationship with the committee, the executive focused on its general relief campaign, generating approximately $12,000 a month.[153] By 1922, the fund had raised a total of nearly $390,000 in cash and collected clothing, tools, and medical supplies with a value of $100,000.[154] Chastened by the cost and complexity of rescuing Jewish orphans, the Canadian-Jewish-European Orphans Committee disbanded after the final group of children arrived in Canada.

The fund continued to raise money throughout the rest of 1921 and began a new campaign to buy food to send to Soviet Russia. However, once the war between Poland and Russia ended, the JDC was quickly able to expand its network of relief activities throughout Eastern Europe. The end of armed conflict, the establishment of basic public order, and the massive infusion of aid provided by the JDC suggested that the relief crisis was over.[155] When the JDC began to issue reports about Jewish refugees anxious to emigrate, the prospect of assisting relatives and friends to immigrate to Canada galvanized Winnipeg's Jewish community. Western Canada's Jewish Fund for the Relief of War Sufferers attempted to combine relief work with assistance to

Jewish immigrants—in late 1921 it was renamed the Jewish War Victims and Immigrant Aid Fund, and in 1922 it became the Jewish Relief and Immigrant Aid Society—but by 1923 it had virtually ceased to function. Recognizing that a separate organization was needed to mobilize the support of members of the Jewish community to lobby the federal government to admit Jewish immigrants and assist them to settle in Canada, by 1919 communal activists such as Marcus Hyman, Fanny Cherniack, J.A. Cherniack, Max Mains, Ben Miller, and Israel Rusen who served on the executive of the fund were also devoting their time to the Hebrew Immigrant Aid Society. In 1920, when the Canadian Jewish Congress established the Jewish Immigrant Aid Society of Canada, the Hebrew Immigrant Aid Society was reorganized as its western branch. Within a year, as public concern about immigration issues quickly superseded support for raising money for the relief of war victims, the Western Branch of the Jewish Immigrant Aid Society of Canada in effect displaced the fund. By 1923, its last year of operation, the activities of the Jewish Relief and Immigrant Aid Society were limited to sending remittances and raising money to support "two Orphans' Homes opened in the name of 'Winnipeg'" in Ukraine.[156]

The tensions and conflicts that animated disputes over communal governance of charity in the Jewish community and later fundraising to provide aid to Jewish war victims were difficult to resolve. Schooled in communitarian values and ideals, Jewish activists who belonged to socialist organizations such as Poale Zion or were members of mutual aid societies believed that communal decision making should be based upon democratic principles and practices, that every member of the Jewish community had an equal right to participate in founding and governing organizations established to protect the vulnerable. Having honed their organizational skills and powers of persuasion at countless mutual aid association meetings or debates at political events, they believed that positions of leadership should be held by individuals elected because they had demonstrated not only that they could carry out executive responsibilities but also that they understood the importance of being accountable to those who placed them in positions of trust. Motivated by a commitment to communal solidarity, they viewed the North End Relief Society, the United Hebrew Relief, and Western Canada's Jewish Fund for the Relief of War Sufferers as organizations that embodied deeply held principles of mutual aid and reciprocal obligation, the responsibility of Jews to contribute to the well-being of each other.

The affluent and wealthy "South End" Jews who controlled the Hebrew Benevolent Association, founded the United Hebrew Charities and the Central Relief for European Jews, and briefly supported Western Canada's Jewish Fund for the Relief of War Sufferers also believed that they had a responsibility to contribute to the well-being of vulnerable members of the Jewish community. However, their commitment to charity was based upon a traditional understanding of *tzedakah*, that Jews had a religious obligation to assist the poor. Talmudic teaching emphasized that assisting the poor was "essentially a collective or communal" responsibility carried out under the auspices and control of synagogues that dispensed charity to those judged to be deserving.[157] This concept of collective responsibility empowered the wealthy; just as members of congregations who made major donations to build and operate synagogues and purchased the most expensive seats acquired power and status and were invariably elected as its officers, so too practitioners of traditional *tzedakah* assumed that wealth entitled donors to establish and control charitable organizations.

For Max Steinkopf, Hiram Weidman, Moses Finkelstein, and many other "South End" Jews, the belief that wealth conferred power was reinforced by their success in business. As owners of profitable businesses, they had unimpeded authority to make investment decisions and manage employees. Although they were members of the Jewish community, they inhabited a privileged social realm within it and participated in social networks far removed from the day-to-day lives or concerns of Jews in the North End.[158] As members of organizations such as B'nai B'rith and the Winnipeg Zionist Council, they respected and followed democratic procedures, but their commitment to democracy was selective: they tended to participate in exclusive organizations whose members respected their wealth and status and deferred to their leadership. They were reluctant to submit to decisions made by broadly based organizations that represented the concerns and aspirations of recent Jewish immigrants, organizations whose members elected leaders based upon their prominent roles in the mutual aid associations, cultural activities, Yiddish schools, and political meetings that comprised the secular social networks of the North End. To them, demonstrated commitment to shared goals was more important than wealth and status. However, as Winnipeg's Jewish community undertook to establish social welfare institutions, it was forced to find ways of benefiting from the financial support of the affluent and wealthy while preserving the democratic principles and practices that made widespread participation in communal governance viable.

CHAPTER 6

Winnipeg's Jewish Social Welfare Institutions

On 29 February 1920, a large crowd assembled on Matheson Avenue near the northern boundary of Winnipeg to celebrate the official opening of a new building to house the Jewish Orphanage. Built and furnished at a cost of close to $136,000, the Tudor-style, three-storey building situated on a five-and-a-half-acre site could accommodate 125 children.[1] The new orphanage was carefully designed to ensure that it incorporated the most modern construction techniques and materials as well as progressive ideas about the institutional care of children. Once the lot was purchased, the board of directors of the Jewish Orphanage and Children's Aid Society of Western Canada commissioned the Manitoba Association of Architects to hold a competition to select the best three designs. The board chose a design submitted by the prominent Winnipeg architectural partnership of Woodman and Cubbidge. In July 1919, the firm sent an architect to accompany the superintendent of the orphanage, Louis Greenberg, on a tour of orphanages in the United States.[2] Greenberg, raised in a Brooklyn orphanage and previously the assistant director of the Marks Nathan Jewish Orphans Home in Chicago, selected eighteen Jewish orphanages to visit, institutions that tempered custodial care with comfortable physical surroundings and programs that nurtured and enriched the lives of children.[3] Following their return to Winnipeg, the architect amended his plans to incorporate Greenberg's recommendations.

For many Jewish families, the dislocation of immigration and the hardship of settlement exacted a toll on their children. Without the support of close relatives, the dissolution of families because of the death of one or both parents, or the illness, disability, or desertion of a parent, often made children dependent on charitable assistance. Women with children could turn to Jewish communal charities for assistance, but aside from making informal arrangements for foster care the Jewish community had no means of caring for orphans or the children of single parents unable to care for them. Under provincial legislation, the police were authorized to apprehend "neglected and dependent" children and bring them before a judge empowered to entrust them to the care of a children's aid society. These societies became the children's legal guardians, which gave them the authority to place children entrusted to their care in a "home or shelter."[4]

In the spring of 1912, rumours began to circulate in Winnipeg's Jewish community that Winnipeg's Children's Aid Society was placing a "large number" of Jewish children in the care of Christian institutions, the Children's Home or St. Joseph's Orphanage.[5] Not only would these children be raised by staff who had no understanding of their language, religion, or culture, but also—because the custodians were accustomed to enforcing conformity to British Canadian values and beliefs—the children would inevitably be influenced by Christian religious instruction and lose their Jewish identity. The solution was to establish a Jewish orphanage to rescue Jewish children placed in the care of Christian institutions and to provide a home for future dependent children. However, echoing the dispute between supporters of the United Hebrew Charities and the North End Relief Society over who had a legitimate mandate to speak for or act on behalf of the Jewish community, in 1912 two factions began to plan to establish Jewish orphanages.

Speaking at a general meeting of the B'nai B'rith Lodge on 20 June 1912, R.S. Robinson, an affluent businessman, proposed that its members follow the lead of chapters in the United States and build a Jewish orphanage.[6] Robinson stated that, if the lodge undertook to build an orphanage, then he would donate a large building lot in the North End.[7] The members of the lodge "enthusiastically" endorsed his proposal and appointed Robinson, Max Steinkopf, M.J. Finkelstein, Hiram Weidman, A.H. Aronovitch, M.H. Saunders, and Lester Rice to a committee to develop a plan to establish an orphanage.[8] However, in September 1912, before the committee met to prepare its report to the members of the lodge, Lena Fenson invited eighteen North End Jewish women to attend a meeting to discuss establishing an orphanage. They decided to recruit additional members and begin raising money by charging monthly dues of twenty-five cents.[9] On 12 October, they established the Hebrew Ladies' Orphan Home Association, and within three weeks it had a membership of 200 women and raised $400.[10]

The committee appointed by the B'nai B'rith Lodge did not meet until the spring of 1913. At the meeting, Robinson announced that he was prepared to make a substantial donation if the orphanage was named in memory of Esther Robinson, his recently deceased mother. The members of the committee were reluctant to name the orphanage after an individual but at his request agreed not to mention his offer when it submitted its recommendation to the membership. Since the Hebrew Ladies' Orphan Home Association was completing preparations to open an orphanage in a rented house, when the lodge held a meeting on 17 July 1913, the committee recommended to the members that they abandon their plan to build a Jewish orphanage.[11] To the surprise of members of the committee, Robinson responded to their report by repeating his offer to make a donation if the orphanage was named after his mother. When it became clear that a majority of the members accepted the committee's recommendation and were not prepared to support his plan, Robinson announced that he had already decided to proceed and had "an organization behind him." Arguing that it would not be in the "best interest[s]" of the Jewish community to have two orphanages, A.H. Aronovitch proposed a meeting of representatives of B'nai B'rith, the organization that Robinson had established to support his proposed Esther Robinson Jewish Orphanage, and the Hebrew Ladies' Orphan Home Association to negotiate an agreement to work together to build an orphanage.[12]

The meeting was held on 23 July 1913. Robinson announced that he would donate $5,000 to a building fund if his mother's name was "incorporated into the official name of the institution."[13] His offer was given serious consideration—a donation of $5,000 was tempting—but representatives of B'nai B'rith and the Hebrew Ladies' Orphan Home Association were reluctant to name a communal institution after an individual; they believed that the orphanage should be built by and operated in the name of the Jewish community. To overcome their resistance, Robinson increased his offer to $10,000, threatening that if it was not accepted he would donate the money to an orphanage in Toronto or Montreal. After a lengthy discussion, the representatives agreed to report to their respective organizations that they had failed to reach an agreement.[14]

Although Robinson and his supporters had agreed to attend the meeting as a courtesy to their lodge brothers, as far as they were concerned, compromise was not an option; the only purpose of the meeting was to secure the support of B'nai B'rith and the Hebrew Ladies' Orphan Home Association for an orphanage named after Esther Robinson. They were not willing to take into consideration points of view or interests that differed from their own.

In essence, though those points of view or interests reflected the concerns of a women's organization with a rapidly growing membership and a fraternal organization seeking an opportunity to make a contribution to the welfare of dependent children, they believed that their right to make decisions was more important than building consensus in the Jewish community.

A clear indication that Robinson was determined not to compromise is that, prior to the meeting, he enlisted the support of Henry A. Isaacs, president of the Shaarey Shomayim congregation, to hold a meeting later the same day at the synagogue. The stated purpose of the meeting was to establish the Esther Robinson Jewish Orphanage. Chaired by Isaacs, the meeting elected an executive composed of David Balcovske as president, Max Goldstein as vice-president, R.S. Robinson as treasurer, Dora Robinson (his daughter) as honorary secretary, as well as forty-one directors.[15] Although the executive was dominated by men, by encouraging women to enter the public sphere and participate in communal affairs, the Hebrew Ladies' Orphan Home Association had established a precedent that could not be ignored: of the forty-one directors chosen, twenty were women.[16] With few exceptions, all of the members of the board lived in Central and South Winnipeg. At the meeting, a spokesperson for the board announced that plans were under way to apply for a provincial charter and purchase a property in the North End to house the orphanage until enough money could be raised to build a permanent facility.[17]

The members of B'nai B'rith were shocked to discover that Robinson had proceeded with his plans before the lodge had an opportunity to consider a report at the meeting of 23 July. At the request of twenty-six members of the lodge, the president, Lester Rice, held an emergency meeting the following evening to discuss Robinson's offer and the outcome of the attempt to seek an agreement to join forces with the Hebrew Ladies' Orphan Home Association to build an orphanage. The members passed a resolution—the vote was fifty-seven in favour and five against—rejecting Robinson's offer, followed by a second resolution pledging to support the Hebrew Ladies' Orphan Home Association's plan to build "The Canadian Jewish Orphanage."[18]

Within days, the directors of the Esther Robinson Jewish Orphanage distributed a notice informing the Jewish community that they had purchased two houses on Robinson Street in the North End. In response, a newly formed committee composed of representatives of the Hebrew Ladies' Orphan Home Association and the B'nai B'rith Lodge announced that the Canadian Jewish Orphans' Home "has secured One [*sic*] of the largest houses in North Winnipeg" to house an orphanage.[19] Concerned that these competing claims would undermine support for an ambitious $100,000 fundraising campaign to build an orphanage, a home for the aged, and a Jewish hospital, the organization committee of the Canadian Jewish Orphans' Home invited the president of the Esther Robinson Jewish Orphanage to attend a "mass meeting" so that both organizations could explain their plans to the Jewish community.[20] At the meeting, held on 26 August 1913, Robinson attempted to explain his actions, but he could not overcome the resentment of those who believed that he had pursued his personal agenda at the expense of the Jewish community. The "quite stormy" meeting culminated in a unanimous vote in favour of a resolution pledging "financial and moral support to the Canadian Jewish Orphans [*sic*] Home."[21]

Buoyed by this public mandate, on 22 September 1913, the Canadian Jewish Orphans' Home began operations in a rented house at 113 Selkirk Avenue. Undeterred by widespread public endorsement of the home, a month later, on 23 November, the Esther Robinson Jewish Orphanage opened in two adjacent houses, one for girls and one for boys (73 and 75 Robinson Street), purchased with a $3,000 donation from Robinson. Questions were immediately raised about duplication and whether members of the Jewish community should be called on to make donations to support two orphanages.[22] In June 1914, the organization committee of the Canadian Jewish Orphans' Home sent a letter to the president of the Esther Robinson Jewish Orphanage suggesting a meeting to discuss amalgamation. However, though the representatives of the two orphanages held three meetings, they could not agree on a name. The representatives of the Canadian Jewish Orphans' Home suggested various ways of honouring his mother, but Robinson was adamant that Esther Robinson remain a prominent part of the name of the orphanage.

In 1914, the Esther Robinson Jewish Orphanage applied for incorporation.[23] Under the terms of the Children's Act, incorporation gave the orphanage the authority to become the legal guardian of and to care for "neglected, abandoned or orphaned children."[24] Consequently, in addition to orphans and the children of desperate or incapacitated parents placed in its care, often on the recommendation of the United Hebrew Charities or the North End Relief Society, the orphanage became responsible for children referred by provincial courts or the Associated Charities, the City of Winnipeg's relief agency.[25] By February 1915, the orphanage was caring for thirty-eight children at a total cost of $550 a month.[26] The orphanage relied on donations and an annual "tag day" organized by the Ladies' Aid to fund its annual expenditures. In addition, as an incorporated charity, it received annual grants of $750 from the Province of Manitoba and $500 from the City of Winnipeg, subsidies that provided 22.5 percent of its income.[27]

Following the rejection of its proposal to amalgamate with the Esther Robinson Jewish Orphanage, the Canadian Jewish Orphans' Home continued to operate as a separate entity. It was managed by an organization committee chaired by A.H. Aronovitch. Although the Canadian Jewish Orphans' Home owed its existence to the organizational skills and efforts of the members of the Hebrew Ladies' Orphan Home Association, men were assumed to have greater access to potential donors who could make large contributions to a building fund. Consequently, the organization committee of the Canadian Jewish Orphans' Home established two subcommittees. Nine men, including A.H. Aronovitch and Lester Rice, president of B'nai B'rith, comprised a finance committee, which focused on plans for a campaign to raise $100,000. A house committee, which consisted of three men and thirteen women who belonged to the Hebrew Ladies' Orphan Home Association, was responsible for managing the day-to-day operation of the orphanage. Following the outbreak of the First World War, it quickly became apparent that it would be impossible to raise enough money to build an orphanage. The finance committee abandoned its plans for a capital campaign, and by 1914 the Hebrew Ladies' Orphan Home Association, which had between 800 and 900 members, assumed primary responsibility for soliciting donations for operating expenses.[28] Bazaars, raffles, and dances were held, and canvassers visited the homes of members to collect monthly dues. Since the organization committee had not incorporated the orphanage, it did not qualify for government funding, and its continued operation depended on the fundraising efforts of the Hebrew Ladies' Orphan Home Association. By September 1914, the rented house at 113 Selkirk Avenue was full, and the organization committee decided to move the orphanage to a larger facility, two semi-detached houses at 327 and 329 Manitoba Avenue. By 1916, the Canadian Jewish Orphans' Home was caring for twenty children.[29]

In 1916, the Jewish community was preoccupied with raising money for the Winnipeg Jewish Fund for the Relief of War Sufferers. This growing financial commitment combined with ongoing fundraising for the United Hebrew Relief made it difficult for supporters of the two orphanages to raise enough money to cover their operating expenses. With the financial support of the large membership of the Hebrew Ladies' Orphan Home Association, the Canadian Jewish Orphans' Home remained debt free, but the Esther Robinson Jewish Orphanage began to accumulate a large deficit. Robinson's divisive promise to donate $10,000 to build a Jewish orphanage had resulted in a $3,000 contribution to the purchase of two houses, but mortgage payments and interest on the orphanage's line of credit consumed 19 percent of operating expenses.[30] Although they had pledged their support, Robinson and his allies were not prepared to subsidize the operation of the orphanage. As the prospect of building an orphanage became increasingly remote, and the Esther Robinson Jewish Orphanage's financial problems became public knowledge, donors argued that supporting two orphanages was too high a price for the Jewish community to pay to indulge a wealthy man's desire to name an institution in memory of his mother.

In October 1916, the organization committee of the Canadian Jewish Orphans' Home approached the board of directors of the Esther Robinson Jewish Orphanage with a second proposal to amalgamate. The organization committee proposed establishing a new orphanage that would assume the liabilities of the Esther Robinson Jewish Orphanage and raise $5,000 to repay Robinson's $3,000 donation and provide $2,000 for operating expenses.[31] On 14 October, representatives of the two orphanages met to discuss amalgamation. They agreed to financial terms and elected a provisional executive that decided to operate the new institution, the Jewish Orphanage and Children's Aid of Western Canada, at the Robinson Street site. The new orphanage held its official opening on 12 November.[32]

Aware that the feud between the two orphanages had created a serious rift in the Jewish community, the provisional executive called a public meeting on 5 February 1917 to secure public endorsement of the new orphanage and to elect a permanent board of directors. The board elected at the meeting was crafted to strike a balance between men and women, districts where members resided, and former supporters of both orphanages. The thirty-nine-member board, composed of nineteen women and twenty men, included members of the Hebrew Ladies' Orphan Home Association from the North End, members of the B'nai B'rith Lodge from Central and South Winnipeg who had supported the Canadian Jewish Orphans' Home, as well as Robinson and four other founders of the Esther Robinson Jewish Orphanage.[33] The four-member executive elected by the board included two vice-presidents, Kate Kirshner, a resident of the North End, who represented the Hebrew Ladies' Orphan Home Association, and Sinai Bere, a resident of the South End, who had been a director of the Esther Robinson Jewish Orphanage. Conscious of the need to quickly raise the $5,000 needed to fulfill the terms of amalgamation, E.R. Levinson, a prominent lawyer who had been instrumental in negotiating the agreement between the two orphanages, was elected president, and David Spivak, a successful businessman who lived in the North End, was elected treasurer.[34] Levinson, one of the few members of B'nai B'rith who lived in the North End, had recently replaced Lester Rice as president of the lodge. Maintaining a close relationship with the lodge was considered indispensable; many of its affluent members had supported the Canadian Jewish Orphans' Home, and the lodge was a potential source of major donors and fundraisers.[35]

After five years of dissension, a single organization supported by a broad cross-section of the Jewish community had a public mandate to operate a Jewish orphanage. The first task of the new board was to recruit an experienced professional to manage the orphanage. Based upon the advice of the secretary of the Grand Lodge of the B'nai B'rith in Chicago, in April 1917 the board hired Louis Greenberg as superintendent and his wife, Florence, as matron. Greenberg had not only the training and experience to improve the standard of care provided by the orphanage but also the credentials and stature to publicize the contribution that it could make to the welfare of the most vulnerable members of the Jewish community and the importance of building a modern, permanent facility to care for them.

The amalgamation had overcome much of the ill feeling created in the Jewish community, but the orphanage still relied on canvassing, monthly membership dues, and a bazaar run by the members of the Hebrew Ladies' Orphan Home Association, renamed the Ladies' Society of the Jewish Orphanage and Children's Aid of Western Canada, to generate over half of its revenue.[36] Facing increasing costs for food and burdened by interest payments on over $4,000 in liabilities from the Esther Robinson Jewish Orphanage that consumed 28 percent of its income, the orphanage needed more revenue. Concerned that too many members of the Winnipeg Jewish community were indifferent to the orphanage's financial problems, the board decided that the solution to its revenue problem was to act on its mandate to serve Jewish communities throughout western Canada. It authorized Greenberg to carry out a publicity campaign to inform the approximately 13,000 Jews living in Fort William, rural Manitoba, Saskatchewan, Alberta, and British Columbia that the new orphanage not only served their communities but also could become a future home for 500–1,000 orphans from Europe.[37] His campaign not only generated more donations by the end of 1917 but also led to the formation of branches of dues-paying members of the Ladies' Society in Fort William, Plum Coulee, Winkler, and the district of Kildonan in Manitoba and Regina in Saskatchewan.[38]

Six months after his arrival in Winnipeg, Greenberg was forced to deal with a major crisis. The orphanage, caring for thirty-five children, was overcrowded. When a number of the children became seriously ill, the City of Winnipeg Health Department condemned the houses on Robinson Street as a health hazard.[39] In October 1917, the orphanage was relocated to a house that the board rented at 1280 Main Street. Initially, the thirteen-room house had ample space, but admissions steadily increased, and by August 1918 sixty-one children were living in the orphanage.[40] Overcrowding—many children were sharing "cots"—together with the orphanage's financial problems convinced the board to launch a campaign to raise $100,000 to build a spacious, fireproof orphanage equipped with the most modern sanitary facilities.

In preparation for the campaign, the board appointed seventy-five honorary directors throughout western Canada, and the Ladies' Society launched a drive to recruit additional members, increasing its membership from approximately 850 to 1,500. The campaign, which took place in early September 1918, raised close to $40,000 in cash and $40,000 in pledges due once construction of the orphanage began. The board immediately began to make plans to raise the remaining $20,000, but at the end of September the Spanish influenza epidemic hit Winnipeg. Since public gatherings or canvassing posed a health

13. Rehearsal of a performance to raise money for the Winnipeg Jewish Orphanage building fund, c. 1918.

risk, the board decided to suspend fundraising until it had purchased a site and finalized a contract with a construction company. In February 1919, the board purchased a five-and-a-half-acre lot for $25,600, and once Woodman and Cubbidge had finalized the plans it called for tenders to construct the building.[41] The board chose Sutherland Construction as the general contractor; however, with the high level of unemployment in Winnipeg, it wanted to ensure that the project assisted Jewish businesses and provided employment for Jewish workers. Consequently, it gave contracts to the Jewish-owned Winnipeg Plumbing Company and the Electric Construction Company.[42] In total, the board estimated, the new orphanage would cost $100,000.

Construction, delayed because of the Winnipeg General Strike, began on 5 July 1919. At a ceremony held on 10 August, a crowd of 2,500 witnessed the official laying of the cornerstone. Adopting the scheme of "selling" bricks, the board used the ceremony to renew its fundraising campaign. It raised nearly $12,500 at the ceremony, including a winning bid of $2,100 for the cornerstone submitted by Mrs. J. Gurman of Melfort, Saskatchewan.[43] The sale of bricks and canvassing for donations continued throughout the fall, and on 17 November a delegation from the board met with Premier T.C. Norris to request a capital grant. Informing the premier that over $43,000 was needed to build and furnish the orphanage, the delegation asked for the largest grant that "the province could spare."[44] The provincial government contributed $5,000 to the building fund. When the capital campaign concluded, receipts totalled nearly $122,000: $85,150 from donors in Winnipeg, $6,410 from towns in Manitoba, $15,360 from Saskatchewan, $5,660 from Alberta, and $1,750 from Fort William.[45] However, the final cost of building and furnishing the orphanage was $136,000, and the board was forced to borrow $20,000, a debt that it was unable to repay in full until 1923.[46]

14. J. Gurman of Melfort, Saskatchewan, whose donation of $2,100 gave her the honour of laying the cornerstone of the Winnipeg Jewish Orphanage, 10 August 1919.

The orphanage opened on 29 February 1920. Following religious services conducted by Israel Kahanovitch, the rabbi of Beth Jacob synagogue and the chief rabbi of western Canada, and Herbert J. Samuel, the rabbi of Shaarey

Zedek synagogue, a large crowd heard brief addresses from the lieutenant governor, the premier, the attorney general, and the mayor of Winnipeg.[47] On behalf of the board, E.R. Levinson, president of the orphanage, thanked the Jewish community for its generous support and declared the orphanage officially open. Once the opening ceremony ended, eighty-five children in the care of the Jewish Orphanage and Children's Aid of Western Canada entered their new home.[48]

A Modern Jewish Orphanage

Built in the Tudor style, the building was widely praised because its exterior resembled a large private residence rather than a typical institution. During a tour arranged for newspaper reporters, Greenberg emphasized that the building had been planned as a "complete home" that combined the highest standards of physical care with ample provision for children's educational and spiritual development.[49] In addition to large dining rooms, dormitories, and small bedrooms for younger children, the orphanage had classrooms, playrooms, a library, a living room, and an auditorium for religious services, films, and concerts. Supplementing the education that school-age children received at neighbourhood public schools, the orphanage provided Hebrew lessons and religious instruction. A choir and a band provided children with opportunities to develop their musical abilities, and the orphanage's spacious grounds, which included tennis courts, a playground, and sports fields for

15. Winnipeg Jewish Orphanage, c. early 1920s.

baseball, football, skating, and hockey, provided facilities for physical activities. Under the supervision of a committee of physicians and dentists, the orphanage provided medical care in a clinic, a dental room, and a twelve- bed hospital staffed by two nurses.[50]

Until 1926, the orphanage only admitted children between two and sixteen years of age.[51] Because the board did not believe that the orphanage had the facilities or resources to care for children under the age of two, it sent them to the Children's Home of Winnipeg. However, in 1926, the orphanage was forced to admit six infants between the ages of six weeks and eight months who could not be placed in other institutions. Embarrassed that the orphanage was not caring for Jewish infants, the board changed its policy and in 1928 built a two-storey annex to house an infants' ward and a boys' dormitory. Unlike older children, infants were placed with adoptive parents whenever possible.

Throughout the 1920s, most of the children admitted to the orphanage were not really orphans; either they were "half-orphans," or they had been "abandoned" by their parents. For example, in 1926, only twenty-six of the 102 children in the orphanage were orphans; twenty-four children had a mother, and twenty-two children had a father. Most of the thirty children identified as abandoned either had a parent who was mentally ill or they had been entrusted to the care of the orphanage by the Juvenile Court for "correction" or by the Children's Aid Society because of parental neglect.[52] Some desperate parents used the orphanage as a temporary refuge because they were chronically ill or disabled, as did widows and widowers forced to choose between working and taking care of their children.[53]

As a result, the number of children in the orphanage fluctuated; in addition to orphans and "half-orphans," who were permanent residents, a small proportion of the children admitted lived there until a change in financial circumstances or a court order enabled their father, mother, or parents to reclaim them.[54] In some cases, parents reclaimed their children but were forced to return them to the orphanage.[55] When reviewing applications for admission, the orphanage attempted to determine whether children had relatives who could be persuaded to take care of them. Failing that, the admissions committee tried to establish if orphans had inheritances or were the beneficiaries of life insurance policies that could be used to defray the cost of their care. Whenever possible, parents or guardians who could afford to do so were expected to pay for the care of their children, and if surviving parents remarried and refused to accept custody of their children they were expected to contribute a "reasonable sum" to the orphanage each month for their room and board.[56]

The orphanage focused on the children's religious education—the older boys prayed in the orphanage synagogue every weekday morning, and all of the children attended services together with members of the public on Friday nights and Saturdays—and the "development of a sound individuality, the building of character."[57] Boys were encouraged to "help around the Home in many ways, making themselves useful and reliable," and girls were "taught the practical duties of cooking, serving, and general housekeeping."[58] All children were "taught the value of thrift" by encouraging them to maintain savings accounts. To instill the value of individual enterprise, they were given limited opportunities to earn money and encouraged to compete to win cash awards for proficiency in Hebrew. Aside from building character, individual responsibility, thrift, and a work ethic, the primary concern of the orphanage's education committee was to ensure that the children received "modern schooling in the Hebrew language" and that the orphanage educated them in the "principles of the Jewish religion and Jewish national aspirations."[59] Once the children reached the age of sixteen, the board's vocational committee attempted to "assign the boy or girl to a class of employment to which he or she was suited."[60] However, the orphanage did not teach children practical skills to prepare them for employment in trades; instead, it relied on nearby public schools to prepare them for productive employment.

The orphanage relied on Jewish business owners to place children leaving the orphanage in "proper employment." Hiring children from the orphanage, the president suggested, was their "first duty." Employers, he enthused, "will always find them disciplined, obedient, obliging and industrious." The children, he stated, "have been equipped to take their places at the workers [*sic*] bench, at the factory or in the office."[61] According to a volunteer involved in finding

16. Residents of the Winnipeg Jewish Orphanage with Superintendent Aaron Osovsky and Fanny Osovsky, c. early 1920s.

employment for the children, the girls found employment as hairdressers or worked for furriers, and the boys worked in the clothing industry.[62] However, using funds from an education fund established by the Bronfman family, a few boys "of a scholarly bent" were given an "opportunity for higher education," and they received scholarships to attend a theological seminary in Chicago.[63]

The orphanage enjoyed widespread public participation in its management, fundraising, and operations. In addition to a forty-one-member board of directors, the 2,000-member Ladies' Society maintained a membership base that extended from Port Arthur to Vancouver. The society collected each member's six-dollar annual dues and created an honour roll to record the contributions of the Jewish women of western Canada to building the orphanage and to recognize donors who gave money for operating expenses. The orphanage commissioned a film to publicize the institution in theatres throughout western Canada, providing potential donors with vivid images of the quality of care that the children received and their activities. In addition to fundraising, groups of Winnipeg members of the Ladies' Society met at the orphanage each week to mend children's clothing and maintain its supply of linen. A second women's organization, the Ladies' Auxiliary, which had about seventy-five members, established a number of committees to offer assistance at the orphanage.[64] They included a mothers' committee to mentor girls and teach them how to sew; an after-care committee that assumed responsibility for the welfare of children after they left the orphanage, offering "advice and assistance when necessary"; a child welfare committee; a kindergarten committee, whose members ran the orphanage's preschool program; and a vocational committee, "which develops the child in study or work to which it is best suited."[65] The Ladies' Auxiliary also managed children's activities at the orphanage. In addition to teaching dancing, assisting the children to perform Purim plays, and organizing public performances by the orphanage's choir and band, its members ran a story hour, a reading club, a branch of the Girl Guides, and a Boys and Girls Club.[66]

Established in 1917, a Girls' Auxiliary participated in the fundraising campaign to build the orphanage by raising $1,000 to furnish a library. Once the orphanage was open, it provided books for the library and undertook to raise $200 a month for operating expenses. The 130 members of the Girls' Auxiliary also planned amusements and recreational activities for the children. The members organized monthly entertainments at the orphanage in the winter and annual picnics, sporting events, and automobile rides in the summer. They also took the children to see films at local theatres and assisted the Women's

Auxiliary to stage Purim plays and other dramatic events.[67] The B'nai B'rith Lodge, which operated a summer camp with accommodations for children on a three-acre site on the western shore of Lake Winnipeg, also assisted the orphanage. Every summer children from the orphanage enjoyed a reprieve from their daily routine, a ten-day holiday at the camp.[68]

By the mid-1920s, an institution that ten years earlier had generated division and conflict was firmly embedded in the Jewish community of Winnipeg. Supported by Jewish residents of the North End as well as Central and South Winnipeg, by affluent donors, and by a multitude of volunteers who raised money and organized activities for the children, the orphanage became a source of pride and a symbol of the Jewish community's progressive understanding of child welfare.[69] Like the bitter dispute between supporters of the United Hebrew Charities and the North End Relief Society, foundation of the orphanage was an object lesson of the cost, in terms of money, duplication of effort, wasted time, and fractured relationships that disputes over communal decision making exacted. It also demonstrated what a unified Jewish community could accomplish.

The Jewish Old Folks' Home

This lesson was understood by the founders of the Jewish Old Folks' Home. In 1912, the Jewish community became aware that a number of elderly Jewish immigrants who had recently settled in Winnipeg were destitute. Without children willing or able to support them, they were forced to turn to the United Hebrew Charities or the North End Relief Society. Their plight was unusual, Jewish families invariably assumed responsibility for aged or infirm parents, and it was rare for elderly immigrants not accompanied by children or travelling to join them to settle in Winnipeg. Nevertheless, it was evident that the problem of destitute elderly Jews forced to depend on communal charity would persist. In 1910, the Montreal Jewish community had confronted the same problem and responded by establishing the Hebrew Old People's and Sheltering Home.

In 1912, a group of Jewish women who lived in the North End and Central Winnipeg met to discuss "ways and means" of establishing a home to provide care for "old, helpless, feeble and friendless" Jews.[70] They began to raise money and as a temporary measure made arrangements to pay for the board and room of destitute elderly Jews in private homes. In December 1913, ten women submitted a declaration of association to the provincial government requesting letters patent incorporating the Winnipeg Old Folk's Jewish Home.[71] Led by

President Annie Abromovitch, Vice-President Freda Shatsky, Treasurer Sylvia Shragge, Secretary Bessie Chess, and seven board members, the Winnipeg Old Folk's Jewish Home Association solicited money door to door, sold tickets to a benefit ball, and tried other means to raise enough money to build a home. The association had hoped to join with the organization committee of the Canadian Jewish Orphans' Home to purchase a large lot on Selkirk Avenue near the Red River where both a home and an orphanage could be built, but in early 1914 the president of the organization committee sent a letter advising the association that the committee was not in a position to share the cost.[72]

With the outbreak of the First World War, like the organization committee of the Canadian Jewish Orphans' Home, the association found it even more difficult to raise money. Not only was the public caught up with the war effort, but also, as women, few members of the association had independent incomes or the same access as men to donors who could make sizable donations. To broaden its fundraising, when members of the association elected a new board of directors, they adopted the expedient of recruiting two men—Joseph Genser as president and Morris Nydis as vice-president—to serve on the executive. Chaia Rosenblatt, who together with her husband, Nissel, operated several businesses, served as treasurer.[73] By July 1915, the association had enough money to rent two semi-detached houses at 143 and 145 Euclid Avenue and hire a housekeeper to care for its first residents, five elderly Jewish men and women.[74] Within a year, the home, known as the Old Folk's Immigration Home, had seven residents, three men and four women, ranging in age from sixty to eighty-six.[75] By 1917, the home, which had an annual budget of $3,000, had ten residents.[76]

By 1918, with fifteen residents, the home was filled to capacity and had a waiting list. The board of directors decided to purchase a building for the home that would be large enough to accommodate the growing number of elderly residents. In April 1919, the board held a public meeting to make its case to the Jewish community and seek its support for a fundraising drive. The assembly passed a unanimous resolution giving the board a mandate to proceed, and a small group of donors—including several of the women who founded the Winnipeg Old Folk's Jewish Home Association—contributed $4,550 to launch the fundraising campaign. These donors formed the nucleus of a building committee, which quickly raised $10,000. The committee raised most of the money in Winnipeg. However, like the orphanage, the home, renamed the Jewish Old Folks' Home of Western Canada, had a mandate to serve Jewish communities from Fort William to Alberta. Consequently,

17. Jewish Old Folks' Home, 1919–1940. This facility was closed when a new institution was built.

the building committee expanded its fundraising drive to solicit donations throughout the region.[77]

However, the timing of the campaign made it difficult to raise money. The campaign happened to coincide with the Winnipeg General Strike, and the building committee competed with the fundraising drive to build the new orphanage. Nevertheless, the problem of overcrowding at the Euclid Avenue home was so pressing that, though the board had only half of the purchase price, it decided to spend $20,000 to buy the Cressy Block at 426 and 428 Manitoba Avenue, an apartment building with ten suites, and a seven-room house located on the same lot. It then spent close to $3,900 on renovations, creating a kitchen, two dining rooms, a fifty-seat synagogue, and offices on the main floor, and eighteen bedrooms with space for sixty beds, plus a hospital room, a living room, and bathrooms on the second floor.[78] Although the official opening of the home provided an opportunity to solicit $5,624 in donations, the board was forced to assume an $8,000 mortgage to pay for the apartment building and renovations, a debt not repaid until 1923.[79]

On 16 November 1919, the board of directors of the Jewish Old Folks' Home of Western Canada called a public meeting to present its report and elect a new board. The new board had twenty-five members: fifteen men and ten women, including three of the home's founders. The board elected Jacob Chmelnitsky as president, Sam Cossoy as vice-president, Rebecca Abromovitch as vice-president, and a third man, M. Tessler, as treasurer. Although more women were elected in 1920, giving them a majority on the thirty-six-member board, four of the six executive positions were held by men.[80] Women had played instrumental roles in establishing the home; however, men were considered indispensable to raise money and manage the home. In addition, unlike the orphanage, which drew support from Jewish residents in the North End, Central Winnipeg, and the South End, with the exception of three board members who lived in Central Winnipeg, all of the members of the board elected in 1920 lived in the North End. Although the board attempted to attract the support of the whole Jewish community, throughout the 1920s the home essentially remained a North End institution.

18. Board of Directors, Jewish Old Folks' Home, 1924.

19. Benjamin Sarner, superintendent of the Jewish Old Folks' Home, with male residents, 1920s.

20. Nurse with female residents of the Jewish Old Folks' Home, 1920s.

The prominent Central and South Winnipeg lawyers and businessmen who devoted their time and money to build and sustain the orphanage did not extend their support to the home.

In September 1920, the board appointed Isaac Rosen as director of the home.[81] Rosen, who had arrived in Winnipeg in 1882, was retired and able to serve as a volunteer. To assist him, the board also set up seven committees to manage the home. In addition to a finance committee, it established an investigation committee, which determined whether applicants were eligible for admission and whether they had the means to pay for their care, as well as a house committee, building committee, synagogue committee, and social committee, bodies responsible for the day-to-day management of the home. Burdened with an unwieldy management structure, Rosen did not have the authority to administer the home effectively. Recognizing that it needed a professional manager with a mandate to assume direct control over the operation of the home, in June 1922 the board appointed Benjamin Sarner to replace him.[82] Appointed as superintendent and "collector" (or chief fundraiser), Sarner was to supervise the home's cook, housekeeping staff, and nurse and oversee the delivery of medical care provided by a group of five physicians and two dentists who volunteered their services. Sarner also worked with the Ladies' and Girls' Auxiliaries, whose members enriched the residents' lives by organizing concerts and celebrating holidays with them.[83]

Fundraising to maintain the home was a constant concern. Between 1919 and 1923, the home had an annual operating budget of approximately $16,500.[84] However, as the number of residents rose (from thirty-four in 1923 to forty-two in 1930), the cost of maintaining the home steadily increased.[85] Government support for private institutions that cared for the elderly was limited. The provincial government operated the Portage la Prairie Home for Incurables. Although it mainly cared for "persons afflicted with incurable diseases" or those "unable to care for themselves on account of bodily or mental affliction," it had a separate wing that functioned as a home for the elderly.[86] This institution was intended to serve the entire province. Nevertheless, the provincial government provided operating grants to the St. Boniface Old Folk's Home and the Middlechurch Old Folk's Home but not to the Jewish Old Folks' Home.[87] The City of Winnipeg, obligated by statute to contribute fifty cents a day for the maintenance of each destitute resident of the city admitted to the Home for Incurable, did not pay grants to private old-age homes.[88]

Nevertheless, at the opening ceremony of the home, Mayor of Winnipeg Charles F. Gray was so impressed with the facility that he promised to

21. Members of the Girl's Auxiliary of the Jewish Old Folks' Home, 1920s.

recommend to Winnipeg City Council that it approve an annual operating grant. However, though the province's Public Welfare Commission supported municipal funding of private old folk's homes, when representatives of the board appeared before City Council to request funding, they did not get a sympathetic hearing.[89] Although unsuccessful, the board continued to send delegations to appear before council to request funding. In 1926, a delegation from the board appeared before council once again, arguing that, like the Home for Incurables, the Jewish Old Folks' Home was taking care of a number of "feeble-minded and blind persons" and therefore was entitled to receive funding. The delegation requested an annual grant of $2,000. However, after hearing that the Civic Charities Endorsation Bureau was concerned about the number of residents in the home from rural Manitoba and other provinces as opposed to Winnipeg, City Council decided to defer a decision pending a report from the bureau.[90] Ultimately, on the recommendation of the bureau, in December 1926 City Council decided to give the home financial support for the care of six residents from Winnipeg. City Council concluded that giving the home a per diem of forty cents for each of the six residents—an annual cost of $876—was cheaper than paying for the cost of their care at the Home for Incurables.[91]

The home attempted to generate revenue by assessing whether applicants had the means to pay for their care and imposing appropriate fees. Applicants were asked detailed questions about their property, savings, and whether they had insurance or were members of a mutual aid association. They were also asked to assign all of the property that they possessed to the home and to give the board of directors "all rights" to conduct funerals.[92] Since almost all applicants for admission were destitute, the home did not receive a significant amount of revenue from residents' fees.[93] However, after 1 September 1927, when the federal Old Age Pension was established, it became a dependable if modest source of income. Eligible residents, initially few in number because of the twenty-year Canadian residency requirement, were required to turn over their pensions of $240 a year to the home.[94]

Since neither the Province of Manitoba nor the City of Winnipeg—with the exception beginning in 1926 of small per diem payments—provided financial support, and because few residents' could afford to pay fees, operation of the home depended on continual fundraising. It included holding bazaars and other events as well as soliciting individual donations from members of the Winnipeg Jewish community. Many Jewish families adopted the practice of celebrating engagements and other major events by asking guests to make donations to the home.[95] In addition, every year members of the board went to Vancouver, Edmonton, Saskatoon, and other major centres to appeal for donations while the superintendent travelled throughout rural Manitoba, Saskatchewan, and Alberta. He visited more than ninety small Jewish communities and families to solicit contributions, reminding donors that the institution deserved their support because it served all of the Jews of western Canada.[96] Although their financial contribution was modest, the approximately 100 members of the Girls' Auxiliary organized theatrical revues, dances, and teas that raised hundreds of dollars used to buy medicine for the residents of the home.[97]

With a population of slightly more than 14,500 by the early 1920s, Winnipeg's Jewish community was responsible for maintaining a costly social welfare system. In addition to maintaining the United Hebrew Relief, and having invested over $145,000 to establish an orphanage and a home for the elderly, members of the community were now responsible for raising over $63,000 a year to fund operating expenses. Moreover, though fundraising to assist Jews in Eastern Europe had virtually ceased by 1923, the immigration of Jews to Canada had become a major issue. With an annual budget in 1923–24 of close to $14,000, the Winnipeg-based Western Division of the Jewish

Immigrant Aid Society depended on raising more than $6,500 in donations.[98] Nevertheless, the determined efforts of hundreds of volunteer fundraisers and canvassers ensured that communal social welfare organizations and institutions received sufficient funding to eliminate operating deficits, pay off loans and mortgages, and expand their services. However, their success came at a cost; members of the Jewish community were bombarded with repeated appeals for donations and membership dues as well as numerous requests to buy tickets for benefit concerts and theatrical performances or to attend fundraising bazaars, raising concerns that competition for financial support was beginning to create donor fatigue, which could jeopardize the continued operation of the social welfare services that the Jewish community had sacrificed so much to establish.

The Federated Budget Board

The broader British Canadian community was experiencing similar problems. As a report on Winnipeg's social welfare agencies noted, "it was generally recognized that the practice of approximately forty agencies making individual appeals each year, or oftener, resulted in a great waste of time, effort, and money, in addition to being frequently ineffective as far as institutions are concerned."[99] In April 1919, twenty-five British Canadian social welfare agencies and institutions formed the Central Council of Social Agencies to coordinate the delivery of social welfare services. It claimed a mandate to evaluate Winnipeg's social welfare needs and make recommendations concerning the "undertaking of additional work by any existing organization or any new organization" and to "further the education of public opinion" to achieve "greater efficiency in public welfare work."[100] Together with the Winnipeg Board of Trade, which supported making the charitable sector more efficient by implementing sound business practices, the Central Council was anxious to rationalize both fundraising and expenditures on social welfare.

The Central Council concluded that a "federated budget"—an annual, centralized fundraising campaign that, in addition to soliciting donations from the wealthy donors whom many social welfare agencies traditionally relied on, would appeal to the "smaller giver" whom fundraisers had a "tendency to overlook"—could raise more money than a "multiplicity of appeals."[101] Centralized fundraising would not only be more efficient—member agencies would no longer have to spend parts of their annual budgets soliciting donations, and volunteers could devote their time and energy to assisting social welfare agencies to provide services rather than raising money—but it would also "submerge class and religious prejudices" by fostering public support for the "betterment of the community as a whole."[102] In addition, a federated budget would result in a "fairer distribution of funds": access to social welfare services would no longer depend on whether or not an agency or institution succeeded at fundraising, and the distribution of funds to member agencies and institutions would be based upon objective standards, an evaluation of their financial management and administrative capacity to deliver services that fulfilled the needs of the community.[103] This objective scrutiny, supporters of the federated budget plan argued, would reassure donors; they would no longer have the responsibility of determining whether a social welfare agency was spending charitable donations responsibly. Admission to the campaign and annual audits would provide a seal of approval confirming that participating social agencies deserved the public's support.

In 1921, the Central Council and the Winnipeg Board of Trade each passed a resolution to appoint seven of its members to constitute an interim Federated Budget Board.[104] Although the Jewish Orphanage was a member of the Central Council, it did not send representatives to every meeting, and no one from the Jewish community was present when it decided to join with the Board of Trade to establish a Federated Budget Board. Nevertheless, the boards of directors of the Jewish Orphanage, Jewish Old Folks' Home, and United Hebrew Relief were aware that support for annual centralized fundraising was growing: by April 1922, the number of social welfare agencies and institutions that belonged to the Central Council had increased to forty, and reports of the establishment of the Federated Budget Board and its plan to launch its first annual campaign in November were published in Winnipeg's daily newspapers.[105]

The Federated Budget Board's plan to launch its annual campaign created a dilemma for the Jewish community. With the exception of lobbying City Council and the provincial government for the same capital or operating grants that other social welfare organizations and institutions received, the boards of the United Hebrew Relief, Jewish Orphanage, and Jewish Old Folks' Home assumed that, having established a system of communal social welfare, the Jewish community would continue to make whatever sacrifices were necessary to raise the money needed to maintain it. Intensely proud of the Jewish community's commitment to the social welfare of its vulnerable members, they were determined to preserve their autonomy. Nevertheless, the boards recognized that their competing fundraising drives were beginning to strain the goodwill of donors and would inevitably lead to an unacceptable decline in operating revenue. Rather than jeopardize what the Jewish community had achieved, they were prepared to consider some form of cooperation to combine their fundraising activities. They were aware that in 1916 Jewish charities in both Toronto and Montreal had established federations of Jewish philanthropies whose executives ran an annual fundraising campaign and made allocations to individual organizations and institutions.[106] However, preoccupied with consolidating the finances of the recently established Jewish Orphanage and the Jewish Old Folks' Home, and attempting to raise more money to enable the United Hebrew Relief to deal with an increase in demand for assistance, communal leaders had not held serious discussions to lay the foundation for an agreement on joint fundraising.

Consequently, in October 1922, with the launch of the Federated Budget Board's first annual fundraising campaign fast approaching, the boards of directors of the United Hebrew Relief, Jewish Orphanage, and Jewish Old Folks' Home were forced to make a decision: apply to join the campaign or continue to fundraise independently. For many members of the Jewish community, the issue was autonomy; if admitted as beneficiaries of the campaign, then social welfare agencies were required to submit an annual report of their finances and a "detailed statement" of the operating revenue that they needed for the coming year.[107] The budget committee of the Federated Budget Board would then determine how much each social welfare agency was entitled to receive and establish the campaign goal. In an editorial, the *Israelite Press* weighed the advantages and disadvantages of joining the board. Acknowledging that membership would mean that an organization dominated by British Canadians would have the authority to scrutinize how the United Hebrew Relief, Jewish Orphanage, and Jewish Old Folks' Home spent money, the editor attempted to allay fears that this would lead to outside interference in the internal affairs of the Jewish community. Emphasizing that the Jewish community would benefit from stable funding, he recommended that these institutions participate in the campaign.[108]

Many members of the Jewish community remained unconvinced. In a series of public meetings, supporters of the United Hebrew Relief and Jewish Old Folks' Home initially rejected a proposal to join the campaign, and members of the Jewish Orphanage deferred a decision until a committee prepared a report on the work of federated budget organizations in other cities.[109] However, with the board campaign set to begin in two weeks, proponents of joining the board quickly mobilized support to call a public meeting to give the whole Jewish community an opportunity to participate in making a decision. Within days, the boards of directors of all three organizations met, agreed to choose three delegates each to prepare a proposal to join the campaign, and organized a public meeting for 7 November 1922 to present it for discussion and a final decision. Opinion at the meeting was deeply divided, but ultimately a majority voted in favour of joining the campaign. Many opponents believed that submitting financial information on the operations of the three institutions would expose the Jewish community to unwelcome and possibly hostile scrutiny, but they were undoubtedly reassured by the knowledge that Alan Bronfman, president of the Jewish Orphanage, who chaired the meeting, and Max Steinkopf were members of the executive committee of the Federated Budget Board. Also, since contributors to the campaign could assign their donations to the agency of their choice, advocates of participation in it could argue that donors who supported Jewish social welfare organizations and institutions could continue to do so. Immediately after the meeting, the boards of the United Hebrew Relief, Jewish Orphanage, and Jewish Old Folks' Home quickly submitted applications to become beneficiaries of the Federated Budget Board's campaign.[110]

Their applications were speedily approved.[111] Less than a week after they were submitted, the Federated Budget Board placed an ad in the *Winnipeg Tribune* listing the United Hebrew Relief, Jewish Orphanage, and Jewish Old Folks' Home among the thirty social welfare agencies and institutions that would benefit from its $450,000 campaign.[112] In addition, the Jewish community was given the right to appoint two members to the board.[113] The board campaign, which took place 21–24 November 1922, exceeded expectations. Approximately 1,500 canvassers, including volunteers from the Jewish community, raised $451,213 in cash and pledges.[114] Ultimately, the board collected $406,257 and disbursed $382,079 to the thirty social welfare agencies and institutions that had participated in the campaign.[115] Jewish social welfare agencies and institutions received close to $49,000: United Hebrew Relief $10,000, Jewish Orphanage $28,000, and Jewish Old Folks' Home $10,800.[116] The board's allocation of $10,000 to the United Hebrew Relief covered almost all of its annual expenditures. However, neither the Jewish Old Folks' Home nor the Jewish Orphanage received full funding.

In part, this was because both institutions received revenue in the form of maintenance fees. The Jewish Old Folks' Home received a modest amount of revenue from the few residents who could pay for their care. Similarly, fees paid by parents and guardians of children accounted for approximately 6 percent of the Jewish Orphanage's revenue. In addition, the orphanage received $500 from the City of Winnipeg and $750 from the Province of Manitoba. The budget committee of the Federated Budget Board deducted these amounts when determining its allocations to both institutions. However, both the home and the orphanage were subject to much larger reductions in funding because of their mandates to serve Jewish communities throughout western Canada. The Federated Budget Board had been established to fund Winnipeg's social welfare agencies and institutions, and its campaign appealed to donors to help the "homeless, the sick, the handicapped and the fallen" of the community.[117] Consequently, the board adopted a policy of only allocating funds to support residents of Winnipeg. Since the Jewish Old Folks' Home and Jewish Orphanage served Jewish communities outside Winnipeg, this policy had a major impact on the board's funding of both institutions. The budget committee's allocation to the home was reduced by approximately $5,000. As a result, in 1922–23, the allocation to the home comprised approximately two-thirds of its annual expenditures. Similarly, since about 38 percent of the children in the Jewish Orphanage came from outside Winnipeg, its allocation was reduced by approximately one-third.[118] However, the boards of both institutions were aware of the Federated Budget Board's policy when they agreed to join the campaign. When the 1922-23 campaign concluded, they once again made plans for their annual fundraising tours of Jewish communities throughout western Canada.[119]

The success of the Federated Budget Board's first fundraising campaign silenced or won over most of those within the Jewish community who had argued against participation in it. Although they had only a few days to prepare, volunteers from the Jewish community who quickly organized contingents of canvassers to go door to door in Jewish neighbourhoods and approach Jewish businessmen to solicit donations were pleased that nearly $49,000 had been allocated to Jewish social welfare agencies. As the 1923–24 campaign approached, the Jewish community had every reason to be optimistic. In November 1923, the Federated Budget Board announced that its goal for the 1923–24 campaign was to raise $465,000 to be distributed among thirty-eight social welfare agencies and institutions.[120] Based upon the budget committee's preliminary allocations, the United Hebrew Relief could expect to receive $9,250, the Jewish Old Folks' Home $10,800, and the Jewish Orphanage $25,000.[121] In preparation for the campaign, a newly established body, the Jewish Central Budget Committee, coordinated the organization of a Jewish Division of Canvassers.[122] It consisted of a thirteen-member "Central Committee" responsible for canvassing Jews in Central and South Winnipeg, a fifteen-member "North End Residential Committee" composed of team captains responsible for organizing a canvass of Jewish neighbourhoods in the North End, and a twenty-eight-member "Jewish Business Men's Select Committee," which included a number of prominent businessmen and physicians.[123]

However, the Federated Budget Board's 1923–24 campaign was a disappointment. An initial tally suggested that the campaign had raised approximately $375,000, but many pledges had not been paid, and the final total was $330,863, far short of the goal of $465,000.[124] The enthusiasm of the first campaign was absent, and the number of donors dropped from 30,855 to 26,525.[125] Faced with a substantial shortfall, the board attempted to avoid cutting its preliminary allocations by reducing its funding commitment from a twelve-month to an eleven-month period by holding the 1924–25 campaign a month earlier. As a result, the 1923–24 allocation to the United Hebrew Relief decreased from $9,250 to $8,370, the Jewish Old Folks' Home from $10,800 to $9,900, and the Jewish Orphanage from $25,000 to $22,913.[126] The Federated Budget Board was troubled by the decrease in both the number of donors and the amount collected; much would depend on the success of the 1924–25 campaign. The Jewish Central Budget Committee was also concerned about the impact of the outcome of the campaign on the Jewish community's social welfare agencies and institutions, but it was confronted with a potentially more serious problem. In December 1923, the *Manitoba Free Press* reported that the Jewish Division of Canvassers had collected $28,735 in donations.[127] This sum was $12,448 less than the amount that the Federated Budget Board allocated to the United Hebrew Relief, the Jewish Old Folks' Home, and the Jewish Orphanage. Although the newspaper did not make this comparison, information on the board's allocations was readily available, and an informed reader could easily conclude that the Jewish community was not contributing its fair share of donations.

Accompanied by an extensive publicity campaign emphasizing that "Thousands in Need of Help Are Waiting Anxiously for Your Answer to Their Appeal. Don't Fail Them Now!" the Federated Budget Board launched its 1924–25 campaign to raise $445,000 on 4 November. Once again the campaign failed to achieve its objective; the number of donors declined from 26,525 the previous year to 23,450, and it raised only $307,072.[128] After deducting $25,000 for administration and expenses and making an allowance of $25,000 for unpaid pledges, the budget committee was left with $260,000 to allocate to thirty-seven social welfare agencies and institutions.[129] Although a larger number of pledges than anticipated were paid, yielding an additional

$17,680 for allocations, extensive reductions in funding were unavoidable. For the following twelve months, the budget committee allocated $6,000 to the United Hebrew Relief, $7,200 to the Jewish Old Folks' Home, and $22,000 to the Jewish Orphanage, reductions that amounted to more than 22 percent of the previous year's total funding.[130] Since both the home and the orphanage had managed to pay off their building debts, they were able to cope with a reduction in funding by reducing operating expenditures and appealing to their supporters throughout western Canada for donations, but this recourse was not available to the United Hebrew Relief. With expenditures of approximately $9,000 a year, the decrease in Federated Budget Board funding placed the agency in a precarious financial position, forcing its board of directors to appeal to Winnipeg's Jewish community for donations.

Faced with fewer donors and continuing decreases in contributions, the executive of the Federated Budget Board reluctantly came to the conclusion that it could not continue to fund thirty-seven social welfare agencies and institutions. In his annual statement, Douglas Scott, chairman of the board, attributed the drop in public support for campaigns to a widespread perception that many of the agencies and institutions did not deserve the funding that they received. He announced that a survey was needed to determine which ones were meeting genuine needs in the community.[131] To dispel concerns that the survey might be subject to undue influence from members of the board, and to assure the public that it would be based upon expert analysis, in April 1925 the board commissioned Edward T. Devine, a professor of social economy at Columbia University and a former general secretary of the New York Charitable Society, to complete a social audit of the thirty-seven agencies and institutions that it funded.[132]

Devine completed his social audit in March 1925.[133] Based upon its recommendations, the Federated Budget Board reduced the number of social agencies and institutions it funded from thirty-seven to twenty-three. The United Hebrew Relief was one of the social agencies dropped from the list.[134] According to Devine, "the few Jewish families" assisted by the agency were the "only exception" to a social welfare policy whereby relief was dispensed either by the City of Winnipeg's Social Welfare Commission or by "churches, benevolent societies, or private individuals at their own expense." Since Catholics or Protestants did not receive relief from "funds subscribed through the Federated Budget Board," he concluded, "*I see no convincing reason why this anomaly should be continued.*"[135]

The decision of the Federated Budget Board not only forced the United Hebrew Relief to increase its fundraising to achieve self-sufficiency but also undermined the efforts of the Jewish Central Budget Committee to persuade members of the Jewish community that they had a responsibility to support the board's annual campaign. In an appeal published in Yiddish and English, the committee chastised members of the Jewish community for their failure to volunteer as canvassers or donate amounts at least equivalent to the funding that the board allocated to Jewish social welfare institutions. "Would you allow others to pay for the upkeep of our institutions?" the pamphlet chided. "Have we lost our pride and self-respect? Do we realize the consequences of our negligence and indifference?"[136] The committee's insistent message was unambiguous: unless the Jewish community changed its attitude to the campaign, it would become impossible to claim that the Jewish Old Folks' Home and Jewish Orphanage were entitled to receive funding.

The Federated Budget Board's publicity for the launch of the 1925–26 campaign to raise $310,000 also communicated an urgent message. Emphasizing that the board, acting on the advice of Devine, "an authority on Community Funds and a man of world-wide experience in charitable work," had narrowed its focus to funding twenty-three institutions "worthy of confidence" because they are well managed and "meet legitimate needs," it declared that the board was at a "crossroads."[137] Unless the campaign achieved its objective, the minimum amount needed to provide the remaining twenty-three social agencies and institutions with enough money to operate for twelve months, the board would disband, and donors would once again be subjected to the "old expensive week-in and week-out collecting and begging appeals for funds."[138]

The Federated Budget Board's campaign did not achieve its objective, but it raised $288,277. After expenses, the board had $264,210 to disburse; effective 1 November 1925, it allocated $6,000 to the Jewish Old Folks' Home and $21,408 to the Jewish Orphanage.[139] Compared with the allocations made for the previous eleven months, this represented a reduction of $1,854 in funding for the home and $2,592 for the orphanage. These reductions put additional pressure on the boards of both institutions to increase revenues. In addition to appealing to supporters throughout western Canada, the home placed more emphasis on carefully investigating whether those who applied for admission could afford to contribute to the cost of their care, and the orphanage increasingly relied on fees paid by parents and guardians.[140] However, members of the Jewish community were not in a position to complain about the drop in funding; reports released shortly after the conclusion of the campaign suggested that contributions collected by Jewish canvassers were almost 30 percent lower than the amount that they had raised the previous year.[141]

The discrepancy between the amount that Jewish donors contributed to Federated Budget Board campaigns and the funding that it allocated to the Jewish Old Folks' Home and the Jewish Orphanage illustrated the complexities of balancing Jewish communal autonomy with integration into British Canadian society. For prominent Jewish businessmen such as Max Steinkopf and Hyman Yewdall, who represented the Winnipeg Board of Trade on the Federated Budget Board and served on its budget committee, the participation of Jewish social welfare agencies and institutions in the board's annual campaigns, the establishment of the Jewish Central Budget Committee, which elected two representatives to the board, and the organization of a Jewish Division of Canvassers were stepping stones that would promote integration of the Jewish community. They would send a clear message to Winnipeg's British Canadian leaders that Jews, widely thought to be exclusively concerned with their own communal interests, wanted to make a contribution to the welfare of the broader community. Similarly, joining the Central Council of Social Agencies provided representatives of the Jewish Orphanage and United Hebrew Relief with opportunities to work with colleagues from British Canadian social welfare agencies and institutions and to demonstrate that, far from being bound by parochial beliefs about charity, they also wanted to promote the professionalization of social work and modernize the delivery of social services.[142] In addition, since the council was entitled to appoint twelve of its members to the Federated Budget Board, affiliation offered Jewish social welfare agencies and institutions a means of increasing the number of representatives of the Jewish community on the board.[143]

However, repeated shortfalls in the Jewish community's donations to the Federated Budget Board's campaign undermined the credibility of its Jewish members. Their determination to help the board achieve its goal of building public support for a city-wide campaign to fund social welfare agencies and institutions throughout Winnipeg was self-evident; however, campaign results suggested that they did not have sufficient support in the Jewish community to act or make claims on its behalf. Opinions within the Jewish community differed on why the shortfall in contributions persisted. For some, it occurred because too many Jews "simply fail[ed] to understand" how the Federated Budget Board worked or the benefits that they derived from it. According to the *Jewish Post*, more public education was needed: "The majority of our people do not seem to be aware that the Jewish Orphanage last year drew

$19,000 and the Jewish Old Folks' Home $6000 from the Budget." In addition, "welfare services are rendered to Jews by the hospitals, by the Institute of the Blind, and other institutions receiving Budget support."[144] The *Israelite Press*, however, claimed that the shortfall was the result of a failure of leadership. Pointing to a lack of canvassers, it asked "where are the leaders of the Jewish Community?" More money would be raised, it suggested, if the directors of the Jewish Old Folk's Home, Jewish Orphanage, and organizations such as B'nai B'rith and Hebrew Sick Benefit Society fulfilled their responsibilities to organize an effective canvass.[145] Whatever the explanation for the shortfall, or the best remedy, communal leaders recognized that it exposed the Jewish community to "criticism and recrimination." It was "humiliating to make excuses" to British Canadians; the reputation of the Jewish community was at stake. Citing opinions expressed by members of the boards of the orphanage and home that, if the Jewish community did not increase its contribution to the Federated Budget Board, then both institutions must withdraw from the campaign. The *Jewish Post* agreed that the results of the 1927–28 campaign would be decisive.[146]

The Jewish community's contributions to the 1927–28 Federated Budget Board campaign and subsequent campaigns continued to be a public embarrassment, but the Jewish Old Folks' Home and Jewish Orphanage did not withdraw from the board. Although donations to annual campaigns steadily increased—$291,798 in 1926–27, $321,898 in 1927–28, $331,819 in 1928–29, and $325,859 in 1929–30—contributions from the Jewish community decreased.[147] Despite concerns that the honour of the Jewish community was "at stake," and despite repeated reminders that Jews had a duty to contribute at least the same amount that the home and orphanage received from the board ("anything less would be unfair to other contributors"), the shortfall grew. Between November 1926 and November 1930, annual allocations averaged $25,650, but contributions from the Jewish community declined, from approximately $20,000 in the 1927–28 campaign to $10,000 in the 1929–30 campaign.[148] Thwarted by the indifference of Jewish donors to appeals to honour and duty, or the assertion that the board should be supported because it "brings all races and creeds together in a common movement for a common good," the organizers of the Jewish Division of Canvassers decided to disband.[149] In the 1930–31 campaign, Jewish canvassers joined teams organized by British Canadian organizations. As the *Jewish Post* explained, the Jewish Division had been created because a "friendly rivalry and competitive spirit would spur each team to do its upmost." However, "it had the insidious effect of inviting comparisons between Jews and others in regard to moneys [*sic*] collected [and] moneys [*sic*] spent on sectional charity." This led to the "injection of prejudice in regard to a matter which should have been of general unprejudiced communal interest."[150]

A lack of understanding of the role of the Federated Budget Board and the benefits that the Jewish community received from the funding that it provided to the Jewish Old Folks' Home and Jewish Orphanage undoubtedly contributed to the shortfall in donations, as did the failure of the members of the Jewish Central Budget Committee to recruit enough canvassers. However, other factors led members of the Jewish community to question whether the board brought "all races and creeds together in a common movement for a common good." First, though the board's first campaign was initially judged a success, tallies released shortly after it ended suggesting that donors had contributed $451,213, exceeding its goal of $450,000, the final amount totalled $406,000 because many pledges could not be collected. Furthermore, in the next three campaigns, public support for the "common good" steadily declined; the problem of unpaid pledges persisted, the number of donors dropped, and total donations fell from $330,863 in 1923–24 to $288,277 in 1925–26. Consequently, it became increasingly difficult for Jewish supporters of the Federated Budget Board to persuade members of the Jewish community that the decision to give up communal autonomy and become part of a city-wide, centralized, annual fundraising campaign controlled by and dependent on the support of British Canadians was advantageous.

Second, many Jewish donors had been led to believe that supporting the Federated Budget Board's campaign meant that the Jewish Old Folks' Home and Jewish Orphanage would receive "full funding." Unaware of the funding implications of the distinction between the elderly and orphans who were residents of Winnipeg and those who came from Jewish communities outside the city, they were disappointed to learn that board allocations to both institutions covered only two-thirds of their operating expenses. Furthermore, the decision in 1925 to stop funding the United Hebrew Relief provided additional evidence that, despite the claims of its Jewish members, far from basing its funding decisions upon the demonstrated need for the services provided by social welfare agencies and institutions, the board was treating the Jewish community unfairly.

Finally, beginning in 1923, Federated Budget Board funding of Jewish social welfare services steadily decreased. Allocations to the United Hebrew Relief, Jewish Old Folks' Home, and Jewish Orphanage, which totalled

$48,800 in 1922–23, dropped to $41,183 in 1923–24 and to $35,200 in 1924–25. In 1925–26, the decision not to fund the United Hebrew Relief led to a further reduction, while the home and orphanage received $27,408. Their funding dropped to $25,760 in 1926–27, increased slightly to $26,000 in 1927–28, and then decreased to $25,700 in 1928–29 and to $25,143 in 1929–30.[151] Consequently, far from eliminating the "duplication and expense" of competing "tag days, subscriptions, bazaars, and innumerable charity affairs," as board funding of Jewish social welfare services fell, donors in the Jewish community were once again bombarded with increasingly urgent appeals for donations.[152]

Despite widespread dissatisfaction with the Federated Budget Board, the boards of directors of the Jewish Old Folks' Home and Jewish Orphanage continued to support participation in the annual campaign throughout the 1930s.[153] However, by 1927, it became evident that the Jewish community had to deal with the problem of competing appeals for donations. In addition to the board campaigns, members of the Jewish community were being asked to make donations to the United Hebrew Relief, raise money to supplement board funding of the home and orphanage, and support the Western Division of the Jewish Immigrant Aid Society, the Peretz and Talmud Torah schools, the Young Men's Hebrew Association, and a number of Zionist organizations such as the Jewish National Fund and Hadassah. Leaders of the United Hebrew Relief, Jewish Old Folks' Home, and Jewish Orphanage recognized that, unless some regulation of communal appeals for donations was established, funding of the Jewish community's social welfare assistance and services would be jeopardized. As the *Jewish Post* declared, "Winnipeg's Jews are not tired of giving. They are tired of being pestered with a continual and unending round of appeals."[154]

The Jewish Charities Endorsation Bureau and the Mount Carmel Clinic

In March 1927, M.J. Finkelstein, president of the Jewish Orphanage, Aaron Osovsky, superintendent of the orphanage, and S. Hart Green, honorary president of the United Hebrew Relief, drafted a constitution for a new organization, the Jewish Charities Endorsation Bureau. Its purpose was to "establish an authoritative and representative" committee to "prevent indiscriminate collections of funds for National, Philanthropic and Charitable purposes." The bureau, to be elected by an annual meeting attended by two representatives of every Jewish organization that chose to become affiliated, would review all applications for endorsation. If an investigation of the organization determined that it was "worthy" of public support, then the bureau would issue a permit to raise funds.[155] In addition to building donor confidence by certifying that organizations granted permits by the bureau had been thoroughly investigated and educating members of the Jewish community to make donations only to officially sanctioned causes, it would attempt to control the timing of fund-raising drives and events to prevent conflicts, particularly with the Federated Budget Board's annual campaign. At a meeting held on 19 April 1927, representatives of thirty Jewish organizations approved a motion establishing the bureau and elected an eighteen-member board of directors. Almost all of the directors were representatives of the United Hebrew Relief, Jewish Old Folks' Home, and Jewish Orphanage.[156] Within months, however, the bureau faced a major challenge to its authority when the founders of the Mount Carmel Clinic refused to comply with its decision not to grant a permit to hold a fundraising drive to raise money to construct a new building.

For many members of the Jewish community, medical care was unaffordable. By 1912, three Yiddish-speaking physicians had established practices.[157] They charged modest fees; however, for poor Jewish families and numerous hard-pressed working-class families subsisting on as little as $600 a year, a charge of $1.50 for office visits was often beyond their means.[158] Instead, they sought medical assistance in hospital outpatient departments. Although the treatment was free, outpatient departments were overcrowded, and in addition to lengthy wait times Jews and other Eastern European immigrants not fluent in English frequently experienced difficulty describing their symptoms to physicians or understanding their instructions about treatment.[159] Many poor Jewish women took advantage of the nursing care provided by the Margaret Scott Nursing Mission. Established in 1904, the mission's trained nurses visited homes in low-income neighbourhoods in Central Winnipeg and the North End. Primarily concerned with the health of women and children, they offered pre- and postnatal care and advice on nutrition and hygiene.[160] However, even if they received medical attention, poor Jewish families were often unable to afford the medication prescribed. Out of desperation, some poor Jews visited the Presbyterian Church's Mission to the Jews. Although they were subjected to religious indoctrination to convert them to Christianity, the mission operated a free dispensary.[161]

Some mutual aid societies offered their members free medical care. Beginning in 1906, members of the Hebrew Sick Benefit Association—and subsequently members of at least three other mutual aid societies—could see a physician without charge.[162] However, since these societies depended on the regular payment of dues, poor Jews, the elderly, the disabled, the chronically ill, the unemployed, and women who were single parents of young children could not fulfill their membership responsibilities. In 1915, a report that increasing numbers of poor Jews were seeking medical assistance from the Presbyterian Church's Mission to the Jews led to the organization of the Winnipeg Hebrew Free Dispensary.[163] Located in a house at 326 Selkirk Avenue, one of the main thoroughfares of the North End, the dispensary opened on 2 May 1915. Open to all, "without any distinction of race, creed or color," the dispensary treated patients six mornings a week. It was staffed by a nurse, five physicians, and a dentist who volunteered their services. In addition to free medical care, the dispensary provided patients with medication without charge.[164] Between 10 May and 20 September that year, the dispensary treated 1,822 patients and filled 2,400 prescriptions.[165] Dependent on donations and a Women's Auxiliary that raised money by sponsoring teas and other fundraising events, the dispensary attempted, without success, to get a grant from Winnipeg City Council to pay for the drugs that it provided.[166]

Its founders hoped that the dispensary would lead to the establishment of a Jewish hospital. However, after three or four years, it ceased operations, and Jews who could not afford to pay for physicians' services were once again forced to turn to hospital outpatient departments for treatment.[167] In the early 1920s, the post–First World War revival of Jewish immigration contributed to a significant increase in the number of Jews treated in outpatient departments. In 1925, the *Israelite Press* noted that, though Jews comprised approximately 8 percent of the population of Winnipeg, 1,175 or 29 percent of the 4,058 patients treated in the outpatient department of the Winnipeg General Hospital in 1923 were Jewish. Similarly, though the vast majority of Winnipeg residents had been born in Great Britain, that year 832 Jewish children were treated in the outpatient department of the Winnipeg Children's Hospital compared with 981 children of British origin.[168] This disproportionate use of free hospital outpatient departments, the *Israelite Press* argued, led the public to believe that Jews were misusing publicly funded medical services. Jews, the newspaper reminded its readers, had a tradition of caring for the poor. It was not only a question of pride but also a means of self-defence; at a time when foreigners were viewed with suspicion, the enemies of immigration would use evidence of the overuse of public services to argue against allowing Jews to immigrate to Canada.[169] The solution was to establish a free medical clinic where Jews who could not afford to pay for the services of a physician or the medication that they needed would be treated by Jewish doctors and nurses fluent in Yiddish.

In February 1925, the Jewish Medical Society of Winnipeg elected a committee to investigate establishing a "hospital service for the Jewish Community."[170] Founded in October 1919, the society provided a forum for Jewish physicians to discuss medical issues as well as reach agreements on the delivery of professional services in the Jewish community.[171] Building upon a well-established practice of Jewish physicians volunteering their services at the Jewish Orphanage and the Winnipeg Hebrew Free Dispensary, the society decided to formalize the delivery of medical services in Jewish charitable institutions. In November 1919, members of the society agreed that "each and every doctor take charge" of providing medical care to the residents of the Jewish Old Folks' Home.[172] Through agreements with the Hebrew Sick Benefit Association and a number of other mutual aid societies, physicians who belonged to the society treated hundreds of members of the Jewish community free of charge. The decision to investigate setting up a Jewish hospital was an extension of the well-established principle that physicians had a responsibility to ensure that members of the Jewish community who could not afford to pay for their services had access to free health care provided by medical professionals fluent in Yiddish.

In May 1925, the Jewish Medical Society issued an invitation to attend a conference to discuss establishing a "Jewish Free Clinic."[173] Representatives of twenty-six "mutual aid societies, organizations and synagogues" were informed that physicians and pharmacists were prepared to volunteer their services, but $4,000 would be needed to equip the clinic, and once it opened it would cost $3,000 a year to operate.[174] Convinced that raising this amount was feasible, they elected an eighteen-member committee to make plans for a fundraising campaign. Despite widespread support for a clinic, the committee was slow to act. Frustrated with its lack of progress, in August 1925 the Hebrew Sick Benefit Association, the Austrian Hebrew Association, the Independent B'nay Abraham Sick Benefit and Free Loan Association, and the Independent Sick Benefit Association, together with eleven other Jewish organizations, held a meeting to take charge of the fundraising campaign for the clinic.[175] In addition to raising $1,850, attendees elected a campaign committee that launched a membership drive.[176] By November, canvassers had visited 1,200 homes, soliciting donations and enrolling 675 members who pledged to pay an annual membership fee of three dollars.[177] Encouraged by the amount that it raised in donations from individuals and mutual aid societies, as well as the revenue that its growing membership would generate, the campaign committee began preparations to open a clinic in early 1926.[178]

Aggrieved that the committee that they had helped to establish in May 1925 had been upstaged by a "new movement," in December 1925 a group of Jewish physicians and pharmacists, including members of the Jewish Medical Society, issued a public statement asserting that it was premature to open a clinic; not enough money had been raised, and it was bound to fail. Under the circumstances, they announced, they would not support the new clinic.[179] Undeterred, the campaign committee proceeded with its plans, and on 2 February 1926 the Mount Carmel Clinic began treating patients in a rented house at 263 Pritchard Avenue.[180]

22. Mount Carmel Clinic, Pritchard Avenue, 1929–1929.

The clinic consisted of a reception area, two examining rooms, and a pharmacy. Its mandate was to treat all members of the Jewish community who could not afford to pay for medical care. Assisted by a full-time nurse, eight physicians—including Oscar Margolese, a physician with twenty years of experience, and H. Herschman, who both belonged to the Jewish Medical Society, W. Heringer, and a number of recent graduates of the University of Manitoba's Faculty of Medicine—volunteered their services. Joseph Wilder, who persuaded the National Drug Company to donate a supply of medicine, and a team of seven pharmacists filled prescriptions free of charge. Within months of opening, the clinic also began to distribute free eyeglasses. In its first three and a half months, the clinic treated over 750 patients, including twenty-five in their homes. Committed to the "principle of free, friendly treatment without the taint of 'charity-giving,'" the clinic welcomed all patients "not in a position to pay for private medical attention."[181] Its founders quickly demonstrated that their critics had misjudged the willingness of members of the Jewish community to support a facility that provided free medical care; between September and March 1926, they raised nearly $6,000. The clinic was not only free of debt but also had a cash reserve of almost $1,000.[182]

The composition of the Mount Carmel Clinic's board of directors reflected its close relationship with the Jewish community's mutual aid societies. The clinic's mandate to provide free medical care was closely aligned with the societies' commitment to the principles of mutual aid. Leaders of the Hebrew Sick Benefit Association and a number of other mutual aid societies not only had been instrumental in establishing the committee that had founded the clinic but they also had drawn on their financial reserves to make donations and encouraged their members to participate in fundraising.[183] In addition to "other persons" who could be elected at annual general meetings, of the twenty-eight communal organizations entitled to appoint two delegates to the board of directors, twenty were mutual aid societies, and two were mutual aid society Ladies' Auxiliaries.[184] To broaden its support in the Jewish community, shortly after the clinic opened, a group of women who had founded the clinic established a Ladies' Auxiliary that organized annual tag days and other fundraising events.[185]

By the spring of 1926, the clinic's small staff of volunteer physicians began to experience difficulty coping with the steady stream of patients seeking treatment.[186] Sensing that numerous editorials, articles, and personal testimonials in the *Israelite Press* praising Mount Carmel and the dedication of its medical staff might have persuaded many of the physicians who had publicly refused to support plans to establish a clinic to reconsider, the clinic's founders took steps to persuade them to volunteer.[187] Dr. Oscar Margolese, a founding member of the Jewish Medical Society, was able to reassure his colleagues that the clinic was operating efficiently and providing high-quality medical care. In addition, physicians and pharmacists were guaranteed a role in management of the clinic. Its act of incorporation, given royal assent on 23 April 1926, stated that its medical staff were entitled to appoint three of the twelve members of the executive of the board of directors.[188] On 13 May, at the first annual meeting held after the act was passed, Dr. H.D. Isaacs became second vice-president, and Dr. M.S. Hollenberg and Joseph Wilder were elected to the executive. The board of directors released a detailed financial statement published in the *Israelite Press* and *Jewish Post*. The statement confirmed that the clinic had ample revenue from donations and was operating with a surplus.[189]

In June 1926, the *Israelite Press* reported that the board of directors of the Mount Carmel Clinic and the physicians and pharmacists who had opposed establishing a clinic had come to an understanding and were now prepared to pledge their support.[190] This reconciliation was timely, for the clinic needed additional medical staff to cope with a dramatic increase in patients. The clinic, which treated 1,915 patients in 1926, provided medical care to 3,336 or approximately 20 percent of the Jewish community in 1927. It also dispensed 3,500 prescriptions compared with 1,500 the year before.[191] It soon became apparent that the house that the clinic was renting could not accommodate such a large number of patients and that the medical staff needed more equipment. Conscious of the high cost of constructing a new building to provide a permanent home for the clinic, the board of directors adopted the expedient of renovating the rented house. In May 1928, it dutifully applied to the Jewish Charities Endorsation Bureau for a permit to launch a $10,000 fundraising campaign on 10 June to pay for renovations and purchase medical equipment.[192]

The members of the bureau unanimously agreed to approve the permit. However, shortly after its fundraising campaign began, the board of directors of the clinic decided to abandon its plan to renovate the house that it was renting and instead raise money to construct a modern medical facility. The board concluded that spending thousands of dollars on renovations to a rented house was a poor investment. A new building, with space for dental care, more examining rooms, a laboratory, an x-ray machine, and a room for minor surgery, would enable the medical staff to improve the quality and range of services provided. Although a new building would cost much more than $10,000, the board was encouraged by the success of the Jewish Orphanage's recent fundraising campaign to build an annex for infants. In March 1928, the Jewish Charities Endorsation Bureau had approved a request from the orphanage to raise $15,000, but its fundraising campaign had exceeded its goal by thousands of dollars.[193] Confident that it could raise enough money, the board of directors of the clinic decided to solicit donations to build a new clinic.

The decision to amend the fundraising campaign provoked a swift response from the bureau. It sent a letter to the clinic's board of directors requesting an explanation of why it had disregarded the conditions of its campaign permit. This led to a meeting between representatives of the clinic and the bureau to discuss how to resolve what appeared to be a breach of the bureau's policy on communal fundraising. They agreed that the clinic would submit a second application for a permit to raise money, one for a new building. However, when members of the bureau met to consider the clinic's application, they expressed concern that, based upon past experience, the Jewish community could not afford to establish an institution burdened by a large mortgage. Representatives of the clinic assured them that the "cost of [a] new building would not exceed $12,000" and that its board of directors would not sign a contract to begin construction until the full amount had been raised.[194] When members of the bureau expressed scepticism that a suitable building could be constructed for $12,000, the clinic's representatives agreed to submit architect's drawings and estimates from contractors to confirm that their plan was feasible.

The clinic subsequently commissioned Max Blankstein, a prominent Jewish architect, to prepare plans and received bids from two contractors. Representatives of the clinic presented the plans and two contractors' estimates, the first for $17,000 and the second for $19,000, at the bureau's next meeting. A number of members of the bureau "well versed in building matters" suggested that the cost of a "properly constructed building" built to the architect's specifications would be "far in excess" of $19,000. Together with the cost of equipment for the new clinic and operating funds of between $6,000 and $7,000, they argued, the Jewish community would be called on to contribute approximately $35,000.[195] If the campaign did not succeed in raising this amount, and doubts were expressed that it could, then the Jewish community would be forced to assume responsibility for a debt that it could not afford. Arguing that the bureau had been established to protect the Jewish community by "foreseeing and preventing just such mistakes," after a "full and thorough discussion" of the clinic's application, members of the bureau voted two in favour and fourteen against granting the clinic a permit for a building campaign.[196]

The clinic's board of directors was outraged by this decision. According to the *Jewish Post*, the board members had a persecution complex. They attributed the decision to "hostility, bias, prejudice, in fact everything except honest conviction," but the editor asserted that this claim was incorrect.[197] However, the board had some justification for questioning the bureau's neutrality. Twelve of the twenty-three members of the bureau were either current or past members of the boards of directors of the Jewish Orphanage and Jewish Old Folks' Home. M.J. Finkelstein, president of the bureau, was also president of the Jewish Orphanage and chairman of the Jewish Section of the Federated Budget Board campaign. Considering that the orphanage, which had accumulated an operating deficit of nearly $8,500, had a major stake in the success of the board's 1928 campaign, members of the clinic's board might reasonably have concluded that the bureau's decision to reject their application for a permit was based upon a desire to prevent its building campaign from competing with the Jewish Section's appeal for donations that would benefit the orphanage.[198] Furthermore, the bureau justified its decision not to give the clinic a permit by arguing that it had a responsibility to protect the Jewish community from being burdened with excessive debt. Given the size of the orphanage's deficit, the clinic's board undoubtedly wondered why in March 1928 the orphanage was given a permit to raise $15,000 whereas, a few months later, the debt-free clinic was turned down.

In September 1928, the board of directors of the Mount Carmel Clinic decided to withdraw from the Jewish Charities Endorsation Bureau. It applied to the city for a permit to construct a building valued at $18,000, appointed a campaign committee, and made plans to proceed with a fundraising drive. Reaction to its decision to defy the bureau was mixed. In a blistering editorial, the *Jewish Post* accused the board of "irresponsibility and selfishness." As a member of the bureau, the clinic had "pledged itself to obey its decisions, to respect its authority and to maintain its aims and objects." Accusing the clinic of a "breach of faith" with other Jewish organizations and institutions and the selfish pursuit of its own interests at their expense, the editorial called on the bureau to "conduct a vigorous publicity campaign" to educate the public. If members of the Jewish community fully understood the importance of the bureau's work overseeing communal fundraising, then they would understand that the clinic "was in the wrong" and refuse to donate money to its building campaign.[199]

Although the *Israelite Press* conceded that the bureau had a responsibility to reject applications for permits for fundraising not beneficial to the Jewish

23. Board of Directors, Mount Carmel Clinic, 1929.

community, it questioned whether it should prevent an institution such as the clinic, which had so many supporters, from raising money for a cause in which they believed. More attuned to the activities and views of members of the Hebrew Sick Benefit Association and the other mutual aid societies represented on the clinic's board of directors, the *Israelite Press* reminded the bureau that its influence depended on whether or not the public recognized its authority. The bureau, it warned, should be careful not to arouse the anger of the people against it.[200]

Neither the clinic's dispute with the Jewish Charities Endorsation Bureau nor the *Jewish Post*'s declaration that, "taking everything into consideration, it would be a good thing if the present campaign proved to be a failure" undermined its building campaign.[201] The 350 members of the clinic's Ladies' Auxiliary—which in 1927 had raised enough money to purchase a building lot on Selkirk Avenue East on the banks of the Red River—pledged to raise $3,000 and ultimately collected $3,150. Many of the Clinic's 1,600 members went door to door to solicit donations, and a number of mutual aid societies donated lump sums. The clinic's plan to build a Jewish hospital resonated with donors who had been forced to seek medical attention in the outpatient departments of the Winnipeg General and Children's Hospitals. Moreover, the clinic's policy of not distinguishing between poor and low-income, working-class Jews but providing free treatment to all patients who could not afford to pay for private medical care appealed to many donors. Although members of the Jewish community had generously supported the Jewish Old Folks' Home and Jewish Orphanage, institutions that served a relatively small number of vulnerable elderly and orphaned Jews, countless donors responded enthusiastically to the clinic's building campaign because they either numbered among its more than 3,000 patients or expected to seek treatment in the future. By 16 June 1929, when the clinic's board of directors invited members of the Jewish community to attend a ceremony laying the cornerstone of the new building, the campaign had achieved its objective.[202] Confounding critics, the clinic's campaign committee had raised enough money to complete construction of the new building without incurring a mortgage.[203]

24. Mount Carmel Clinic, 1929–1982.

The new Mount Carmel Clinic opened in the fall of 1929. Now that the building campaign was over, the board of directors reconsidered its decision to withdraw from the Jewish Charities Endorsation Bureau. Nothing would be gained by continuing to refuse to accept the authority of the bureau. Moreover, reinstatement would enable the clinic to apply for permits to raise money to cover its annual operating expenditures. Bureau approval could only enhance the clinic's legitimacy and contribute to the success of its fundraising. However, when the board petitioned the bureau for reinstatement, its members exacted a price: first, an admission by the board that the bureau "was right in refusing to issue a permit last year to the Clinic for its building campaign"; second, an acknowledgement that, without a permit, it was "impossible" for the clinic to "proceed with its proposed annual maintenance campaign."[204] Once the clinic's board confirmed that the bureau's decision to refuse to approve a permit for a building campaign had been justified and that submitting to its authority was crucial to the clinic's future financial viability, members of the bureau voted unanimously to reinstate the clinic. At its next meeting, the bureau approved the clinic's application for a permit for its annual fundraising campaign.

Although the new clinic was not the Jewish hospital that the founders and supporters of the Winnipeg Hebrew Free Dispensary had envisioned, it offered a broad range of medical services. Physicians had access to laboratory and x-ray facilities to assist them to diagnose patients. Volunteer pharmacists filled patients' prescriptions at the clinic's pharmacy. The clinic also provided physiotherapy and "electro-therapy" treatments.[205] In addition, it conducted eye examinations and supplied patients with eyeglasses. On the second floor, an eye, ear, and nose specialist performed tonsillectomies, and dentists provided basic dental care. Although the new clinic opened at the onset of the economic depression of the 1930s, it developed a successful strategy to raise operating funds. In addition to almost $1,200 in donations, the clinic's annual tag day and carnival yielded almost $4,500, 72 percent of its annual budget.[206] In addition, after two years of lobbying, the clinic's board of directors persuaded the provincial government in 1934 to provide an annual grant of $500.[207] The Mount Carmel Clinic became an indispensable part of the Jewish community. Serving nearly 20 percent of Winnipeg's Jews, the clinic provided free medical care to both poor and low-income patients, and this policy endeared it to donors who recognized that it was not so much a charity as an institution that embodied the principles of mutual aid that had inspired the formation of the Jewish community's fifty-six mutual aid societies.

The reinstatement of the Mount Carmel Clinic as a member of the Jewish Charities Endorsation Bureau was a turning point in the governance of the Jewish community's social welfare institutions. The founding and development of the Jewish Orphanage, Jewish Old Folks' Home, and Mount Carmel Clinic revealed that the provision of social welfare depended on the initiative of groups of volunteers, frequently women, who established organizations that raised money to open temporary facilities and then build permanent institutions. However, as the resolution of the conflict between two rival Jewish orphanages demonstrated, the Jewish community had little tolerance for self-appointed leaders who attempted to use their wealth to exercise control over communal decisions about social welfare. To succeed, the founders of the orphanage, home, and clinic understood that they had to adhere to clearly established democratic principles, most importantly that all interested members of the community had a right to participate in making decisions about the provision of social welfare.

Whether elected to boards, general members or members of Ladies' Auxiliaries, participants at annual meetings, or donors, supporters of the United Hebrew Relief, Jewish Orphanage, Jewish Old Folks' Home, and Mount Carmel Clinic became part of distinct social networks. Intensely loyal to and protective of the interests of their organization or institution, they jealously guarded their autonomy. Although the commitment of supporters enabled each organization or institution to overcome obstacles and become a vital component of the Jewish community's social welfare system, it inhibited the formation of an overarching communal body with the authority to regulate fundraising. Proclaimed as a solution to the problem of endless rounds of competing fundraising campaigns and a means of providing the United Hebrew Relief, the Jewish Orphanage, and the Jewish Old Folk's Home with stable funding, participation in the annual campaigns of the Federated Budget Board quickly proved to be disappointing. In addition to making contributions to the campaigns, members of the Jewish community were asked to compensate for decreases in allocations to the relief agency, orphanage, and home. And, in 1925, when the board excluded the United Hebrew Relief from the annual campaign, the Jewish community was once again called on to donate money to fund all of the organization's expenses.

Determined not to sever their relationship with the British Canadian community by withdrawing the Jewish Orphanage and Jewish Old Folks' Home from the annual campaigns of the Federated Budget Board, supporters proposed a hybrid solution: continuing to participate in the city-wide campaign and reverting to a measure of communal autonomy by establishing a new organization, the Jewish Charities Endorsation Bureau, to regulate all other fundraising in the Jewish community. Although it demonstrated its effectiveness by regulating campaigns to raise money for operating expenses and, in the case of the orphanage, fundraising to build an annex, its decision to refuse to grant the Mount Carmel Clinic a permit for a building campaign undermined its authority. This decision was widely perceived as an attempt to sacrifice a popular initiative—building a new clinic to provide free medical care to more than 3,000 members of the Jewish community, for the most part residents of the North End—in order to protect previously established organizations and institutions. Defying the bureau, in what amounted to a public endorsement of its right to raise money to build a new clinic, the board of directors of Mount Carmel Clinic organized a highly successful building campaign.

Competition for donations did not end with the reinstatement of the clinic. However, with all four of the Jewish community's social welfare organizations and institutions as members, the Jewish Charities Endorsation Bureau had the authority to coordinate communal fundraising in order to stagger the timing of campaigns and prevent conflicts. Coordinating communal fundraising became increasingly important as the economic depression of the 1930s worsened and as contributions to the Federated Budget Board's annual campaigns decreased. In 1935–36, the annual campaign, now called the Winnipeg Community Chest, collected $256,409—compared with $325,859 in 1929–30—of which $238,755 was distributed to member organizations and institutions.[208] Allocations to the Jewish Old Folks' Home and Jewish Orphanage, which received $25,143 in 1929–30, dropped to $12,000.[209] Consequently, the relief agency, orphanage, home, and clinic depended more than ever on maintaining the loyalty of their supporters to survive. However, with widespread unemployment, individual Jewish donors and mutual aid societies were hard pressed to make donations. Increasingly, through the bureau, the leaders of the Jewish community's organizations and institutions that depended on public appeals for donations reached an understanding: although cooperation compromised their autonomy, it was mutually advantageous. In 1938, in what the *Jewish Post* proclaimed was the "dawn of a new era" in communal governance, the Jewish Charities Endorsation Bureau was transformed into the Jewish Welfare Fund.[210] After more than twenty-five years of competition for donor support, the leaders of the relief agency, orphanage, home, and clinic agreed to participate in a unified annual campaign.[211] Out of necessity, a system of social welfare created and sustained by thousands of volunteers and donors who shared a commitment to the well-being of vulnerable members of the Jewish community but were often divided by their loyalty to different organizations and institutions came under the authority of one communal body. The Jewish Welfare Fund ushered in a new era; however, as its mandate evolved from control over funding to centralized planning of social services, it displaced the social activism and widespread mobilization of support for the provision of social welfare that had defined communal solidarity throughout a formative period in the development of Winnipeg's Jewish community.

CHAPTER 7

"Opening the Door": The Western Division of the Jewish Immigrant Aid Society

After the First World War, the first priority of the Canadian government's immigration policy was to attract immigrants from Great Britain. However, the resumption of passenger ship service from Europe to Canada raised concerns about an influx of immigrants from Eastern Europe. In 1920, William Cory, acting deputy minister of immigration and colonization, instructed Frederick Blair, the department's secretary, to monitor the number of "aliens," immigrants from European countries, arriving in Canada. Blair's report revealed that in 1920 immigration from preferred European countries—Belgium, France, Holland and Scandinavia—had increased from 2,232 to 3,703, an increase of 66 percent. But it also revealed a surge of immigration from Poland, Romania, and Russia, from 95 to 4,494.[1] For both Cory and Blair, of particular concern was the small but increasing number of Jews arriving from Eastern Europe.

Fleeing the Polish-Russian war, pogroms, and widespread famine, Jewish refugees from Ukraine, Belorussia, and Poland—many with the assistance of husbands or relatives in Canada who sent money or prepaid railway and steamship tickets—travelled to Antwerp and Le Havre. Determined to stem what Cory and Blair believed was the beginning of a large influx of Jews "whose coming is regarded more in the light of a catastrophe than anything else," immigration officers were instructed to rigorously apply the department's "continuous journey" regulation to detain Jewish immigrants arriving on the next steamship.[2]

The application of PC 23, the continuous journey regulation, which had never been applied to Europeans, was quickly followed by PC 918, which demanded that all non-British immigrants have a passport—a regulation that had rarely been applied before the First World War—and the strict application of PC 924, which required that all immigrants possess a minimum of twenty-five dollars.[3] By December 1920, immigration officials had detained 650 Jews, more than half of the 1,210 Jewish immigrants who arrived from Eastern Europe between April and November 1920.[4] These restrictive measures were the first of repeated attempts throughout the 1920s to restrict Jewish immigration to Canada. Unlike the pre–First World War period, when Jewish immigrants seeking admission into Canada faced few government restrictions, successive ministers responsible for immigration, who either shared the anti-Semitic views of senior officials such as Cory and Blair or found it expedient to allow them to effectively take control of the implementation of immigration policy, sanctioned changes in regulations or administrative directives designed to prevent Jews from settling in Canada. That Canada admitted 41,800 Jews between 1920 and 1931 was largely because the newly formed Jewish Immigrant Aid Society (JIAS) persistently lobbied both ministers responsible for immigration and their officials to negotiate concessions that permitted categories of Jewish immigrants to settle in Canada that the government was determined to exclude.[5]

Mobilizing the Jewish Community to "Open the Door"

The detentions shocked and alarmed Jews across Canada. Throughout the fall of 1920, the Montreal-based JIAS appealed detention orders. Most of the Jewish immigrants who could prove that they were joining husbands, fathers, or close relatives legally resident in Canada were ultimately admitted. However, department officials were determined to bar the entry of young Jewish men without relatives in Canada who had been detained because they did not possess twenty-five dollars upon arrival. Although the association offered to post bonds to guarantee that they would not become "public charges," sureties that immigration officials had often accepted prior to 1914, department boards of inquiry rejected their appeals and issued orders for their deportation on the first available Canadian Pacific Ocean Services steamship returning to Antwerp. In November 1920, the department deported thirty-five Jewish detainees followed days later by a second group of twenty-six.[6]

For the executive of Winnipeg's Hebrew Immigrant Aid Society, news of the deportations "came like a thunderbolt clear from the sky."[7] Having been informed that all of the detainees with relatives in western Canada had been released, members of the executive had been hopeful that further appeals would secure the freedom of the rest of the detainees. Advised that a delegation composed of representatives of the Canadian Jewish Congress and the Jewish Immigrant Aid Society had arranged a meeting with Minister of Immigration and Colonization James A. Calder to request a suspension of deportations, the executive of the Hebrew Immigrant Aid Society struck a committee to call on Jewish communities throughout western Canada to send telegrams to Calder appealing for the release of the detainees.[8] By 10 December 1920, twenty-four communities had sent telegrams.[9] Writing on behalf of the "Jewish Citizens of Winnipeg," S. Hart Green urged the minister of immigration and colonization to allow the detainees to remain in Canada: "To Deport These Immigrants Back To The Horrors From Which They Have Escaped Would Be A Crime Against Humanity."[10] Ultimately, the JIAS secured the release of 1,306 of the 1,788 Jewish immigrants detained, and 232 were deported.[11]

The vast majority of Winnipeg's adult Jews were recent immigrants. Narratives of making the difficult decision to emigrate; leaving behind elderly parents, siblings, relatives, and friends; shared experiences of encounters with unscrupulous middlemen who preyed on immigrants; coping with numerous obstacles that impeded the journey; and the sheer exhaustion of travelling for weeks before reaching Winnipeg were integral parts of family life. These narratives were not simply memories to be shared with children and friends. Through exchanges of letters and messages carried by *landslayt*, friends and acquaintances who had immigrated to Canada, Winnipeg's Jews maintained close ties with their hometowns in Eastern Europe. Many members of Winnipeg's Jewish community had made it possible for members of their families to join them in Winnipeg, were in the process of making arrangements to send tickets or money to Eastern Europe, or were planning to do so. Consequently, discussions of immigration issues, how to assist immigrants to come to Canada, whether the Canadian government's immigration policy impeded the admission of Jews, and which forms of support they needed to begin new lives in Winnipeg were ongoing parts of family and communal life.

Winnipeg's Hebrew Immigrant Aid Society

Responding to a surge in the number of Jewish immigrants arriving in Winnipeg, in 1912 a group of communal activists founded the Hebrew Immigrant Aid Society.[12] Initially, the society focused on raising money to provide short-term assistance to immigrants until they found employment. When unemployment increased in 1913–14, the society opened a *folkskich* ("public kitchen") on Selkirk Avenue, a dining room that offered meals at very low prices. Over a thirteen-month period, the *folkskich* served 42,000 meals.[13] To assist immigrants to find employment, in 1915 the society established an employment bureau and encouraged immigrants to settle on one of western Canada's Jewish agricultural colonies. In addition, it established committees to help immigrants learn English, assist women to find employment, and arrange accommodation.[14]

Although it was focused on the well-being of Jews who arrived in Winnipeg, the Hebrew Immigrant Aid Society was also concerned with the Canadian government's immigration policy, particularly measures that could restrict Jewish immigration. In 1913, the society sent a petition to the minister of the interior requesting the reduction or abolition of the twenty-five dollars that each immigrant was required to possess to be admitted into Canada.[15] The outbreak of the First World War and the resulting rapid decline in transatlantic migration temporarily diverted the society's attention from the government's immigration policy. Anticipating that the war would end within twelve to eighteen months, in March 1915 the executive of the society held a meeting to enhance its organizational capacity. Based upon prewar levels of Jewish immigration, the executive expected that once immigration resumed a large number of Jews would come to Canada. Its members elected a five-person executive and expanded the board of directors to twenty-three. Adopting the name Hebrew Immigrant Aid Society of Canada, the executive mandated its vice-president, Herman (Chaim) Saltzman, to recruit members throughout western Canada. Travelling from Port Arthur and Fort William in western Ontario to Vancouver, within a year Saltzman established fifteen branches that recruited 770 members. He also increased the society's membership in Winnipeg to 585.[16] To consolidate its support in Winnipeg's Jewish community, in April 1915 Ben Sheps, president of the society, invited mutual aid societies, clubs, and other communal organizations to appoint two delegates each to attend conferences to discuss immigration issues.[17]

However, as the war continued, providing relief to Jews in Eastern Europe became a more pressing issue than immigration. Although the Hebrew Immigrant Aid Society of Canada continued to function, raising money to assist war sufferers absorbed most of the time and energy of communal activists in Winnipeg and throughout western Canada. Many communal leaders believed that it was essential to support both organizations, that relieving the distress of Jews in Eastern Europe was an urgent priority, but that when the war finally ended immigration would resume, and a strong organization would be needed to ensure that Jewish immigrants would be admitted into Canada and given assistance on arrival. By 1917, Marcus Hyman, secretary of the Hebrew Immigrant Aid Society of Canada, became chairman of Western Canada's Jewish Fund for the Relief of War Sufferers, and E.A. Cohen served as a board member of both the society and the fund. Within two years, Hyman and seven of the members of the board of directors of the society were simultaneously members of the executive committee of the fund.[18]

25. Ben Sheps, President of the Hebrew Immigrant Aid Society of Canada and President and Vice-President of the Western Division of the Jewish Immigrant Aid Society of Canada.

Between 1912 and 1920, leaders of the Hebrew Immigrant Aid Society of Canada were drawn exclusively from the North End. Wary of an organization whose president, Ben Sheps, was a Labour Zionist and whose vice-president, Herman (Chaim) Saltzman, was a socialist, prominent "South Enders" such as Max Steinkopf, David Balcovske, Bernard Shragge, and A.H. Aronovitch, who had assumed leadership roles in establishing the United Hebrew Charities and Jewish Orphanage, did not actively support the society.[19] One important exception was M.J. Finkelstein, who provided the society with legal advice. In January 1914, he drafted a letter on behalf of the society expressing concern that immigration department officials were planning to apply PC 918, a regulation requiring that all immigrants produce a passport, to Jews. The letter, which explained in detail why Russian Jews were unable to obtain passports, emphasized that application of the regulation would exclude about "ninety per cent of the Jewish immigrants who leave Russia for the purpose of seeking a new home where they can live under a flag of freedom." Sent to Jewish communities in Montreal, Toronto, and other large cities, the letter was intended to mobilize support for "prompt, energetic and united action" to make the federal government aware of the injustice of the regulation.[20]

In 1916, Finkelstein was nominated to serve as president of the society but declined because of other commitments.[21] However, in August 1916, Finkelstein and Sheps collaborated to organize the Western Jewish Conference. Held in Winnipeg, the conference was intended to promote the establishment of a Canadian Jewish Congress, a nation-wide assembly that would further the goal of a Jewish homeland in Palestine, support efforts to raise money for the relief of war sufferers, and make plans to prepare for postwar Jewish immigration.[22] Their collaboration continued at the founding convention of the congress, held in March 1919 in Montreal. Finkelstein and Sheps were elected to serve on the national executive as representatives of Winnipeg's Jewish community: Finkelstein was elected as one of the three vice-presidents, and Sheps was elected as one of the three secretaries.[23] In addition to the future of Palestine, which delegates debated at length, immigration emerged as the most important issue facing Canadian Jews. At the urging of S.W. Jacobs, MP, delegates passed a resolution in favour of "an open door for all immigrants." The resolution instructed the executive to establish a national organization with branches in all cities and ports of entry to assist Jewish immigrants.[24]

The Western Division of the Jewish Immigrant Aid Society

The founding convention of the congress was a resounding success, but delegates neglected to provide the new organization with the financial support that its executive needed to establish a national office and hire staff to implement its agenda. Consequently, more than a year passed before an interim executive was finally elected, in June 1920.[25] Elected general secretary, H.M. Caiserman, who also served as general secretary of the Canadian Jewish Congress, immediately sent a letter to branches of the congress throughout Canada urging them to begin raising money to support the JIAS.

The Canadian Jewish Congress resolution on immigration and its sponsorship of the JIAS were clear statements that immigration issues were vital to all Canadian Jews and comprised an unmistakable call for all supporters of the congress to work on behalf of the new organization. In Winnipeg, Sheps began the process of reconstituting the near-dormant Hebrew Immigrant Aid Society as the Western Division of JIAS (WDJIAS). M.J. Finkelstein together with Sheps and a number of other former members of the executive and board of directors of the Hebrew Immigrant Aid Society—Marcus Hyman, Morris Triller, Max Mains, William Keller, Joseph A. Cherniack, Fania Cherniack, Isaac Ludwig, and Mark Shinbane—became founding members of the new organization. Finkelstein as well as Sheps, Hyman, Triller, and Cherniack had been delegates to the founding convention of the Canadian Jewish Congress. They were joined by three other delegates: Myer Averbach, Joseph Hestrin, and Sam Green. With the exception of Finkelstein (a General Zionist) and

Triller (non-aligned), all six of the former delegates who became founding members of the WDJIAS were either socialists or members of Poale Zion. Despite the Canadian Jewish Congress's endorsation and promotion of the JIAS, unlike M.J. Finkelstein, Max Steinkopf, Hiram Weidman, H.E. Wilder, and three other General Zionists who served as delegates did not respond to Caiserman's appeal.[26]

Although the detention of Jewish immigrants had generated widespread concern about the future of Jewish immigration, the founding members of the WDJIAS faced a difficult task. In the summer of 1920, communal activists were still preoccupied with raising money for Western Canada's Jewish Fund for the Relief of War Sufferers. Many of the founding members of the WDJIAS—Ben Sheps, Joseph A. Cherniack, Fania Cherniack, Marcus Hyman, Isadore Hurwitz, Israel Rusen, M. Abraham, and Max Mains—were serving as members of the executive of the fund. Marcus Hyman, chairman of the fund, and Max Mains, its general secretary, were immersed in plans to hold a fundraising campaign, the second campaign of the year, to bring Ukrainian Jewish orphans to Canada.[27] Undaunted, the founding members of the WDJIAS elected Sheps as president of an interim executive that launched a membership drive in Winnipeg and sent invitations to Jewish communities throughout Saskatchewan and Alberta to send representatives to a conference in Saskatoon. Held on 29 August 1920, the conference focused on plans to establish branches of the JIAS throughout western Canada. To support the efforts of communal activists in Jewish communities throughout western Canada to establish branches, Sheps recruited ten volunteers in Winnipeg to speak at public meetings. Within weeks, branches were established in Calgary, Medicine Hat, Brandon, and Fort William.[28]

A month later Sheps was able to report that "the people are very much aroused": 300 members who paid membership fees of five dollars had been recruited in Winnipeg, and a "Monster Mass Meeting" to be addressed by Dr. Korolnick, a speaker from New York, was planned for 20 October 1920, at which "we hope to make a large collection."[29] Sheps also reported that members of the executive were "interviewing every organization in our city, to get pledges from them" and enrol their members.[30] To boost the recruitment of members, Sheps requested that, whenever a passenger ship arrived, Caiserman instruct JIAS's office in Quebec City to send him a list of Jewish immigrants bound for western Canada: "Your office wired to Winnipeg about the arrival of relatives, and the said family . . . made forty members for our society in two days."[31] He also requested that Caiserman send copies of minutes of meetings of the national executive to every branch "as this will prove to the people of Western Canada that you are doing some active work" and demonstrate the importance of raising money.[32] Expressing the view of the interim executive that "immigration assistance is much more constructive relief than sending money to Europe at present," Sheps urged the national executive to recommend an amalgamation of JIAS and the Associated Jewish War Relief Societies of Canada. Arguing that "the feeling in Western Canada is very much in favour of the said amalgamation," he emphasized that "it would save a lot of expenses, and it would increase our army of workers."[33]

With a growing membership and new branches opening throughout western Canada, by December 1920 the transformation of the Hebrew Immigrant Aid Society into the WDJIAS was nearly complete. On 5 December 1920, the interim executive convened a general meeting of its members that confirmed Sheps as president and elected an executive and board of directors.[34] Although they had been preoccupied with organizational work and fundraising, the leaders of the WDJIAS also began to define how the society could effectively represent the interests and concerns of its members. In October and November 1920, they submitted a series of proposals to the national executive; they included suggestions that it open an office in Ottawa to deal with immigration appeals, investigate the possibility of establishing a new agricultural colony in western Canada for Jewish immigrants, and create a link with the Warsaw office of the New York–based Hebrew Immigrant Aid Society (HIAS) so that Canadian Jews could communicate directly by telegram with their relatives in Eastern Europe.[35] The WDJIAS also began to provide services that became vital to its members, pressing the national office of the JIAS to take prompt action to secure the release of members' relatives who had been detained by immigration officials and aiding members who needed information and assistance to bring their relatives to Canada.[36] When Jewish immigrants arrived in Winnipeg, representatives of the WDJIAS met them at the train station and either helped them to find their relatives or assisted them with accommodations and meals until they could find employment.[37] Finally, the WDJIAS used whatever political influence it could deploy to persuade the government to remove obstacles to Jewish immigration.

However, attempts by the JIAS to persuade the Canadian government to adopt an "open door for all immigrants" policy coincided with an upsurge of anti-foreigner sentiment. The government's portrayal of immigrants from Eastern Europe as enemy aliens during the First World War intensified British Canadian prejudices against foreign-born immigrants. As strikes and lockouts escalated throughout the war, from sixty-three in 1914 to 336 in 1919, the government attributed rising labour militancy to the influence of socialist agitators exploiting growing dissatisfaction with wages and working conditions to foment unrest among foreign-born workers; the socialists' goal was to enlist them in revolutionary activity to seize power and abolish capitalism.[38]

Fears of revolutionary activity among immigrants from Eastern Europe escalated during the 1919 Winnipeg General Strike. The Royal North West Mounted Police (RNWMP) concluded that Jewish socialists posed a singular threat to national security. Although the majority of the workers who supported the strike were British Canadian, aside from six British Canadian members of the strike committee, the only supporters of the strike whom RNWMP officers singled out for arrest were four "foreigners," including three Jews—Michael Charitonoff, Samuel Blumenberg, and Shloime (Solomon) Almazoff.[39] According to the RNWMP, Jewish support for the strike extended far beyond the activities of a few Jewish radicals: "The Jewish element of Winnipeg are taking a very active interest in the strike, even those who have nothing in common with the labour movement are devoting their time to augmenting this movement."[40]

Preoccupied with the threat of foreign radicals, James Calder and his fellow cabinet ministers approved amendments to the Immigration and Naturalization Acts to broaden the government's powers of deportation, but they recognized that deporting dangerous foreigners was not sufficient; the only way to limit the importation of radical ideas was to restrict the immigration of Southern and Eastern Europeans.[41] Amendments to the Immigration Act enacted in June 1919 included provisions that empowered cabinet to prohibit or limit the admission of "immigrants belonging to any nationality or race."[42]

Although these amendments to the Immigration Act gave the government sweeping powers to bar the admission of Jews and other immigrants from Europe whom it considered undesirable based upon their nationality or race, Calder proceeded cautiously. He and other members of the cabinet were acutely aware that the unpopular Union government could not afford to alienate thousands of voters by implementing a regulation specifically barring Jews or other Eastern European immigrants. Alarmed as he was by RCMP reports "that a number of Jews are holding meetings in the North End of Winnipeg almost every second day" to collect money to be "forwarded to Russia and Poland for the purpose of bringing all the poor Jews" to Canada, even Frederick Blair, a determined opponent of Jewish immigration, was aware of the political realities.[43] If it were not for the large number of Jews with relatives living in Eastern Europe, he explained, "it is quite possible that the bars would be put up and these people would be excluded altogether."[44]

In his official declarations, Calder was careful to reassure the Jewish community that the immigration department did not view "Jewish immigration as undesirable." Immigration law and regulations, he declared, "are being applied to all people irrespective of nationality, race or creed. Jews are in no sense discriminated against."[45] However, whereas immigration officials had instructions to exercise discretion when applying regulations concerning continuous journeys and passports to preferred immigrants from Scandinavia, Holland, Belgium, France, and Switzerland, they were told to apply rigorously the same regulations to detain and deport Jews.[46] But detentions and deportations were last resorts; the government's goal was to discourage Jews from embarking from European ports by impressing on steamship companies the importance of making prospective immigrants aware that immigration officers were under strict instructions to enforce continuous journey and passport regulations. Blair took pains to emphasize that, since Canada did not recognize the communist government of the Soviet Union, officials would not accept passports it issued and refugees who did manage to obtain identity papers from the Latvian or Lithuanian government or the government of any other country that allowed them to stay as temporary residents were inadmissible because they could not comply with the continuous journey regulation.[47] To ensure that the department was able to monitor effectively the flow of Jewish immigration to Canada, Blair instructed immigration officials at ocean ports to "add the word 'Jew'" in conjunction with "Polish, Russian etc." in the column on ships' landing manifests identifying the immigrant's race.[48]

Having armed immigration officers with the continuous journey, passport, and beginning in November 1920 a series of regulations increasing the landing amount to $250, Calder, Cory, and Blair were confident that the department's restrictive measures would contain the flow of Jewish immigrants from Eastern Europe.[49] However, they had underestimated the desperation of thousands of Jews living in Eastern Europe and the determination of their relatives and friends in Canada to assist them to find a safe haven in Canada. Appointed in 1920 by Western Canada's Jewish Fund for the Relief of War Sufferers, Chaim Saltzman, accompanied by Simon Belkin, a representative of the Canadian Alliance of Ukrainian Jews, travelled to the Soviet Union to supervise the distribution of aid and persuade government officials to permit

Jews to emigrate.[50] They carried 3,000 letters from Canadian Jews, including many from Winnipeg, that were distributed throughout Ukraine offering to assist their relatives and friends to emigrate.

On their return to Canada, Saltzman and Belkin addressed public meetings, informing Canadian Jews of the plight of Jews in Ukraine. At a meeting held in Winnipeg in August 1921 attended by more than 1,000, Belkin reported that pogroms had displaced thousands of Jews who were living in overcrowded cities with little hope of getting the medical attention, shelter, or food that they desperately needed.[51] Throughout 1921, thousands of Jewish refugees fled Russia, making their way to Warsaw or Bucharest, where they could collect money sent from Canada to offices of the New York–based Hebrew Immigrant Aid Society that could be used to purchase railway and steamship tickets or pick up from steamship company agents prepaid tickets sent by relatives and friends.[52]

Although the immigration department had strict rules preventing Canadian residents from giving money to immigrants arriving in Canada to enable them to show that they had $250, for a small fee they could circumvent this restriction by transferring funds through the HIAS to friends and relatives in Eastern Europe. The immigration department was also stymied by changes in the political landscape of Eastern Europe. On arriving in Bucharest, Jewish refugees who crossed the border between Ukraine and Romania illegally discovered that the Russian consul who had been appointed by the tsarist government before the revolution was willing to provide them with the passports that they needed to enter Canada.[53] Similarly, under the Treaty of Riga between Poland and the Soviet Union negotiated in October 1920, large swaths of western Belorussia and Ukraine became Polish territory; as a result, hundreds of thousands of Russian Jews became eligible for Polish citizenship. In Warsaw, the HIAS handled Polish passport applications for Jewish emigrants, and many of the thousands of Jews waiting in Antwerp and Rotterdam for passage to Canada were able to obtain passports from Polish consulates.[54]

In Winnipeg, the executive of the WDJIAS was unwilling to accept that the government's widely publicized policy of encouraging agriculturalists to settle in Canada enabled Poles, Ukrainians, and Russians to enter Canada but excluded Jews. In February 1921, Ben Sheps invited delegates from Jewish communities in western Canada to attend a conference in Saskatoon. Included among the forty delegates were representatives of twelve Jewish agricultural colonies. The primary purpose of the conference was to discuss creating employment opportunities for Jewish immigrants from Eastern Europe. In an address to the delegates, Yiddish journalist Vladimir Grossman urged them to devise means to place Jewish immigrants on existing farms and assist them to organize new agricultural colonies.[55] On behalf of 400 Jewish farmers, the delegates passed a resolution that Sheps sent to Prime Minister Arthur Meighen. Emphasizing that Canada had "vast possibilities for colonization" and needed agriculturalists, the delegates pointed to the success of western Canada's 400 Jewish farmers who had transformed wilderness into "splendid farming settlements."[56] They appealed to the prime minister to remove obstacles to the immigration of Jews from Eastern Europe, "where life is a terror for them and they must . . . by necessity flee from those countries where they were born and brought up, but which afford them no protection."[57]

The resolution was referred to Blair, the department's expert on Jewish immigration, for comment. In a memorandum prepared for Cory, Blair reviewed the results of the department's recent survey of eighteen Jewish agricultural colonies that had been established in western Canada.[58] Although the acreage under cultivation had doubled, in his report Blair chose to emphasize that the number of Jewish farmers on the five largest colonies had declined from 239 in 1910 to 201 in 1920.[59] He concluded that, given the poor record of the Jewish agricultural colonies, the department should not encourage "the movement of Jewish people from Europe to Canada in the hope that they will settle and stay on the land."[60]

However, the government's restrictive measures did little to stem the flow of Jewish immigrants to Canada. As soon as the transatlantic shipping season opened, the immigration of Jews from Eastern Europe to Canada soared. A total of 1,393 Jews arrived in February and March 1921—over twice the number who had arrived in the previous ten months—and the number steadily increased throughout the spring, summer, and fall. By 31 December 1921, Jewish immigration totalled 7,255, compared with 1,438 for the same period in 1920.[61] Blair's short-term solution to the escalation of Jewish immigration was to order the rigorous enforcement of the department's continuous journey, $250 landing amount, and passport regulations. Between May and November 1921, immigration officers detained close to 1,800 Jewish immigrants arriving in Canada. Nearly 1,000 were detained either because they had been delayed in Antwerp waiting for their ship to sail or for money to arrive from Canada, and therefore were deemed to have interrupted their journey, or because they had not travelled by a continuous journey from Russia. Many of those in compliance with the continuous journey regulation were detained because they did not have enough money.[62] Blair also found a way to invalidate passports issued by the Polish government, its consuls, or the Russian consul in Bucharest. In July 1921, cabinet approved an order-in-council requiring that all passports include a visa issued by a British diplomatic or consular official, a measure that invalidated the passports of hundreds of Jewish immigrants in transit.[63] Although the department had assured the JIAS that the new regulation would not apply to immigrants who began their journeys before 15 August 1921, officials began detaining Jewish immigrants in early September.[64]

By 1921, the JIAS was better prepared to deal with large-scale detentions. Bolstered by over $40,000 in membership dues and donations—including $1,300 from Winnipeg—and close to $35,000 in grants from the Jewish Colonization Association as well as the Hebrew Immigrant Aid Society and the Joint Distribution Committee, the JIAS had the financial resources to pay daily maintenance fees that the government charged for immigrants held in detention, legal fees, and medical expenses and to post bonds to secure the release of immigrants who did not have $250 on landing or were in transit to the United States.[65] Over a seven-month period beginning in October 1921, the Ottawa Bureau of the JIAS dealt with 436 appeals of Board of Inquiry deportation orders involving 1,271 Jewish immigrants. Except for eleven cases, all of its appeals were successful, resulting in the release of 1,247 detainees.[66]

Fortunately the detentions coincided with an impending federal election, and the JIAS recognized that the government was politically vulnerable. C.C. Ballantyne, the minister of marine and fisheries, campaigning for re-election in a Montreal constituency with a large Jewish population, informed Prime Minister Meighen that "my life has been made almost unbearable by prominent Jewish citizens in my division asking me to use whatever influence I may possess with the Minister of Immigration to have some of these jewish [*sic*] immigrants admitted." Ballantyne quickly received assurances that "all cases coming from his electoral district are being considered in the most generous and favourable light possible."[67] The detentions were not simply a political liability in Montreal; they also became an issue in constituencies with large numbers of Jewish voters in central Toronto and North End Winnipeg.[68] In December 1921, days before the election, the minister of immigration and colonization issued an order to release 300 Jewish detainees.[69] Ultimately, of the 1,874 Jewish immigrants detained, only 218 were deported.[70]

The surge in Jewish immigration in 1921—an increase of over 400 percent—and the success of the JIAS in appealing deportation rulings based upon the very regulations enacted to restrict Jewish admission angered Blair. He made his views clear in a response that he was asked to prepare to a letter from "four prominent Jewish citizens" forwarded by Edmund Bristol, a cabinet minister who represented a Toronto constituency with a large number of Jewish voters. Referring to the humanitarian crisis unfolding in Poland, the letter pointed out that Jewish refugees found it impossible to comply with the department's passport and continuous journey regulations, and Blair vented his frustration to the deputy minister: "The enclosure to Mr. Bristol's letter is one of the documents that makes my blood warm even in cold weather. It is the same old story of Jewish attempts to maintain their position that they must have special treatment on the ground of 'terrible atrocities, etc.'" Their intent, he concluded, was to make Canada "a refuge for the several hundred thousand Jewish refugees and others in and about Poland."[71]

The WDJIAS hoped that the election of a Liberal government in December 1921 would lead to a liberalization of immigration policy. In January 1922, a "mass meeting" of the association addressed by E.J. McMurray, the newly elected Liberal MP for North Winnipeg, passed a resolution addressed to Prime Minister W.L. Mackenzie King reminding him that the government of Sir Wilfrid Laurier had carried out a "broadminded immigration policy [that] created a period of splendid prosperity in our country." The WDJIAS called on the prime minister to re-establish a "sane, liberal, progressive immigration policy" by cancelling regulations that prevented the admission of Jewish immigrants who did not possess $250 but whose relatives were prepared to post bonds guaranteeing that they would not become public charges.[72] King, however, did not consider immigration policy a priority. Although his cabinet was sworn in on 29 December 1921, the post of minister of immigration and colonization was either left vacant or filled on a temporary basis by Senator Hewitt Blostock until 20 February 1922, when Charles Stewart was appointed acting minister.[73] Finkelstein, who believed that department officials W.J. Black, Frederick Blair, and W.D. Little were anti-Semites, had hoped that the election of a Liberal government would lead to their replacement.[74] However, they not only kept their positions but also increased their influence over immigration policy.

In early 1922, Blair pondered how to increase the flow of immigrants from Great Britain and preferred countries while simultaneously preventing as many Jews as possible from arriving in Canada. His dilemma was that the JIAS had considerable success securing the release of Jewish immigrants who had been detained for violation of the continuous journey and passport regulations, and their relatives found ways to send them the $250 that they needed to show immigration officers when they arrived in Canada. The solution was to prevent Jewish immigrants from leaving Europe. Although the immigration department had stationed officers in Antwerp and Le Havre, they were not empowered to deny immigrants the right to enter Canada.

In May 1922, Blair finalized a strategy to both increase immigration and reduce the number of Jewish immigrants embarking from Europe. Within weeks of Stewart's appointment, Blair secured his approval of two new regulations. PC 1041 stipulated that all immigrants arriving from Europe possess a passport stamped with a visa issued by a Canadian immigration officer stationed in Europe.[75] PC 717 cancelled the requirement that immigrants possess $250 on landing but limited immigration from Europe to "bona fide" male agriculturalists with sufficient means to begin farming, farm labourers with a reasonable prospect of employment, and female domestic servants. PC 717 also restricted the admission of family members to wives and children; brothers, sisters, parents, and minors joining a married or unmarried sister were no longer admissible.[76] In effect, the regulations opened the door to an increase in immigration from Great Britain and the United States but restricted the entry of immigrants from Europe by imposing an occupation test and limiting family sponsorship to wives and minor children.

In practice, the immigration officers whom the department stationed in Antwerp, The Hague, Cherbourg, Paris, Bremen, Hamburg, Bucharest, Danzig, Libau, Rivne, and Riga, together with the physicians whom the department appointed to conduct medical examinations, transferred the inspection and screening of immigrants from Canada's ports of entry to European cities.[77] The immigration officers had instructions to "relax" regulations when inspecting immigrants from preferred countries but to apply them rigorously to Jews.[78] Transferring inspections of immigrants to Europe proved to be effective. In May 1922, the month that the regulations were approved, 411 Jewish immigrants were admitted into Canada; admissions decreased to 262 in June and to 166 in August.[79] Between June and December 1922, Canada admitted 1,590 Jewish immigrants compared with 5,799 during the same period in 1921.[80] The regulations were renewed in January 1923. In total, between January and December 1923, 3,475 Jewish immigrants were admitted into Canada via ocean ports compared with 3,388 in 1922 and 8,009 in 1921.[81] The screening of Jewish immigrants in Europe was so effective that the detention of Jewish immigrants at Canada's ocean ports ceased.[82] Expressing his satisfaction with the decision to abandon the requirement that immigrants possess $250 and instead select them on the basis of "the much more effective and scientific occupation test," the deputy minister, W.J. Egan, commented that Canada was now able to encourage the admission of "those classes and races suited to, and required for, the settlement and development of Canada" and to exclude those deemed undesirable.[83]

Negotiating the First Quota

The appointment in August 1923 of James A. Robb as minister of immigration and colonization encouraged the JIAS to believe that he might ignore the opposition of department officials and be receptive to proposals to increase Jewish immigration. Samuel Jacobs, MP for George-Étienne Cartier, a Montreal constituency with a large Jewish population and the honorary president of the JIAS, and Robb had served together in the House of Commons since 1917 and were both Laurier loyalists. Once Robb was appointed minister of immigration and colonization, Jacobs did not hesitate to raise the issue of Jewish refugees. Recognizing the difficulty of attempting to persuade Robb to seek cabinet approval of changes to restrictive regulations, Jacobs decided to appeal to the minister on humanitarian grounds. In September 1923, Jacobs asked for a meeting with Robb in Montreal. The previous month Jacobs had received a request from the Paris office of the Jewish Colonization Association (JCA) to raise the issue of Jewish refugees with the Canadian government.[84] In preparation for the meeting, Frederick Blair, whose views on Jewish immigration were well known in the department, was asked to write a memorandum on the admission of Jewish refugees. In it, Blair stated that "it is manifestly impossible for Canada to open the door to the tens of thousands of these refugees." He emphasized that "this view is not based on racial grounds, but on our ability to absorb them."[85] However, Robb decided to ignore the advice of his officials. When Jacobs, accompanied by Lyon Cohen, president of the Canadian Committee of the Jewish Colonization Association (CCJCA), appealed to the minister to grant a permit to admit 1,000 Jewish refugees from Russia stranded in

26. Samuel W. Jacobs, Member of Parliament (Cartier, Montreal), 1917–1938, and Honorary President of the Jewish Immigrant Aid Society of Canada, 1920–1938.

27. M.A. Gray, General Secretary of the Western Division of the Jewish Immigrant Aid Society of Canada.

Romania, assuring him that the CCJCA would guarantee that none of the immigrants would become a public charge, Robb "readily agreed to admit them" at the "rate of 100 persons per week."[86] On 2 December 1923, the first group of Jewish refugees stranded in Romania—twelve men, thirty-four women, and thirty-seven children—arrived in Montreal.[87]

Although the CCJCA had assumed full responsibility for the refugees, it was not equipped to meet their settlement needs once they arrived. In November 1923, Lyon Cohen wrote to branches of the Jewish Immigrant Aid Society to enlist their support. Emphasizing that the work of caring and finding employment for the refugees "cannot be accomplished without the co-operation of Jews throughout the Dominion," he asked Morris A. Gray, secretary of the Western Division of the Jewish Immigrant Aid Society, to "assist in the revival" of the Winnipeg organization.[88] The WDJIAS was far from dormant. In an attempt to ensure that immigrants sent to Winnipeg had better prospects of finding employment, in May 1923 Gray travelled to Halifax to interview refugees arriving on the steamship *Madonna*. Gray selected those who either had friends or relatives in Winnipeg or western Canada or had work experience that would enable them to find jobs and accompanied them on the train journey west.[89]

By May 1923, the WDJIAS employment committee had found work for 145 immigrants, but settlement costs, particularly for accommodation, forced the society to expand its appeal for donations of money and clothing and hold fundraising events.[90] The cost of maintaining an immigrant shelter, a sixteen-room house that provided accommodation for a maximum of thirty-five to forty refugees—who stayed a minimum of two weeks and as long as six months—and served thousands of meals, together with rent subsidies and loans, accounted for over 80 percent of WDJIAS annual expenditures on refugee settlement.[91] However, as the number of Jewish immigrants arriving in Winnipeg declined—from approximately 1,245 in 1921–22 to 301 in 1922–23—its executive found it difficult to persuade members of the Jewish community who had enthusiastically supported the reorganization of the

28. M.A. Gray and members of Winnipeg's Jewish community welcome Jewish refugees, 1924.

society in 1920, believing that it foreshadowed a return to pre–First World War levels of immigration, to continue to support the organization.[92] Informed that 6,000 refugees from Ukraine stranded in Romania would be admitted into Canada, in December 1923 the executive of the WDJIAS organized a conference of representatives of Jewish organizations that established the Emergency Immigrant Aid Committee, a temporary working group with a mandate to begin preparations to receive the refugees. When the first contingent of sixty-two refugees arrived on 5 January 1924, they were greeted at the CPR station by a crowd of over 1,000 people.[93]

In an attempt to mobilize additional support for the work of caring and finding employment for the refugees, on 31 December 1923 Lyon Cohen sent a letter to the delegates who had been selected to attend the annual convention of the Zionist Organization of Canada to be held in January 1924 in Toronto. Cohen urged the delegates to attend a dominion emergency immigration conference scheduled for the last day of the convention.[94] Thirty-four delegates, including Rabbi Israel Kahanovitch, Max Steinkopf, and H.E. Wilder, a member of Winnipeg's Emergency Immigrant Aid Committee, attended the immigration conference, at which Cohen appealed to the delegates to support

JIAS branches across Canada. The delegates unanimously passed resolutions calling for the unification of all settlement work under the auspices of the JIAS and the distribution of refugees across Canada: 40 percent to Montreal, 30 percent to Toronto and throughout Ontario, and 30 percent to Winnipeg and western Canada.[95]

The emergency immigration conference spurred Winnipeg's Emergency Immigrant Aid Committee to hold a conference to reorganize the WDJIAS. On 11 February 1924, thirty-three representatives appointed by seven mutual aid societies, the Montefiore Club, and the Independent Order of B'nai B'rith met to reconstitute the WDJIAS.[96] They elected a new executive that included elements of continuity—S. Hart Green, a former member of the board of directors was elected president, replacing Ben Sheps, who became a vice-president—but it also reflected growing acceptance of the importance of immigration among members of the Jewish community who had not previously supported the WDJIAS. Two prominent General Zionists, Herbert J. Samuel, the rabbi of Shaarey Zedek synagogue, and H.E. Wilder, who had been delegates at the founding convention of the Canadian Jewish Congress in 1919 but had not responded to its general secretary's appeal to all members to help establish branches of the JIAS, were elected as chairmen of committees. In addition, two prominent businessmen, Moses Haid and A.H. Aronovitch, were elected to the executive.[97] The newly elected executive established seven committees to organize and oversee the society's operations: a house committee to manage the immigrant shelter, a publicity committee, a distribution committee responsible for arranging transportation to send refugees to Jewish communities throughout western Canada, a ladies' committee to take care of female refugees staying in the shelter and supervise the preparation and serving of meals, a reception committee to greet refugees when they arrived in Winnipeg, an employment committee that helped refugees to find jobs, and a loan committee to lend refugees money to pay for their first month's rent and buy food until they found employment and enable skilled workers to purchase tools and equipment.[98] A night school run by the WDJIAS provided Jewish refugees with an opportunity to learn English. The WDJIAS also assumed responsibility for the refugees' medical needs; it organized a rotation of five physicians who provided their services free of charge and the society paid for their medication.[99]

Between January and April 1924, a total of 275 refugees arrived in Winnipeg.[100] Since seasonal unemployment peaked during the winter months, the timing of the arrival of the refugees made it difficult for the WDJIAS to find employment for them. As S. Hart Green noted, "employment is very scarce in Winnipeg, and it is next to impossible to find permanent jobs here for any of the refugees." Some of the refugees found temporary work, but the small amounts that they earned were "not nearly enough to support themselves and [their] families."[101] Of the approximately fifty families that settled in Winnipeg, many consisted of widows and small children.[102] More than a third of the refugees (107) were entrusted to the care of Jewish communities and agricultural colonies in rural Manitoba, Saskatchewan, Alberta, or sent to Vancouver, but in "many cases" both the host communities and the refugees were "dissatisfied" and returned to Winnipeg.[103] Unable to cope with the cost of paying for train fares, buying winter clothing, and making loans to refugees travelling to Jewish communities outside Winnipeg, in addition to assisting those who settled in the city, the executive of the WDJIAS appealed to the CCJCA to reimburse it for expenses of a "national character," expenditures incurred to distribute refugees throughout western Canada.[104] As the number of refugees arriving in Winnipeg continued to increase—by September 1924 an additional 340 had arrived—the WDJIAS found it difficult to raise money and became increasingly dependent on subsidies from the national office of the JIAS.[105] Most of the refugees who had arrived in Winnipeg had "gone through all kinds of hardship and misery during the ten years of war, starvation, massacres and epidemics," and they needed food, shelter, clothing, and time to recover before attempting to find employment.[106] The arrival of the refugees also coincided with "one of the worst economic depressions" in the history of western Canada; during the winter months, "hundreds of unemployed were marching the streets of Winnipeg seeking employment."[107] Many of the refugees were widows with small children who had little work experience. Overall, a tiny number of the refugees "were of the type that could be called self-supporting."[108]

Having promised the government that none of the Jewish refugees would become a public charge, the WDJIAS took every precaution to ensure that the refugees did not apply for municipal relief and come to the attention of the Winnipeg office of the Commissioner of Immigration for Western Canada. When they arrived in Winnipeg, the refugees were warned that applying for municipal relief would lead to deportation and advised that, if they found themselves in dire straits, they could turn to the WDJIAS for assistance. Periodically, a small number became destitute and returned to the sheltering home. When it was full, the WDJIAS provided them with cash payments for food and rent as well as clothing.[109] Jewish refugees could also become public charges and risked deportation if they were unable to pay their hospital bills.

Consequently, the WDJIAS assumed responsibility for the full costs of their hospital care.[110]

On 25 November 1924, the last group of the 900 Jewish refugees from Romania destined for western Canada arrived in Winnipeg.[111] When the Paris office of the JCA had asked the CCJCA to approach the Canadian government about the possibility of admitting Russian Jews stranded in Romania, it had specified 1,000 refugees. But the agreement between the department and the CCJCA, which stated that the refugees would be admitted at the "rate of one hundred per week," did not specify a deadline or a total number.[112] The CCJCA assumed, and Deputy Minister of Immigration W.J. Egan appeared to agree, that the "quota" consisted of 5,000 Jewish refugees. However, by June 1924, when approximately 1,100 Jewish refugees had arrived, it became apparent to the CCJCA that it had overestimated the number of Jewish refugees stranded in Romania. On 11 June, Cohen accompanied by Jacobs met with the minister and Egan to ask that, on the understanding that "we do not exceed the entire number of our quota," the CCJCA be permitted to modify the terms of the agreement with the department to include Russian Jews stranded in Constantinople as well as Jewish refugees, including many with relatives in Canada, who had travelled to Western European ports but could not proceed because they could not comply with Canadian immigration regulations.[113] Robb was sympathetic and instructed his deputy minister to find a means of modifying the quota agreement.

According to Egan, the Jews stranded in Western Europe were not genuine refugees because most of them had left Russia with the permission of the Soviet government, but he was bound by the minister's decision.[114] After lengthy negotiations with Cohen and Jacobs, Egan agreed that under the quota agreement the CCJCA could include 1,200 "self-supporting immigrants" with relatives in Canada.[115] Although Egan did not confirm the amendment of the quota agreement in writing, in July 1924 the CCJCA authorized the JIAS to begin registering Canadian Jews who wanted to bring their relatives to Canada. To ensure that members of each Jewish community had a fair opportunity to get a permit to admit their relatves to Canada, the JIAS apportioned permits to each Jewish community based upon its population: Montreal received 540, Toronto 330, and Winnipeg and western Canada 240.[116] To fulfill its commitment to the department that "only desirable immigrants" would be admitted into Canada, the JIAS established its own selection process. Canadian Jews who wanted to bring relatives to Canada registered with the national office in Montreal, the WDJIAS in Winnipeg, or the Emergency Immigrant Aid

Committee in Toronto. Once the Paris office of the JCA certified that the relatives were approved, applicants were invited to complete a form requesting a permit, pay a ten dollar processing fee, and deposit money—twenty-five dollars for an individual, fifty dollars for a couple, and seventy-five dollars for a family of three or more—to demonstrate that they had sufficient funds to support their relatives for at least a month. The JIAS then directed them to agents for one of the three steamship companies designated by the department to purchase tickets.[117] After the tickets were purchased, the JIAS submitted a list of names of relatives to the immigration department, identifying who should be issued permits, or letters of admission, under the quota.

Frustrated by the government's restrictions on Jewish immigration, Winnipeg's Jews welcomed the amendment to the quota agreement. Although the Winnipeg Jewish community's share of the permits was relatively small, up to 100 families were given the opportunity to bring relatives to Canada who were stranded in Europe because they could not comply with the continuous journey, passport, and occupational regulations. The amended quota agreement also offered hope that the government might repeal PC 717 and subsequent regulations that restricted family reunification to wives and minor children.

On 10 September 1924, Jacobs and Belkin met with Egan and the minister of immigration and colonization to discuss final arrangements for the departure of the permit holders from Western Europe. The representatives of the CCJCA were stunned to learn that Egan had persuaded the minister to withdraw the department's agreement to amend the quota. Citing growing unemployment and protests from labour organizations against high levels of immigration, Egan informed Jacobs and Belkin that "public sentiment" was against increased immigration. Robb hinted that, if unemployment decreased in the spring of 1925, he might reconsider.[118] He affirmed that the original quota agreement remained in effect; Russian Jews stranded in Romania would continue to be admitted on compassionate grounds, but all others had to comply with immigration regulations.

Egan's decision placed both the CCJCA and the JIAS in an impossible position: hundreds of applicants had been assured that the immigration department would admit their relatives to Canada. They had purchased tickets and deposited money for them believing that they would soon arrive in Canada. Although the CCJCA pointed out that under the terms of the quota agreement the JCA had sent a total of 3,395 Jewish refugees stranded in Romania to Canada, it was widely criticized for failing to live up to its commitment to secure the admission of the 1,200 Jewish refugees stranded in Western Europe and betraying the trust of Canadian Jews who hoped to bring their relatives to Canada. On the defensive, Cohen and Jacobs decided to seek an interview with Egan to secure 1,605 permits, the balance of the 5,000 that they believed the minister had approved.[119] In an attempt to mobilize political support for the admission of relatives of Canadian Jews before the interview, Cohen contacted "leaders of the Jewish community in Winnipeg" to advise them to meet with Prime Minister Mackenzie King when he stopped in the city as part of his tour of western Canada.[120] Accompanied by E.J. McMurray, the Liberal MP for North Winnipeg, a delegation of three appointed by the WDJIAS called on the prime minister, who invited them to join him for lunch on his private railway car. The three, considered by King to be "good sensible men, very reasonable and all political friends," asked for the "admission in certain contingencies of near relations" of Canadian Jews.[121] The delegation reported to Cohen that the prime minister responded to their request "very favourably" and promised to discuss their concerns with the minister of immigration and colonization when he returned to Ottawa. This encouraged Cohen to believe that Egan would be forced to reconsider his decision and approve 1,605 permits.[122]

The meeting with the prime minister together with the persistent efforts of Jacobs to persuade Robb to reverse his decision on the quota agreement produced results. In February 1925, Robb agreed to reinstate the agreement and instructed Egan to meet with Cohen and Jacobs to settle the number of permits that would be issued and how applications would be processed. After a series of conferences, Egan, Cohen, and Jacobs came to an understanding that the immigration department would issue 1,605 permits to admit the relatives of Canadian Jews, that the JIAS would be responsible for screening and submitting all applications for permits to the department for approval, and that 40 percent of the permits would be allocated to Montreal, 30 percent to Toronto, and 30 percent to Winnipeg and western Canada.

However, despite both Robb's assurances to Cohen and Jacobs and the terms and conditions of the original quota agreement, Egan was determined to restrict the number of Jewish refugees who could be admitted into Canada. Although he waived the occupational "test" that restricted admission to agriculturalists and domestic servants, he stipulated that all of the 1,605 Jewish refugees had to comply with both the continuous journey and the passport regulations, and only wives and children under the age of eighteen would be admitted.[123] Determined to persuade Egan to waive those regulations and broaden the definition of family members admissible under the quota, Cohen travelled to Ottawa to meet with the deputy minister.

Fortuitously, Cohen's appeal coincided with a personal plea from E.J. McMurray, the solicitor general of Canada, to Prime Minister King to reconsider the government's policy on the admission of relatives of Canadian residents. In April 1925, McMurray wrote to King to warn him that, unless the government changed its policy of refusing to admit relatives of Canadian residents, the Liberals risked losing crucial political support throughout western Canada. Citing his own North End Winnipeg constituency, in which "about fifty per cent of the population are English speaking by birth and the other fifty per cent of European extraction . . . [with] the Ukrainian, Pole, Russian, German and Jew predominating," he emphasized that many of his constituents wanted to bring "their near relatives, such as sons and daughters, brothers and sisters, fathers and mothers," to Canada. McMurray blamed Egan for the resentment of the government building among the foreign-born population whose votes would "decide pretty nearly the result of the election" in many constituencies in Manitoba, Saskatchewan, and Alberta: "The Deputy Minister has become a law unto himself and rules autocratically." McMurray complained that unless something was done to control Egan "I will be defeated in my own constituency." Emphasizing that the issue of the admission of relatives "affects our collective welfare as a party," McMurray suggested that it be discussed by cabinet.[124]

Facing a resurgence of support for the Conservative Party and conscious of the need to persuade Liberal voters in western Canada who had defected to the Progressive Party in the 1921 election to return to the Liberal Party, King was acutely aware that his government could not afford to alienate any blocs of voters. As McMurray suggested, Egan could not continue to be "a law unto himself": political intervention was needed. In a complete about-face, Egan removed all of the conditions that he had imposed on the admission of Jewish refugees. In May 1925, he informed the JIAS that he had instructed his officials to admit all of the categories of relatives of Canadian residents that it wished to include under the balance of the quota agreement subject only to a medical examination.[125] By early June, all of the 1,605 permits had been allocated, and the Jewish refugees stranded in European ports began to leave for Canada.

In addition to providing assistance to the 600 Jewish refugees who remained in Winnipeg and the 300 who travelled to Jewish communities throughout western Canada, in March and April 1925 the WDJIAS was preoccupied with helping Jews in Winnipeg who wanted to bring their relatives to Canada to complete application forms for the 300 permits allocated to the

Winnipeg Jewish community.[126] Applicants were required to sign a bond of indemnity guaranteeing that their relatives would not become public charges, provide information about where their relatives would live and whether work had been found for them, and pay a fee of ten dollars to the WDJIAS for the cost of processing their applications. In exceptional cases, the WDJIAS gave loans to applicants to pay for steamship tickets. For example, M.A. Gray accepted a deposit of $100 from a twenty-year-old seamstress who wanted to bring her father, stepmother, and their infant to Canada and authorized a loan for $230.50 to pay for the balance of the cost of their steamship tickets. "The girl being a good dressmaker earns from ten to fifteen dollars per week. Half of her salary will be applied on account of our loan to her for transportation for her parents."[127] Assisting refugees and completing administrative tasks were time consuming; over an eighteen-month period, the executive of the WDJIAS held eighty-five meetings, and its seven committees met once or twice a week.[128]

The Second Quota Agreement

After all of the 1,605 permits were allocated, the JIAS still had close to 1,500 applications on file. The WDJIAS alone had received three times the number of applications that it approved. Sensing that they should take advantage of the political situation to press the government to agree to a second quota, Cohen and Jacobs met with Egan on 11 June 1925 to ask for an additional 3,000 permits to admit relatives of Canadian Jews still stranded at Western European ports.[129] Egan assured them that the immigration department would grant a second quota of 3,000 refugees, but by July neither the CCJCA nor the JIAS had received a letter confirming an agreement.[130] Returning to Ottawa on 2 July, Cohen and Jacobs attempted to finalize an agreement with Egan, who would only concede that, for the purposes of planning, the JIAS could expect to receive a quota of 2,500. Consequently, it announced that members of the Jewish community could submit applications for permits to bring their relatives to Canada, and by the end of September the society had reviewed and submitted to the immigration department over 2,000 applications.[131] However, none of the applications was approved, and the national office could offer the WDJIAS, which had been allocated 25 percent of the expected 2,500 permits, little information about the delay. Based upon past experience, the only way to deal with Egan's intransigence was to make an appeal to the minister of immigration. With a federal election under way, Jacobs had little difficulty persuading the minister that hundreds of Jewish voters in Montreal, Toronto, and Winnipeg would punish the Liberals at the polls if the government did not fulfill what was widely believed to be a promise to admit their relatives to Canada.

Nevertheless, Egan was able to convince the minister to limit the number of relatives of Canadian Jews admitted under the new quota. In early October 1925, Egan wrote to the JIAS stating that the immigration department had decided to admit into Canada a total of 1,500 relatives of Canadian Jews. He stated that the department was prepared to waive the occupational requirement but specified that the immigrants had to pass a medical exam and a literacy test, possess a valid passport, and comply with the continuous journey regulation. However, Egan did grant the JIAS a concession: the categories of eligible relatives listed in the letter expanded the definition of eligible family members included in the previous agreement. In addition to wives and children, parents and grandparents, unmarried adult children, nieces and nephews, and widowed daughters, stepdaughters, and nieces, as well as their children, the department was willing to admit "similar relatives" of an applicant's wife and complete family units joining parents, brothers and sisters, and aunts and uncles.[132] The expanded definition of eligible family members broadened the scope of the agreement, but the inclusion of compliance with the continuous journey requirement meant that refugees stranded in European ports were not admissible. However, Cohen and Jacobs were able to persuade Egan to issue 217 permits to Jewish refugees stranded in European ports, and the remaining 1,289 permits were allocated to Jewish immigrants from Eastern Europe travelling directly from their countries of origin.[133]

Held on 29 October 1925, the federal election resulted in a second but more precarious Liberal minority government. With only ninety-nine Liberal MPs elected—King and eight cabinet ministers were defeated—the survival of the Liberal government depended on the support of two Labour MPs, J.S. Woodsworth and the newly elected MP from North Winnipeg, A.A. Heaps.[134] As E.J. McMurray had predicted, Jewish voters in North End Winnipeg viewed the 1925 federal election as a plebiscite on the Liberal government's immigration policies. Heaps, a former upholsterer employed by the Canadian Pacific Railway, who had represented the North End on

29. A.A. Heaps, Member of Parliament (Winnipeg North), 1925–1940, and Honorary President of the Jewish Immigrant Aid Society of Canada, 1926–1940.

Winnipeg City Council for eight years, was nominated by the Independent Labour Party. Arrested for sedition in 1919 for his role as a leader of the Winnipeg General Strike, Heaps had established a reputation as a defender of the interests of the working class who understood the concerns of Winnipeg's North End Jewish community. Campaign literature distributed by the party's Jewish Campaign Committee emphasized that Heaps was one of "our own."[135] His election campaign focused on McMurray's failure to persuade the Liberal government to adopt an open door policy, a promise that McMurray had made when he contested a 1923 by-election, and the government's record of impeding Jewish immigration. After the election of Heaps, the *Israelite Press* commented that "by their vote the Jewish people indicated that for them the question of Immigration is still paramount."[136]

S.W. Jacobs, who had never hesitated to declare publicly that he would vote for any party that would "relax the immigration regulations," now had an ally, a fellow Jewish MP equally determined to take advantage of the Liberals' precarious minority standing in the House of Commons to pressure the government to agree to a new quota of Jewish immigrants for 1926.[137] On 12 January 1926, the national executive of the JIAS met in Montreal to discuss a new quota. Having accepted 2,500 applications for permits, the national office of the JIAS was having difficulty explaining why the society had only been granted 1,500 permits. In addition, when the immigration department issued the permits, it ignored its agreement with the JIAS on how to distribute them, with the "result that Western Canada, which was entitled to 25% of the permits, secured only about 15%, while the Province of Ontario, instead of getting 30% received more than 45% of the 1500."[138] Referring to the anger of the executive of the WDJIAS over the distribution of permits, A. Levin, president of the JIAS, warned Jacobs that both the unity and the "very life" of the society were at risk.

Levin had reason to be concerned about the unity of the JIAS. The president of the WDJIAS accused the national office of "grabbing our proportion of the permits." This was not merely "an absolute breach of faith"; if the WDJIAS did not receive assurances that western Canada would be treated fairly in the future, the executive decided, then it would function "entirely separate and apart from any Montreal affiliation" and attempt to negotiate its own quota with the immigration department.[139] This was not an idle threat. Like the national office, which relied on Jacobs, honorary president of the JIAS, to use his political influence on its behalf, Heaps was more than willing to advocate on behalf of the WDJIAS. After attending a meeting of the national executive in Montreal, M.A. Gray and S. Hart Green stopped in Ottawa to meet with Heaps. Following their meeting, Heaps met with Charles Stewart, the acting minister of immigration and colonization, and Frederick Blair, the acting deputy minister. Heaps had requested the meeting to raise a specific issue: the release of 156 outstanding permits to the WDJIAS, part of western Canada's share of the 1,500 allocated to the JIAS in October 1925. Heaps took advantage of his meetings with Stewart and Blair to make the case for a new quota.[140] As a basis for discussion, Heaps presented them with the draft of an agreement establishing a quota for 1926.[141]

His objectives were, first, to secure an agreement for 1926 that would enable the JIAS to recommend the admission of as many immigrants as possible who would not have to comply with the immigration department's restrictive regulations and, second, in addition to the 156 outstanding permits, to guarantee that western Canada would receive 25 percent of the quota.[142] The draft agreement became the basis for discussions between the minister and Jacobs, who represented the interests of the JIAS, and Cohen, acting on behalf of the Paris office of the JCA.

Believing that the minister "was in a good mood," Jacobs was confident that he would be able to secure the 1,000 permits that the JIAS needed to clear its backlog of outstanding applications and that Stewart would agree to a new quota for 1926 of 3,000 Jewish immigrants.[143] Cohen, enlisting the support of Jacobs, appealed to the minister on humanitarian grounds to include 500 of the estimated 6,000 Jewish refugees still stranded in European ports.[144] After extensive discussions—still resentful of the "treatment we have previously received at the hands of our Montreal head office," the executive of the WDJIAS was reluctant to give its approval—on 19 February 1926 the immigration department and JIAS finalized an agreement. The WDJIAS, JIAS, and CCJCA had reason to be satisfied with the agreement. However, though Heaps and Jacobs had been able to exercise considerable political leverage, the terms and conditions of the agreement suggested that Stewart's "good mood" was tempered by Blair's reluctance to grant any concession on immigration to the Jewish community.

The quota agreement between the minister of immigration and colonization and the JIAS stated that the department would issue 250 permits a month between January and December 1926, a total of 3,000, 1,000 fewer than Jacobs expected.[145] In a report to Gray on his discussions with Stewart and Blair, Heaps noted that there was "no chance" of persuading them to agree to a quota of 4,000, and in fact he had "had a very hard struggle to get it raised to this number."[146] Heaps did succeed in securing a clause in the agreement stating that the JIAS would give "precedence" to "the 156 Western cases" and that the WDJIAS would still be entitled to receive 25 percent of the quota or 750 permits.[147] This clause addressed the WDJIAS executive's concerns, but it meant that under the agreement the JIAS would receive only 2,844 new permits.

The terms and conditions of the admissibility of relatives reflected Blair's adamant insistence that Jewish immigrants comply with the immigration department's restrictive regulations. Heaps and Jacobs were able to persuade Blair to expand the categories of relatives eligible for admission under the quota; in addition to all of the categories of relatives included in the October 1925 agreement, grandparents were now able to bring two or more orphaned grandchildren to Canada, and the JIAS was permitted to include 200 heads of families in the quota.[148] But the agreement specified that, though the immigration department was prepared to waive the occupational requirement, half (1,500) of the Jewish immigrants admitted under the quota had to comply with the passport and continuous journey regulations.[149] Blair was well aware that Jewish refugees, a type of Jewish immigrant whom he particularly reviled, would be inadmissible.

After three days of meetings with Charles Stewart, in which S.W. Jacobs and Lyon Cohen made "strong representations" to admit Jewish refugees stranded in Europe, the minister agreed to include 300 refugees in the JIAS quota, fewer than the 500 whom Cohen had requested, but for the Paris office of the JCA this was a welcome contribution to alleviating the protracted Jewish refugee problem in Europe.[150] In his letter authorizing their admission into Canada, Blair stated that beginning in April the department would issue fifty permits a month to Jewish refugees recommended by the Paris office of the JCA. However, to ensure that admission of the 300 refugees did not contribute to increased Jewish immigration in the future, Blair specified that only family units were eligible "rather than the head of a family being brought now and his wife and children following later."[151]

For members of the executive of the WDJIAS, Cohen's action was yet another example of the high-handed behaviour of the national leadership of the JIAS and its disregard for their views and problems.[152] Under mounting pressure to secure permits to enable applicants in Winnipeg and Jewish communities throughout western Canada to be reunited with their relatives, they were frustrated to learn that 300 fewer relatives would be admitted under the quota. They were also concerned about the additional cost of assisting more

Jewish refugees to settle in Winnipeg. Jewish communities throughout western Canada had generously donated $6,559 to assist the Jewish refugees who had arrived in Winnipeg in 1924. However, once the focus of Jewish immigration shifted from refugees to relatives of Canadian Jews who assumed responsibility for their "reception, maintenance and care," donors no longer believed that their financial contributions were needed; in the first six months of 1925, donations declined to $612.[153]

While revenue from donations plummeted, the cost of assisting refugees rapidly increased. In the first six months of 1925, expenditures on "Immigrant Aid," which had amounted to $6,506 in 1924, totalled $5,586.[154] The executive of the WDJIAS was alarmed by the possibility of another influx of refugees especially when, in February 1925, S.B. Haltrecht, the general manager of the JIAS, responded to the request for an additional subsidy of $5,000 by suggesting that the refugees "who came over in 1924 are now part and parcel of the Canadian Jewish community and each locality is expected to look after its own poor."[155] The executive members of the WDJIAS were outraged that the general manager of the national office of the JIAS in Montreal, which had received $78,000 from the American Jewish Congress and other US-based Jewish organizations, responded to their financial plight by preaching self-sufficiency, especially since they had been assured that the JIAS had an ample reserve fund.[156]

Haltrecht further antagonized the executive of the WDJIAS by provoking a dispute over application fees. The national office of the JIAS charged applicants a twenty dollar fee and solicited a donation of up to $100 in the form of a membership fee as means of financing its operations. Haltrecht expected the WDJIAS to do the same: charge applicants twenty dollars, remit ten dollars to the national office of the JIAS to pay for administrative expenses, and deal with its financial shortfall by also collecting a membership fee from each applicant. In a letter to A. Levin, president of the JIAS, S. Hart Green explained that in January 1926 the executive of the WDJIAS had reluctantly increased the application fee to twenty dollars because it was desperately short of revenue but that it could not afford to send half of it to the national office. As for imposing a membership fee, Green pointed out that "we simply have not the class of applicants that you apparently have in Montreal and are not in a position to charge like you do."[157] Instead of sending money to the national office, Green reiterated that the WDJIAS was in financial difficulties; it was being forced to cut back on relief work, and "we doubt very much if we will be able to continue our work . . . unless we have some financial assistance from the East."[158] In his reply, Levin was firm; the WDJIAS could not expect to receive a subsidy from the JIAS; rather, it had a clear obligation to send money to Montreal.

Since the national office refused to continue providing subsidies to support destitute Jewish refugees, the executive of the WDJIAS reluctantly decided to ask applicants for permits to make donations.[159] Notifying an applicant that a permit to admit his brother-in-law, wife, and two children had been issued, Gray advised him that, since a "great many" of the immigrants who came to Canada under the auspices of the JIAS "are out of work and must be supported by the Society, we are compelled to ask for a donation from all those people that we serve and assist in securing permits for their relatives, to be able to continue with our work."[160] However, by the end of 1926, only a small number of the Jewish refugees who had arrived in 1924 were still financially dependent on the WDJIAS. Moreover, since only twenty-eight of the Jewish refugees admitted under the 1926 quota settled in Winnipeg, the WDJIAS could afford to stop asking for donations. As the number of applications for permits increased throughout 1926, the executive of the WDJIAS recognized that its dispute with the national office over fees threatened to jeopardize Gray's administrative relationship with Haltrecht and impede the processing of permits. Consequently, it relented and adopted a policy of remitting half of the twenty dollar application fee to the national office and kept ten dollars "to pay for the stenographer and other office expenses and to maintain those immigrants that require help."[161]

Throughout 1926, Gray's time was devoted to processing applications for permits. After ensuring that an application form was filled out correctly—mistakes spelling the names of relatives could cause lengthy delays—and verifying that the applicant had the means both to post a bond of indemnity and to afford steamship and railway tickets, the executive of the WDJIAS reviewed and signed the applications that it approved and sent them to the national office.[162] Once Haltrecht verified that the relatives identified in the applications were eligible for admission based upon the categories of family relationships included in the quota agreement, he submitted them to the immigration department for approval. The department then sent the approved permits to Haltrecht, who forwarded them to Gray. Each permit, valid for five months, was assigned to a specific steamship company. On receipt of the permits, Gray contacted the applicants, handed them the permits in person, and urged them to purchase the tickets as soon as possible. When they purchased tickets, applicants gave their permits to the relevant steamship company, which sent them to one of its agents in Europe for delivery to the ticket holders, who then presented them to a Canadian immigration officer. Once the ticket holders passed medical examinations, an immigration officer issued visas confirming that they were admissible into Canada.

Although the quota agreement included a provision that allowed the JIAS, under extenuating circumstances, to apply for a three-month extension of a permit, it was imperative to use each permit that the immigration department issued before it expired. Gray monitored each permit allocated to the WDJIAS to ensure that applicants purchased steamship tickets as soon as they received their permits and the ticket holders passed their medical exams. Since the demand for permits far exceeded the number allocated to the WDJIAS, Gray acted swiftly to reclaim any unused permits. With the agreement between the immigration department and the JIAS due to expire at the end of 1926, he was determined to make maximum use of the share of permits allocated to the WDJIAS. He sent unused permits to Haltrecht, who returned them to the immigration department for cancellation. Once a permit was cancelled, Gray could then submit an application for a new permit to replace it.

As the processing of applications for permits progressed, it became apparent that the 1926 quota of 3,000 Jewish immigrants was inadequate. Unexpectedly, King belatedly heeded the advice that McMurray had given in April 1925 to broaden the definition of relatives of Canadian residents eligible for admission into Canada. McMurray's warning that the Liberals would pay a political price at the polls if they did not change the government's immigration policy remained relevant a year later. Anticipating the possibility of an early election, King attempted to bolster support for the Liberal Party among immigrant voters by implementing PC 534. Approved in April 1926, PC 534 amended PC 183, introduced in January 1923, which restricted the admission of family members to wives and children under the age of eighteen.[163] Providing that a Canadian resident "satisfied the Minister of his willingness to receive and care for such relative[s]," the new regulation permitted the admission of a father or mother, an unmarried son or daughter eighteen years of age or older, and an unmarried brother or sister. The regulation also permitted the admission of "a person who has satisfied the Minister that his labour or service is required in Canada."[164]

At first, the leaders of the CCJCA and JIAS welcomed the new regulations. By permitting Canadian Jews to sponsor their parents, unmarried adult children, and unmarried brothers and sisters, PC 534 promised to reduce the number of applications for permits issued under the quota. This would enable the JIAS to focus on securing permits for nieces or nephews, widowed nieces and their unmarried children, stepdaughters and their unmarried children, and grandchildren. However, when Haltrecht wrote to the immigration department to seek clarification of PC 534, he was informed that, "while the present agreement with your Society remains in effect, the provisions of the Order-in-Council mentioned will not be extended to such cases."[165] Blair was adamant that, since "these relatives and more were included in the quota," there was no reason to allow Jews to apply for their admission under PC 534.[166] The senior officials of the immigration department were in agreement; to do so would contradict the very purpose of the quota—to limit the number of Jewish immigrants admitted into Canada. Since under the terms of PC 534 Egan had the authority to approve or reject applications to sponsor relatives, the JIAS had no alternative but to accept the immigration department's decision.

In mid-1926, the political landscape of Canada abruptly changed. On 28 June 1926, King asked the governor general to dissolve Parliament and call an election. When the governor general refused his request, King resigned. The governor general then asked Arthur Meighen, leader of the Conservative Party, to form a government. Meighen's government was short-lived. On 2 July, it lost a crucial vote in the House of Commons, and the governor general accepted Meighen's advice to dissolve Parliament. However, Meighen still had the constitutional authority to govern until the next election. On 13 July, Meighen appointed Sir Henry Drayton as acting minister of immigration and colonization. After his appointment, Jacobs met with R.B. Bennett, the minister of finance, to discuss extending the family sponsorship provisions of PC 534 to Jewish immigrants. Although he was a Conservative partisan, Bennett held Jacobs in high esteem.[167] Bennett used his influence with Drayton to ask him to allow Jewish residents of Canada to benefit from the provisions of PC 534.[168] Overruling his deputy and assistant deputy ministers, on 10 August Drayton instructed Egan to apply PC 534 to "bona fide Jewish applicants despite the Quota arrangement."[169] After a delay of several weeks, in late September, Egan instructed his officials to accept applications from Jewish residents to sponsor their relatives under PC 534.[170]

In the interim, with the federal election under way, the executive of the JIAS decided to take advantage of the Conservatives' desire to broaden its electoral base by requesting an additional 1,000 permits. On 1 September 1926, a delegation that included A. Levin, president of the JIAS, and S.B. Haltrecht met with Sir Henry Drayton, also serving as acting prime minister.[171] They asked him to approve an additional 1,000 permits for 1926, including 100 for heads of families.[172] Drayton was non-committal and sought the advice of

Frederick Blair. According to Blair, "to grant an additional 1000 is to invite an application for more." Ignoring the immigration department's bias in favour of immigration from Great Britain and Western Europe, Blair stated that by granting quotas the immigration department was practising discrimination in favour of Jews: "I think every person who looks at the facts fairly must come to the conclusion that Jewish people are either worth more to Canada or have a greater claim on Canada than other races and are, therefore, entitled to special privileges."[173] Concluding that PC 534 provided Jewish residents with ample opportunities to sponsor their relatives, Drayton decided that there was no need to approve an additional 1,000 permits.

Held on 14 September 1926, the federal election resulted in a Liberal majority. Jacobs and Heaps were re-elected, but they were no longer in a strategic position to exact concessions from the government on immigration policy. To cement an alliance between the Liberals and nine Liberal Progressive MPs—former members of the Progressive Party who had coordinated their election campaigns with the Liberal Party—on 25 September King appointed Robert Forke, their titular leader, as minister of immigration and colonization. Since a meeting of the national executive of the JIAS was scheduled for early December, the leaders of the CCJCA and JIAS decided to take advantage of the presence of delegates from Toronto and Winnipeg to assemble a large delegation to meet with the minister.

The meeting took place on 13 December 1926. In addition to Heaps and Jacobs, the delegation included A. Levin representing the JIAS, Lyon Cohen representing the CCJCA, M.A. Gray representing the WDJIAS, and the president of the Toronto branch of the JIAS.[174] The minister was accompanied by Deputy Minister W.J. Egan and most of his senior staff. Emphasizing that the CCJCA and JIAS would continue to select desirable immigrants, Cohen asked the minister to continue the quota agreement for another year.

It quickly became apparent that Forke was not prepared to discuss a new quota. Replying to Cohen, he stated that he would like to grant the request of the delegation but was bound by the provisions of the Immigration Act, which, Blair interjected, prohibited establishing quotas.[175] The political climate had clearly changed, and the King government no longer had a political incentive to renew the quota agreement. In the absence of any political direction from the prime minister, Forke simply deferred to his senior officials on matters of immigration policy, and he made it clear that he was not prepared to continue to discuss the legality or the merits of the delegation's request. He did suggest, however, that a smaller delegation meet with his officials to determine if the immigration department could in "some way" accommodate their request for a means of facilitating Jewish immigration.[176]

On 16 December 1926, a delegation composed of three MPs—Jacobs, Heaps, and Joseph Thorson—together with Cohen and Belkin representing the CCJCA, and Levin and Haltrecht representing the JIAS, met with Egan and Blair.[177] Blair set the tone of the meeting by asserting that quotas were illegal. Moreover, not only were they "unfair if given to one race" and not others, but also, since most Jewish immigrants settled in urban areas, a quota that facilitated their admission into Canada was contrary to the main purpose of the government's immigration policy, to encourage the admission of agriculturalists. When Cohen was finally able to ask Egan what the immigration department was prepared to do to respond to their request, Egan replied that he intended to enforce strictly the Immigration Act and its regulations. Claiming that Jews received a third of the permits issued under PC 534, he argued that it was "sufficient to meet the need[s] of Jewish immigrants." As for immigrants who could not qualify for admission under PC 534 because convincing evidence could not be provided that their "labour or service is required in Canada," Egan announced that, if an MP was prepared to recommend a constituent's application for the admission of such an immigrant to the department, the minister had issued instructions authorizing him to issue a permit. However, he emphasized that permits would be issued only for immigrants who could comply with the continuous journey and passport regulations.[178] Although all three MPs were concerned that their offices would be flooded with applications, Heaps and Jacobs recognized that this application of PC 534 would enable Canadian Jews to sponsor a limited number of their relatives to come to Canada, including heads of families who, once established, could in turn sponsor their wives, minor children, parents, unmarried adult children, and unmarried brothers and sisters.

In May 1927, Heaps made a final attempt to persuade the minister of immigration to agree to a quota. On 7 May, Heaps, accompanied by S. Hart Green, met with Forke and Egan in the minister's office. Although Egan acknowledged that he had "not received a single complaint from anyone in connection with our (WDJIAS's) work during the last three years, either in the work of the refugee movement or the handling of permits," he stated that the government was not willing to agree to any quota, and all Jewish immigrants had to comply with existing regulations.[179] In his report to the WDJIAS executive, Heaps stated that, though he and Green had been unable to secure an agreement on a quota, "some good was done by having the Deputy Minister make a statement praising the work of the Society in Western Canada."[180] Heaps was referring to Egan's "intimation" that the issue of a quota would be "given further consideration at a later date," but he was also mindful that a good working relationship with Egan would facilitate what was to become a new dimension of WDJIAS activity, the submission by Heaps of applications for permits under PC 534 to admit "a person who has satisfied the Minister that his labour or service is required in Canada."

Heaps and Jacobs resolved to take full advantage of Forke's instructions to Egan to issue permits to applicants if their MP confirmed that the labour or service of the immigrant identified in the application was required in Canada.[181] Throughout 1927 and 1928, Gray acted as a conduit for applications for permits that Heaps submitted to the immigration department. For example, in March 1928, Heaps secured a permit for the married brother-in-law of one of his constituents and in October 1928 a permit for the widowed sister and her two children of another constituent on the understanding that she would "remain in his home or some other home as a housekeeper, for a period of five years."[182] The permits usually authorized the admission of more than one immigrant—in June 1928, Heaps secured seven permits admitting twenty-eight immigrants—but the immigration department subjected applications that listed multiple immigrants to closer scrutiny. Consequently, Heaps advised Gray that focusing on heads of families would be more effective: "In the future my policy will be to bring out first the head of the family and then the rest can come out under ordinary regulations later. In that case there will be less difficulty for me & I can get many more through."[183]

However, Egan quickly realized that the strategy to prioritize heads of families would ultimately increase the number of Jewish immigrants admitted into Canada. In September 1928, Heaps advised Gray that "the Department insist now upon families coming as a unit so it will only be in exceptional cases that a head will come on his own."[184] Gray was under continuous pressure to forward applications to Heaps, especially from constituents who met with him to ask for his help when he was in Winnipeg. Egan did not impose a limit on the number of permits that the immigration department was prepared to issue on the recommendation of an individual MP, but each case consumed a great deal of time for Heaps, especially when it involved an immigrant from the Soviet Union. When the Soviet government stopped issuing "proper passports" to Jewish emigrants, the immigration department refused to approve applications for permits to admit immigrants from the Soviet Union unless the applicant was able to post a $1,500 bond issued by a bonding company to guarantee that the immigrant would not become a public charge for a five-year period.[185] Heaps was very successful at getting applications for permits approved, but he cautioned Gray to screen applicants carefully. Referring to a difficult case, he asked, "now Gray why in the name of common sense should you or I go to all this trouble and making other cases harder to get through?"[186] When Gray sent him a batch of forty applications, Heaps cautioned him not to accept any more applications until he had an opportunity to deal with the ones that he had received.[187]

But the number of Jewish immigrants admitted under the permit system was far fewer than those admitted under the quotas. Between October 1926 and April 1928, Heaps secured eighty-five permits—under the quota in 1926, the JIAS had allocated 750 permits to western Canada—and Jacobs obtained 143.[188] In addition, in 1928, the immigration department established a new system of medical examinations. Seven Canadian physicians were stationed at European ports to examine immigrants before they boarded steamships.[189] The new system of medical examinations had an immediate impact on Jewish immigration. The board of directors of the JIAS became concerned that "hundreds of Jews who have been permitted in the past to come to this country were now being rejected for various reasons." The board concluded that this was "suggestive of a policy of the Canadian government that tends to exclude Jewish immigration to Canada."[190] The board asked Heaps and Jacobs to intervene. In September 1928, they met with the minister, Blair, and A.L. Jolliffe, Chief Controller of Chinese Immigration, to discuss the large number of Jewish immigrants detained at Riga and Danzig.[191] The minister agreed to send an official to investigate, and as a result the Jewish immigrants who had been rejected were re-examined, and "eventually almost all were permitted to come forward."[192]

Nevertheless, the new system of medical inspections and beginning in 1928 renewed enforcement of passport regulations reduced the number of Jewish immigrants arriving at Canadian ports from 4,749 in 1927 to 3,532 in 1928 and 3,353 in 1929.[193] The decline in Jewish immigration to Canada affected the activities of the WDJIAS. Jewish immigrants arriving in Winnipeg declined from over 1,000 in 1924–25 to approximately 500 a year between 1 April 1926 and 31 March 1930.[194] Moreover, unlike the refugees, the Jewish immigrants who arrived after 1927 were sponsored by relatives or friends and did not depend on the WDJIAS for food, clothing, and accommodation.

Whereas in 1924 the WDJIAS spent approximately $7,200 helping Jewish refugees, in 1928 and 1929 its expenditures on relief, hospital bills, and other forms of assistance totalled $1,729.[195] Consequently, though some of Gray's work involved assisting Heaps to apply for permits, he had more time to devote to other activities. For example, Gray assisted members of the Jewish community to apply for birth certificates that they needed to qualify for the Old Age Pension as well as passports, naturalization certificates, and visas to enter the United States.[196] Using his contacts with steamship companies, he was also able to take advantage of their networks of agents in Europe to assist Winnipeg Jews to send money to friends and relatives. In response to inquiries from Europe and the United States, Gray conducted numerous searches to locate relatives in Winnipeg and throughout western Canada who had lost touch with their families.[197] The WDJIAS also continued to run an employment service, helping immigrants to find work in Winnipeg or on farms.

Over time, Gray established an effective working relationship with Thomas Gelley, the division commissioner of the immigration department in Winnipeg. By 1929, Gray was able to secure permits on behalf of Heaps from Gelley directly, substantially increasing the number of permits distributed through the WDJIAS.[198] Gelley's office also notified Gray when Jewish immigrants who had become public charges were summoned to appear before boards of inquiry for deportation hearings. At the hearings, the Legal Aid Department of the WDJIAS was invariably able to persuade the adjudicators to cancel deportation orders for the immigrants by providing assurances that the WDJIAS would pay their hospital bills or find employment for them.[199]

Although members of Winnipeg's Jewish community continued to turn to the WDJIAS for advice and assistance—in a one-year period, Gray either spoke to or corresponded with 1,565 individuals—both its membership and its donations declined.[200] By 1925, the postwar optimism that the JIAS could persuade the government to revert to its pre-1914 immigration policy, which had permitted tens of thousands of Jewish immigrants to come to Canada, had dissipated. The quota agreements were a significant achievement, but they transformed the WDJIAS into an intermediary that provided a service to eligible sponsors; in exchange for application fees and donations, Gray submitted a limited number of applications for permits to the national office of the JIAS. In addition, by 1926, most of the refugees who arrived in Winnipeg were self-supporting. Consequently, the WDJIAS was no longer able to justify public appeals for donations, the fundraising campaigns that had been so effective in mobilizing membership support in the past. Despite the important services that it continued to provide, when the government refused to grant a quota for 1927, the WDJIAS, an organization that had been founded to persuade the government to adopt an "open door" immigration policy, was reduced to processing no more than 130 applications for permits a year and offering advice on how to sponsor relatives.[201] Once an organization with a mass membership, a large cohort of volunteers, and a permanent administrative assistant, by 1927 the WDJIAS depended on the dedication of its four-member executive and the countless hours of time that M.A. Gray, its general secretary, and a small group of volunteers donated to keep its office running.[202]

By April 1929, the WDJIAS was in dire financial straits. Between May 1927 and April 1929, its revenue, which had amounted to $12,208 from May 1925 to June 1927, dropped to $2,221. However, expenditures in the same period, which included $1,497 for office expenses and telegraph and cable costs, plus $1,729 for relief and hospital bills, totalled $3,226. The WDJIAS no longer received donations from the public or subsidies from the national office of the JIAS and became almost entirely dependent on donations from applicants for permits.[203] Since its financial survival depended on drawing on a rapidly diminishing reserve fund that would be depleted by the end of 1929, the executive of the WDJIAS decided to ask Heaps to appeal to the national executive of the JIAS for assistance. However, the JIAS was struggling with its own financial problems.[204] Nevertheless, effective 1 March, the national executive decided to provide the WDJIAS with an operating grant of $100 a month, which together with the "small contributions" from Winnipeg Jews in return for assistance with permits enabled Gray to continue to rent an office, pay for administrative expenses, and provide "absolutely necessary relief."[205]

On 30 December 1929, W.L. Mackenzie King appointed Charles Stewart to replace Robert Forke as minister of immigration and colonization. Heaps, who together with Jacobs had persuaded Stewart in 1926 to agree to a quota on Jewish immigration, was optimistic that he could persuade the minister to give the leaders of the JIAS a sympathetic hearing.[206] Heaps travelled to Ottawa three weeks before the 20 February start of the parliamentary session to meet with Stewart. But King and his government were becoming increasingly aware of the economic consequences of the October 1929 stock market crash. By early 1930, unemployment rates, below 3 percent between 1927 and 1929, tripled and continued to increase throughout the year.[207] When Heaps met with Stewart, the minister proved to be just as intransigent as his predecessor, rejecting any suggestion that Jewish immigration be increased.

Responding to growing public concern about worsening economic conditions and rising unemployment, a week after its election in July 1930, the Conservative government of R.B. Bennett adopted PC 1957, a regulation that placed unprecedented restrictions on immigration from Europe.[208] PC 1957 rescinded PC 534, the regulation that for nearly four years had enabled Jewish residents of Canada to sponsor their relatives and either MPs or "persons of standing" to recommend the admission of Jewish immigrants, and cancelled all permits that had been issued prior to 14 March 1930.[209] The implementation of PC 1957 had an immediate impact on Jewish immigration. The board of directors of the JIAS noted that the regulation affected "over three thousand of our people in Russia, Poland and Roumania [*sic*] who were either in possession of permits and ready to go or were expecting permits."[210] The wives and minor children of Jewish residents of Canada were still admissible, but by January 1931 Jewish immigration from Europe plummeted: a total of 214 Jewish immigrants arrived in Canada in 1931 compared with 3,702 in 1930.[211]

The arrival of Jewish immigrants in Winnipeg became a rare event. Between 1 April 1931 and 31 March 1932, a total of sixteen Jewish immigrants arriving from Europe stated that Manitoba was their destination compared with 534 in the same period in 1929–30 and 354 in 1930–31.[212] Aside from assisting Winnipeg Jews who encountered difficulties sponsoring wives and children to file appeals, the WDJIAS could do little to fulfill its mandate to promote Jewish immigration to Canada. As unemployment increased and small businesses struggled to survive, supporters of the WDJIAS, demoralized by the government's restrictions on immigration, found it difficult either to afford or to justify paying membership dues or making the donations that the society needed to continue to function. By 1932, its financial situation was precarious; Gray reported that "there is no money in the treasury" to pay for the office rent or the telephone and that, since it was "not an opportune time to go campaigning" for donations, the executive of the WDJIAS was likely to decide "that the whole thing will be closed down."[213]

Unlike the JIAS, supported by wealthy Montreal Jews such as Lyon Cohen and Samuel Bronfman, none of the affluent members of Winnipeg's Jewish community came to the aid of the WDJIAS.[214] Nevertheless, despite its financial problems, the society persevered largely because M.A. Gray, in addition to his responsibilities as a city councillor, was prepared to volunteer his time on a daily basis.[215] Aside from assisting Winnipeg Jews to obtain visas to visit or reside in the United States and sending remittances and parcels to

Eastern Europe, the WDJIAS was forced to deal with the growing number of recent Jewish immigrants at risk of deportation.

As unemployment increased in Winnipeg, so did the risk of becoming a public charge. Under pressure from municipal governments facing rapidly escalating costs of relief, W.A. Gordon, minister of immigration and colonization, authorized his officials to initiate deportation proceedings as soon as the department received notification that an immigrant had become a public charge. For Gordon, immigrants from Europe were a particular concern: "With regard to foreign-born immigrants who have become a public charge . . . deportations are being effected just as promptly as passports can be made available to send the deport back to his native country."[216] Deportations for being a public charge, which totalled 444 from 1 April 1928 to 31 March 1929, increased to 2,106 in the same period in 1929–30, to 2,245 in 1930–31, to 4,507 in 1931–32, and to 4,916 in 1932–33.[217] The WDJIAS warned recent immigrants of the danger of applying for relief—the City of Winnipeg Relief Department routinely reported all applicants who were not citizens to the district commissioner of immigration who initiated deportation proceedings—and few did so, but as unemployment increased the society was forced to use its meagre resources to provide a growing number of destitute Jews with assistance.[218] However, when immigrants were unable to pay their hospital bills, it was often difficult for Gray to intervene in time to prevent hospital administrators from reporting them to the immigration department as public charges. In 1932–33, representatives of the WDJIAS appeared before ten boards of inquiry on behalf of Jewish immigrants and in all cases successfully appealed deportation orders by assuming responsibility for their hospital bills.[219]

However, facing insolvency, the executive of the WDJIAS realized that it did not have the resources to dispense relief and continue to pay immigrants' hospital bills. A partial solution was to assist Jewish immigrants who had lived in Canada for five years, and therefore were eligible for citizenship, to apply for their naturalization papers. As Canadian citizens, if they became public charges, they would not be vulnerable to deportation. Between April 1932 and May 1933, the WDJIAS "prepared applications for naturalization papers for 65 people . . . and in some cases, especially the refugees, the $5.00 fee was advanced by the society in order that we are protected in the event of these people becoming a public charge, in which case the society would be responsible."[220]

Eleven years after communal activists in Winnipeg's Jewish community reconstituted the Hebrew Immigrant Aid Society of Canada as the Western Division of the Jewish Immigrant Aid Society as part of a nation-wide campaign to persuade the government to adopt an "open door" immigration policy, the WDJIAS was reduced to preventing the deportation of Jewish immigrants who had settled in Winnipeg. Nevertheless, between 1920 and 1930, with the support of the WDJIAS, the JIAS succeeded in circumventing a series of regulations crafted to restrict Jewish immigration to Canada. Without the persistent lobbying of ministers of immigration by S.W. Jacobs, Lyon Cohen, and A.A. Heaps, and the determination of the members of the executives and general secretaries of both societies to maintain effective working relationships with Black, Egan, Blair, and other senior officials of the immigration department, most of the 41,800 Jews who came to Canada in this period under quota agreements or on permits would never have been admitted.[221] Many of the approximately 2,500 Jewish immigrants who settled in Winnipeg were women and children welcomed by husbands and fathers who, after long separations, had eagerly prepared for their arrival. But for the majority, especially the refugees, from their arrival at the railway station to their application for naturalization certificates, the services provided by the WDJIAS enabled them to find their place as new members of Winnipeg's Jewish community.[222]

CONCLUSION

The immigrants who established Winnipeg's Jewish community came to Canada in an era of limited government responsibility for social welfare. With few exceptions, elected representatives at the municipal, provincial, and federal levels of government subscribed to the doctrine that individuals were responsible for their well-being and opportunity. The Immigration Act reinforced this doctrine, and immigrants admitted into Canada were expected to be self-sufficient. Those who became public charges before they acquired citizenship and out of desperation applied for municipal relief, or were admitted to hospital and could not pay for their medical care, were summarily deported. The prevailing view of the role of the government in this pre–welfare state era was that its primary responsibility was to promote economic growth and development by facilitating the investment of capital and not to support those who failed to be self-sufficient. To do so would require higher rates of taxation to fund relief or pay for medical care, a tax burden that would discourage investment and inhibit economic growth. Moreover, assisting those who failed to become self-sufficient would undermine their work ethic by reducing their motivation to accept whatever terms and conditions of employment they were offered.

Jewish immigrants readily accepted the prevailing doctrine of individual responsibility. Having made the difficult decision to emigrate, they were fully prepared, and indeed welcomed the opportunity, to live in a society in which, unlike in Tsarist Russia (which subjected Jews to debilitating restrictions that forced them to live in poverty), hard work could lead to self-sufficiency and even prosperity. But they were also acutely aware that misfortunes were an inevitable part of life, that circumstances beyond an individual's control, such as an illness, a disability, the death of a family's main income earner, the death of a parent or both parents, or infirmity in old age, could erode or destroy self-sufficiency. With the exception of a small minority who acquired sufficient wealth to protect their families from these misfortunes, the overwhelming majority of members of Winnipeg's Jewish community had low or modest incomes. Consequently, accumulating savings was so difficult that common occurrences, such as an interruption of income or unexpected medical expenses, posed serious threats to a family's financial security. Recognizing that they were all vulnerable to the same misfortunes and did not have the financial resources to protect themselves or their families, Jewish immigrants established a system of communal social welfare.

Based upon the principle of communal solidarity, that acting collectively members of Winnipeg's Jewish community could protect each other from life's misfortunes, between 1903 and 1926, Jewish immigrants established over fifty mutual aid societies, a charity that provided assistance to the poor, three social welfare institutions (an orphanage, a home for the aged, and a medical clinic), and two organizations, one that sent hundreds of thousands of dollars to aid Jewish victims of war in Eastern Europe and one that assisted Jewish immigrants and hundreds of refugees to settle in Winnipeg. Their organizational activism extended the scope of communal solidarity beyond Winnipeg to include western Canada; both the Jewish Old Folks' Home and the Jewish Orphanage were supported by and served Jewish communities throughout the region. Similarly, Winnipeg's Jewish community became the organizational centre of both Western Canada's Jewish Fund for the Relief of War Sufferers and the Western Division of the Jewish Immigrant Aid Society of Canada, two associations that linked the work of Jewish communal activists in Winnipeg and Jewish communities in rural Manitoba, Saskatchewan, and Alberta to national and international efforts to aid Jews throughout Europe.

However, as this history of the establishment and development of the Jewish community's social welfare organizations and institutions demonstrates, at various times disputes over communal governance undermined communal solidarity. Whereas Jewish activists who belonged to mutual aid societies or supported socialist organizations such as Poale Zion believed that communal governance should be based upon democratic principles and practices, that leaders should be elected by and held accountable to members of the community, many of Winnipeg's Jewish notables assumed that they were entitled to leadership positions. Unwilling to accept a system of communal governance that denied them the leadership positions that they thought they deserved, with the exception of the Jewish Orphanage, they either chose not to make donations to support communal social welfare or, in the case of the Central Relief for European Jews, used fundraising to bargain for influence over the decisions of Western Canada's Jewish Fund for the Relief of War Sufferers.

Nevertheless, ultimately, democratic principles and practices prevailed. By the 1920s, Jewish immigrants arriving in Winnipeg became members of a community with an elaborate system of social welfare. Met at the train station by representatives of the Western Division of the Jewish Immigrant Aid Society, Jewish immigrants without friends or relatives in Winnipeg were escorted to a refuge where they were given meals and advice about finding accommodation and employment. They quickly learned that the Jewish community's system of social welfare—the benefits provided by mutual aid societies, charitable assistance to the poor, institutional care for orphans, the children of single parents, and the elderly, and free medical care—offered them a substantial measure of social security. With the protection that the social welfare system provided from potentially devastating financial effects of misfortunes, Jewish immigrants could plan for the future. Joining a mutual aid society that provided free loans gave them an opportunity to borrow money to make otherwise unaffordable household purchases, invest in businesses, or pay for steamship tickets to bring family members and relatives to Canada. Once established, they had ample opportunities to make their own contributions to communal solidarity by becoming members or supporters of one of the Jewish community's numerous societies, organizations, institutions, and associations.

Unquestionably, communal solidarity played a crucial role in the settlement and integration of Jewish immigrants. It enabled them to rebuild their lives, achieve a measure of financial security, and become contributing members of their new community. It also proved to be resilient. In the 1930s, it protected many members of the Jewish community from the ruinous effects of a decade-long economic depression. Despite high rates of unemployment and a substantial decline in business income, with the exception of the Western Division of the Jewish Immigrant Aid Society, the Jewish community's mutual aid societies, the United Hebrew Relief, the Jewish Old Folks' Home, the Jewish Orphanage, and the Mount Carmel Clinic continued to function. Countless Jewish families experienced severe hardship during the Depression, but very few Winnipeg Jews applied for relief; mutual aid societies continued to pay benefits, and, though the United Hebrew Relief had difficulty raising enough money to deal with the increase in the number of requests for assistance, the Jewish community's charity continued to support the destitute.

A survey of the more recent history of Winnipeg's Jewish community suggests that communal solidarity evolved after the Depression. By the 1960s, all of the more than fifty mutual aid societies had ceased to exist, casualties of increasing affluence, welfare state income assistance benefits such as unemployment insurance, and changes in banking practices that increased the availability of personal loans. By the 1950s, memberships began to decline. The sons and daughters of the founders and members of mutual aid societies, the beneficiaries of their parents' commitment to communal solidarity, did not have the same compelling financial incentive to become members, nor, having grown up in Winnipeg, could they identify with an older generation's need for the companionship provided by a "society," an organization of immigrants whose lives and experiences were so different from their own. Unable to attract new members, once old age and the deaths of their founders and initial members reduced their memberships to the point that they were no longer financially viable, these societies dissolved.[1]

The United Hebrew Relief continued to assist destitute Jews until 1942, when changes in the practice of social work led to the establishment of the United Hebrew Social Service Bureau. Staffed by professional social workers, the bureau assumed the United Hebrew Relief's responsibility for assisting the poor, integrating financial aid with counselling and other services to help families in crisis situations resolve their problems. After a long debate about the comparative advantages of foster care and institutional care, in 1948 the Jewish Orphanage closed. The bureau, renamed the Jewish Family Service Bureau in 1951, became responsible for the placement and supervision of Jewish orphans in foster care. Incorporated in 1952 as the Jewish Child and Family Service, it was granted legal authority to serve as a Jewish children's aid society.

Beginning in 1947, when the federal government reluctantly approved the admission of Jewish war orphans, the United Hebrew Social Service Bureau began assisting Jewish immigrants by arranging accommodation for them; providing them with food, clothing, and English classes; and helping them to find employment. Dormant since 1941, the Western Division of the Jewish Immigrant Aid Society (WDJIAS) of Canada was reorganized after the Second World War to support a Canadian Jewish Congress initiative to bring Holocaust survivors to Canada. The WDJIAS helped Winnipeg Jews to locate family members living in displaced persons camps, arranged for the shipment of parcels and the transfer of money to Europe, and assisted them to apply to sponsor their relatives to come to Canada. It also supported the "Tailor Project," a contract labour scheme that brought skilled Jewish garment and fur workers living in displaced persons camps and their families to Canada.[2] Once the postwar Jewish refugee crisis eased and the federal government reinstated its pre-1930 policy of encouraging immigration from Europe, the WDJIAS disbanded, and the Jewish Child and Family Service became the Jewish community's immigrant settlement agency.

Although both the Jewish Old Folks' Home and the Mount Carmel Clinic continued to function, both institutions were affected by changes in the demography of the Jewish community. Throughout the 1930s, the proportion of Winnipeg's Jewish population over the age of sixty-five steadily increased.[3] Unable to accommodate all of the elderly Jews who applied for admission, the board of directors of the home discussed plans to build a larger, more modern building in the North End, but launching a fundraising campaign during the Depression was not considered feasible. However, stimulated by wartime production, by 1940 increased levels of employment and business activity convinced the board that it could raise the $100,000 needed to purchase land and construct a modern facility. Enlarged five times to accommodate more residents, by the 1980s the Jewish Old Folks' Home, renamed the Sharon Home, no longer offered the type of accommodation and the range of medical and therapeutic services that the Jewish community wanted to provide to its elderly members. In 2001, the Sharon Home opened the first phase of the Saul and Claribel Simkin Centre in the South End, which, after almost fifty years of post–Second World War urban migration, had displaced the North End as the demographic centre of the Jewish community.

The post–Second World War migration of Winnipeg's Jews to the South End also affected the demand for medical services provided by the Mount Carmel Clinic. As the Jewish population of the North End declined, fewer patients visited the clinic. But the demand for free medical care was also affected by prosperity—increasingly, members of the Jewish community could afford to pay for physicians' and dentists' services—and changes to Manitoba's health-care system. In 1938, the provincial government passed legislation establishing Manitoba Blue Cross, a voluntary, non-profit, medical insurance plan that covered the cost of hospital care. Launched on 1 January 1939, the plan had 15,000 members by 1941. In the next decade, enrolment steadily increased. By the end of 1957, when the federal government passed the Hospital Insurance and Diagnostic Services Act, the first step in establishing Medicare, 46 percent of Manitoba's eligible residents had Blue Cross coverage.[4] Taking advantage of federal funding for health-care services, in 1958 the Manitoba government introduced hospital insurance, replacing Blue Cross with a system that provided free hospital care and diagnostic services to all residents of the province. And in 1969, three years after the federal government passed the Medical Care Act, the Manitoba government added physicians' services to the province's system of free health-care coverage.

Although the arrival of Jewish orphans and displaced persons together with an influx of immigrants from Europe temporarily increased the demand for free medical care, by the 1950s very few patients visited the Mount Carmel Clinic. However, redefining its mandate, in the late 1950s and 1960s the clinic pioneered the development of community-based health care, a holistic approach to delivering medical services. In addition to free access to physicians, dentists, diagnostic services, and medication, the clinic established a range of services such as a day hospital, a well-baby program, family planning, and counselling. The Jewish Welfare Fund continued to provide financial support, and the clinic was able to depend on a small number of Jewish physicians who volunteered their time, but increasingly its clientele reflected the multi-ethnic diversity of the North End. With the introduction of Medicare, which enabled the clinic to appoint full-time physicians, and funding provided by government operating grants and agencies such as the United Way, the clinic continued its transformation into a facility that provided a wide range of community-based medical services.

Few of the Jewish immigrants who established Winnipeg's Jewish community could have imagined that their children and grandchildren would live in a society in which the government was responsible for universal health care, provided various forms of income assistance, and funded social services. Certainly, the establishment of the welfare state reduced much of the need for Winnipeg's Jews to engage in collective action to protect each other from life's misfortunes. However, though the organizational landscape of Winnipeg's Jewish community changed, the legacy of the generation of Jewish immigrants who embraced communal solidarity endured. After the 1930s, communal solidarity evolved, but it continued to shape the development of social welfare in Winnipeg's Jewish community.

ACKNOWLEDGEMENTS

Growing up in Winnipeg's North End, I frequently went to the Mount Carmel Clinic on Selkirk Avenue to visit my mother, the executive director. During my visits, I often looked at a framed collection of photographs of the thirty-two men and women who had served on the clinic's board of directors in 1929. I was, of course, intrigued by their old-fashioned clothing but I was also struck by their sense of purpose. They were, my mother informed me, the men and women who had led a fundraising drive to build a "hospital" to provide free medical care to members of the Jewish community.

Much later, when I became interested in the history of immigration to Canada and the formation of Winnipeg's Jewish community, I became aware that very little had been written about the men and women who had established the Mount Carmel Clinic or indeed the other institutions, organizations, and societies that had assumed collective responsibility for the welfare of the thousands of Jewish immigrants who settled in Winnipeg. Recovering the history of the contribution this remarkable generation of activists and volunteers made to the formation of Winnipeg's Jewish community proved to be a time-consuming quest. This book could not have been written without the assistance of staff at numerous archives I visited in Canada and the United States. I am particularly indebted to Stan Carbone and Vanesa Harari of the archives of the Jewish Heritage Centre of Western Canada in Winnipeg and Janice Rosen and the staff of the Alex Dworkin Canadian Jewish Archives in Montreal. Their prompt responses to numerous requests for information and efforts to make documents available during my visits are greatly appreciated.

I also want to thank the staff of the University of Manitoba Press. David Carr's enthusiasm, Jill McConkey's patient advice as I honed the manuscript, and Glenn Bergen's editorial guidance confirmed that I made a wise choice of publishers.

This book would not have been written without the support and encouragement of my family. My children, Jacob, Daniel, and Anna, made time in their busy academic schedules to provide incisive comments on drafts of the manuscript. Above all, Kathy's conviction that writing about communal solidarity in Winnipeg's Jewish community was especially important because it affirmed that we all are responsible for each other sustained me from the beginning of my research to completion of the book.

NOTES

Introduction

1 Simon Kuznets, "Immigration of Russian Jews to the United States: Background and Structure," *Perspectives in American History* 9 (1975): 50. Calculated from Table V, section A. Jewish emigration from Russia began earlier, but 1881 is regarded as a turning point, the beginning of a mass exodus that ended in 1914.

2 Gerald Tulchinsky, *Canada's Jews: A People's Journey* (Toronto: University of Toronto Press, 2008), 8.

3 Details of the demography and growth of Winnipeg's Jewish community can be found in Chapter 3.

4 Gerald Tulchinsky, *Branching Out: The Transformation of the Canadian Jewish Community* (Toronto: Stoddart, 1998), 10.

5 In 1932, the Mount Carmel Clinic Board of Directors had forty-five members. *Jewish Post*, 4 February 1932.

Chapter 1: Jewish Life in the Pale of Settlement

1 Approximately 7,300 of the nearly 9,000 Jewish immigrants who settled in Winnipeg from 1882 to 1914 came from the Pale of Settlement (the second largest number, 655, came from Romania).

2 John D. Klier, "Russian Jewry on the Eve of the Pogroms," in *Pogroms: Anti-Jewish Violence in Modern Jewish History*, ed. John D. Klier and Shlomo Lambroza (Cambridge, UK: Cambridge University Press, 1992), 5; Simon Kuznets, "Immigration of Russian Jews to the United States: Background and Structure," *Perspectives in American History* 9 (1975): 70, calculated from Table VII, section A.

3 Klier, "Russian Jewry," 5.

4 Calculated from population figures in ibid.

5 Eli Lederhendler, "Classless: On the Social Status of Jews in Russia and Eastern Europe in the Late Nineteenth Century," *Contemporary Studies in Society and History* 50, no. 2 (2008): 509.

6 Ibid., 514–15. Yoav Peled states that there were "390,000 Jewish workers in the Pale, including over 240,000 handicraft workers, over 45,000 factory workers and over 100,000 day laborers and agricultural workers." Yoav Peled, *Class and Ethnicity in the Pale: The Political Economy of Jewish Workers' Nationalism in Late Imperial Russia* (New York: St. Martin's Press, 1989), 74.

7 Henry Rosenthal, "Agricultural Colonies in Present Day Russia," in *The Jewish Encyclopedia: A Descriptive Record of the Earliest Times to the Present Day*, ed. Isadore Singer (New York: Funk and Wagnalls, 1901), 1: 252–56.

8 Klier states that in 1881 "just over 80 percent" of the 2.9 million Jews in the Pale lived in towns or *shtetlekh* and that the remainder "resided in the countryside in peasant villages." Klier, "Russian Jewry," 5.

9 Kuznets, "Immigration of Russian Jews," 63, Table VI, section A. The calculation of the increase in total population is based upon figures for European Russia, an area larger than the Pale.

10 Ibid., calculated from Table VI, section B.

11 Arcadius Kahan, "Impact of Industrialization on the Jews in Tsarist Russia," in *Essays in Jewish Social and Economic History*, ed. Roger Weiss (Chicago: University of Chicago Press, 1986), 50, Table A 2.

12 Kahan estimates that, by the end of the nineteenth century, 27–28 percent of women were employed. Ibid., 6.

13 Salo W. Baron, *The Russian Jew under Tsars and Soviets*, 2nd ed. (New York: Macmillan, 1976), 95.

14 Kuznets states that "perhaps a fifth to a quarter of the population [was] at miserably low economic levels," and, reviewing literary and documentary evidence, Lederhendler concludes that "over a third was pauperized." Kuznets, "Immigration of Russian Jews," 79; Lederhendler, "Classless," 518.

15 Baron notes that, in a thirty-year period beginning in 1858, the Russian economy experienced eighteen years of depression. Baron, *The Russian Jew*, 95.

16 Heinz-Dieter Lowe, *The Tsars and the Jews: Reform, Reaction, and Anti-Semitism in Imperial Russia, 1772–1917* (Chur, Switzerland: Harwood, 1993), 56.

17 Ibid., 63.

18 Ibid., 70–71; Yohanan Petrovsky-Shtern, *Jews in the Russian Army, 1827–1917* (Oxford: Oxford University Press, 2009), 175.

19 Eugene M. Avrutin, *Jews and the Imperial State: Identification Politics in Tsarist Russia* (Ithaca, NY: Cornell University Press, 2010), 95, 108–15.

20 Baron, *The Russian Jew*, 48.

21 Brian Horowitz, *Jewish Philanthropy and Enlightenment in Late-Tsarist Russia* (Seattle: University of Washington Press, 2009), 257n43.

22 Benjamin Nathans, *Beyond the Pale: The Jewish Encounter with Late Imperial Russia* (Berkeley: University of California Press, 2002), 354, Table 14; Michael Stanislowski, "Russian Jewry, the Russian State, and the Dynamics of Russian Emancipation," in *Paths of Emancipation: Jews, States, and Citizenship*, ed. Pierre Birnbaum and Ira Katznelson (Princeton, NJ: Princeton University Press, 1995), 278.

23 S.M. Dubnow, *History of the Jews in Russia and Poland* (Philadelphia: Jewish Publication Society of America, 1946), 2: 222, 413–14. All members of the conscript's family were responsible for payment of the fine.

24 Baron, *The Russian Jew*, 67.

25 Lowe, *The Tsars and the Jews*, 93.

26 Shaul Stampfer, "Patterns of Internal Jewish Migration in the Russian Empire," in *Jews and Jewish Life in Russia and the Soviet Union*, ed. Yaccov Ro'I (Abingdon: Routledge, 1995).

27 In 1844, the Russian government abolished the *kahal*, the council that traditionally governed Jewish communities. Avrutin, *Jews and the Imperial State*, 25–27; Antony Polonsky, *The Jews in Poland and Russia, Volume I, 1350–1881* (Oxford: Littman

Library of Jewish Civilization, 2010), 52. Crown rabbis were mandated by the state to collect census data and enforce government regulations.

28 David Vital, *A People Apart: The Jews in Europe, 1789–1939* (Oxford: Oxford University Press, 1999), 352.

29 For an overview of the *Haskalah* movement, see Immanuel Etkes, "Haskalah," in *The YIVO Encyclopedia of Jews in Eastern Europe*, ed. Gershon David Hundert (New Haven, CT: Yale University Press, 2009), 1: 681–88.

30 Polonsky, *The Jews in Poland and Russia, Volume I*, 419–20. ORPE is an abbreviation of the acronym for the society's name in Russian.

31 Jewish emigration from the Russian Empire began earlier, but 1881 is generally regarded as the beginning of the era of mass transatlantic migration via Western European countries to North America that ended in 1914.

32 David Weinberg identifies these intellectuals as members of a "transitional generation." David H. Weinberg, *Between Tradition and Modernity* (New York: Holmes and Meier, 1996), 1–28.

33 Ibid., 145–216; Vital, *A People Apart*, 389–400.

34 For an account of the origin and evolution of the Bund, see Henry J. Tobias, *The Jewish Bund in Russia: From Its Origins to 1905* (Stanford, CA: Stanford University Press, 1972).

35 By 1900, the Bund had established 274 branches with 34,000 members, and by 1905 Poale Zion had a membership of "about 25,000." Israel Kolatt, "Po'Alei," in *Encyclopedia Judaica*, 2nd ed., ed. Michael Berenbaum and Fred S. Skolnik (Detroit: Macmillan Reference USA, 2007), 16: 245; David Blatman, "Bund," in Hundert, ed., *The YIVO Encyclopedia*, 1: 276.

36 Daniel Soyer, *Jewish Immigrant Associations and American Identity in New York, 1880–1939* (Cambridge, MA: Harvard University Press, 1997), 18.

37 Their dominance was reinforced by the deeply ingrained deference of the poorly educated for "beautiful" or learned Jews, elite religious scholars whose membership was "transmitted from generation to generation among the leading families." Shaul Stampfer, "Heder Study, Knowledge of Torah, and the Maintenance of Social Stratification," in Shaul Stampfer, *Families Rabbis, and Education: Traditional Jewish Society in Nineteenth-Century Eastern Europe* (Oxford: Littman Library of Jewish Civilization, 2010), 164–65.

38 David E. Fishman, *The Rise of Modern Yiddish Culture* (Pittsburgh: University of Pittsburgh Press, 2005), 5. Fishman notes that "the Haskalah's negative attitude toward Yiddish as a *zhargon* became the norm among Jews who considered themselves modern and enlightened." Ibid., 6.

39 For a brief survey of prominent nineteenth-century Hebrew writers, see Baron, *The Russian Jew*, 126–27; for a discussion of Hebrew newspapers and periodicals, see Avraham Greenbaum, "Newspapers and Periodicals," in Hundert, ed., *The YIVO Encyclopedia:* 1, 1264–65.

40 Quoted in Horowitz, *Jewish Philanthropy*, 37.

41 The 1897 Russian census identified Jews based upon their religion and nationality (language). Isaac M. Rubinow, *Economic Condition of the Jews in Russia* (New York: Arno Press, 1975), 488na.

42 Fishman, *The Rise of Modern Yiddish Culture*, 22–25.

43 Ibid., 7.

44 Ibid.

45 Ibid., 8.

46 Kenneth Moss, "Printing and Publishing after 1800," in Hundert, ed., *The YIVO Encyclopedia*, 2: 1468.

47 Fishman, *The Rise of Modern Yiddish Culture*, 12; Moss, "Printing and Publishing," 1467; Jeffrey Veidlinger, *Jewish Public Culture in the Late Russian Empire* (Bloomington: Indiana University Press, 2009), 100–11.

48 Fishman, *The Rise of Modern Yiddish Culture*, 12.

49 Ibid.

50 Sarah Abrevaya Stein, *Making Jews Modern: The Yiddish and Ladino Press in the Russian and Ottoman Empires* (Bloomington: Indiana University Press, 2004), 31.

51 Ibid.; Scott Ury, "Der Fraynd," in Hundert, ed., *The YIVO Encyclopedia*, 1: 547; Fishman, *The Rise of Modern Yiddish Culture*, 13.

52 Antony Polonsky, "Warsaw," in Hundert, ed., *The YIVO Encyclopedia*, 2: 1997; Stein, *Making Jews Modern*, 49.

53 Ury states that "some researchers" claim that because of these practices 10 percent of the Jewish population of the Russian Empire had access to a Yiddish newspaper. Ury, "Der Fraynd," 547.

54 Veidlinger, *Jewish Public Culture*, 27, 36–37.

55 Fishman, *The Rise of Modern Yiddish Culture*, 49.

56 Veidlinger, *Jewish Public Culture*, 37.

57 Fishman, *The Rise of Modern Yiddish Culture*, 51–52; Ezra Mendelsohn, *Class Struggle in the Pale: The Formative Years of the Jewish Workers' Movement in Tsarist Russia* (Cambridge: Cambridge University Press, 1970), 122–23.

58 For a discussion of Jewish libraries, see Veidlinger, *Jewish Public Culture*, 24–66.

59 Ibid., 39–40.

60 Ibid., 34, quoting Falek Zolf, *Di leste fun a dor: Heymishe geshtaltn* (Winnipeg: Israelite Press, 1952), 189.

61 Veidlinger, *Jewish Public Culture*, 74.

62 Ibid., 59, Table 2.2.

63 Mendelsohn, *Class Struggle in the Pale*, 118–21.

64 Ibid., 122.

65 Ibid., 59, 57, calculated from Table 2.2.

66 Ibid., 54.

67 The curriculum of the *heder* or traditional Jewish "primary school" focused on teaching boys fundamental elements of the Torah, Mishnah, Talmud, and religious liturgy.

68 Antony Polonsky, *The Jews in Poland and Russia, Volume II, 1881–1914* (Oxford: Littman Library of Jewish Civilization, 2010), 367.

69 Veidlinger, *Jewish Public Culture*, 142.

70 Paola Bertolone, "The Text of Goldfadn's *Di kishefmarkherin* and the Operetta Tradition," in *Yiddish Theater: New Approaches*, ed. Joel Berkowitz (Oxford: Littman Library of Jewish Civilization, 2003), 79.

71 Seth L. Wolitz, "Forging a Hero for the Jewish Stage: Goldfadn's *Bar Kokhba*," *Shofar* 20, no. 3 (2002): 56.

72 Veidlinger, *Jewish Public Culture*, 208–14.

73 Ibid., 196–202.

74 Seven of the twenty members of the Hirschbein Troupe were women. Ibid., 188, Figure 12.

Chapter 2: Social Welfare and Communal Governance

1 David G. Dalin, "*Tzedakah* with Dignity: Jewish Charity and Self-Help in Rabbinic Tradition," *Conservative Judaism* 51, no. 3 (1999): 3.

2 Salo W. Baron, *The Russian Jew under Tsars and Soviets*, 2nd ed. (New York: Macmillan, 1976), 107.

3 Mordechai Zalkin, "Charity," in *The YIVO Encyclopedia of Jews in Eastern Europe*, vol. 1, ed. Gershon David Hundert (New Haven, CT: Yale University Press, 2009), 307, 309.

4 According to Russian government sources, in 1881 there were 187 "such almshouses." Heinz-Dietrich Lowe, "From Charity to Social Policy: The Emergence of Jewish 'Self-Help' Organizations in Russia, 1800–1914," *East European Jewish Affairs* 27, no. 2 (1997): 55n7.

5 Mordechai Nadav, *The Jews of Pinsk, 1506–1880*, ed. Mark Jay Mirsky and Moshe Rosman (Stanford, CA: Stanford University Press, 2008), 455, 458. In his 1907 study, Isaac Rubinow identified 665 committees for the care of the sick, 500 societies for the distribution of food, seventy-two societies for the distribution of clothing, and fifty-one societies for assisting poor brides. Isaac M. Rubinow, *Economic Condition of the Jews in Russia* (New York: Arno Press, 1975), 573.

6 Zalkin, "Charity," 308.

7 Isaac Levitats, *The Jewish Community in Russia, 1844–1917* (Jerusalem: Posner and Sons, 1981), 164–65.

8 Dalin, "*Tzedakah* with Dignity," 4–5.

9 Ibid., 17–18.

10 Zalkin, "Charity," 308.

11 Baron, *The Russian Jew under Tsars and Soviets*, 107; Shaul Stampfer, *Families, Rabbis, and Education: Traditional Jewish Society in Nineteenth-Century Eastern Europe* (Oxford: Littman Library of Jewish Civilization, 2010), 91; Natan Meir, "From Communal Charity to National Welfare: Jewish Orphanages in Eastern Europe before and after World War I," *East European Jewish Affairs* 39, no. 1 (2009): 19, 23.

12 Dalin, "*Tzedakah* with Dignity," 18–19.

13 Marcos Silber, "Credit," in Hundert, ed., *The YIVO Encyclopedia*, 1: 362.

14 David Vital, *A People Apart: The Jews in Europe, 1789–1939* (Oxford: Oxford University Press, 1999), 302.

15 Meir, "From Communal Charity to National Welfare," 22; Stampfer, *Families*, 86–89.

16 David E. Fishman, *The Rise of Modern Yiddish Culture* (Pittsburgh: University of Pittsburgh Press, 2005), 76; Nadav, *The Jews of Pinsk*, 358.

17 Eli Lederhendler, *The Road to Modern Jewish Politics: Political Tradition and Political Reconstruction in the Jewish Community of Tsarist Russia* (New York: Oxford University Press, 1989), 138–39.

18 Ibid., 140–42.

19 Ibid., 145, 149.

20 For a discussion of the development of social welfare in nineteenth-century Western European Jewish communities, see Derek J. Penslar, *Shylock's Children: Economics and Jewish Identity in Modern Europe* (Berkeley: University of California Press, 2001).

21 Natan M. Meir, *Kiev, Jewish Metropolis: A History, 1859–1914* (Bloomington: Indiana University Press, 2010) 215–16, 233.

22 Stampfer, *Families*, 93.

23 Ibid., 94, Table 4.1, and 100, Table 4.2.

24 Ibid., 91.

25 Meir, "From Communal Charity to National Welfare."

26 The number of Jewish hospitals in "European Russia increased from 53 in 1880 to 130 in 1908." Lisa Rae Epstein, "Caring for the Soul's House: The Jews of Russia and Health Care 1860–1914" (PhD diss., Yale University, 1995), 174.

27 By 1912, the ORPE had twenty-nine branches and 5,800 members. Brian Horowitz, *Jewish Philanthropy and Enlightenment in Late-Tsarist Russia* (Seattle: University of Washington Press), 8.

28 Adele Lindenmeyr, *Poverty Is Not a Vice: Charity, Society, and State in Imperial Russia* (Princeton, NJ: Princeton University Press, 1996), 203–04. Suspicious of all forms of voluntary association, prior to 1897 the Russian government allowed Jewish communities to establish charities, but they were illegal.

29 Ibid., 205.

30 Stampfer, *Families*, 96; Meir, "From Communal Charity to National Welfare," 23; Levitats, *The Jewish Community in Russia*, 76.

31 Meir, "From Communal Charity to National Welfare," 23; Nadav, *The Jews of Pinsk*, 462. In Kiev, female philanthropists established a variety of social welfare services. Meir, *Kiev, Jewish Metropolis*, 237–45.

32 Meir, "From Communal Charity to National Welfare," 25; Levitats, *The Jewish Community in Russia*, 167.

33 Meir, *Kiev, Jewish Metropolis*, 84.

34 Ibid., 72–73, 80–85. Meir states that philanthropists sought recognition from both the Jewish community and the Russian government. See 214–15, 233–34.

35 Ibid., 72–73.

36 Ibid., 73.

37 Ibid., 290–95.

38 Jonathan Frankel, *Prophecy and Politics: Socialism, Nationalism, and the Russian Jews, 1862–1917* (Cambridge, UK: Cambridge University Press, 1981), 145, 148, 172; Vital, *A People Apart*, 417–18.

39 For example, in 1912, 83 percent of the Vilna Jewish community's "medical" budget was allocated to two hospitals and a home for the aged; the remainder funded a soup kitchen, the distribution of free food, and shelters. Levitats, *The Jewish Community in Russia*, 167.

40 Lowe, "From Charity to Social Policy," 61.

41 By 1889, members of self-help societies included stocking makers, printers, tailors, carpenters, locksmiths, and cigarette makers. Ezra Mendelsohn, *Class Struggle in the Pale: The Formative Years of the Jewish Workers' Movement in Tsarist Russia* (Cambridge, UK: Cambridge University Press, 1970), 41, 64.

42 Lowe, "From Charity to Social Policy," 61. Mendelsohn states that the traditional *hevrot* and the *kassy* "were clearly in opposition, representing as they did two entirely different worlds." Mendelsohn, *Class Struggle in the Pale*, 44.

43 According to data from the Jewish Colonization Society, at the end of the nineteenth century, women and girls comprised 29.5 percent of the industrial labour force in the Pale of Settlement. Arcadius Kahan, "The Impact of Industrialization in Tsarist Russia on the Socioeconomic Conditions of the Jewish Population," in *Essays in Jewish Social and Economic History*, ed. Roger Weiss (Chicago: University of Chicago Press, 1986), 62, Table A10.

44 For a discussion of the role of economic dependence of women in marriage, see ChaeRan F. Freeze, *Jewish Marriage and Divorce in Imperial Russia* (Hanover: Brandeis University Press, 2002).

45 Ibid., 66–67, 117–24.

46 Mendelsohn, *Class Struggle in the Pale*, 65–66.

47 Zvi Gitelman, "A Century of Jewish Politics in Eastern Europe: The Legacy of the Bund and Zionist Movement," in *The Emergence of Modern Jewish Politics: Bundism and Zionism in Eastern Europe*, ed. Zvi Gitelman (Pittsburgh: University of Pittsburgh Press, 2003), 17.

48 Jeffrey Veidlinger, *Jewish Public Culture in the Late Russian Empire* (Bloomington: Indiana University Press, 2009), 43; Mendelsohn, *Class Struggle in the Pale*, 80, 80n3.

49 This figure likely includes both traditional *gemilut hasadim* and modern self-help societies. Lowe, "From Charity to Social Policy," 63.

50 Silber, "Credit," 362.

51 Ibid.

52 Lowe, "From Charity to Social Policy," 64–65. Lowe notes that, counting the families of members, by 1913 "40–50 per cent of the Jewish population of the Pale" had access to credit. See 65.

53 Levitats, *The Jewish Community in Russia*, 153, calculated from Table 5.

54 Calculated from figures in Lowe, "From Charity to Social Policy," 65.

55 Ibid., 64; Theodore Norman, *An Outstretched Arm: A History of the Jewish Colonization Association* (London: Routledge and Kegan Paul, 1985), 47.

56 Lowe, "From Charity to Social Policy," 65; Levitats, *The Jewish Community in Russia*, 150.

57 Lowe, "From Charity to Social Policy," 65.

58 Silber states that in the Pale of Settlement artisans made up 36 percent of the membership of savings and loan cooperatives, and merchants and peddlers made up 32.6 percent. Silber, "Credit," 362.

59 Frankel, *Prophecy and Politics*, 157.

60 Christoph Gassenschmidt, *Jewish Liberal Politics in Tsarist Russia, 1900–1914: The Modernization of Russian Jewry* (New York: New York University Press, 1995), 39, 42.

61 The Zionists' decision to contest the 1907 election independently prompted Jewish liberals to form the Jewish People's Group. Antony Polonsky, *The Jews in Poland and Russia, Volume II, 1881–1914* (Oxford: Littman Library of Jewish Civilization, 2010), 64.

62 Under an emergency decree, between 1906 and 1909, military courts issued nearly 2,700 death sentences and sent over 22,000 into administrative exile. Richard Wortman, "Nicholas II and the Revolution," in *The Revolution of 1905 and Russia's*

Jews, ed. Stefani Hoffman and Ezra Mendelsohn (Philadelphia: University of Pennsylvania Press, 2008), 41–42.

63 Vladimir Levin, "The Jewish Socialist Parties in Russia in the Period of Reaction," in Hoffman and Mendelsohn, eds., *The Revolution of 1905*, 112–13; Gassenschmidt, *Jewish Liberal Politics*, 70.

64 Levin, "The Jewish Socialist Parties," 123–25.

65 Quoted in Samuel A. Portnoy, *Vladimir Medem: The Life and Soul of a Legendary Jewish Socialist* (New York: Ktav Publishing House, 1979), 444.

66 Gassenschmidt, *Jewish Liberal Politics*, 86.

67 Alexander Orbach, "The Jewish People's Group and Jewish Politics in Tsarist Russia, 1906–1914," *Modern Judaism* 10, no. 1 (1990): 11.

68 Vladimir Levin, "Orthodox Jewry and the Russian Government: An Attempt at Rapprochement, 1907–1914," *East European Jewish Affairs* 29, no. 2 (2009): 187–204.

69 Gassenschmidt, *Jewish Liberal Politics*, 86–92.

70 Levin, "The Jewish Socialist Parties," 118–26.

71 Gassenschmidt, *Jewish Liberal Politics*, 99.

72 Robert Weinberg, "The Russian Right Responds to 1905: Visual Depictions of Jews in Postrevolutionary Russia," in Hoffman and Mendelsohn, eds., *The Revolution of 1905*, 55–69.

73 Gassenschmidt, *Jewish Liberal Politics*, 109; Veidlinger, *Jewish Public Culture*, 135–36.

74 Gassenschmidt, *Jewish Liberal Politics*, 108, 117.

75 For a discussion of the concept of a "generational consciousness," see Robert Wahl, *The Generation of 1914* (Cambridge, MA: Harvard University Press, 1979), 210.

Chapter 3: Jewish Immigration and Settlement in Winnipeg

1 Library and Archives Canada (hereafter LAC), RG 76, Immigration, Passenger Lists, 1865–1922, T4788, (hereafter Passenger Lists). In addition to the Epsteins, ten other Jewish immigrants who arrived on the *Lake Michigan* stated that they intended to settle in Winnipeg.

2 Simon Kuznets, "Immigration of Russian Jews to the United States: Background and Structure," *Perspectives in American History* 9 (1975): 50, calculated from Table V, section A.

3 Ibid., 43, calculated from Table II. The estimate of 84,100 Jewish immigrants in the period 1880–1914 is based upon census and immigration data and assumes that births accounted for approximately 40 percent of the growth of the Jewish population of Canada between 1881 and 1901. Canada, *Census of Canada, 1880–81* (Ottawa: Maclean, Roger, and Company, 1882) (hereafter *Census, 1880–81*); Canada, *Fourth Census of Canada, 1901* (Ottawa: S.E. Dawson, Printer to the King, 1902) (hereafter *Fourth Census, 1901*); Department of Immigration and Colonization, *Report of the Department of Colonization and Immigration for the Fiscal Year Ended March 31, 1929* (Ottawa: F.C. Acland, 1930), 12, Table 2; 13, Table 3 (hereafter *Report, 1929*).

4 A total of 197 came from various other countries, and 177 migrated to Winnipeg from other provinces, primarily Quebec and Saskatchewan. Approximately half of the Jewish immigrants from England and the United States were the children of Jews who had emigrated from Russia, and 38 percent of Jews born in other Canadian provinces were the children of Russian Jews. This estimate of Jewish immigrants is

calculated from enumeration records of the 1916 census of the prairie provinces for North, Central, and South Winnipeg. *Census of Prairie Provinces, Population and Agriculture, Manitoba, Saskatchewan, Alberta, 1916* (Ottawa: King's Printer, 1918) (hereafter *Census, 1916*).

5 For a discussion of the pre-1881 history of Winnipeg's Jewish community, see Arthur A. Chiel, *The Jews in Manitoba: A Social History* (Toronto: University of Toronto Press, 1961), 10–24; and Allan Levine, *Coming of Age: A History of the Jewish People of Manitoba* (Winnipeg: Heartland Associates, 2009), 27–41.

6 *Census, 1880–81*, 1: 196, Table II. Based upon the 1880 and 1881 editions of *Henderson's Winnipeg Directory*, Harry Gutkin identified twenty-six Jews. At least three of the Jewish men identified were married. Harry Gutkin, *Journey into Our Heritage: The Story of the Jewish People in the Canadian West* (Toronto: Lester and Orpen Dennys, 1980), 18.

7 A.J. Arnold, "The Earliest Jews in Winnipeg, 1874–1882," *Beaver Magazine* 54, no. 2 (1974): 5; Mark Wischnitzer, *To Dwell in Safety: The Story of Jewish Migration since 1800* (Philadelphia: Jewish Publication Society of America, 1948), 46.

8 *Census, 1916.*

9 Canada, *Census of Canada, 1890–91* (Ottawa: S.E. Dawson, 1893), 231, Table IV (hereafter *Census, 1890–91*).

10 *Census, 1916*; *Fourth Census, 1901*, 291, Table IX.

11 Between 1900–01 and 1904–05, Jewish immigration to Canada averaged 3,458 people per year. It increased to 5,248 between 1905–06 and 1909–10 and to 7,276 between 1910–11 and 1913–14. *Report, 1929*, 12, Table 2; 13, Table 3.

12 Enumeration records, *Census, 1916*. Immigration to Canada from Europe virtually ended as a result of the outbreak of the First World War in August 1914. A total of 1,254 Jewish immigrants arrived in Winnipeg in 1913, 654 in 1914, 44 in 1915, and 31 in 1916.

13 Ibid., xxi, Table 8.

14 Immigration Act, 1906, ss. 28.

15 Ninette Kelley and Michael Trebilcock, *The Making of the Mosaic: A History of Canadian Immigration Policy*, 2nd ed. (Toronto: University of Toronto Press, 2010), 62–166.

16 According to the 1897 Russian census, Jews engaged in agricultural pursuits in the Pale of Settlement (including the fifteen *gubernii* of European Russia plus Congress Poland) comprised 2.9 percent of the labour force. Since this occupational category included forestry, hunting, and fishing, the proportion of Jews with farming experience living in the Pale was considerably less. Simon Kuznets, "Immigration of Russian Jews to the United States: Background and Structure," *Perspectives in American History* 9 (1975), 73, Table VIII; Herman Rosenthal, "Agricultural Colonies," in *The Jewish Encyclopedia*, vol. 1, ed. I. Singer (New York: Funk and Wagnalls, 1906), 252–56.

17 An Act Respecting Immigrants and Immigration, S.C. 1869, c. 10; An Act Respecting Immigrants and Immigration, S.C. 1906, c. 19; An Act Respecting Immigration, 1909–10, c. 27.

18 Referring to labourers in 1905, William Van Horne, chairman of the Board of Directors of the CPR, declared that "what we want is population. . . . Let them all come in. There is work for all." Quoted in Kelley and Trebilcock, *The Making of the Mosaic*, 141.

19 "Annual Report of the Department of the Interior for 1914," *Sessional Papers, 1915*, no. 25 (hereafter "Report, 1914"), 18, Table V.

20 None of the 178 Jewish immigrants destined for Winnipeg admitted in September and October 1913 were agriculturalists. Occupations of the men ranged from labourers to skilled workers such as carpenters or butchers, and single women invariably claimed to be domestics. Married women self-identified as housewives. Passenger Lists, T4804–T4806, T4750–T4751.

21 For example, see C.A. Magrath, *Canada's Growth and Some Problems Affecting It* (Ottawa: Mortimer Press, 1910); and J.S. Woodsworth, *Strangers within Our Gates; Or Becoming Canadians* (Toronto: F.C. Stephenson, 1909; reprinted, Toronto: University of Toronto Press, 1971). For a discussion of anti-Semitism in Canada in this period, see Gerald Tulchinsky, *Canada's Jews: A People's Journey* (Toronto: University of Toronto Press, 2008), 126–45.

22 Kelley and Trebilcock, *The Making of the Mosaic*, 124–34.

23 W.D. Scott, "Immigration and Population," in *Canada and Its Provinces: A History of the Canadian People and Their Institutions*, vol. 7, ed. Adam Shortt and Arthur G. Doughty (Toronto: Publishers Association of Canada, 1914), 590.

24 Kelley and Trebilcock, *The Making of the Mosaic*, 145–59.

25 Scott, "Immigration and Population," 571, 588–98. Between 1902–03 and 1913–14, when 68,866 Jews immigrated to Canada, immigration officials rejected, primarily on medical grounds, only 714 or 1 percent of the total number admitted. "Report, 1914," 75, 76.

26 *Report, 1929*, 13, Table 3.

27 See Chapter 7.

28 A total of 66,170 Jewish immigrants arrived in Canada between 1904–05 and 1914–15. *Report, 1929*, 12, Table 2; 13, Table 3.

29 Canada, *Sixth Census of Canada, 1921*, vol. 1 (Ottawa: F.A. Acland, King's Printer, 1924), 493, Table 27; Statistics Canada, R.H. Coates, and William D. Euler, *Seventh Census of Canada, 1931* vol. 2 (Ottawa: Dominion Bureau of Statistics, Department of Trade and Commerce, 1933), 435, Table 33.

30 Louis Rosenberg and M. Weinfeld, *Canada's Jews: A Social and Economic Study of Jews in Canada in the 1930s* (Montreal: McGill-Queen's University Press, 1993), 333, Table 197.

31 Constructed in 1884, the first CPR station was too small by 1904 to accommodate the volume of passenger traffic. Union Station, Winnipeg's second railway station, opened in 1912, but before the 1920s it was not a major immigrant terminus.

32 "Winnipeg Canadian Pacific Railway Station," *Canada's Historic Places*, http://www.historicplaces.ca/en/rep-reg/place-lieu.aspx?id=6345&pid=13321&h=Winnipeg,CP R,Station.

33 A description of the hotel's amenities can be found in the *Railway and Shipping World*, July 1904.

34 Robert Vineberg, "Welcoming Immigrants at the Gateway to Canada's West: Immigration Halls in Winnipeg, 1872–1975," *Manitoba History* 65 (2011): 13–17.

35 Alan F.J. Artibise, *Winnipeg: A Social History of Urban Growth, 1874–1914* (Montreal: McGill-Queen's University Press, 1975), 179–80.

36 Testimony of J. Bruce Walker, Commissioner of Immigration for Western Canada, 10 October 1916, in Great Britain, *Royal Commission on the Natural Resources, Trade,*

and Legislation of Certain Portions of His Majesty's Dominions, vols. 15–16 (London: HMSO, 1917), 47.

37 Vineberg, "Welcoming Immigrants," 18.

38 Ibid., 17–18; *Manitoba Free Press*, 1 June 1904.

39 Artibise, *Winnipeg*, 134, Table 8.

40 Ibid., 10, 134, Table 8.

41 Statistics Canada, *Population of Prairie Provinces,* 113, Table 13 https://www66.statcan.gc.ca/eng/1921/192101490113_p.%20113.pdf.

42 Reuben Bellan, *Winnipeg's First Century: An Economic History* (Winnipeg: Queenston, 1978), 53.

43 C.P. Wright and J.S. Davis, "Canada as a Producer and Exporter of Wheat," *Wheat Studies* 1, no. 8 (1925): 280, Table XII.

44 Between 1895 and 1914, the number of contractors increased from 20 to 228. Mavis E. Gray, "The Great Wheat Boom: The Winnipeg Construction Industry, 1896–1914" (MA thesis, University of Manitoba, 1997), 80.

45 Ibid., 55–57.

46 Bellan, *Winnipeg's First Century*, 79.

47 Artibise, *Winnipeg*, 10, 13, Table 8.

48 Ibid., 132, Table 7.

49 Ibid., 137.

50 Ibid., 141, 142, Table 12.

51 Ibid., 143, Table 13. The remainder, 18 percent, were Roman Catholic or Greek Orthodox.

52 Ibid., 23.

53 Don Nerbas, "Wealth and Privilege: An Analysis of Winnipeg's Early Business Elite," *Manitoba History* 47 (2004): 42–64.

54 Ibid., 44–49.

55 Artibise, *Winnipeg*, 25.

56 Ibid. As of January 1910, nine of Winnipeg's nineteen millionaires had served on City Council, including two as mayor. Ibid., 33.

57 Ibid., 69–72, 88–101, 113–23.

58 Ibid., 225, 223–45.

59 W.T. Easterbrook and Hugh G.J. Aitkin, *Canadian Economic History* (Toronto: University of Toronto Press, 1988), 493.

60 Calculated from profiles of members of the Legislative Assembly. Manitoba Historical Society (hereafter MHS), MHS Resources: Memorable Manitobans, http://www.mhs.mb.ca/docs/people/. For example, in 1921, Winnipeg had a population of 179,097 or 29 percent of the total population of Manitoba.

61 Ibid.

62 Ibid.

63 James Blanchard, "Rodmond P. Roblin, 1900–1915," in *Manitoba Premiers of the 19th and 20th Centuries*, ed. Barry Ferguson and Robert Wardhaugh (Regina: Canadian Plains Research Center, 2010), 119, 136.

64 Ibid., 123; Jim Blanchard, *Winnipeg 1912* (Winnipeg: University of Manitoba Press, 2005), 89, 93.

65 *The Parliamentary Guide*, ed. Ernest J. Chambers (Ottawa: Mortimer, 1908), 370.

66 Gerald Friesen, *The Canadian Prairies: A History* (Toronto: University of Toronto Press, 1984), 276; Artibise, *Winnipeg*, 85, 116–19.

67 MHS, Memorable Manitobans.

68 Artibise, *Winnipeg*, 167.

69 Blanchard, *Winnipeg 1912*, 80–95.

70 "The Act of Incorporation, Constitution, Rules and Regulations, and List of Members of the Manitoba Club," Winnipeg, 1913, Peel's Prairie Provinces https://www.google.ca/search?q=Peel%E2%80%99s+Prairie+Provinces+&ie=utf-8&oe=utf-8&client=firefox-b&gfe_rd=cr&dcr=0&ei=EKu2Wp3SD-yfXpyIqHA&gws_rd=cr; Alan Metcalfe, *Canada Learns to Play: The Emergence of Organized Sport, 1807–1914* (Toronto: McClelland and Stewart, 1987), 33.

71 MHS, Memorable Manitobans.

72 Alan Levine, *The Exchange: 100 Years of Trading Grain in Winnipeg* (Winnipeg: Peguis, 1987), 37–38.

73 Nerbas, "Wealth and Privilege," 55, Table 3, 56; Blanchard, *Winnipeg 1912*, 50, 131–34, 256–59. For examples of music and art clubs, see Artibise, *Winnipeg*, 34.

74 J.S. Woodsworth, *My Neighbour* (Toronto: University of Toronto Press, 1972), 46.

75 A. Ross McCormack, "Networks among British Immigrants and Accommodation to Canadian Society: Winnipeg, 1900–1914," in *Immigration in Canada: Historical Perspectives,* ed. Gerald Tulchinsky (Toronto: Copp Clark Longman, 1994), 214.

76 The only exception was a lodge for women, the Daughters of England. Ibid.

77 Doug Smith, *Let Us Rise! An Illustrated History of the Manitoba Labour Movement* (Vancouver: New Star Books, 1985), 14–19.

78 Doug Smith, *The Winnipeg Labour Council, 1894–1994: A Century of Labour Education, Organization, and Agitation* (Winnipeg: Manitoba Labour Education Centre, 1994), 6, 9.

79 Smith, *Let Us Rise!*, 27–30.

80 Ibid., 18–20, 22–23.

81 George Emery and J.C. Herbert Emery, *A Young Man's Benefit: The IOOF and Sickness Insurance in the United States and Canada, 1860–1929* (Montreal: McGill-Queen's University Press, 1999), 33–35, Tables 2.3 and 2.4.

82 J.S. Ewart, "Inaugural Presidential Address," in *Report of the Canadian Club of Winnipeg, 1904–1906*, 11, 32.

83 Ibid., 8. Between 1904 and 1920, nine of the club's sixteen presidents were members of the business elite, ten belonged to the Manitoba Club, and eight belonged to both the Manitoba Club and the St. Charles Country Club. MHS, Memorable Manitobans.

84 J.B. Mitchell, Honourary Secretary, *Fourth Report of the Canadian Club of Winnipeg*, 1907–1908 (hereafter *Fourth Report*), 7.

85 *Report of the Canadian Club of Winnipeg, 1904–1906*, 5.

86 Ibid.

87 Ibid., 9. Between 1904 and 1916, almost all of the members of the club were "barristers, brokers, dentists, doctors, insurance and real estate agents, journalists, and managers." Wade A. Henry, "W. Sanford Evans and the Canadian Club of Winnipeg, 1904–1919," *Manitoba History* 27 (1994): 12n28

88 *Fourth Report*, 7. By 1913, the Women's Club had 1,652 members.

89 *Fifth Annual Report of the Canadian Club of Winnipeg, 1908–1909*, 8–10.

90 Woodsworth, *Strangers within Our Gates*, 128; George Fisher Chipman, "Winnipeg: The Melting Pot," *Canadian Magazine* 33, no. 5 (1909): 414; J.S. Woodsworth, "The Immigrant Invasion after the War—Are We Ready for It?," in *Eleventh Annual Report of the Canadian Club of Winnipeg, 1914–1915*, 30.

91 Quoted in Murray Donnelly, *Dafoe of the* Free Press (Toronto: University of Toronto Press, 1968), 72.

92 Chipman, "Winnipeg," 410.

93 Woodsworth, *Strangers within Our Gates*, 76, 80, 84.

94 Artibise, *Winnipeg*, 142, Table 12.

95 Woodsworth, *Strangers within Our Gates*, 96, 110, 112, 115, 129.

96 Quoted in Donnelly, *Dafoe of the* Free Press, 73.

97 Woodsworth, *Strangers within Our Gates*, 127.

98 Ibid.

99 Ibid.

100 Ibid. Woodsworth also referred to Jews' "sordid materialism." Woodsworth, *My Neighbour*, 107.

101 Nerbas, "Wealth and Privilege," 44, 45.

102 Woodsworth, *Strangers within Our Gates*, 127.

103 Ibid.

104 Ibid.

105 Ibid.

106 Artibise, *Winnipeg*, 161, 216, 234, 235, 239.

107 John Carling and E.H. St. Denis, *Census of Manitoba, 1885–6* (Ottawa: Maclean, Roger, 1887), n.p., Table III (hereafter *Census, 1885–6*); *Census, 1916*, 143, Table VI.

108 *Census, 1885–6*, n.p., Table III.

109 *Fourth Census of Canada, 1901*, 290–91, Table XI. Most of the Austro-Hungarians were Galicians.

110 Enumeration records, *Census, 1916*. By 1916, a small number of Jews (283) lived in Elmwood, a district east of the Red River included in the Winnipeg North census district.

111 Ibid., 142–43, Table VI.

112 *Census, 1901*, 290–91, Table XI.

113 Ibid.

114 Canada, enumeration records, *Fifth Census of Canada, 1911* (Ottawa: Printer to the King, 1912) (hereafter *Census, 1911*).

115 Enumeration records, *Census, 1916*.

116 Ibid. British Canadians comprised 33 percent followed by Poles (16.6 percent), Ukrainians (21.6 percent), and German-speaking immigrants from Austria-Hungary and Germany (11.5 percent).

117 Ibid.

118 Artibise, *Winnipeg*, 158. In 1921, 86 percent of Winnipeg's Jews lived in the North End, and in 1931 88.7 percent lived there. Canada, *Sixth Census of Canada, 1921*, vol. 2 (Ottawa: F.A. Acland, 1924), 377, Table 26; Louis Rosenberg, *A Population Study of*

Winnipeg's Jewish Community (Montreal: Canadian Jewish Congress, 1946), 12, Table III.

119 Enumeration records, *Census, 1916*.

120 *Census 1890–91*, 230, Table IV.

121 *Census, 1916*, 142–43, Table VI. Almost all of Central Winnipeg's Jewish residents lived between Pacific Avenue and the CPR railway.

122 Ibid.

123 *Census, 1890–91*, 230, Table IV; *Fourth Census, 1901*, 30, Table VII.

124 *Census, 1916*, 142–43, Table VI.

125 Enumeration records, ibid.; Daniel Stone, "Moving South: The Other Jewish Winnipeg before the Second World War," *Manitoba History* 76 (2014): 2–10.

126 A. Ross McCormack, *Reformers, Rebels, and Revolutionaries: The Western Canadian Radical Movement, 1899–1919* (Toronto: University of Toronto Press, 1977), 77–97.

127 Chipman, "Winnipeg," 414. This portrayal of Galician voters ignored widespread voting list manipulation and vote buying involving British Canadians throughout Manitoba. Blanchard, *Winnipeg 1912*, 61–64.

128 Woodsworth, *Strangers within Our Gates*, 239.

129 McCormack, *Reformers, Rebels, and Revolutionaries*, 93.

130 Roz Usiskin, "The Winnipeg Jewish Community: Its Radical Elements, 1905–1918," *MHS Transactions* 3, no. 33 (1976–77): 13.

131 *Israelite Press*, 30 April 1915, quoted in ibid., 14.

132 Orest T. Martynowych, "Ukrainian Section of the Socialist Party of Canada/Social Democratic Party of Canada," Centre for Ukrainian Canadian Studies, University of Manitoba. Contemporary sources estimated that between 12,000 and 35,000 workers marched in the parade.

133 Woodsworth, *Strangers within Our Gates*, 128.

134 Paul Burrows, "'Apostle of Anarchy': Emma Goldman's First Visit to Winnipeg in 1907," *Manitoba History* 57 (2008): 5.

135 Ibid., 4; *Winnipeg Telegram*, 11 April 1907.

136 *Voice*, 19 April 1907; Burrows, "'Apostle of Anarchy,'" 6.

137 LAC, RG 76, Immigration, Vol. 513, File 800111, correspondence, J.H. Ashdown to Frank Oliver, 9 April 1908.

138 Immigration Act, 1910, R.S., 1927, c. 93, s. 3, ss. (n).

139 Marilyn Barber, "Nationalism, Nativism, and the Social Gospel: The Protestant Church Response to Foreign Immigrants in Western Canada, 1897–1914," in *The Social Gospel in Canada*, ed. Richard Allen (Ottawa: National Museum of Canada, 1975), 189.

140 Ibid.

141 United Church Archives (hereafter UCA), Methodist Church of Canada, Board of Home Missions, Fond 14, Box 7, File 1, All People's Mission, Winnipeg, 1906–07, correspondence, J.V. Kovar to James Allen, 28 February 1907.

142 *Christian Guardian*, 3 January 1906, quoted in G.N. Emery, "The Methodist Church and the 'European Foreigner' of Winnipeg: The All People's Mission, 1889–1914," *MHS Transactions* 3, no. 28 (1971–72): 5.

143 UCA, Methodist Church of Canada, Board of Home Missions, Fond 14, Box 7, File 1, All People's Mission, Winnipeg, 1906–07, correspondence, J.V. Kovar to James Allen, 28 February 1907.

144 UCA, Methodist Church of Canada, Board of Home Missions, Fond 14, Box 7, File 3, All People's Mission, 1908–09.

145 Ibid.

146 UCA, Methodist Church of Canada, Board of Home Missions, Fond 14, Box 7, File 1, correspondence, J.S. Woodsworth to James Allen, 8 July 1907; ibid., File 2, J.S. Woodsworth, "All People's Mission," spring 1908?.

147 UCA, Methodist Church of Canada, Board of Home Missions, Fond 14, Box 1, File 9, correspondence, J.H. Ashdown to James Allen, 20 April 1909.

148 George Fisher Chipman, "The Refining Process," *Canadian Magazine* 33, no. 6 (1909): 548.

149 S.C. Murray, *The Challenge of Our Prairie Provinces* (Toronto: Committee of the Forward Movement, Presbyterian Church, 1920), n. pag.

150 UCA, Presbyterian Church, Board of Home Missions, Fond 123, Box 2, File 18.

151 Geraldine Carol Russin, "The Ukrainian United Church in Winnipeg, Manitoba, 1903–1961: A History of a Unique Religious Experience" (MA thesis, University of Manitoba, 1999).

152 S.B. Rohold, *The Jews in Canada*, 2nd ed. (Toronto: Board of Home Missions, Presbyterian Church, 1913), 15.

153 Ibid., 19.

154 Ibid., 22.

155 Ibid., 23; Peter Bush, *The Presbyterian Church in Canada's Mission on the Prairies and North, 1885–1925* (Winnipeg: Watson and Dwyer, 2000), 202–03. The church opened a mission at 153 Magnus Avenue and an assembly hall at 215 Jarvis Avenue. *Manitoba Free Press*, 31 January 1919.

156 Woodsworth, *Strangers within Our Gates*, 268–69, Appendix 4.

157 Emery, "The Methodist Church," 11. The Robertson Memorial Institute and the Mission to the Jews, which opened in 1911, served far fewer immigrants.

158 Artibise, *Winnipeg*, 201.

159 Donnelly, *Dafoe of the* Free Press, 57.

160 Ibid., 57–58, 72; UCA, Methodist Church of Canada, Board of Home Missions, Fond 14, Box 7, File 1, J.S. Woodsworth, "All People's Mission" report, received 13 November 1907.

161 Artibise, *Winnipeg*, 204.

162 *Tenth Annual Report of the Canadian Club of Winnipeg, 1913–1914*, 24.

163 Artibise, *Winnipeg*, 200–01. Woodsworth estimated that in 1907 "about four hundred" adult foreigners attended evening classes. Woodsworth, *Strangers within Our Gates*, 238.

164 Chipman, "The Refining Process," 550.

165 *Eleventh Annual Report of the Canadian Club of Winnipeg, 1914–1915*, 15.

166 Daniel Hiebert, "Class, Ethnicity, and Residential Structure: The Social Geography of Winnipeg, 1901–1921," *Journal of Historical Geography* 17, no. 1 (1991): 56–86.

167 Levine, *Coming of Age*, 124–27; Henry Trachtenberg, "Peddling, Politics, and Winnipeg's Jews, 1891–1895: The Political Acculturation of an Urban Immigrant Community," *Histoire sociale/Social History* 57 (1996): 176–77.

168 Enumeration records, *Census, 1916*.

169 Passenger Lists, T4795–T4803.

170 Artibise, *Winnipeg*, 123, Table 5. In 1886, 783 workers were employed in construction; by 1911, the number had increased to 10,715. Gray, "The Great Wheat Boom," 63.

171 See Chapter 1 for a discussion of Jewish employment in the Pale of Settlement.

172 Eaton's hired Jewish women to work in the mail order department but not as sales clerks. Sharon Chisvin, ed., *Jewish Life and Times*, vol. 7 (Winnipeg: Jewish Historical Society of Western Canada, 1998), 69–70.

173 McCormack, "Networks among British Immigrants," 216–17.

174 "Winnipeg Development and Industrial Bureau," in *Gateway City: Documents on the City of Winnipeg, 1873–1913*, ed. Alan F.J. Artibise (Winnipeg: Manitoba Records Society Publications and University of Manitoba Press, 1979), 156.

175 Artibise, *Winnipeg*, 123.

176 Ibid., 128.

177 Enumeration records, *Census, 1916*.

178 Ibid.

179 Ibid.

180 Ibid.; Harry Gale, "The Jewish Labour Movement in Winnipeg," in *First Annual Publication: A Selection of Papers Presented in 1968–1969* (Winnipeg: Jewish Historical Society of Western Canada, 1970), 3–4; Roz Usiskin, "'The Alien and the Bolshevik in Our Midst': The 1919 Winnipeg General Strike," in *Jewish Life and Times*, vol. 5 ed. Arnold R. Rogers (Winnipeg: Jewish Historical Society of Western Canada, 1988), 38.

181 Gale, "The Jewish Labour Movement," 4.

182 Enumeration records, *Census, 1911*.

183 Mary McKinnon, "Trade Unions and Employment Stability at the Canadian Pacific Railway, 1903–1929," in *Origins of the Modern Career*, ed. David Mitch, John Brown, and Marco D.H. van Leeuve (Aldershot, UK: Ashgate, 2004), 127.

184 Enumeration records, *Census, 1916*.

185 Ibid.

186 Employers routinely paid young workers less while they were being trained. For example, printers between the ages of fifteen and nineteen earned twelve to thirteen cents an hour, whereas the hourly rate for those over the age of twenty was between twenty and twenty-six cents.

187 Jacob and Crowley was owned by Ben Jacob, a Jewish immigrant from Russia, and a Christian, John Crowley, who came to Winnipeg from Toronto. Levine, *Coming of Age*, 114.

188 Enumeration records, *Census, 1916*.

189 Enumeration records, *Census, 1911*; enumeration records, *Census, 1916*.

190 Although information about rabbis' salaries is not available, based upon their education and occupation, they are considered professionals. The term "middle class" refers to individuals who earned at least $200 more than highly paid workers. In determining the number of merchants, dealers, and so on who were middle class, I have estimated that about one-third of them earned at least $1,200 annually.

191 The balance, 18 percent in Central Winnipeg and 19 percent in South Winnipeg, was comprised of merchants, dealers, and so on with working-class incomes.

192 For example, Max Krolik lived in a prestigious apartment building that he co-owned on Wardlaw Avenue built in 1905 at a cost of $25,000. Krolik had a jewellery store

on Main Street and was a part owner of a trust company. In 1916, census enumerators did not enter incomes for other Jewish residents of Wardlaw (Herman Steinkoff [*sic*], Max Steinkoff [*sic*], Nathan Korman, Louis Goldstein, Samuel Rosner, and Isaac Moscovitz), but in 1911 five of their neighbours earned between $1,920 and $3,500 a year. In 1911, a house on McMillan Avenue was advertised for sale at $6,000, and one on Balmoral Place was advertised for $12,000. *Winnipeg Tribune*, 22 April and 24 April 1911. For a discussion of the quality and price of houses in the South End, see Artibise, *Winnipeg*, 156, Table 8, and 167–68.

193 In 1911, approximately 94 percent of Jewish men had an occupation compared with 21.4 percent of Jewish women. Considering that few Jewish women over the age of twenty-two worked outside the home, it could be argued that this comparatively low level of participation in the workforce reflected the cultural values that shaped male and female gender roles rather than a lack of employment opportunities.

194 In 1913, Woodsworth reviewed the cost of living in Winnipeg and estimated the amount that a family needed to maintain a basic standard of living. I have adjusted his figures to take into consideration the rate of inflation between 1911 and 1913. Artibise, *Winnipeg*, 308–11, Appendix D; Canada, Department of Labour, *Report of the Board of Inquiry into the Cost of Living in Canada* (Ottawa: J. de Tache, 1915), 75.

195 This figure is based upon a sample of 206 income earners. If earners between the ages of fifteen and twenty are included, the average income of Jewish male workers drops to $537. Enumeration records, *Census, 1911*.

196 Ibid.

197 Ibid.

198 This figure is based upon a sample of 400 Jewish immigrants over the age of eighteen. Enumeration records, *Census, 1916*.

199 MHS, St. John's High School. http://www.mhs.mb.ca/docs/sites/stjohnshighschool.shtml.

200 By 1916, only nine Jews had graduated from professional programs offered by the University of Manitoba, four physicians and five lawyers. Harry Medovy, "The Early Jewish Physicians in Manitoba," *Manitoba Historical Society Transactions* 3, no. 29 (1972–73): 23–40; enumeration records, *Census, 1916*.

Chapter 4: Government Charitable Assistance and the Emergence of Jewish Social Welfare

1 Library and Archives Canada (hereafter LAC), RG 76, Immigration, Vol. 187, File 65412, correspondence, W.D. Scott to J.M. Cosgrove, 17 January 1911.

2 Under the 1906 Immigration Act, immigrants could be deported within two years of arriving in Canada; this term was increased to three years in 1910. Immigration Act, 1906, ss. 33; Immigration Act, 1910, ss. 40. Inmates of jails or prisons and those who advocated violent political change were also subject to deportation.

3 The requirement of three years of residency was in effect from 1868 to 1914. In 1914, the required period of residency was increased to five years. Naturalization Act, 1914, ss. 2 (a).

4 For a discussion of individualism, see Allan Smith, "The Myth of the Self-Made Man in English Canada," *Canadian Historical Review* 59, no. 2 (1978):189–219.

5 *Manitoba Free Press*, 10 February 1912, quoted in Alan F.J. Artibise, *Winnipeg: A Social History of Urban Growth, 1874–1914* (Montreal: McGill-Queen's University Press, 1975), 188. The Associated Charities was founded by "six men from the Board

of Trade and six from the Grain Exchange." Mrs. Sandford Evans, "A Message from Winnipeg," in *Addresses before the Canadian Club of Toronto*, vol. 8 (Toronto: Warwick Brothers and Rutter, 1911), 237.

6 Artibise, *Winnipeg*, 188.

7 Testimony of John Howard Toynbee Falk, 9 October 1916, in Great Britain, *Royal Commission on the Natural Resources, Trade, and Legislation of Certain Portions of His Majesty's Dominions*, vols. 15–16 (London: HMSO, 1917), 38–40 (hereafter *Royal Commission*). Falk testified that even the highest wage rate for unskilled labour, 27.5 cents an hour, was "not sufficient to enable a married man to bring up a family adequately," 40.

8 In 1911–12, the officers of the Associated Charities who served on its governing council included three millionaires, William Robinson, president; J.H. Ashdown, treasurer; and N. Bawlf. Over half of the seats on the council were held by members of the business elite. City of Winnipeg Archives (hereafter CWA), Associated Charities of the City of Winnipeg, *Fourth Annual Report, 1912*. In 1911–12, 430 donors contributed $13,324 to the bureau. A small number of individual and corporate donors (forty-eight) gave $100 or more. Their contributions comprised 60 percent of all donations. In addition to donations, the City of Winnipeg provided the bureau with an operating grant of $3,000.

9 According to the policy of the Associated Charities, jobs in Winnipeg were reserved for married men. Ibid., 25.

10 Falk acknowledged that men employed by farmers in the winter months often worked for room and board. *Royal Commission*, 38.

11 *Winnipeg Tribune*, 25 September 1906.

12 Evans, "A Message from Winnipeg," 240.

13 In 1912, the Associated Charities reported that 38 of the 619 single men who applied for assistance had been deported, or their names had been referred to the Winnipeg commissioner of immigration. Approximately one-third (214) had been in Canada for less than three years. CWA, Associated Charities of the City of Winnipeg, *Fourth Annual Report, 1912*, 22, 25.

14 It appears that few families were willing to risk deportation by applying for assistance. *Royal Commission*, 39. Between 1907 and 1914, the Canadian government deported 3,480 immigrants for being public charges. Department of the Interior, "Report of the Department of the Interior for 1914," *Sessional Papers, 1915*, no. 25, 78 (hereafter "Report, 1914").

15 LAC, RG 76, Immigration, Vol. 187, File 65412, correspondence, W.D. Scott to J.M. Cosgrove, 17 January 1911; Journals of the Legislative Assembly of Manitoba, vol. 46, *Sessional Papers , 1913–14*, no. 19, 692–93 (hereafter *Journals, 1913–14*).

16 Between 1907 and 1914, 423 immigrants were deported because of tuberculosis. "Report, 1914," 78.

17 For a discussion of the influence of eugenics on official views of immigration and mental illness, see Angus McLaren, *Our Own Master Race: Eugenics in Canada, 1885–1945* (Toronto: McClelland and Stewart, 1990). Between 1906 and 1914, 1,093 immigrants were deported because of insanity or mental weakness. "Report, 1914," 78.

18 Aside from a federal subsidy and proceeds from the sale of provincial lands, most of the province's revenues came from fees. In 1915, taxation generated approximately 15 percent of the provincial government's revenues. Most of the tax revenue came

from succession duties and a corporation tax. The wealthy believed that these forms of taxation penalized success and reduced investment in the economy. *Journals of the Legislative Assembly of Manitoba*, vol. 48, "Public Accounts," *Sessional Papers, 1916,* no. 1, n.p. (hereafter *Journals, 1916*).

19 S.M. 1875, 38 Vict., c. 48, II.

20 Ibid., VII, VIII, IX.

21 *Manitoba Free Press*, 28 May 1910.

22 Ibid. The debt amounted to $14,062.95. The province and the city provided grants totalling $8,500, and the balance of $5,562.95 came from donations.

23 *Journals, 1913–14*, 692–93. The hospital's statement of receipts and expenditures included a cash balance of $78,454.39.

24 Ibid. In 1920, the daily fees for treatment in the Winnipeg General Hospital were $1.75 in a public ward, $2.75–$3.09 in a semi-private ward, and $6.00 in a private ward. Henderson Directories, *Henderson's Winnipeg Directory* (Winnipeg: Henderson Directories, 1920), 29.

25 *Journals, 1913–14*, 692–93.

26 S.M. 1873, 37 Vict., c. 7, XCIX (3), *Revised Statutes of Manitoba, 1913*, vol. 1, c. 28, ss. 17–24, and *Revised Statutes of Manitoba, 1913*, vol. 2, c. 30, s. 26 (a), s. 35.

27 The City of Winnipeg also paid for indigent children educated by the School for the Deaf, a residential institution operated by the provincial government.

28 *Journals, 1916*, 27, 102, 103. The provincial government's fiscal year ended 30 November 1915.

29 CWA, *City Comptroller's Annual Report, 1914–1915*, 56–58, 66 (hereafter *City Report, 1914–1915*).

30 See Chapter 3 for a discussion of Winnipeg city councillors' views on public expenditures on social welfare.

31 CWA, *City Comptroller's Annual Report, 1911–1912*, 52–53 (hereafter *City Report, 1911–1912*); CWA, *City Report, 1914–1915*, 56–58.

32 *Revised Statutes of Manitoba, 1913*, vol. 1, s. 24. In 1910, the City of Winnipeg established an Investigation and Collections Department to recover the costs of treatment of patients admitted to public wards.

33 CWA, *City Report, 1914–1915*, 56.

34 CWA, *Associated Charities of the City of Winnipeg, Fourth Annual Report, 1912*, 27 (hereafter *Associated Charities, 1912*). Twenty-eight were married. They included three wives of ministers and the wife of J.S. Woodsworth.

35 Ibid., 16.

36 Ibid.

37 Ibid., 25.

38 Ibid., 31–32; CWA, *City Report, 1911–1912*, 53.

39 CWA, *Associated Charities, 1912*, 28.

40 Ibid.

41 Ibid., 30.

42 Ibid., 13.

43 Ibid., 32.

44 Winnipeg employers opposed the legislation. The manager of the Manitoba Iron Works claimed that "legislation of this kind would wipe out every industrial plant in

Winnipeg." Quoted in Doug Smith and Manitoba Labour Education Centre, *The Winnipeg Labour Council, 1894–1994: A Century of Labour Education, Organization, and Agitation* (Winnipeg: Manitoba Labour Education Centre, 1994), 8.

45 S.M. 1910, 10 Ed. VIII, vol. 1, c. 81, Schedule, 1 (a) (1), 1 (3).

46 In 1916, amendments to the act increased compensation to injured workers to 55 percent of their average earnings, and the monthly payment to surviving spouses rose to twenty dollars a month plus five dollars a month for each child under the age of sixteen to a maximum of forty dollars a month. S.M. 1916, 6 Geo. V, vol. 1, c. 33, s. (1) (b) (c), s. (5).

47 S.M. 1916, 6 Geo. V, vol. 1, c. 69, s. 2.

48 Veronica Strong-Boag, "'Wages for Housework': Mothers' Allowances and the Beginnings of Social Security in Canada," *Journal of Canadian Studies* 14, no. 1 (1979): 25–26. In 1919, all of the recipients of the Mothers' Allowance were either widows or women whose husbands were in mental asylums. Manitoba Legislative Assembly, "Third Annual Report of the Manitoba Mothers' Allowance Commission," *Sessional Papers, 1918–19*, no. 52, 4–5 (hereafter "Mothers' Allowance Commission, 1918–19").

49 "Mothers' Allowance Commission, 1918–19," 8; Aleda Winnifred Turnbull, "Progressive Social Policy in Manitoba, 1915–1939" (MA thesis, University of Manitoba, 1980), 85.

50 "Mothers' Allowance Commission, 1918–19," 8.

51 S.M. 1916, 6 Geo. V, vol. 1, c. 69, s. 3.

52 Applicants had to provide "full information as to property, assets, liabilities insurance and income from any sources." Manitoba, Royal Commission on the Administration of the Child Welfare Division, *Report of the Royal Commission Appointed by Order-in-Council Number 747–28 to Inquire into the Administration of the Child Welfare Division of the Department of Health and Public Welfare* (Winnipeg: Department of Health and Welfare, 1929), 16.

53 Since women who were not naturalized risked deportation if they applied for the Mothers' Allowance, this restriction on eligibility likely had little practical effect.

54 S.M. 1916, 6 Geo. V, vol. 1, c. 69, s. 2. Beginning in 1917 a married person could apply to the Court of King's Bench for a divorce on the grounds of adultery.

55 "Mothers' Allowance Commission, 1918–19," 3, 16.

56 In 1919, the visitors had a caseload of approximately 400 families. Ibid., 9. Application approval rates varied from 64 percent to 88 percent between 1917 and 1919. Cancellation rates varied from 6 percent to 12 percent in the same period.

57 S.M. 1916, 6 Geo. V, vol. 1, c. 69, s. 2.

58 "Mothers' Allowance Commission, 1918–19," 7.

59 The amount of the allowance increased when children turned four and eight. See "Monthly Schedule of Allowances," ibid., 7. A mother of two children between the ages of four and seven received approximately sixty-four dollars a month. According to the Minimum Wage Board, in 1919 women in female-dominated occupations were paid twelve dollars per week or approximately fifty dollars a month. Manitoba Legislative Assembly, "Report of Activities of Minimum Wage Board from November 30th, 1918 to November 30th, 1919," Public Works Department, Annual Report for 1919, *Sessional Papers, 1918–19*, no. 52, 68–73.

60 For a discussion of Jewish immigrant employment and entrepreneurship, see Chapter 3.

61 In 1906, Winnipeg's relief officer stated that the "Jews . . . look after their poor pretty well." *Manitoba Free Press*, 25 September 1906. The fourth annual report of the Associated Charities of Winnipeg noted that 68 of the 1,026 "cases dealt with" in 1911–12 were "Hebrews," but it did not state whether they were among the 232 applicants who received assistance. CWA, *Associated Charities, 1912*, 16, 18. In 1910, the Hebrew Benevolent Society stated that it had formally requested that, "whenever a Jew appeals for assistance to the relief officer, he be directed" to the association. Quoted in *Winnipeg Tribune*, 13 January 1910. Nevertheless, between June 1909 and January 1910, the Associated Charities spent seventy-five dollars providing assistance to sixteen Jewish families. *Winnipeg Tribune*, 24 January 1910. In 1917–18, 2 of the 191 recipients of the Mothers' Allowance were "Hebrew" women, and in 1918–19, 13 of the 413 recipients were Jews. "Mothers' Allowance Commission, 1918–19," 10.

62 In 1894, the chair of the City of Winnipeg Market, License and Health Committee, which dealt with applications for relief, stated that Jews "would not work" and were of "no use to the country." Quoted in Henry Trachtenberg, "Peddling, Politics, and Winnipeg's Jews, 1881–1895: The Political Acculturation of an Urban Immigrant Community," *Histoire sociale/Social History* 57 (1996): 176–77.

63 Arthur A. Chiel, *The Jews in Manitoba: A Social History* (Toronto: University of Toronto Press, 1961), 31.

64 Ibid.

65 Based upon 275 adults, the federal government allocated a total of $1,375 to assist Jewish refugees. Between May and September 1882, William Hespeler, Winnipeg's immigration agent, transferred $495.56 to the relief committee. A.J. Arnold, "The Earliest Jews in Winnipeg," *Beaver Magazine* 54, no. 2 (1974): 10.

66 Arnold notes that, according to the 1883 *Henderson's Winnipeg Directory*, the occupations of Jews included an upholsterer, a capmaker, a watchmaker, an expressman, a bricklayer, as well as labourers, carpenters, clerks, and tailors. Ibid., 11.

67 *Manitoba Free Press*, 8 January 1883. This article is reprinted in Harry Gutkin, *Journey into Our Heritage: The Story of the Jewish People in the Canadian West* (Toronto: Lester and Orpen Dennys, 1980), 47–48. An article published the following day stated that "five or six" Jewish families who had rented accommodations were also destitute. *Manitoba Free Press*, 9 January 1883.

68 *Manitoba Free Press*, 8 January 1882. Some of the men interviewed at the immigration shed stated that they had worked for a contractor in Portage la Prairie the previous summer but had not been paid. *Manitoba Free Press*, 9 January 1882.

69 A few weeks later Winnipeg City Council approved the expenditure of an additional $200. *Manitoba Free Press*, 30 January 1883.

70 *Manitoba Free Press*, 10 January 1883.

71 *Manitoba Free Press*, 18 January 1883. Hamilton stated that twenty dollars in donations remained.

72 *Manitoba Free Press*, 14 February 1883.

73 Although the Citizens' Relief Committee distribution of donated fuel, food, and clothing played a significant role in alleviating the distress of the Jewish refugees, compared with the $1,200 contributed by Winnipeg's small Jewish community, the $250 donated by the Toronto Anglo-Jewish Association, the $1,375 given by the federal government, and the $300 donated by Winnipeg City Council, the amount of money that it raised through its public appeal appears to have been comparatively small.

74 See Chapter 3. Between 1883 and 1899, Jewish immigration to Winnipeg averaged about twenty-seven immigrants a year. Enumeration records, *Census of Prairie Provinces, Population and Agriculture, Manitoba, Saskatchewan, Alberta, 1916* (Ottawa: King's Printer, 1918) (hereafter *Census, 1916*).

75 Chiel, *The Jews in Manitoba*, 72–73. The boundaries of Central Winnipeg are defined in Chapter 3.

76 Ibid., 73.

77 *Jewish Post*, 15 April 1992. In what was to become a familiar pattern of religious dissent, small groups of dissident Orthodox Jews who in turn disagreed with the form of Judaism practised by the Sons of Israel established their own congregations: the Anshay Roosia, the Milchige, and the Shtall Shulach. Allan Levine, *Coming of Age: A History of the Jewish People of Manitoba* (Winnipeg: Heartland Associates, 2009), 63.

78 *Manitoba Free Press*, 29 April 1884; quoted in Chiel, *The Jews in Manitoba*, 74.

79 Chiel, *The Jews in Manitoba*, 77.

80 *Winnipeg Tribune*, 20 March 1890. Five of the members of the committee had settled in Winnipeg before 1881. They included Abraham Benjamin, Phillip Brown, George Frankfurter, David Ripstein, and Simon Ripstein.

81 Archives of Manitoba (hereafter AM), M584, Minutes of the Board of Management, Shaarey Zedek synagogue, 4 August 1889.

82 Ibid., 25 August 1889.

83 Chiel, *The Jews in Manitoba*, 80.

84 AM, M584, Minutes of the Board of Management, Shaarey Zedek synagogue, 29 December 1890.

85 Ibid.

86 Ibid.

87 *Manitoba Free Press*, 29 January 1894; *Winnipeg Tribune*, 29 January 1894.

88 Levine, *Coming of Age*, 66.

89 *Winnipeg Tribune*, 27 January 1894.

90 *Winnipeg Tribune*, 2 May 1900. In 1900, Rosh Pina appointed Rabbi Abraham Singerman with an annual salary of $900: $300 guaranteed by the congregation, $300 for overseeing *kashrut* (Jewish "dietary laws"), and $300 from fees for performing marriages and circumcisions.

91 *Winnipeg Tribune*, 29 January 1894, 31 January 1884.

92 Levine, *Coming of Age*, 66.

93 Chiel, *The Jews in Manitoba*, 81.

94 *Manitoba Free Press*, 7 November 1903.

95 Chiel, *The Jews in Manitoba*, 84.

96 Ibid., 84–85.

97 *Fusgeyers* were young Jews who left Romania by foot between 1900 and 1901 hoping to immigrate to Great Britain or North America.

98 Gutkin, *Journey into Our Heritage*, 125.

99 *Manitoba Free Press*, 29 April 1884.

100 At least six of the seven members of the executive of the Montefiore Hebrew Benevolent Society were German Jews who settled in Winnipeg before 1882. Ibid.

101 *Manitoba Free Press*, 29 March 1887.

102 See dedication ceremony, Shaarey Zedek synagogue, in *Proceedings of the Grand Lodge of Manitoba, Ancient, Free, and Accepted Masons*, vol. 3, part 1, 1889–90, 7–9.

103 *Manitoba Free Press*, 26 November 1891. The society sent the family to Grand Forks, a small community in North Dakota located 235 kilometres south of Winnipeg.

104 *Winnipeg Tribune*, 22 May 1894.

105 This estimate is based upon the cost of purchasing land and constructing the Shaarey Zedek ($10,000) and Rosh Pina ($3,900) synagogues, the assumed cost of purchasing the building used to house the Sons of Israel congregation between 1890 and 1892 (total approximately $15,000), and $4,000 for salaries, Torah scrolls, and room rentals. *Winnipeg Tribune*, 20 March 1890, 25 August 1893. By 1894, the Jewish community had about 800 members.

106 *Manitoba Free Press*, 26 November 1891.

107 *Manitoba Free Press*, 15 January 1892.

108 According to the *Manitoba Free Press*, "having at all times shown the greatest sympathy with and for their race," the Jewish immigrants considered Fonseca a "fitting person" to represent them. Ibid. Fonseca promptly wrote to W.H. Baker of the Baron de Hirsch Institute in Montreal. LAC, MG 28, V 83, Jewish Colonization Association, correspondence, William Fonseca to W.H. Baker, 15 January 1892.

109 *Manitoba Free Press*, 26 January 1892. The society appears to have been short-lived.

110 For a discussion of the role of prominent members of the Jewish community in mobilizing political support for the Liberal and Conservative Parties, see Henry Trachtenberg, "Ethnic Politics on the Urban Frontier: 'Fighting Joe' Martin and the Jews of Winnipeg, 1893–1896," *Manitoba History* 35 (1998): 2–14.

111 Chiel, *The Jews in Manitoba*, 80, 132.

112 *Winnipeg Tribune*, 13 June 1898.

113 *Canadian Jewish Times*, 19 December 1913, in *A Biographical Dictionary of Canadian Jewry, 1909–1914: From the* Canadian Jewish Times, ed. Lawrence F. Tapper (Teaneck, NJ: Avotaynu, 1992), 181. By 1898, the society had 140 members. *Winnipeg Tribune*, 7 December 1898.

114 *Manitoba Free Press*, 15 December 1906.

115 *Pioneer Winnipeg Women's Work, 1883–1907* (Winnipeg: Winnipeg Telegram, 1907), 38; *Manitoba Free Press*, 6 January 1904.

116 In 1904, the Shaarey Zedek Ladies' Aid Society used the proceeds of its annual dance to assist destitute Jews, and any "surplus" was donated to the St. Boniface and Winnipeg General Hospitals. The society's disposition of money not needed to fund its own charitable work did not take into consideration whether the Rosh Pina Ladies' Aid Society and the Hebrew Benevolent Society needed more money to assist immigrants or destitute Jews in their care.

117 LAC, MG 28, V 86, Jewish Family Services of the Baron de Hirsch Institute, Vol. 5, File 1, Minutes of the Board of Directors of the Baron de Hirsch Institute, 22 July 1900, 6 August 1900.

118 Although Jewish charities struggled to raise money, in 1900 a group of Jewish merchants, which included three prominent members of the Shaarey Zedek synagogue, raised close to $350 for the Canadian Patriotic Fund. *The Manitoba Free Press* claimed that it was "the largest fund yet raised among Manitoba Jews for charitable purposes." *Manitoba Free Press*, 18 April 1900, quoted in Chiel, *The Jews in*

Manitoba, 132–33. The Shaarey Zedek Ladies' Aid Society raised twenty-five dollars. *Winnipeg Tribune*, 12 March 1900. The Canadian Patriotic Fund was established in January 1900 to assist the widows and children of Canadian soldiers killed in South Africa.

119 *Winnipeg Tribune*, 30 June 1901.

120 Ibid.

121 Established in 1898, the Winnipeg Zionist Society had 100 members. *Winnipeg Tribune*, 12 April 1898. Chiel notes that the Zionist movement "helped to bring together Jews from many and diverse backgrounds." Chiel, *The Jews in Manitoba*, 157. Speakers at the meeting also called for a Jewish homeland in Palestine. *Winnipeg Tribune*, 18 May 1903.

122 A second meeting sponsored by the Young Zionists Athletic Club was held a week later. *Winnipeg Tribune*, 18 May 1903. The club was established in 1903 to "encourage Canadian patriotism and to improve the physical, spiritual, social and economic condition of its members." Chiel, *The Jews in Manitoba*, 155.

123 *Winnipeg Tribune*, 11 July 1903. Born in Romania, Dr. Moses Gaster became the chief rabbi of the Sephardic Communities of British Jews in 1887.

124 Fred Skolnik and Michael Berenbaum, eds., *Encyclopaedia Judaica*, vol. 17 (Detroit: Macmillan Reference USA in association with the Keter Publishing House, 2007), 381.

125 By 1907, the society's president and vice-president were Jewish immigrants from the Austro-Hungarian Empire.

126 Chiel, *The Jews in Manitoba*, 132.

127 *Manitoba Free Press*, 16 July 1907. No additional information about the society's activities or membership is available, but about 300 people attended its 1907 annual picnic. Ibid. The Winnipeg Free Hebrew School (Talmud Torah) was eventually built in 1913 at a cost of about $65,000. Manitoba Historical Society, Historic Sites of Manitoba, http://www.mhs.mb.ca/docs/sites/germansocietybuilding.shtml.

128 Approximately 112 Jewish immigrants arrived in Winnipeg from Russia in 1902 and 201 in 1903. Enumeration records, *Census, 1916*.

129 *Manitoba Free Press*, 21 April 1905.

130 Chiel, *The Jews in Manitoba*, 134; *Manitoba Free Press*, 6 December 1905.

131 H.E. Wilder, ed., *The Hundredth Anniversary Souvenir of Jewish Emancipation in Canada and the 50th Anniversary of the Jew in the West* (Winnipeg: Israelite Press, 1932), 28. Wilder notes that "hundreds" attended the school.

132 *Winnipeg Tribune*, 13 November 1905; *Manitoba Free Press*, 6 December 1905.

133 In early December, Jewish fundraisers complained that Winnipeg's Christians had expressed "little interest" in the "terrible calamities that are befalling the Russian Jews." *Manitoba Free Press*, 8 December 1905. This prompted twenty-two individuals and twenty-one businesses outside the Jewish community to donate approximately $470. Business owners, who made half of the donations, were possibly motivated by commercial interests rather than humanitarian concerns. *Winnipeg Tribune*, 20 December 1905.

Chapter 5: Communal Charity, Mutual Aid, and International Relief

1 H.E. Wilder, ed., *The Hundredth Anniversary Souvenir of Jewish Emancipation in Canada and the 50th Anniversary of the Jew in the West* (Winnipeg: Israelite Press, 1932), 28.

2 Ibid., 28, 29. According to Wilder, the first stream of Jewish immigrants arrived from Russia in 1882 and the second stream from Romania between 1898 and 1903.

3 Ibid., 28.

4 Enumeration records, *Census of Prairie Provinces, Population and Agriculture, Manitoba, Saskatchewan, and Alberta, 1916* (Ottawa: King's Printer, 1918) (hereafter *Census, 1916*).

5 The average age of adult Jewish immigrants who settled in Winnipeg is based upon a sample of 400 immigrants over the age of eighteen. Enumeration records, *Census, 1916*.

6 Arthur A. Chiel, *The Jews in Manitoba: A Social History* (Toronto: University of Toronto Press, 1961), 119.

7 By 1908, the Yiddish Dramatic Club had thirty-two members. Harry Gutkin, *Journey into Our Heritage: The Story of the Jewish People in the Canadian West* (Toronto: Lester and Orpen Dennys, 1980), 175–77.

8 *Israelite Press*, 4 March 1915, 21 September 1917, 12 October 1917, and 1 February 1918. Cited in Roseline Usiskin, "Toward a Theoretical Reformulation between Political Ideology, Social Class, and Ethnicity: A Case Study of the Winnipeg Jewish Radical Community" (MA thesis, University of Manitoba, 1978), 170.

9 For a discussion of the debate over Jewish schools, see Chiel, *The Jews in Manitoba*, 92–105.

10 *Israelite Press*, 11 July 1912, 24 February 1914. Cited in Harvey H. Herstein, "The Growth of the Winnipeg Jewish Community and the Evolution of Its Educational Institutions" (MA thesis, University of Manitoba, 1964), 65, 101.

11 Chiel notes that Jews were delegates at party conventions as early as 1887. Chiel, *The Jews in Manitoba*, 170.

12 Henry Trachtenberg, "'The Old Clo' Move': Anti-Semitism, Politics, and the Jews of Winnipeg, 1882–1921" (PhD diss., York University, 1984).

13 Ibid., 449–52. First proposed in 1906, the Arlington Street bridge did not open until 1912.

14 Ibid., 521.

15 Roz Usiskin, "The Winnipeg Jewish Community: Its Radical Elements, 1905–1918," *MHS Transaction*, Series 3, no. 33 (1976–77): 7–11. In 1915, supporters of the "Free Society" established Branch No. 564 of the Arbeiter Ring. Founded in New York in 1892, Der Arbeiter Ring (Workmen's Circle) became a national organization in 1900. By 1908, it had branches in Winnipeg, Montreal, and Toronto. Daniel Soyer, *Jewish Immigrant Aid Associations and American Identity in New York, 1880–1939* (Detroit: Wayne State University Press, 2001), 66–70.

16 See Chapter 3.

17 Alan F.J. Artibise, *Winnipeg: A Social History of Urban Growth, 1874–1914* (Montreal: McGill-Queen's University Press, 1975), 225.

18 See Chapter 2.

19 Revised Statutes of Manitoba, 1913, vol. 1, c. 27, s. 2 (a) (b).

20 Ibid., s. 2.

21 Archives of Manitoba (hereafter AM), Q24621, Memorandum of Association, Hebrew Sick Benefit Association of Winnipeg, January 1907. The three brothers were Abraham, Reuben, and Solomon Cohen.

22 *Jewish Post*, 13 February 1925.

23 Ibid.; Jewish Heritage Centre Archives (hereafter JHCA), File 9F8, Constitution of the Hebrew Sick Benefit Association, 1931?, 25–27.

24 However, Bobrover Hilsfarein, the Nikolieff Aid Association, and the Independent Free Loan Association paid Dr. Ben Victor an annual fee to provide medical care to their members. The Manitoba Museum (hereafter TMM), Rose Victor (oral history), Master Tape no. 429, 2 July 1972.

25 JHCA, File Jewish Organizations, Letters Patent, no. 25587, 9 January 1916.

26 *Israelite Press*, 27 October 1922.

27 TMM, Louis Hendin (oral history), Master Tape no. 266, 12 May 1972. Hendin, a member of the Propoisker Hebrew Society, served as the loan association's secretary and vice-president. The society made financial contributions to a number of Jewish organizations and institutions, including the Old Folk's Home, the Jewish orphanage, and the Mount Carmel Clinic.

28 See the annual financial statement of the Linitzer Sick Benefit Society in Legislative Assembly of Ontario, *The Report of the Registrar of Friendly Societies of Ontario* (Toronto: Clarkson W. James, 1923), 244–45.

29 Chiel, *The Jews in Manitoba*, 114; *Jewish Post*, 13 February 1925; Fred Narvey, "Personal Perspective on the Leftist Theatre of the 1930s," in *Jewish Radicalism in Winnipeg, 1905–1960*, ed. Daniel Stone (Winnipeg: Jewish Heritage Centre of Western Canada, 2002), 83.

30 Founded in 1924 by sixteen members, the Achdus Free Loan Association initially provided loans of twenty-five dollars. When the association's membership reached "over 200," its maximum loan was $100. "The Achdus Free Loan Association Celebrates Golden Anniversary of Service," *Western Jewish News*, 7 November 1974.

31 Ibid.

32 The Achdus Free Loan Association did not impose penalties if a member missed payments, and loans could be forgiven. In 1926, Winnipeg's thirty-two Jewish free-loan associations had "over $200,000.00" in capital. Arthur Daniel Hart, ed., *The Jew in Canada* (Toronto: Jewish Publications, 1926), 234.

33 The Kiev Free Loan and Aid Association was an exception. Four of the thirty petitioners who requested letters patent were women. JHCA, File Jewish Organizations, Letters Patent, no. 25597, 8 January 1916.

34 See Chapter 3; Roz Usiskin, "Winnipeg's Jewish Women of the Left: Traditional and Radical," in Stone, ed., *Jewish Radicalism*, 106–121.

35 *Pioneer Winnipeg Women's Work, 1883–1907* (Winnipeg: Winnipeg Telegram, 1907), 42.

36 *Canadian Jewish Times*, 11 April 1913.

37 JHCA, File Jewish Organizations, Letters Patent, no. 28233, 29 August 1917. Elmwood is a neighbourhood located across the Red River from the North End. In 1916, it was home to 283 Jews. Enumeration records, *Census, 1916*.

38 Other *landsmanshaftn* included the Besarabier Free Loan Association (Bessarabia *gubernia*), the Kovno Lithuanian Free Loan Association (Kovno, Kovno *gubernia*), the Nikolieff Aid Association (Nikolayev, Kherson *gubernia*), the Mizerich Free Loan Association (Mezerich, Grodno *gubernia*), the Pavolotch Loan Association (Pavoloch, Kiev *gubernia*), the Varatinchini Free Loan Association (Varachin, Poltave *gubernia*), the Voliner Free Loan Association (Volynia, *gubernia*), and the Yedinitzer Friends Association of Winnipeg (Yedinitz, Bessarabia *gubernia*).

39 AM, G 7406, File 27, Charters Granted under the Charitable Associations Act.

40 Ibid.

41 According to the 1926 census, approximately 4,400 Jewish men lived in Winnipeg. Detailed information on membership in Winnipeg's Jewish mutual aid associations is not available. The estimate of 3,800 members is based upon the following: membership in the Hebrew Sick Benefit Association (480), the Kiev Free Loan and Aid Association (216), the Achdus Free Loan Association (200), the Hebrew Free Loan Association (150), the Bnay Ezra Free Loan Association (125), and the Arbeiter Ring Sick Benefit Association (84) totalled 1,225. *Jewish Post*, 13 February 1925; JHCA, 8, File 11, Achdus Free Loan Association/Kiev Free Loan Association; *Western Jewish News*, 7 November 1974; *Canadian Jewish Times*, 7 February 1913; *Israelite Press*, 27 October 1922; Roz Usiskin, "The Winnipeg Jewish Radical Community: Its Early Formation, 1905–1918," in *Jewish Life and Times: A Collection of Essays* (Winnipeg: Jewish Historical Society of Western Canada, 1983), 158. At least three mutual aid associations had women's auxiliaries: the Hebrew Sick Benefit Association, the Kiev Free Loan and Aid Association, and the Achdus Free Loan Association. Assuming that they had a combined membership of 100 (approximately 10 percent of the number of male members), and conservatively estimating that an average of fifty members belonged to the fifty other mutual aid societies, membership in Winnipeg's Jewish mutual aid associations totalled approximately 3,825.

42 *Manitoba Free Press*, 5 January 1892; *Winnipeg Tribune*, 11 May 1908.

43 *Winnipeg Tribune*, 19 January 1909. Requests for assistance increased in the winter months when seasonal unemployment was high.

44 The delegation was referred to the city's relief officer. Ibid. All of the members of the delegation—Moses Finkelstein, Ben Zimmerman, David Ripstein, Hiram Weidman, and Abraham Lechtzier—were affluent businessmen who lived in Central Winnipeg.

45 *Manitoba Free Press*, 15 January 1910.

46 *Winnipeg Tribune*, 24 January 1910. In the 1911–12 fiscal year, the City of Winnipeg allocated $35,325 to twenty-three charitable institutions. City of Winnipeg Archives (hereafter CWA), City Comptroller's Annual Report, 1911–12, Schedule no. 11, 62.

47 *Winnipeg Tribune*, 24 January 1910.

48 *Canadian Jewish Times*, 19 December 1913. In February 1913, twenty of its members established a legal precedent by applying for letters patent under the Charitable Associations Act. JHCA, File Jewish Organizations, Letters Patent, no. 20447, 11 November 1913.

49 *Canadian Jewish Times*, 19 December 1913, 9 January 1914.

50 Ibid., 19 December 1913.

51 Ibid., 3 February 1911. Winnipeg Lodge No. 650 of B'nai B'rith, a Jewish fraternal order, was established in 1909 by a group of thirty-six founding members, who included Rabbi Levin and Hiram Weidman. Almost all of the founders were professionals or businessmen, and over 70 percent of them lived in Central or South Winnipeg. Hart, ed., *The Jew in Canada*, 435.

52 *Winnipeg Tribune*, 27 February 1911.

53 Shragge had pledged $100, Finkelstein and Balcovske fifty dollars each. Ibid.

54 In 1913, when the two congregations merged, the *Canadian Jewish Times* reported on 24 January 1913 that the 600 members of the reconstituted Shaarey Zedek synagogue include "some of the wealthiest Jews in the city."

55 A total of 9,023 Jews lived in Winnipeg in 1911. For a discussion of the distribution of Jewish residents in Winnipeg, see Chapter 3.

56 They included A.H. Aronovitch, Abraham Berg, Lazar Berger, Jacob A. Chmelnitsky, Moses Finkelstein, David Finn, Abraham Levinson, Lester Rice, Bernard Shragge, Herman Steinkopf, and Hiram Weidman. With the exception of Finn and Berg, who lived in the North End, and Berger and Steinkopf, who resided in the South End, all of the members of the board lived in Central Winnipeg.

57 The term "charitable organizations" likely referred to mutual aid associations.

58 *Winnipeg Tribune*, 13 March 1911.

59 Ibid.

60 Tensions between more affluent, established Jews and recent Jewish immigrants were not unique to Winnipeg. In Montreal, conflicts between "uptown" Jews, who assumed that they were best qualified to lead the Jewish community, and leaders of "downtown" working-class Jews were a prominent feature of communal politics. See Henry Srebrnik, *Creating the Chupah: The Zionist Movement and the Drive for Jewish Communal Unity in Canada, 1898–1921* (Boston: Academic Studies Press, 2011).

61 Chiel, *The Jews in Manitoba*, 136–37.

62 JHCA, File Jewish Organizations, Letters Patent, no. 22566, 18 March 1914.

63 Ibid., Letters Patent, no. 23451, 26 October 1914. The letters patent of the United Hebrew Charities listed thirty-six names.

64 *Israelite Press*, 4 October 1915. The Ladies' Auxiliary affiliated with the United Hebrew Charities was founded in May 1915. Ibid., 7 July 1916. The size of the board was subsequently reduced to fifteen directors plus a five-member executive. JHCA, 10, File 9, Bylaws of the United Hebrew Relief, n.d.

65 Statutes of Manitoba, 1916, 6 Geo. V, vol. 2, c. 140.

66 Ibid., s. 11.

67 JHCA, 10, File 9, Bylaws of the United Hebrew Relief, s. 1, n.d.

68 *Israelite Press*, 7 July 1916. Support for the charity also came from outside Winnipeg; twenty-six of its members lived in rural communities. The Ladies' Auxiliary collected $2,333 on behalf of the United Hebrew Relief. Hart, ed., *The Jew in Canada*, 226.

69 *Israelite Press*, 16 November 1917, 22 July 1919.

70 *Jewish Post*, 23 September 1927.

71 Eric Lohr, "The Russian Army and the Jews: Mass Deportation, Hostages, and Violence during World War I," *Russian Review* 60 (2001): 404–419.

72 Ibid., 416.

73 *Winnipeg Tribune*, 28 March 1907.

74 *Manitoba Free Press*, 8 April 1907.

75 Chiel, *The Jews in Manitoba*, 140; *Israelite Press*, 29 October 1914.

76 Nine of the ten members of the committee lived in the North End.

77 *Israelite Press*, 29 October 1914. Quoted in Herstein, "The Growth of Winnipeg's Jewish Community," 29.

78 Ibid.

79 Michael Beizer, "The American Joint Distribution Committee," in *The YIVO Encyclopedia of Jews in Eastern Europe*, vol. 1, ed. Gershon David Hundert (New Haven, CT: Yale University Press, 2009), 39.

80 Saltzman and Gutkin were members of Branch No. 169 of the Arbeiter Ring (Marxists), and Gray belonged to Branch No. 506 (Socialist Zionists). The fifth member was Abraham Slobinsky.

81 *Israelite Press*, 12 October 1915. Quoted in Herstein, "The Growth of Winnipeg's Jewish Community," 30. The term "subway" refers to the Main Street railway underpass beneath the CPR main line, which divided the North End from Central Winnipeg.

82 Wilder, ed., *The Hundredth Anniversary Souvenir*, 33; JHCA, uncatalogued file, Immigrant Aid and Relief, 1920, letterhead of Western Canada's Jewish Fund for the Relief of War Sufferers. In 1920, the executive established a *landsmanshaftn* committee to coordinate fundraising with mutual aid associations. The Hebrew Sick Benefit Society donated $2,000 to the fund. *Canadian Jewish Review*, 7 September 1923.

83 Initially, the city was divided into nine districts, but by 1922 there were thirteen.

84 In 1917, the tag day involved thirty captains who supervised teams composed of ten women. *Winnipeg Tribune*, 19 September 1917. Winnipeg City Council contributed $2,500. CWA, Minutes of City Council, 1915, 527.

85 JHCA, uncatalogued file, Immigrant Aid and Relief, 1920, financial statement dated 29 October 1920.

86 Ibid.

87 *Canadian Jewish Chronicle*, 19 December 1919.

88 JHCA, uncatalogued file, Immigrant Aid and Relief of War Sufferers, 1918, correspondence, Marcus Hyman to B. Zukerman, 26 June 1918; ibid., Immigrant Aid and Relief, 1920, letterhead, Western Canada's Jewish Fund for the Relief of War Sufferers.

89 Representatives of the branches were members of the fund's executive committee.

90 The fund raised $50,000 in 1916 and $48,000 in 1917. *Winnipeg Tribune*, 19 September 1917; *Canadian Jewish Chronicle*, 21 September 1917.

91 Antony Polonsky, *The Jews in Poland and Russia*, vol. 3 (Oxford: Littman Library of Jewish Civilization, 2012), 34–42.

92 The North End had the highest death rate in the city. See Esyllt W. Jones, *Influenza 1918: Disease, Death, and Struggle in Winnipeg* (Toronto: University of Toronto Press, 2007), 58–63. JHCA, uncatalogued file, Western Canada's Jewish Fund for Relief of War Sufferers, 1919, correspondence, Max Mains to A. Zucker, 9 April 1919.

93 *Canadian Jewish Chronicle*, 19 December 1919.

94 Between 1 April and 31 October 1919, the fund raised $16,707 or approximately $2,400 a month, half of the monthly amount raised in 1918. For a discussion of postwar economic conditions in Winnipeg, see Reuben Bellan, *Winnipeg's First Century: An Economic History* (Winnipeg: Queenston, 1978), 144–60.

95 The Winnipeg branch of the Ukrainian Verband was established in 1919 to assist Jewish war victims in Ukraine. Because of the civil war, the JDC was unable to organize relief work in Ukraine and consequently focused on sending aid to Romania and Poland. Some Winnipeg Jews with close ties to Jewish communities in Ukraine considered this unacceptable. JHCA, uncatalogued file, Western Canada's Jewish Fund for Relief of War Sufferers, 1919, correspondence, Baruch Zuckerman to Max Mains, 19 November 1919.

96 Ibid., correspondence, Max Mains to A. Zucker, 9 April 1919.

97 Ibid.

98 Hart, ed., *The Jew in Canada*, 526–27.

99 Ibid., 527.

100 Chiel, *The Jews in Manitoba*, 140–44.

101 Almost half of the adult population (3,481) of the Jewish community attended the meeting. Chiel, *The Jews in Manitoba*, 143. Finkelstein and Weidman were founders of the United Hebrew Charities.

102 Ibid., 144.

103 Sheps was president of the Hebrew Immigrant Aid Society.

104 In November 1919, Steinkopf, Finkelstein, and Weidman campaigned for H.E. Wilder, nominated to represent the North End on Winnipeg City Council. His opponent, John Queen, was supported by the union movement, members of Poale Zion, and the Social Democratic Party. In many respects, the electoral contest was a referendum on the Winnipeg General Strike. Wilder had opposed the strike, whereas Queen had been one of its leaders. Steinkopf, running for re-election as a Winnipeg School Board trustee, was defeated by Rose Alcin, a member of the Social Democratic Party. Trachtenberg, "'The Old Clo' Move,'" 813–30. One factor that contributed to his defeat was his inability to address Jewish audiences in Yiddish.

105 JHCA, uncatalogued file, Western Canada's Jewish Fund for Relief of War Sufferers, 1919, correspondence, Max Mains to B. Zuckerman, 1 November 1919.

106 Wilder, ed., *The Hundredth Anniversary Souvenir*, 35.

107 JHCA, uncatalogued file, Western Canada's Jewish Fund for Relief of War Sufferers, 1919, correspondence, Max Mains to B. Zuckerman, 31 December 1919; *Manitoba Free Press*, 2 January 1920.

108 JHCA, uncatalogued file, Western Canada's Jewish Fund for Relief of War Sufferers, 1919, correspondence, Max Mains to B. Zuckerman, 31 December 1919; *Manitoba Free Press*, 2 January 1920.

109 *Manitoba Free Press*, 2 January 1920. The committee also placed an ad in the *Manitoba Free Press*, 3 January 1920.

110 JHCA, uncatalogued file, Immigrant Aid and Relief, 1920, correspondence, Max Mains to B. Zuckerman, 6 February 1920.

111 Ibid., correspondence, Max Mains to B. Zuckerman, 19 January 1920.

112 Ibid., correspondence, Max Mains to B. Zuckerman, 24 February 1920.

113 Ibid., correspondence, letterhead of campaign committee, n.d. Neiman Weidman, Hiram Weidman's son, also joined the committee.

114 Ibid., correspondence, Max Mains to B. Zuckerman, 24 February 1920. The fund established a medical branch to solicit medical supplies or donations of money from physicians and pharmacists throughout western Canada. Ibid., correspondence, form letter from Dr. C.J. Bermack, 20 May 1920.

115 Hart, ed., *The Jew in Canada*, 513.

116 In 1919, when Hadassah was founded, Lillian Freiman became chairwoman; she was elected president in 1921. Srebrnik, *Creating the Chupah*, 199–201.

117 In 1919, A.J. Freiman was elected chairman of the Provisional Executive Committee of the Zionist Organization of Canada, formerly known as the Federation of Zionist Societies of Canada. He became president in 1921. Ibid., 102n19.

118 Hart, ed., *The Jew in Canada*, 276.

119 Meighen became prime minister on 10 July 1920. Since Blair was adamantly opposed to Jewish immigration, it is unlikely that he would have agreed to meet with Freiman without political direction to do so. For a discussion of Blair's attempts to prevent Jewish immigration, see Chapter 7.

120 Harvard University Library, Jewish People's Relief Committee, Correspondence, 1915-1924, v. 6, F. C. Blair to Mrs. A. J. Freeeman [*sic*], 24 July, 1920. http://nrs.harvard.edu/urn-3:FHCL:975737?n=196

121 *Winnipeg Tribune*, 18 August 1920.

122 Ibid., 2 September 1920. Manitoba and Saskatchewan had five representatives on the committee, Alberta four, and British Columbia two.

123 In 1919 and 1920, the Zionist movement collected $458,000. Srebrnik, *Creating the Chupah*, 233.

124 Max Mitchell, co-owner of Mitchell Hay and Grain Company, subsequently became a member of Central Relief for European Jews.

125 Lady Borden, the wife of the prime minister; Lady Laurier, the widow of a former prime minister; Lady Davis, married to Sir Mortimer Davis, a wealthy Jewish philanthropist; and Rachel Workman, the wife of a wealthy member of the Montreal Jewish community served as honorary vice-presidents. JHCA, uncatalogued file, Immigrant Aid and Relief, 1920, letterhead, Canadian-Jewish-European Orphans Committee.

126 JHCA, uncatalogued file, Immigrant Aid and Relief, 1920, letterhead, Western Canada's Jewish Fund for the Relief of War Sufferers. Max Mitchell also served on the committee.

127 *Winnipeg Tribune*, 12 November 1920.

128 JHCA, uncatalogued file, Immigrant Aid and Relief, 1920, correspondence, Isadore Hurwitz to Sam Berger, secretary of the Canadian-Jewish-European Orphans Committee, 18 November 1920. Hurwitz was elected secretary of the fund on 31 October 1920 when Mains refused to run for another term.

129 Applicants were asked to provide the following information: name, type and size of residence, state of health, and number, ages, and occupations of children. Ibid., Statement of Applicant.

130 Hart, ed., *The Jew in Canada*, 516.

131 *Winnipeg Tribune*, 14 October 1920; JHCA, uncatalogued file, Immigrant Aid and Relief, 1920, correspondence, Isadore Hurwitz to Sam Berger, 9 January 1920.

132 *Winnipeg Tribune*, 26 August 1921. Seven children were adopted by families in western Canada and five in Winnipeg.

133 JHCA, uncatalogued file, Immigrant Aid and Relief, 1920, correspondence, Max Mains to A. Garelick, secretary of the Jewish People's Relief Committee, 19 August 1920.

134 Ibid., correspondence, Max Mains to A. Garelick, 6 September 1920; Max Mains to B. Zuckerman, 6 September 1920.

135 Ibid., correspondence, Isadore Hurwitz to Sam Berger, 3 November 1920.

136 Ibid., correspondence, Isadore Hurwitz to Sam Berger, 18 November 1920.

137 Ibid., correspondence, Isadore Hurwitz to Sam Berger, 25 November, 14 December, and 23 December 1920.

138 Ibid., correspondence, Sam Berger to Isadore Hurwitz, 7 December 1920; Isadore Hurwitz to Sam Berger, 23 December 1920.

139 Ibid., telegram, Sam Berger to Isadore Hurwitz, 22 December 1920.

140 Ibid., correspondence, Sam Berger to Isadore Hurwitz, 25 December 1920; Hart, ed., *The Jew in Canada*, 515. Berger claimed that Dr. Heifetz had passport problems.

141 JHCA, uncatalogued file, Immigrant Aid and Relief, 1920, correspondence, Isadore Hurwitz to Sam Berger, 29 December 1920; Immigration and Relief, 1921–23, telegram, Isadore Hurwitz to Sam Berger, 4 January 1921. Saltzman had accompanied a shipment of clothing that the fund had sent to Eastern Europe.

142 Ibid., correspondence, Isadore Hurwitz to Sam Berger, 9 January 1921.

143 Ibid., correspondence, Sam Berger to Isadore Hurwitz, 27 January 1921.

144 Hart, ed., *The Jew in Canada*, 516.

145 JHCA, uncatalogued file, Immigration and Relief, 1921–23, correspondence, Isadore Hurwitz to B. Zukerman, 30 March 1921.

146 Ibid.

147 Ibid.

148 Ibid.

149 Ibid., correspondence, Isadore Hurwitz to B. Zukerman, 12 April 1921.

150 Ibid.

151 Ibid.

152 Ibid.

153 Between 1 January 1920 and 30 March 1921, the fund raised $259,000 in cash and donations of clothing, medical supplies, and so on. Ibid., correspondence, Isadore Hurwitz to B. Zuckerman, 30 March 1921.

154 Hart, ed., *The Jew in Canada*, 526.

155 Between August 1921 and the end of December 1922, the JDC spent more than $8 million on relief work in the Soviet Union. Zoza Szajkowski, "Private and Organized American Jewish Overseas Relief (1914–1938)," *American Jewish Historical Quarterly* 57, no. 1 (1967): 64.

156 JHCA, Fond 124, File 3, Jewish Immigrant Aid Society, unsigned form letter sent by the secretary of the Jewish Relief and Immigrant Aid Society, 18 September 1923. The homes were said to be located in "Sagaidaki" and "Zacharewka." The letter stated that, "if we cannot, or do not feel disposed to, do our duty towards relief in general, we must on no account shirk our duty to the Homeless Orphans."

157 David G. Dalin, "*Tzedekah* with Dignity: Jewish Charity and Self-Help in Rabbinic Tradition," *Conservative Judaism* 51, no. 3 (1999): 5–6.

158 For profiles of Steinkopf, Weidman, and Finkelstein, see Hart, ed., *The Jew in Canada*, 389, 174, and 128.

Chapter 6: Winnipeg's Jewish Social Welfare Institutions

1 Arthur Daniel Hart, ed., *The Jew in Canada* (Toronto: Jewish Publications, 1926), 228.

2 Ibid.

3 David Himmel, *A Camp Story: The History of Lake of the Woods and Greenwoods Camps* (Charleston, SC: History Press, 2012), 17–18.

4 Revised Statutes of Manitoba, 1913, vol. 1, c. 30, ss. 20–22, ss. 30–32, s. 36.

5 Jewish Heritage Centre Archives (hereafter JHCA), JHC 10, File 10, H.E. Wilder, "Historical Sketch: The Jewish Orphanage and Children's Aid of Western Canada," n.d., 1.

6 Allan Levine, *Coming of Age: A History of the Jewish People of Manitoba* (Winnipeg: Heartland Associates, 2009), 169–70.

7 Wilder, "Historical Sketch," 1.

8 Ibid. All of the members of the committee were residents of Central and South Winnipeg who belonged to either Shaarey Shomayim synagogue or Shaarey Zedek synagogue. The two synagogues merged in 1913. Three of the members of the committee—Aronovitch, Rice, and Steinkopf—were founders of the United Hebrew Charities.

9 *Canadian Jewish Review*, 7 September 1923.

10 Ibid. The executive consisted of Lena Fenson, president; Sarah Schiller, treasurer; Celia Calof, corresponding secretary; and Fanny Schiller, financial secretary.

11 Wilder, "Historical Sketch," 2–3.

12 Ibid.

13 Ibid., 3.

14 Ibid.

15 *Winnipeg Tribune*, 24 July 1913. Three of the directors—H. Weidman, David Balcovske, and B. Bloom—had accompanied Robinson to the meeting with representatives of B'nai B'rith and the Hebrew Ladies' Orphan Home Association.

16 Ibid. The board of directors was less representative than its size suggests; it included seventeen married couples.

17 Ibid.

18 Wilder, "Historical Sketch," 4.

19 Ibid., 5.

20 *Winnipeg Tribune*, 23 August 1913.

21 Wilder, "Historical Sketch," 5.

22 Wilder, "Historical Sketch," 6.

23 Archives of Manitoba (hereafter AM), AM Q24611, Application to Incorporate the Esther Robinson Jewish Orphanage and Children's Aid Society, 1914. The orphanage was incorporated on 4 April 1914. With the exception of Dora Robinson (Robinson's daughter), all of the signatories were male residents of Central or South Winnipeg.

24 Revised Statutes of Manitoba, 1913, vol. 1, c. 30, ss. 20–22.

25 In February 1915, the orphanage was caring for five wards. Wilder, "Historical Sketch," 8.

26 Ibid.

27 Between 1 December 1915 and 31 October 1916, the orphanage had an income of $5,538.05. Individual donations amounted to $2,612.09, and the tag day raised $800. "Financial Statement, Esther Robinson Jewish Orphanage," Legislative Assembly of Manitoba, *Sessional Papers, 1917*, 623; *Winnipeg Tribune*, 28 October 1914.

28 *Canadian Jewish Review*, 7 September 1923.

29 The children, eleven boys and nine girls, were between the ages of four and fourteen. With the exception of two children born in Manitoba and one in the United States, all were immigrants from Russia. Enumeration records, *Census of Prairie Provinces, Population and Agriculture, Manitoba, Saskatchewan, Alberta, 1916* (Ottawa: King's Printer, 1918) (hereafter *Census, 1916*).

30 "Financial Statement, Esther Robinson Jewish Orphanage," Legislative Assembly of Manitoba, *Sessional Papers, 1917*, 623.

31 Wilder, "Historical Sketch," 9. Robinson subsequently refused repayment and suggested that the $3,000 be used to reduce the orphanage's financial liability for the properties on Robinson Street.

32 *Winnipeg Tribune*, 10 November 1916. A petition submitted to the provincial government to change the name of the Esther Robinson Jewish Orphanage to the Jewish Orphanage and Children's Aid of Western Canada was approved on 15 November 1917. JHCA, File Jewish Organizations, Letters Patent, no. 2433, 15 November 1917.

33 Twenty seats on the board were subsequently reserved for women. In recognition of its role in establishing the orphanage, the Ladies' Society, which succeeded the Hebrew Ladies' Orphan Home Association, was entitled to appoint twelve members of the board. JHCA, JHC 10, File 2, Sec. 4, Constitution of the Jewish Orphanage and Children's Aid of Western Canada.

34 *Canadian Jewish Review*, 7 September 1923. Robinson was joined by Moses Haid, Benjamin Levinson, Sinai Bere, and Solomon Goldman. With the exception of Levinson, they all lived in Central or South Winnipeg.

35 The lodge, which had nearly 500 members in 1921, likely had about 400 members in 1917. *Canadian Jewish Review*, 16 December 1921, 7 September 1923.

36 JHCA, JHC 10, File 1, Jewish Orphanage and Childrens [*sic*] Aid of Western Canada, Report for Year 1917, 21 (hereafter Jewish Orphanage, 1917).

37 *Winnipeg Tribune*, 17 August 1918; Canada, *Sixth Census of Canada, 1921*, vol. 1 (Ottawa: F.A. Acland, 1924).

38 JHCA, JHC 10, File 1, Jewish Orphanage, 1917, 71–72.

39 Six children became ill with diphtheria. AM, GR 1557-A0014, Questionnaire Submitted to the Public Welfare Commission, 6 January 1919.

40 *Winnipeg Tribune*, 17 August 1918.

41 AM, GR 1557-A0014, Financial Statements for the Ten Months Ended 31st October 1921, Jewish Orphanage and Children's Aid Society of Western Canada.

42 *Canadian Jewish Review*, 7 September 1923. Max Koffman owned the Winnipeg Plumbing Company, and Harry Berns and Harry Levant owned the Electric Construction Company.

43 *Winnipeg Tribune*, 11 August 1919.

44 *Winnipeg Tribune*, 8 November 1919.

45 AM, GR 1557-A0014, Financial Statements for the Ten Months Ended 31st October 1921, Jewish Orphanage and Children's Aid Society of Western Canada. The source of $2,468 in miscellaneous contributions and the places of residence of donors of notes totalling $4,505 are not identified.

46 Ibid. The campaign incurred additional expenses for advertising, travel, printing, and so on amounting to $10,000. *Canadian Jewish Review*, 7 September 1923. Greenberg's recommendations resulted in changes to the original plans, which added $18,000 to the final cost. Wilder, "Historical Sketch," 12.

47 *Winnipeg Tribune*, 28 February 1920.

48 The average number of children in the orphanage increased from sixty-six in 1918 to seventy-six in 1919 and to ninety-eight in 1920. AM, GR 1557-A0014, Additional Report for 1918, Comparative Report of the Jewish Orphanage and Children's Aid Society of Western Canada, 1919–20. By February 1919, the house on Main Street was so overcrowded that seven children were placed in temporary care until the new orphanage opened. *Manitoba Free Press*, 28 February 1920.

49 *Winnipeg Tribune*, 28 February 1920.

50 Hart, ed., *The Jew in Canada*, 227–30; AM, GR 1557-A0014, *Jewish Orphanage and Children's Aid of Western Canada* (Winnipeg: Israelite Press, 1920?). Opinions differ on whether the orphanage was a home or an institution. Shortly after the death of their son in May 1920, Florence and Louis Greenberg resigned and returned to Chicago. In July 1920, the board appointed Aaron Osovsky as superintendent. A journalist and community activist, Osovsky had no training or experience in child welfare. Praised as a "fatherly superintendent," he was remembered by many of the former residents of the orphanage as a strict disciplinarian. Reuben Slonim, *Grand to Be an Orphan* (Toronto: Clarke, Irwin, 1983); Levine, *Coming of Age*, 172–75.

51 JHCA, JHC, 10, File 1, Jewish Orphanage and Children's Aid, Report for the Year 1925–26, 9 (hereafter Jewish Orphanage, 1925–26). At the age of sixteen, children normally left the orphanage and found employment.

52 Ibid. The orphanage also supervised "delinquency cases," children who lived with parents or guardians. One of the group of Jewish orphans brought from Ukraine in 1921 stayed in the orphanage.

53 After the death of Samuel Gilman's mother at the age of thirty-two, his father, a Saskatchewan farmer, sent Samuel and his four siblings to the orphanage. Obituary of Samuel Gilman, *Winnipeg Free Press*, 13 May 2009; the Manitoba Museum (hereafter TMM), Pearl Silver (oral history), Master Tape no. 292, 18 March, 1–2 April, and 16 October 1968.

54 Juvenile Court returned children to their parents when it was satisfied that children had reformed and that temporary court orders issued in cases of neglect or marital discord could be withdrawn.

55 Between 1914 and 1926, 33 of the 386 children admitted to the orphanage returned. Jewish Orphanage, 1925–26, 8.

56 JHCA, JHA 10, File 4, Application for Admission, Jewish Orphanage and Children's Aid Society of Western Canada. In 1920, parents and guardians contributed $780, less than 1 percent of the orphanage's income. AM, GR 1557-A0014, Jewish Orphanage and Children's Aid Society of Western Canada, Income and Expenditure for the Year Ended December 31st, 1920. By 1926, this amount had increased to $1,970 or nearly 6 percent of total income and to $10,471 or 27 percent of total income by 1930. JHCA, JHA 10, File 1, Jewish Orphanage 1925–26, 21; Jewish Orphanage and Children's Aid, Report for the Years 1928–29–30, 9 (hereafter Jewish Orphanage, 1928–29–30).

57 JHCA, JHC 10, File 1, Superintendent's Report, Jewish Orphanage, 1928–29–30, 19.

58 Hart, ed., *The Jew in Canada*, 229.

59 Ibid.; JHCA, JHC 10, File 1, Superintendent's Report, Jewish Orphanage 1928–29–30, 20–21.

60 Hart, ed., *The Jew in Canada*, 230.

61 JHCA, JHC 10, File 1, Jewish Orphanage, 1925–26, 5.

62 TMM, Pearl Silver (oral history), Master Tape no. 292, 18 March 1–2 April, and 16 October 1968. In the interview, Silver referred to three of Winnipeg's clothing factories.

63 Hart, ed., *The Jew in Canada*, 230; Jewish Orphanage, 1928–29–30, 20–21. For example, George Ackerman became a cantor, and Reuben Slonim became a rabbi.

64 The Ladies' Auxiliary was established in the spring of 1919. *Canadian Jewish Review*, 7 September 1923.

65 Hart, ed., *The Jew in Canada*, 230; *Canadian Jewish Review*, 7 September 1923.

66 *Canadian Jewish Review*, 7 September 1923.

67 Ibid.

68 Ibid.; *Winnipeg Tribune*, 16 August 1924. Established in 1919, by 1924 the camp provided ten-day holidays for 600 children between the ages of six and seventeen, including fifty children from the orphanage.

69 Of the forty-two officers and members of the board of the orphanage in 1928–29–30, twenty-four lived in the North End, six lived in Central Winnipeg, and six lived in the South End (the residences of four could not be found). Jewish Orphanage, 1928–29–30, 1.

70 Hart, ed., *The Jew in Canada*, 232.

71 AM, Q24670, Declaration of Association, 23 December 1913. The letters patent were issued on 20 March 1914.

72 Wilder, "Historical Sketch," 6.

73 Annalee Greenberg, *The Sharon Home: Building on a Tradition of Caring* (Winnipeg: Sharon Home, 1997), 4; *Canadian Jewish Review*, 27 September 1924.

74 Greenberg, *The Sharon Home*, 4.

75 Enumeration records, *Census, 1916*.

76 Greenberg, *The Sharon Home*, 6. The large house also served as a hostel for Jews visiting Winnipeg. Ibid., 5.

77 Hart, ed., *The Jew in Canada*, 232. See the list of donors, JHCA, JHC 11, File 3, Jewish Old Folks' Home of Western Canada, Historical Survey 1912–23 and Annual Report for 1920–24, 24–42 (hereafter Annual Report for 1920–24).

78 Annual Report for 1920–24, 10; *Winnipeg Tribune*, 6 October 1919.

79 Hart, ed., *The Jew in Canada*, 233; Annual Report for 1920–24, 10.

80 Annual Report for 1920–24, 5–6.

81 *Israelite Press*, 9 September 1920.

82 *Israelite Press*, 1 June 1922.

83 *Canadian Jewish Review*, 7 September 1923.

84 Between 1919 and 1923, the annual operating budget of the home ranged from $14,292 to $18,810. Annual Report for 1920–24, 13.

85 With thirty-five residents, by 1924 the home was full and had a waiting list of fifteen applicants. To accommodate as many applicants as possible, the board adopted the expedient of adding additional beds to its dormitory rooms. *Israelite Press*, 18 January 1924. By 1931, the board concluded that a larger facility was needed, but because of the economic depression fundraising plans were suspended until 1940, when a new home was finally built.

86 Revised Statutes of Manitoba, 1892, vol. 1, cap. 68, s. 6.

87 Manitoba, Provincial Treasurer, Public Accounts 1922–23, 84. Both the Old Folk's Home in Middlechurch and the St. Boniface Old Folk's Home received $2,500. Either the executive of the Jewish Old Folks' Home made no attempt to lobby the provincial government for funding or it did so and was refused.

88 S.M. 1916, 6 Geo. V, vol. 1, cap. 81, s. 13 (1); City of Winnipeg Archives (hereafter CWA), City Comptroller's Annual Report, 1919–20, 55. The city paid $3,853.75 for the "maintenance of patients" to the Portage la Prairie Home for Incurables.

89 Government of Manitoba, *Third and Final Report of the Public Welfare Commission of Manitoba* (Winnipeg: Phillip Purcell, 1920), 29.

90 *Winnipeg Tribune*, 29 May 1926.

91 *Winnipeg Tribune*, 11 December 1926.

92 CWA, Civic Charities Endorsement Bureau, File Jewish Old Folks' Home, Application for Admission, n.d.

93 The Annual Report for 1920–24 did not distinguish residents' fees from donations, but in 1931–32 they amounted to $767.50, slightly more than 7 percent of total income. Ibid., Financial Statement, 31 August 1932.

94 To qualify for a pension, applicants had to prove that they were seventy years of age or older, a British subject, a resident of Canada for twenty years, a resident of Manitoba for a minimum of five years, and virtually destitute. Kenneth Bryden, *Old Age Pensions and Policy-Making in Canada* (Montreal: McGill-Queen's University Press, 1974), 61–62. By 1932, income from pensions amounted to $1,892.45 or 17.7 percent of total income. Within three years, this amount increased to $2,275 but remained the same percentage of total income. CWA, Civic Charities Endorsement Bureau, File Jewish Old Folks' Home, Financial Statement, 31 August 1932 and 31 August 1935.

95 *Israelite Press*, 30 September 1919.

96 *Canadian Jewish Review*, 27 September 1924.

97 Annual Report for 1920–24, 12. For example, in 1923, the Hebrew Ladies' Aid of Moose Jaw, Saskatchewan, contributed fifty dollars to the home. *Israelite Press*, 23 March 1923.

98 JHCA, JHC 116, File 3, Jewish Immigrant Aid Society, Financial Statement, 11 December 1923–31 December 1924. For a discussion of the society, see Chapter 7.

99 Federated Budget Board of Winnipeg, *A Great Community Organization: An Outline of the History, Constitution, Objects, and Accomplishments of the Federated Budget Board of Winnipeg* (Winnipeg: Federated Budget Board, 1926), 5.

100 AM, P 639, File 1, A Brief History of the Welfare Council of Greater Winnipeg.

101 AM, P 639, File 1, Minutes of the Central Council of Social Agencies, 21 February 1921. For a discussion of the "federated appeals" movement in Canada in the 1920s, see Shirley Tillotson, "A New Taxpayer for a New State: Charitable Fundraising and the Origins of the Welfare State," in *Social Fabric or Patchwork Quilt: The Development of Social Policy in Canada*, ed. Raymond B. Blake and Jeffrey A. Keshen (Peterborough: Broadview Press, 2006), 156–57.

102 Federated Budget Board of Winnipeg, *A Great Community Organization*, 9.

103 AM, P 639, File 1, Minutes of the Central Council of Social Agencies, 21 February 1921 (hereafter Minutes of the Central Council of Social Agencies).

104 Minutes of the Central Council of Social Agencies, 22 June 1921; AM, MG 10, A 2, Minutes of the Executive Council of the Winnipeg Board of Trade, 29 September 1921. The Board of Trade resolution referred to establishing a community chest.

105 Minutes of the Central Council of Social Agencies, 24 April 1922. See, for example, *Manitoba Free Press*, 14 October 1922.

106 Hart, ed., *The Jew in Canada*, 195–98, 218–20.

107 Federated Budget Board of Winnipeg, *A Great Community Organization*, 7.

108 *Israelite Press*, 24 October 1922.

109 *Israelite Press*, 3 November 1922.

110 *Israelite Press*, 10 November 1922.

111 *Winnipeg Tribune*, 9 November 1922. Agencies were admitted based upon the following criteria: "(a) The nature of the work carried on. (b) Need for such work in the community. (c) Responsibility of the agency's officers. (d) The financial standing of the agency at the time of application." Federated Budget Board of Winnipeg, *A Great Community Organization*, 7.

112 *Winnipeg Tribune*, 13 November 1922. Three additional agencies, including the B'nai B'rith Fresh Air Camp, were admitted after the campaign began. The camp, which received $2,000 in donations from members of the B'nai B'rith, was allocated $1,500. It served 600 children, including fifty children from the Jewish Orphanage and all children whose mothers received the Mothers' Allowance. *Winnipeg Tribune*, 16 August 1924.

113 The Jewish Central Budget Committee of Winnipeg together with the Winnipeg Council of Women, the Trades and Labour Council, the Rotary Club, the Kiwanis Club, and six other organizations were each entitled to appoint two members to the board. The Board of Trade and the Central Council of Social Agencies were both entitled to appoint a maximum of eleven members. 13 Geo. V, cap. 109, s. 5, s. 6, Acts of the Legislature of Manitoba, 1923, 17th Parliament, 1st Session, vol. 2.

114 *Winnipeg Tribune*, 13 November 1923; Federated Budget Board advertisement, Audited Statement of the Winnipeg Federated Budget, 1922–23. Donors had the option of pledging to contribute a sum in instalments.

115 In November 1923, $65,553 in pledges was still outstanding. In addition, campaign and administrative expenses amounted to approximately $23,000. Ibid. Audited Statement of the Winnipeg Federated Budget, 1922–23. Only one-third of the outstanding pledges was collected. *Winnipeg Tribune*, 27 February 1925; AM, P 3646, United Way of Winnipeg, Federated Budget Board Interim Statement, 30 September 1924.

116 *Winnipeg Tribune*, 13 November 1923; Audited Statement of Winnipeg Federated Budget, 1922–23.

117 *Manitoba Free Press*, Federated Budget Board advertisement, 20 November 1922.

118 Annual Report for 1920–24, 13; Jewish Orphanage, 1925–26, 21.

119 *Israelite Press*, 1 December 1922. For the Jewish Orphanage, the discrepancy between the amount collected from members and donors throughout western Canada and the cost of maintaining "country children" remained a persistent problem. It amounted to $1,588 in 1924, $4,514 in 1925, and $3,512 in 1926. Jewish Orphanage, 1925–26, 21.

120 Five additional social welfare agencies and institutions joined the campaign in 1923. *Manitoba Free Press*, 23 November 1923.

121 *Winnipeg Tribune*, 21 December 1923.

122 See note 108.

123 *Manitoba Free Press*, 24 November 1923. The "Central Committee" included one woman, and two women were among the team captains on the "North End Residential Committee." A.H. Aronovitch, who represented the Winnipeg Board of Trade on the Federated Budget Board, chaired the "Jewish Business Men's Select Committee." Alan Bronfman, who sat on the Federated Budget Board as a representative of the Jewish Central Budget Committee together with Max Steinkopf, was also a member of the committee. A total of ten members of the board of directors of the Jewish Orphanage and five members of the board of directors of the Jewish Old Folks' Home were members of the Jewish Division of Canvassers.

Information on the composition of the board of directors of the United Hebrew Relief in 1923 is not available. However, four members of the Jewish Division of Canvassers belonged to the board of directors of the United Hebrew Relief in 1925.

124 *Winnipeg Tribune*, 21 December 1923, 27 February 1925.

125 *Winnipeg Tribune*, 27 February 1925.

126 *Manitoba Free Press*, 28 February 1925; Statement for the Federated Budget Board for Budget Year 1923–24, period ending 31 October 1924. The allocation to the B'nai B'rith Camp was not reduced; it received $1,500. Allocations totalled $323,189, or $29,380 a month, compared with $389,079, or $32,423 a month, the year before.

127 *Manitoba Free Press*, 5 December 1923.

128 *Manitoba Free Press*, 27 February 1926.

129 *Winnipeg Tribune*, 21 November 1924.

130 *Manitoba Free Press*, 27 February 1926. This percentage is based upon a prorated comparison of funding for an eleven-month period (1 December 1923–31 October 1924) and a twelve-month period (1 November 1924–31 October 1925). The allocation to the B'nai B'rith Camp was reduced from $1,500 to $750.

131 *Manitoba Free Press*, 27 February 1926.

132 "The Social Welfare History Project," http://www.socialwelfarehistory.com/people/devine-edward-t-3/ (accessed 12 May 2015).

133 Edward T. Devine, *Welfare Work in Winnipeg: A Social Audit of Those Welfare Institutions which Participate in the Funding of the Federated Budget Board of Winnipeg* (Winnipeg: Federated Budget Board of Winnipeg, 1925).

134 Others included large institutions such as the Misericordia Hospital, the St. Boniface Hospital, and the Victoria Hospital, a number of social agencies such as the Red Cross Society of Manitoba and the Canadian Social Hygiene Council, and five children's camps, including the B'nai B'rith Fresh Air Camp. *Winnipeg Tribune*, 4 November 1924, 10 November 1925.

135 Devine, *Welfare Work in Winnipeg*, 26.

136 AM, P 3646, United Way of Winnipeg, "Appeal from the Jewish Central Committee," n.d.

137 *Winnipeg Tribune*, 10 November 1925.

138 Ibid.

139 *Manitoba Free Press*, 1 April 1927.

140 Revenue from fees paid by parents and guardians increased from $1,969, or 5.4 percent of total income in 1926, to $8,825, or 24 percent of total income in 1929. Jewish Orphanage, 1925–26, 21; AM, GR 1557-A0014, Jewish Orphanage and Children's Aid Society of Western Canada, Financial Statements as of August 1929.

141 *Winnipeg Tribune*, 24 November 1925. Three service clubs—the Lions, Gyro, and Kiwanis—also raised less than they did the year before. However, the Life Underwriters, Knights of Columbus, and Rotary Club increased the amounts that they raised.

142 AM, P 639, File 4, Minutes of Social Planning Council, 1925–26, Meeting of 24 June 1925. Aaron Osovsky, director of the Jewish Orphanage, gave a report on the Fifty-Second National Conference of Social Work, held in Denver, Colorado, the third successive conference that he attended. The National Council of Jewish Women became a member of the council in 1926. AM, P 639, File 5, Minutes of Social Planning Council, 1925–26, Meeting of 1 November 1926.

143 AM, P 639, File 6, Minutes of Social Planning Council, 1927–28, Meeting of 6 February 1928. Aimee Hart Green, who represented the National Council of Jewish Women, was appointed to represent the council on the board. She was reappointed the following year. In 1930, she was succeeded by Sarah Heppner.

144 *Jewish Post*, 28 October 1927. The Jewish Orphanage received $19,700 in 1926–27. *Manitoba Free Press*, 20 April 1920.

145 AM, P 3646, United Way of Winnipeg, *Israelite Press* article with the headline "Have We Responsible Leaders?," n.d.

146 *Jewish Post*, 28 October 1927.

147 *Manitoba Free Press*, 31 October 1929, 11 March 1930, and 5 March 1931.

148 *Manitoba Free Press*, 28 April 1928, 2 March 1929, 11 March 1930, and 2 March 1931. Accurate figures on the Jewish community's contribution to the campaign are not available. As the *Jewish Post* noted on 28 October 1927, "it is better not to speak too specifically of Jewish subscriptions to the Budget—the record is too poor." However, the *Jewish Post* stated that Winnipeg Jews contributed no more than $20,000 to the 1926–27 campaign, and referring to the need to raise $30,000, the Jewish Section's goal for the 1929–30 campaign, the *Israelite Press* reported that only $10,000 was raised. *Jewish Post*, 11 November 1927, 29 October 1929; AM, P 3646, United Way of Winnipeg, *Israelite Press* article with the headline "Have We Responsible Leaders?," n.d.

149 *Jewish Post*, 31 October 1930.

150 Ibid.

151 *Manitoba Free Press*, 20 April 1928, 2 March 1929, 11 March 1930, and 2 March 1931.

152 For example, in 1925, the United Hebrew Relief made an urgent appeal for donations to assist 100 Jewish families in danger of starvation. *Jewish Post*, 9 October 1925.

153 Funding of the two institutions continued to decrease. For example, in 1936, the Jewish Old Folks' Home received $4,500 and the Jewish Orphanage $7,500. However, the Winnipeg Foundation, a private charity established in 1921, gave an additional $500 to the home and $1,200 to the orphanage. *Winnipeg Free Press*, 27 June 1936, 1 January 1936.

154 *Jewish Post*, 18 February 1927.

155 *Jewish Post*, 25 March 1927.

156 *Jewish Post*, 26 April 1927. Citing the 6 May 1927 issue of the *Israelite Press*, Arthur Chiel states that forty-two Jewish organizations attended the meeting that founded the Jewish Charities Endorsation Bureau. These additional members joined after the bureau was established. Arthur A. Chiel, *The Jews in Manitoba: A Social History* (Toronto: University of Toronto Press, 1961), 146.

157 Harry Medovy, "Early Jewish Physicians in Manitoba," *MHS Transactions*, Series 3, no. 29 (1972–73): 24–29.

158 Detailed information on physicians' fees is not available, but by 1920 Jewish physicians charged two dollars for an office visit and three dollars for a house call. JHCA, JHC 7, File 17, Minute Book, Jewish Medical Society of Winnipeg, October 1920 (hereafter Minute Book).

159 In a one-week period in 1904, the Winnipeg General Hospital treated 110 patients in its outpatient department. *Manitoba Free Press*, 29 August 1904. Before the 1920s, Winnipeg hospitals did not appoint Jewish physicians to staff positions and rarely accepted Jewish medical students as interns. In 1923, a delegation of Jewish medical

students complained that "only one out of eighteen Jewish applicants" who applied for internships was successful. Minute Book, May 1923; Medovy, "Early Jewish Physicians."

160 In 1909, the mission assisted 115 Jewish patients, 10 percent of its caseload. Tamara Miller, "'All Our Friends and Patients Know Us': The Margaret Scott Nursing Mission," in *Prairie Metropolis: New Essays in Winnipeg Social History*, ed. Esyllt W. Jones and Gerald Friesen (Winnipeg: University of Manitoba Press, 2009), 94.

161 The mission opened in 1911. See Chapter 3.

162 See Chapter 5.

163 *Israelite Press*, 1 April 1915.

164 Israel Tessler, letter to the editor, *Winnipeg Tribune*, 13 May 1915.

165 Harvey Herstein notes that physicians also visited patients in their homes. Harvey H. Herstein, "The Growth of the Winnipeg Jewish Community and the Evolution of Its Educational Institutions" (MA thesis, University of Manitoba, 1964), 27n3.

166 *Winnipeg Tribune*, 24 July 1915, 27 September 1915, and 8 March 1917.

167 Available evidence suggests that the dispensary closed in 1918 or possibly 1919.

168 *Israelite Press*, 5 June 1925. A larger number of Ukrainian children were treated at the hospital. Cited in Dee Dee Rizzo, "A History of the Mount Carmel Clinic: An Ethnic and Socio-Economic Perspective" (major paper, Department of Foundations/Administration, University of Manitoba, 1980), 13–14.

169 Ibid.

170 Minute Book, 17 February 1925.

171 The society had twelve founding members. Medovy, "Early Jewish Physicians," 6.

172 Minute Book, 4 November 1919.

173 Minute Book, 17 May 1925.

174 Ibid.; *Israelite Press*, 19 May 1925, cited in Rizzo, "A History of the Mount Carmel Clinic," 16.

175 Minute Book, 28 August 1925.

176 *Israelite Press*, 2 September 1925, cited in Rizzo, "A History of the Mount Carmel Clinic," 17.

177 *Israelite Press*, 13 November 1925, cited in ibid., 18.

178 The Ladies' Auxiliary of the Hebrew Sick Benefit Association donated $500. *Jewish Post*, 7 May 1926.

179 *Israelite Press*, 18 December 1925, cited in Rizzo, "A History of the Mount Carmel Clinic," 19.

180 *Jewish Post*, 14 May 1926.

181 *Jewish Post*, 8 April 1927, Mount Carmel Clinic ad.

182 *Jewish Post*, 14 May 1926; Mount Carmel Clinic Financial Statement, 14 September 1925–31 March 1926.

183 Ibid. Between 14 September 1925 and 31 March 1926, donations from mutual aid societies accounted for about 11 percent of the clinic's income. In October 1926, the Romanian Hebrew Sick Benefit Society organized a bazaar to raise money for the clinic. *Israelite Press*, 1 October 1926.

184 The rest included three synagogues and three women's service organizations that provided assistance to the poor. 16 Geo. V, cap. 114, s. 8, Acts of the Legislature of Manitoba, 1926, 17th Parliament, 5th Session, vol. 2.

185 Ibid. Eleven women and forty men petitioned the provincial government to incorporate the clinic. By the end of April 1926, the Ladies' Auxiliary raised $700. Rizzo, "A History of the Mount Carmel Clinic," 23. A Young Ladies' and a Girls' Auxiliary were established later.

186 Between 2 February and 31 December 1926, the clinic treated 1,915 patients, dispensed 1,500 prescriptions, and provided sixty pairs of eyeglasses. A majority (76 percent) of the patients were women and children. *Jewish Post*, 1 June 1928.

187 Rizzo, "A History of the Mount Carmel Clinic," 23–24.

188 16 Geo. V, cap. 114, s. 11, Acts of the Legislature of Manitoba, 1926, 17th Parliament, 5th Session, vol. 2.

189 *Jewish Post*, 14 May 1926; *Israelite Press*, 14 May 1926.

190 *Israelite Press*, 25 June 1926. By 1927, the clinic's medical staff included seventeen physicians and a dentist. At least six of the physicians belonged to the Jewish Medical Society. *Jewish Post*, 29 April 1927.

191 *Jewish Post*, 1 June 1928.

192 Ibid.

193 *Manitoba Free Press*, 20 March 1928; *Jewish Post*, 30 November 1928. The orphanage ultimately raised $25,000.

194 Jewish Endorsation Bureau, letter to the editor, *Jewish Post*, 30 November 1928.

195 Ibid.

196 Ibid.

197 *Jewish Post*, 2 November 1928.

198 Jewish Orphanage, 1928–29–30, 7. The orphanage paid off its debt in 1924 but had annual operating deficits from 1925 to 1929.

199 *Jewish Post*, 12 October 1928.

200 *Israelite Press*, 22 October 1928, cited in Rizzo, "A History of the Mount Carmel Clinic," 28.

201 *Jewish Post*, 12 October 1928.

202 Rizzo, "A History of the Mount Carmel Clinic," 28.

203 Other than references to its progress, no detailed information about the clinic's building campaign has survived.

204 *Jewish Post*, 15 November 1929.

205 *Winnipeg Tribune*, 12 August 1931.

206 AM, P 2179, File 10, Mount Carmel Clinic, Financial Statement, 31 December 1935. Revenue totalled $6,141.

207 Manitoba, Provincial Treasurer, Public Accounts of Manitoba, 1934–35. Unlike the Jewish Old Folks' Home and Jewish Orphanage, the clinic was unable to persuade the Winnipeg Foundation to provide an annual grant. The clinic's board was also unable to persuade city councillors that, as a charitable institution, it should be exempt from property taxes. *Winnipeg Tribune*, 27 April 1929.

208 *Manitoba Free Press*, 5 March 1931; *Winnipeg Free Press*, 27 June 1936. The Federated Budget Board used the term "Winnipeg Community Fund Campaign" in 1931 and was renamed the Winnipeg Community Chest in 1932.

209 *Winnipeg Free Press*, 27 June 1936. The home received $4,500 and the orphanage $7,500.

210 *Jewish Post*, 28 April 1938.

211 Nevertheless, the home and orphanage continued to receive financial support from the Winnipeg Community Chest. In its first campaign, the Jewish Welfare Fund raised $53,000 from 2,150 donors. Chiel, *The Jews in Manitoba*, 148.

Chapter 7: "Opening the Door": The Western Division of the Jewish Immigrant Aid Society

1 Library and Archives Canada (hereafter LAC), RG 76, Immigration, Vol. 390, File 541782, part 2, memorandum, Frederick C. Blair to William Cory, 29 November 1920. Blair's report compared data from April to October 1920 to those for the same period in 1919.

2 LAC, RG 76, Immigration, Vol. 628, File 962419, correspondence, Frederick C. Blair to P.M. Butler, 10 November; 1920; LAC, RG 76, Immigration, Vol. 390, File 541782, part 2, memorandum, Frederick C. Blair to William Cory, 29 November 1920.

3 Ninette Kelly and Michael Trebilcock, *The Making of the Mosaic: A History of Canadian Immigration Policy*, 2nd ed. (Toronto: University of Toronto Press, 2010), 150–51; PC 23, 7 January 1914. However, PC 23 was intended to bar the admission of adult immigrants but not to prevent Canadian residents from sponsoring their wives and children. LAC, RG 76, Immigration, Vol. 51, File 2183, part 3, 21885, correspondence, F.C. Blair to Leo S. Tobin, White Star–Dominion Line, 16 May 1921; PC 918, 9 May 1910; PC 924, 9 May 1910. On 29 November 1920, the amount that immigrants were required to possess was increased to $250. PC 2930, 29 November 1920.

4 LAC, RG 76, Immigration, Vol. 390, File 541782, part 2, memorandum, Frederick W. Blair to James A. Calder, Minister of Immigration and Colonization, 26 November 1920; Department of Immigration and Colonization, "Report of the Department of Immigration and Colonization for the Fiscal Year Ended March 31, 1921," *Sessional Papers, 1922*, no. 18, 16, Table III (hereafter "Report, 1921").

5 Department of Immigration and Colonization, *Report of the Department of Immigration and Colonization for the Fiscal Year Ended March 31, 1931* (Ottawa: F.A. Acland, 1932), 12–15, Tables 2–5 (hereafter "Report, 1931").

6 Canadian Jewish Congress National Archives (hereafter CJCA), JIAS, Series C, Box 9, File 2042, correspondence, H.M. Caiserman to B. Sheps, 23 November 1920.

7 CJCA, JIAS, Series C, Box 9, File 2042, correspondence, H.M. Caiserman to Secretary, Jewish Immigrant Aid Society of Canada, Winnipeg, 3 December 1920.

8 LAC, RG 76, Immigration, Vol. 390, File 541782, part 2, correspondence, Leon Rosenthal to James A. Calder, 26 November 1920.

9 CJCA, JIAS, Series C, Box 9, File 2042, correspondence, B. Sheps to H.M. Caiserman, 13 December 1920.

10 LAC, RG 76, Immigration, Vol. 390, File 541782, part 2, telegram, S. Hart Green to J.A. Calder, 9 December 1920.

11 Simon Belkin, *Through Narrow Gates: A Review of Jewish Immigration, Colonization, and Immigrant Aid Work in Canada (1840–1940)* (Montreal: Eagle Publishing Company, 1966), 108. Belkin states that 226 escaped custody, two died in detention, and as of June 1921 twenty-two appeal cases were pending.

12 A total of 729 Jewish immigrants arrived in Winnipeg in 1911. This number increased to 862 in 1912 and to 1,254 in 1913. *Census of Prairie Provinces, Population and Agriculture, Manitoba, Saskatchewan, Alberta, 1916* (Ottawa: King's Printer, 1918) (hereafter *Census of Prairie Provinces, 1916*). At the request of twenty-six

petitioners, the society was incorporated on 9 July 1912 as the Hebrew Immigration Progressive Society. Jewish Heritage Centre Archives (hereafter JHCA), File Jewish Organizations, Letters Patent, no. 92329, July 1912.

13 *Israelite Press*, 3 November 1915, cited in Harvey H. Herstein, "The Growth of the Winnipeg Jewish Community and the Evolution of Its Educational Institutions" (MA thesis, University of Manitoba, 1964), 26n3.

14 JHCA, uncatalogued file, Immigrant Aid and Relief, 1915, letterhead, Hebrew Immigrant Aid Society of Canada.

15 *Winnipeg Tribune*, 22 October 1913. In 1913, the Department of the Interior was responsible for immigration.

16 *Israelite Press*, 10 March 1915, cited in Belkin, *Through Narrow Gates*, 89.

17 JHCA, uncatalogued file, Immigrant Aid and Relief, 1915, correspondence, Sam Labovich, Financial Secretary, Workmens' [*sic*] Circle Branch 169, to Hebrew Immigrant Aid Society, 19 April 1915.

18 JHCA, uncatalogued file, Western Canadian Jewish Fund for the Relief of War Sufferers, 1919, letterhead, Western Canada's Jewish Fund for the Relief of War Sufferers; letterhead, Hebrew Immigrant Aid Society of Canada.

19 JHCA, uncatalogued file, Immigrant Aid and Relief, 1915. With the exception of Aronovitch, who arrived in 1905, these Jewish notables came to Canada between 1882 and 1891. Unlike the majority of Winnipeg's Jews who arrived after 1905, they might not have perceived immigration as a pressing issue.

20 David Rome, *Early Documents on the Canadian Jewish Congress: 1914–1921*, Canadian Jewish Archives: New Series No. 1 (Montreal: National Archives, Canadian Jewish Congress, 1974), 1a; JHCA, uncatalogued file, Immigrant Aid and Relief, 1915.

21 JHCA, uncatalogued file, Immigrant Aid and Relief, 1916, correspondence, M.J. Finkelstein to B. Sheps, 1 March 1916.

22 Arthur A. Chiel, *The Jews in Manitoba: A Social History* (Toronto: University of Toronto Press, 1961), 142–43.

23 Henry Felix Srebrnik, *Creating the Chupah: The Zionist Movement and the Drive for Jewish Communal Unity in Canada, 1898–1921* (Boston: Academic Studies Press, 2011), 222. The executive included a vice-president and a secretary for Montreal, Toronto, and Winnipeg.

24 Ibid., 221; Belkin, *Through Narrow Gates*, 94.

25 S.B. Haltrecht, "History of the Jewish Immigrant Aid Society of Canada," in *The Jew in Canada*, ed. Arthur Daniel Hart (Toronto: Jewish Publications, 1926), 490.

26 Isaac Ludwig, Max Ludwig, Israel Hurwitz, Eva Brown, a "Mr. Abraham," School Trustee Rose Alcin, and Israel Rusen, a barrister who had worked for Winnipeg's commissioner of immigration, were also founding members. CJCA, JIAS, Series C, Box 9, File 2042, correspondence, B. Sheps to H.M. Kaiserman [*sic*], 14 August 1920. Profiles of delegates can be found in Roseline Usiskin, "Toward a Theoretical Reformulation between Political Ideology, Social Class, and Ethnicity: A Case Study of the Winnipeg Jewish Radical Community" (MA thesis, University of Manitoba, 1978), 252, Appendix G.

27 The fund's letterhead included a list of the members of its executive. JHCA, uncatalogued file, Immigrant Aid and Relief, 1920, letterhead, Western Canada's Jewish Fund for the Relief of War Sufferers.

28 The Brandon branch had twenty-one members. Its secretary stated that "they will try and enroll every Jew in their town as a member of our organization." CJCA, JIAS,

Series C, Box 9, File 2042, correspondence, B. Sheps to H.M. Caiserman, 5 October 1920.

29 Ibid., correspondence, B. Sheps to H.M. Caiserman, 25 September 1920.

30 Ibid.

31 Ibid.

32 Ibid.

33 Ibid., correspondence, B. Sheps to H.M. Caiserman, 5 October 1920.

34 In addition to Sheps, the executive consisted of William Keller as vice-president, M.W. Triller as treasurer, J. Hestrin as honorary secretary, and R. Klipper as acting secretary. A list of the members of the board of directors has not survived. CJCA, JIAS, Series C, Box 9, File 2042, letterhead, Jewish Immigrant Aid Society of Canada, Western Division.

35 In March 1920, the HIAS opened an office in Warsaw to assist Polish Jews as well as the thousands of Jewish refugees arriving from Russia. Ibid., correspondence, B. Sheps to H.M. Caiserman, 5 October 1920, 15 November 1920, and 23 November 1920. The WDJIAS did not have a representative on the national executive of the JIAS until 1924, when S. Hart Green was elected a national vice-president.

36 Ibid., correspondence, B. Sheps to H.M. Caiserman, 26 October 1920.

37 *Winnipeg Tribune*, 11 September 1920.

38 M.C. Urquhart and Kenneth A.H. Buckley, *Historical Statistics of Canada* (Toronto: Macmillan, 1965), 107; Donald Avery, *"Dangerous Foreigners": European Immigrant Workers and Labour Relations in Canada, 1896–1932* (Toronto: McClelland and Stewart, 1979), 72–74.

39 Reinhold Kramer and Tom Mitchell, *When the State Trembled: How A.J. Andrews and the Citizens' Committee Broke the Winnipeg General Strike* (Toronto: University of Toronto Press, 2010), 165. One of the members of the strike committee, A.A. Heaps, was also Jewish. Born in England, his parents had emigrated from the Kingdom of Poland in the Russian Empire and settled in Leeds.

40 Albert Reames, "Report Re: General Strike in Winnipeg, 25 May, 1919," cited Gerald Tulchinsky, *Canada's Jews: A People's Journey* (Toronto: University of Toronto Press, 2008), 188.

41 S.C. c. 38, s. 7 (1) and 2 (c).

42 S.C. c. 25, s.13 (c).

43 LAC, RG 76, Immigration, Vol. 390, File 541782, correspondence, Superintendent Albert J. Cowdron to Frederick Blair, 15 December 1920.

44 LAC, RG 76, Immigration, Vol. 628, File 962419, correspondence, Frederick C. Blair to P.M. Butler, 10 November 1920.

45 LAC, RG 76, Immigration, Vol. 390, File 541782, correspondence, James A. Calder to C. [*sic*] Caiserman, 16 April 1921.

46 LAC, RG 76, Immigration, Vol. 624, File 947852, Official Circular No. 4 Effective 1 January 1919, and Vol. 628, memorandum, Frederick Blair to William Cory, 1 March 1921.

47 LAC, RG 76, Immigration, Vol. 51, File 2183, part 3, 124921, correspondence, F.C. Blair to William Ballantyne, Canadian Pacific Railway, 2 December 1921. In addition, the immigration department was unwilling to accept Soviet passports because the Soviet Union did not allow citizens who emigrated to return. Consequently, if they became a public charge or committed a criminal offence, they could not be deported from Canada.

48 Ibid., correspondence, F.C. Blair to J.V. Lantalum, Dominion Immigration Agent, St. John 7 February, 1921. Immigrants were identified by country of origin, race, and religion. Therefore, a Polish Jew could be identified as an immigrant from Poland, Polish, and (in the religion column) Jewish. Blair was concerned that annual reports and other department documents that recorded the number of immigrants admitted into Canada could record the admission of a Jew as a Pole or Russian, therefore underreporting the scale of Jewish immigration.

49 PC 2930, 29 November 1920; PC 959, 19 March 1921; PC 2668, 26 July 1921.

50 Belkin, *Through Narrow Gates*, 111–21. In 1921, the Soviet government agreed to permit Jews to emigrate.

51 *Winnipeg Tribune*, 8 August 1921.

52 Zosa Szajkowski, "Private and Organized American Jewish Overseas Relief (1941–1938)," *American Jewish Historical Quarterly* 57, no. 1 (1967): 245, Table 1.

53 Canada did not recognize the Soviet government until 1924.

54 With the assistance of the JCA, the EZRA Committee in Antwerp and the Montefiore Committee in Rotterdam, Jewish aid organizations, assisted Jewish refugees to get passports and purchase steamship tickets. Theodore Norman, *An Outstretched Arm: A History of the Jewish Colonization Association* (London: Routledge and Kegan Paul, 1985), 202.

55 *Canadian Jewish Chronicle*, 4 March 1921. Based in Copenhagen, Grossman was on a cross-country tour to study Jewish life in Canada.

56 LAC, RG 76, Immigration, Vol. 390, File 541782, part 2, Resolution Adopted at a Conference of Representatives of Jewish Communities from Western Canada in Saskatoon, 15 February 1921.

57 Ibid., correspondence, B. Sheps to The Right Honourable Arthur P. Meighen, 21 February 1921.

58 Ibid., memorandum prepared by F.C. Blair for Mr. Cory, 4 March 1921.

59 Ibid. See Belkin, *Through Narrow Gates*, 216, Appendix 6.

60 LAC, RG 76, Immigration, Vol. 390, File 541782, part 2, memorandum prepared by F.C. Blair for Mr. Cory, 4 March 1921.

61 Department of Immigration and Colonization, "Report of the Department of Immigration and Colonization for the Fiscal Year Ended March 31,1920," *Sessional Papers, 1921*, no. 18, 14, Table III (hereafter "Report, 1920"); "Report, 1921," 16, Table III; ibid., "Report of the Department of Immigration and Colonization for the Fiscal Year Ended March 31,1922," *Sessional Papers, 1923*, no. 13, 14, Table III (hereafter "Report, 1922").

62 CJCA, JIAS, Series C, Box 9, File 2194, Jewish Immigrant Aid Society of Canada Manager's Report, May 1921–30 April 1922, 10.

63 PC 2669, 26 July 1921.

64 CJCA, JIAS, Canadian Collection, Box 15, File J395, correspondence, S.B. Haltrecht to S.W. Jacobs, 6 September 1921.

65 CJCA, JIAS, Series C, Box 9, File 2194, Jewish Immigrant Aid Society of Canada Manager's Report, May 1921–30 April 1922, 22–25. The Hebrew Immigrant Aid Society and the Joint Distribution Committee gave grants to enable the JIAS to assist Jewish immigrants destined for the United States. The JIAS posted bonds of $500 to guarantee that if released a detained Jewish immigrant would work on a farm for two years and "not become a factor in the labour market." In 1921, the JIAS posted bonds totalling $13,989.

66 Ibid., 20.

67 LAC, MG 26 I, Arthur Meighen Papers, No. 017436, correspondence, S. Larkin (private secretary to Dr. J.W. Edwards) to Arthur Meighen, 9 November 1921.

68 M.J. Finkelstein attributed the defeat of a Unionist incumbent by a Liberal in Winnipeg's North End to the "immigration issue." The Unionist candidate was "snowed under" in the Jewish section of the constituency. M.J. Finkelstein to S.W. Jacobs, 7 December 1921, quoted in David Rome, *Clouds in the Thirties: On Anti-Semitism in Canada, 1929–1939* (Montreal: Canadian Jewish Congress, 1979), 336.

69 Belkin, *Through Narrow Gates*, 126.

70 CJCA, JIAS, Series C, Box 9, File 2194, Jewish Immigrant Aid Society of Canada Manager's Report, May 1921–30 April 1922, 10. The JIAS successfully appealed eighteen of these deportation orders, enabling the deportees to return to Canada.

71 LAC, RG 76, Immigration, Vol. 628, File 962419, memorandum, F.C. Blair to Mr. Black, 15 December 1921.

72 *Canadian Jewish Chronicle*, 13 January 1922.

73 The post was vacant from 29 December 1921 to 3 January 1922 and from 2 February 1922 to 20 February 1922. Senator Hewitt Bostock served as the acting minister from 3 January 1922 to 2 February 1922. Privy Council Office, *Guide to Ministries since Confederation*, Twelfth Ministry, 29 December 1921 to 28 June 1926, http://www.pco-bcp.gc.ca/mgm/dtail.asp?lang=eng&mstyid=12&mbtpid=1.

74 M.J. Finkelstein to S.W. Jacobs, 7 December 1921, quoted in Rome, *Clouds in the Thirties*, 336.

75 PC 1041, 12 May 1922.

76 PC 717, 9 May 1922.

77 LAC, RG 76, Immigration, Vol. 177, File 59735, memo to train companies, 3 January 1923.

78 LAC, RG 76, Immigration, Vol. 624, File 947852, Official Circular No. 13, 30 June 1922; Vol. 583, File 818219, correspondence, F.C. Blair to T.B. Willans, 29? January 1923; PC 183, 31 January 1923.

79 "Report, 1922," 12, Table III. Admissions in the same months in 1921 were 761 and 1,064.

80 Department of Immigration and Colonization, *Report of the Department of Immigration and Colonization for the Fiscal Year Ended March 31,1923*, Sessional Papers, 1924, no. 13, 12, Table III (hereafter *Report, 1923*).

81 "Report, 1921," 16, Table III; "Report, 1922," 14, Table III; "Report, 1923," 12, Table III.

82 Department of Immigration and Colonization, *Report of the Department of Immigration and Colonization for the Fiscal Year Ended March 31, 1926* (Ottawa: F.A. Acland, 1927), 22 (hereafter *Report, 1926*).

83 Ibid., 6. Egan replaced Black as the deputy minister in October 1923.

84 Mostly from Ukraine, approximately 11,000 Jewish refugees who remained in Romania were threatened with expulsion. The JCA had persuaded the Romanian government to defer taking action until December 1923. Norman, *An Outstretched Arm*, 206–07.

85 LAC, MG 76, Vol. 51, File 2183, part 4, 111908, memorandum written by F.C. Blair, 7 September 1923.

86 Norman, *An Outstretched Arm*, 206–07; Belkin, *Through Narrow Gates*, 133. Belkin was present at the meeting.

87 *Canadian Jewish Chronicle*, 7 December 1923.

88 CJCA, ICA Canada Collection, Box 9, CB 13, JIAS, 1923–24, correspondence, Lyon Cohen to M.A. Gray, 30 November 1923.

89 Ibid., report of the secretary presented at the general executive meeting of the Jewish Immigrant Aid Society in Winnipeg, 10 June 1924, 4.

90 With the support of "twenty-eight Jewish societies," the WDJIAS raised $800 at a benefit concert. *Winnipeg Tribune*, 23 April 1923.

91 The immigrant shelter served over 9,000 meals between January and May 1923. CJCA, ICA Canada Collection, Box 9, CB 13, 3. The WDJIAS spent approximately $6,500. JHCA, JHC 116, F3, statement of cash receipts and disbursements, 11 December 1923 to 31 December 1924. For example, Aaron Bailovsky established a barber shop, investing eighteen dollars of his own money and borrowing the rest from the WDJIAS. JHCA, JHC 116, F7, "Special Report Re Aaron Bailovsky," n.d. The house was located in the North End at 339 Manitoba Avenue.

92 These figures are for Jewish immigrants who stated on arrival that Manitoba was their destination. In 1921, approximately 87 percent of Manitoba's Jews lived in Winnipeg. "Report, 1922," 16–17, Table V; "Report, 1923," 14–15, Table V.

93 LAC, MG 28, V 114, JIAS (Western Division), File 225, report of the Jewish Immigrant Aid Society since its reorganization in December 1923 to 5 April 1924.

94 *Canadian Jewish Chronicle*, 11 January 1924.

95 CJCA, ICA Canada Collection, Box 8, CB 3.2, Immigration to Canada, 1923–40, minutes of dominion emergency immigration conference, 8 January 1924.

96 The Montefiore Club was established in 1911 by young Jewish businessmen. In addition to hosting social and sports activities, it raised money for charitable organizations such as the Jewish Orphanage.

97 CJCA, ICA Canada Collection, Box 8, CB 10, JIAS Officers, 1920–59, WDJIAS letterhead, 1924. Haid served as treasurer, and Aronovitch chaired the loan committee.

98 LAC, MG 28, V 114, JIAS (Western Division), File 225, report of the Jewish Immigrant Aid Society since its reorganization in December 1923 to 5 April 1924.

99 Ibid., File 191, correspondence, M.A. Gray to Dr. Ben Victor and four other physicians, 15 May 1924. The letters thanked the physicians for volunteering their services.

100 CJCA, ICA Canada Collection, Box 9, CB 13, 2, report of the secretary presented at the general executive meeting of the Jewish Immigrant Aid Society in Winnipeg, 10 June 1924.

101 Ibid., correspondence, S. Hart Green to Lyon Cohen, 19 March 1924.

102 *Jewish Post*, 12 June 1925.

103 Ibid.

104 CJCA, ICA Canada Collection, Box 8, CB 12, national expense account of the Jewish Immigrant Aid Society at Winnipeg, to 5 May 1924. The WDJIAS claimed close to $2,100. It received a cheque for $1,000; by December 1924, this amount had increased to $7,000.

105 JHCA, JHC 116, JIAS (Western Division), F3, correspondence, M.A. Gray to S. Hart Green, 11 September 1924 and 3 July 1925. Donations that amounted to $6,559

in 1924 decreased to $612 in the first half of 1925. However, donations of clothing and food increased from $2,500 to $4,000. Between January and June 1925, the WDJIAS received $6,000 from the national office. Ibid., correspondence, George Loos and Company to Executive Committee, Jewish Immigrant Aid Society, Winnipeg, 7 July 1925. The national office of the JIAS received payments from the CCJCA, which was also supported by the Hebrew Immigrant Aid Society and the American Jewish Congress. CJCA, JIAS Canada Collection, Box 15, File 369, correspondence, S. Belkin to Joseph Barondess, 25 September 1924.

106 *Jewish Post*, 12 June 1925.

107 Ibid.

108 Ibid.

109 In a ten-month period, the WDJIAS spent $4,290.45 on relief. LAC, MG 28, V 114, JIAS (Western Division), microfilm reel M4586, File 391, Facts and Figures, 1 July 1925 to 30 April 1926. The Federated Budget Board did not allow the United Hebrew Relief to assist destitute immigrants. However, in March 1925, the Federated Budget Board dropped the United Hebrew Relief from its campaign, and it began to cooperate with the WDJIAS to assist immigrants. For example, in May 1925, the United Hebrew Relief and the WDJIAS agreed to assume joint responsibility for a blind immigrant facing deportation. The WDJIAS undertook to pay the immigrant's rent, and the United Hebrew Relief agreed to pay for food and clothing. Ibid., microfilm reel M4585, File 327, correspondence, M.A. Gray to I.H. Shulman, Secretary, United Hebrew Relief, 12 May 1925.

110 Between 1 July 1925 and 30 April 1926, the WDJIAS paid the hospital bills of thirty-five patients whose stays ranged from three days to fifteen weeks. LAC, MG 28, V 114, JIAS (Western Division), microfilm reel M4586, File 391, Facts and Figures, 1 July 1925 to 30 April 1926.

111 *Jewish Post*, 12 June 1925.

112 CJCA, ICA Canada Collection, Box 9, CB 13, correspondence, W.J. Black to L. Cohen, 29 September 1923.

113 Ibid., CB 15, Quota Agreement, 1923–24, outline of argument by Lyon Cohen in company with S.W. Jacobs at an interview with Robb and Egan, 11 June 1924. Belkin states that 8,000 refugees were stranded at European ports. Belkin, *Through Narrow Gates*, 137.

114 LAC, RG 76, Immigration, Vol. 628, File 962419, memorandum, F.C. Blair to W.J. Egan, 11 June 1924.

115 Belkin, *Through Narrow Gates*, 139.

116 CJCA, ICA Canada Collection, Box 3, AB 2, correspondence, CCJCA to JCA, 15 August 1924.

117 Ibid.

118 Ibid., correspondence, Executive Secretary, CCJCA, to JCA, Paris, 15 September 1924.

119 Belkin, *Through Narrow Gates*, 138. According to the CCJCA's records, a total of 3,075 Jewish refugees travelled to Canada in eleven groups.

120 CJCA, ICA Canada Collection, Box 3, AB 2, correspondence, Executive Secretary, CCJCA, to JCA, 26 November 1924.

121 LAC, MG 26, J13, Diaries of Prime Minister William Lyon Mackenzie King, item 90155, November 1924, http://www.bac-lac.gc.ca/eng/discover/politics-

government/prime-ministers/william-lyon-mackenzie-king/Pages/diaries-william-lyon-mackenzie-king.aspx#f.

122 CJCA, ICA Canada Collection, Box 3, AB 2, correspondence, Executive Secretary, CCJCA, to JCA, 26 November 1924; LAC, MG 28, V 114, microfilm reel M4583, File 194, correspondence, M.A. Gray to S.B. Haltrecht, 6 November 1924.

123 CJCA, ICA Canada Collection, Box 3, AB 2, correspondence, Executive Secretary, CCJCA, to JCA, Paris, immediate family members as defined by PC 183, 31 January 1923.

124 LAC, RG 76, Immigration, Vol. 390, File 541782, part 2, correspondence, Edward McMurray to W.L. Mackenzie King, 28 April 1925.

125 CJCA, JIAS Canada Collection, Box 4, File J117, correspondence, W.J. Egan to S.B. Haltrecht, 1 May 1925.

126 A sample copy of the application form can be found in LAC, MG28, V 114, JIAS (Western Division), microfilm reel M4587, File 604.

127 Ibid., File 609, correspondence, M.A. Gray to S.B. Haltrecht, 30 April 1925. Between December 1923 and June 1925, the WDJIAS disbursed $1,193 in loans to assist immigrants to purchase steamship tickets. JHCA, JHC 123, File 3, WDJIAS Financial Statement, 11 December 1923 to 25 June 1925.

128 *Jewish Post*, 31 July 1925.

129 CJCA, ICA Canada Collection, Box 3, AB 2, correspondence, Executive Secretary, CCJCA, to JCA, Paris, 12 June 1925.

130 Ibid., 13 July 1925.

131 By 15 October 1925, the number of applications submitted to the department reached 2,500. Ibid., 8 December 1925.

132 JHCA, JHC 122, JIAS (Western Division), File 05, correspondence, W.J. Egan to S.B. Haltrecht, 8 October 1925.

133 CJCA, ICA Canada Collection, Box 3, AB 2, correspondence, Executive Secretary, CCJCA, to JCA, Paris, 8 December 1925. As Egan intended, the requirement that all of the 1,500 possess passports created problems for many of the Jewish refugees stranded at Western European ports. Ibid., 28 December 1925.

134 The Liberal government survived the first vote of the new session by three votes. In return for their support, Heaps and Woodsworth demanded that King introduce legislation establishing old age pensions.

135 *Israelite Press*, 27 October 1925, cited in Henry Trachtenberg, "The Winnipeg Jewish Community and Politics: The Inter-War Years, 1919–1939," *Transactions of the Historical and Scientific Society of Manitoba*, Series III, 34–35 (1977–78 and 1978–79): 134.

136 *Israelite Press*, 30 October 1925.

137 *Winnipeg Tribune*, 1 September 1922.

138 CJCA, JIAS Canada Collection, Box 15, File J395, correspondence, A. Levin to S.W. Jacobs, 5 January 1926.

139 CJCA, JIAS Series C, Box 45, File 11089, correspondence, S. Hart Green to S.B. Haltrecht, 30 December 1925.

140 JHCA, JHC 123, JIAS (Western Division), File 3, correspondence, A.A. Heaps to M.A. Gray, 21 January 1926.

141 Ibid., 24 January 1926.

142 The executive of the WDJIAS also wanted the government to give recipients of permits the freedom to buy steamship tickets from a company of their choice. Ibid., correspondence, J.A. Cherniack to A.A. Heaps, 25 February 1926. Although recipients of permits had numerous problems dealing with steamship companies that did not have agents in Winnipeg, the executive was attempting to assist M.A. Gray, an agent for the Baltic American Line, which offered steamship service from Danzig to Halifax. Gray wrote to Haltrecht to request that 25 percent of the permits be assigned to the Baltic American Line. CJCA, JIAS Series C, Box 45, File 11089, correspondence, M.A. Gray to S.B. Haltrecht, 27 February 1926.

143 CJCA, JIAS Canada Collection, Box 15, File J395, correspondence, S.B. Haltrecht to S.W. Jacobs, 27 January 1926.

144 CJCA, ICA, Canada Collection, Box 9, CB 17, correspondence, Lyon Cohen to Charles Stewart, 15 February 1926.

145 Ibid., correspondence, Charles Stewart to Lyon Cohen, 4 February 1926.

146 JHCA, JHC 123, JIAS (Western Division), File 3, correspondence, A.A. Heaps to M.A. Gray, 24 January 1926.

147 Ibid., correspondence, F.C. Blair to S.B. Haltrecht, 15 February 1926.

148 CJCA, ICA, Canada Collection, Box 9, CB 17, correspondence, Charles Stewart to Lyon Cohen, 4 February 1926. The inclusion of heads of families was significant; once established in Canada, they could sponsor their wives and children, thereby ultimately increasing the number of Jewish immigrants admitted under the quota.

149 Ibid.

150 Ibid., correspondence, F.C. Blair to Lyon Cohen, 19 February 1926.

151 Ibid.

152 When members of the executive of the WDJIAS thanked Heaps for his effort to negotiate the quota, it noted that they "would undoubtedly have been crowned with greater success had it not been for the interference of Mr. Lyon Cohen and his colleagues." JHCA, JHC 123, JIAS (Western Division), File 3, correspondence, J.A. Cherniack to A.A. Heaps, 25 February 1926.

153 Ibid., correspondence (WDJIAS financial statement), George Loos and Company to Executive Committee, Jewish Immigrant Aid Society, Winnipeg, 7 July 1925. Members of the Winnipeg Jewish community also donated "four thousand dollars worth of clothing and other supplies." JHCA, JHC 115, JIAS (Western Division), File 11, correspondence, M.A. Gray to S. Hart Green, 3 July 1925.

154 Ibid.

155 CJCA, JIAS, Series C, Box 45, File 1104, correspondence, S.B. Haltrecht to S. Hart Green, 12 February 1926.

156 CJCA, JIAS, Canada Collection, Box 1, LC 1, JIAS, "Financial Statement for the Year Ending April 30th, 1925." In addition to the contribution from the American Jewish Congress, the JIAS received $5,000 from the HIAS, $10,000 from the Joint Distribution Committee, and $53,000 from the Emergency Committee on Jewish Refugees. CJCA, JIAS, Series C, Box 45, File 1104, correspondence, S. Hart Green to A. Levin, 20 April 1926.

157 Ibid., correspondence, S. Hart Green to A. Levin, 20 April 1920.

158 Ibid.

159 In October 1926, Gray submitted a claim for $6,879.47 in expenses for the maintenance of refugees. There is no evidence that it was paid. Ibid., correspondence, M.A. Gray to S.B. Haltrecht, 26 October 1926.

160 LAC, MG 28, V 114, File F 604, microfilm reel M4587, correspondence, M.A. Gray to J.W. Walker, 26 October 1926.

161 Ibid., File 1480, microfilm reel M4594, correspondence, M.A. Gray to Jacob Waid, 18 February 1927.

162 In 1926, the total cost of steamship and railway tickets for two adults and two small children (half fare) to travel from a European port to Winnipeg was $487.10. LAC, MG 28, V 114, JIAS (Western Division), File F 604, microfilm reel M4587, correspondence, M.A. Gray to J.W. Walker, 26 October 1926.

163 PC 534, 8 April 1926.

164 Ibid.

165 LAC, RG 76, Immigration, Vol. 390, File 541782, part 2, correspondence, S.B. Haltrecht to J.S. Fraser, Divisional Commissioner, 11 June 1926; ibid., Vol. 54, File 2240, correspondence, J.S. Fraser to S.B. Haltrecht, 26 June 1926.

166 Ibid., correspondence, F.C. Blair to W.J. Egan, 31 July 1926. Egan was once again serving as deputy minister, and Blair became assistant deputy minister.

167 "If there had to be any Liberals in the House of Commons, I am glad one of them is Sam Jacobs!" R.B. Bennett to S.W. Jacobs, 4 October 1926, quoted in Rome, *Clouds in the Thirties*, 50a.

168 This is inferred from a letter that Jacobs wrote to Bennett in October 1926. In the letter, Jacobs expressed his appreciation for Bennett's help on an immigration matter. Ibid., S.W. Jacobs to R.B. Bennett, 7 October 1926.

169 LAC, RG 76, Immigration, Vol. 390, File 541782, part 2, memorandum, M. Cullen, Private Secretary to the Minister of Immigration and Colonization, to W.J. Egan, 11 August 1926.

170 CJCA, Canada Collection, Box 3, AB 2, correspondence, Canadian Committee to JCA, Paris, 4 October 1926. Drayton remained the minister of immigration and colonization until 25 September 1926.

171 R.B. Bennett to S.W. Jacobs, 4 October 1926, quoted in Rome, *Clouds in the Thirties*, 50a.

172 LAC, MG 28, V 114, JIAS (Western Division), File 210, microfilm reel M4583, correspondence, S.B. Haltrecht to M.A. Gray, 3 September 1926.

173 LAC, RG 76, Immigration, Vol. 390, File 541782, part 2, extract from a memorandum, F.C. Blair to Sir Henry Drayton, 3 September 1926.

174 Belkin, *Through Narrow Gates*, 149. In total, the delegation had twelve members.

175 Ibid., 151.

176 Ibid., 150.

177 Ibid. Thorson, the newly elected MP for Winnipeg Centre, was likely invited by Heaps.

178 Ibid.

179 YIVO Archives, HIAS-HICEM, 245.4 MKM 15.22, Minutes of Executive Committee, WDJIAS, 6 June 1927.

180 Ibid.

181 Canada, House of Parliament, House of Commons, *Report of Select Committee on Agriculture and Colonization* (Ottawa: F.A. Acland, 1928), Minutes of Proceedings, memorandum, Robert Forke to W.J. Egan, 19 October 1926, 60 (here after *Select Committee*).

182 LAC, MG 28, V 114, JIAS (Western Division), microfilm reel M4595, File 1618, correspondence, W.J. Egan to A.A. Heaps, 7 March 1928; microfilm reel M4596, File 1672, correspondence, F.C. Blair to A.A. Heaps, 10 October 1928.

183 Ibid., microfilm reel M4857, File 1912-A, correspondence, A.A. Heaps to M. Gray, 12 June 1928.

184 Ibid., correspondence, A.A. Heaps to M. Gray, 3 October 1928.

185 Ibid., correspondence, A.A. Heaps to M. Gray, 22 February 1928. For a discussion of the complexity and high cost of applying for a Soviet passport, see Boris Morozov, "Out of the Soviet Union: The Exiles and Pompolit," in *Exiled to Palestine: The Emigration of Zionist Convicts from the Soviet Union, 1924–1934*, ed. Ziva Galili and Boris Morozov (London: Routledge, 2006), 32. After five years, an immigrant was eligible to apply for naturalization.

186 LAC, MG 28, V 114, JIAS (Western Division), microfilm reel M4857, File 1912-A, correspondence, A.A. Heaps to M. Gray, 17 October 1928.

187 Ibid., correspondence, A.A. Heaps to M. Gray, 3 October 1928.

188 *Select Committee*, Minutes of Proceedings, 99–100.

189 The physicians were stationed in Antwerp, Danzig, Hamburg, Paris, Riga, and Rotterdam. Ibid., 739.

190 CJCA, JIAS, Administration and Control Records, Box 1, File KA 2, Minutes of Meeting of Board of Directors, 4 September 1928. Jacobs viewed the medical inspections as "subterfuges" to keep Jews out of Canada. S.W. Jacobs to W.J. Egan, 4 September 1928, quoted in Rome, *Clouds in the Thirties*, 54a.

191 LAC, MG 28, V 114, JIAS (Western Division), microfilm reel M4957, File 1912-A, correspondence, A.A. Heaps to M. Gray, 3 October 1928.

192 CJCA, JIAS, Administration and Control Records, Box 1, File KE 1.2, JIAS Ninth Annual Report, 1 May 1928–30 April 1929, 3.

193 Calculated from Department of Immigration and Colonization, *Report of the Department of Immigration and Colonization for the Fiscal Year Ended March 31, 1929* (Ottawa: F.A. Acland, 1930), 24, Table 14 (hereafter *Report, 1929*); *Report of the Department of Colonization and Immigration for the Fiscal Year Ended March 31, 1930* (Ottawa: F.A. Acland, 1931), 22, Table 15 (hereafter *Report, 1930*); CJCA, JIAS, Canada Collection, Box 45, File 1104, W.J. Egan to A. Paull, 4 May 1928.

194 Department of Immigration and Colonization, *Report of the Department of Immigration and Colonization for the Fiscal Year Ended March 31, 1925* (Ottawa: F.A. Acland, 1926), 16–17, Table V (hereafter *Report, 1925*); CJCA, JIAS, Series C, Box 61, File 14676, Immigration Tables, 1 May 1926–10 April 1927; *Report of the Department of Colonization and Immigration for the Fiscal Year Ended March 31, 1928* (Ottawa: F.A. Acland, 1929, 34–35, Table 30; (hereafter Report, 1928); *Report, 1929*, 28–29, Table 30; *Report, 1930*, 38–39, Table 30.

195 JHCA, JHC 123, File 3, WDJIAS Financial Statement, 11 December 1923 to 25 June 1925; YIVO Archives, HIAS-HICEM, 245.4 MKM 15.22, xd-1, correspondence, M.A. Gray to the Executive Committee, JIAS, 27 April 1929.

196 LAC, MG 28, V 114, JIAS (Western Division), microfilm reel M4596, File 1679, correspondence, M.A. Gray to Polish Consulate, Montreal, 28 July 1928 and 31 July 1928.

197 YIVO Archives, HIAS-HICEM, 245.4 MKM 15.22, xd-1, correspondence, M.A. Gray to the Executive Committee, JIAS, 6 November 1930.

198 Ibid. In a one-year period, Gray prepared thirty-eight applications for Heaps (twenty-six permits were issued for ninety immigrants) and submitted 115 applications directly to Gelley ("about 90 permits obtained").

199 CJCA, JIAS Canada Collection, Series C, Box 60, File 14628, correspondence, M.A. Gray to A.J. Paull, JIAS, 14 February 1929. Immigrants appearing before boards of inquiry were likely represented by either S. Hart Green, president of the WDJIAS, or J.A. Cherniack, a vice-president, who were both lawyers.

200 YIVO Archives, HIAS-HICEM, 245.4 MKM 15.22, xd-1, correspondence, M.A. Gray to the Executive Committee, JIAS, 6 November 1930. In January 1929, Gray spoke to more than 500 people, received eighty-two letters and fifteen telegrams, and sent 165 letters and twelve telegrams.

201 Without a quota agreement, branches of the JIAS in Regina, Saskatoon, Edmonton, and Calgary could not continue to operate. CJCA, JIAS Canada Collection, Series C, Box 60, File 14628, correspondence, M.A. Gray to A.J. Paull, JIAS, 30 October 1930; ibid., correspondence, I. Feingut to A.J. Paull, 4 November 1930.

202 When notified that Jewish immigrants were en route to Winnipeg by train, volunteers continued to meet them at the station and provide assistance. The WDJIAS also continued to operate an employment bureau, and one volunteer, H. Cohen, came into the office daily to deal with requests for financial and other forms of assistance. YIVO Archives, HIAS-HICEM, 245.4 MKM 15.22, xd-2, correspondence, M.A. Gray to WDJIAS Executive Committee, 6 November 1930.

203 The WDJIAS received $1,984 in donations for "services rendered" to applicants for permits. As of 1 April 1929, it had a reserve fund of $2,446.77. Ibid.

204 CJCA, JIAS Canada Collection, LC, Box 1, File LC 1, JIAS Eighth Annual Report, 1 May 1927–30 April 1928, 4.

205 YIVO Archives, HIAS-HICEM, 245.4 MKM 15.22, xd-1, correspondence, M.A. Gray to J.A. Cherniack, 3 September 1930. In June 1930, the subsidy was reduced to fifty dollars per month. CJCCCNA, JIAS Canada Collection, Box 60, File 14628, correspondence, M.A. Gray to A.J. Paull, 20 June 1930.

206 "Mr. Heaps claims (this is not for publication) that he can do anything he wants with Mr. Stewart." CJCCCNA, JIAS Series C, Box 59, File 1428, correspondence, M.A. Gray to A.J. Paull, 2 January 1930.

207 David Gower, "A Note on Canadian Unemployment since 1921," *Perspectives on Income and Labour* 4, no. 3, 1992, http://www.statcan.gc.ca/pub/75-001-x/1992003/87-eng.pdf.

208 PC 1957, 14 August 1930.

209 Ibid.

210 CJCA, JIAS Administration and Control Records, Box 1, File KA3, Minutes of Meeting of Board of Directors, 29 August 1930.

211 Calculated from *Report, 1929*, 24, Table 14; *Report, 1930*, 22, Table 15; and *Report, 1931*, 22, Table 15.

212 *Report, 1930*, 38–39, Table 32; *Report, 1931*, 38–39, Table 32; Department of Immigration and Colonization, *Report of the Department of Immigration and Colonization for the Fiscal Year Ended March 31, 1932* (Ottawa: F.A. Acland, 1933), 42–43, Table 33.

213 CJCA, JIAS Canada Collection, Series C, Box 60, File 14628, correspondence, M.A. Gray to A.J. Paull, 26 August 1932 and 8 September 1932.

214 Lyon Cohen had been an honorary president of the JIAS since 1924. In 1931, Samuel Bronfman, the liquor magnate, became an honorary president. As honorary presidents, both served on the executive committee of the JIAS.

215 M.A. Gray was elected as a Labour candidate to Winnipeg City Council in 1930.

216 LAC, RG 76, Immigration, Vol. 395, File 563236, correspondence, W.A. Gordon to D.G. Robinson, Minister of Labour, 6 August 1931.

217 Barbara Roberts, *Whence They Came: Deportation from Canada, 1900–1935* (Ottawa: University of Ottawa Press, 1988), 38, Table 1.

218 Destitute Jews who were citizens could safely apply for relief, but very few did so. Instead, they turned to the United Hebrew Relief. R.C. Bellan notes that, of the 7,016 single men who registered for relief in 1930–31, only 11 were Jewish. Similarly, of the 787 women who registered for relief, only 29 were Jewish. R.C. Bellan, "Relief in Winnipeg: The Economic Background" (MA thesis, University of Toronto, 1941), 184.

219 LAC, MG 28, V 114, microfilm reel M4597, File 1940, correspondence, M.A. Gray to A.J. Paull, 24 May 1933.

220 Ibid. Since wives and children acquired citizenship when married men were naturalized, the naturalization of "65 people" likely meant that between 200 and 250 Jews became citizens.

221 *Report, 1931*, 9–12, Tables 2, 3, 4, and 5.

222 Reliable data on the number of Jewish immigrants who settled in Winnipeg in the 1920s are not available. Most but not all of the annual reports of the immigration department provide data on the number of Jewish immigrants who, on arrival in Canada, informed immigration officers that they were travelling to Manitoba. However, without access to enumeration records from the 1931 census, it is impossible to identify who settled in Winnipeg in the 1920s. The number of Jewish immigrants who settled in Winnipeg between 1920 and 1930 is based upon estimates of how many Jewish wives and children were sponsored by Winnipeg residents, references to the number of Jewish refugees entrusted to the care of the WDJIAS, and how many permits were issued to Winnipeg residents.

Conclusion

1 According to Arthur Chiel, as of August 1956, ten mutual benefit and free-loan associations and nine *landsmanshaftn* were still active. Arthur A. Chiel, *The Jews of Manitoba: A Social History* (Toronto: University of Toronto Press, 1961), 187, Appendix. When they dissolved, four associations—the Kiev Free Loan and Aid Association, the Achdus Free Loan Association, the Bessarabia Free Loan Association, and the Winnipeg Aid Association—donated their remaining funds to the Jewish Foundation of Manitoba. Jewish Foundation of Manitoba, Annual Report 2014, 41, 46, 54.

2 Irving Abella and Harold Troper, *None Is Too Many: Canada and the Jews of Europe 1933–1948* (Toronto: Lester and Orpen Dennys, 1983), 257–74.

3 Louis Rosenberg, *A Population Study of Winnipeg's Jewish Community* (Montreal: Canadian Jewish Congress, 1946), 28, Table X. The number of elderly Jewish residents increased from 3.7 percent of the total population to 6.3 percent.

4 Emmett M. Hall, *Royal Commission on Health Services* (Ottawa: R. Duhamel, Queen's Printer, 1964), 386.

BIBLIOGRAPHY

Primary Sources

Archival Resources

Archives of Manitoba

G7406, File 27, Charters Granted under the Charitable Associations Act

GR1557-A0014, Jewish Orphanage and Children's Aid Society of Western Canada

M584, Minutes of the Board of Management, Shaarey Zedek synagogue

MG 10, A2, Minutes of the Executive Council of the Winnipeg Board of Trade

P639, File 1, A Brief History of the Welfare Council of Greater Winnipeg

P639, File 1, Minutes of the Central Council of Social Agencies

P639, Files 4, 5, and 6, Minutes of the Social Planning Council

P2179, File 10, Mount Carmel Clinic

P3646, United Way of Winnipeg

Q24611, Application to Incorporate the Esther Robinson Orphanage and Children's Aid Society, 1914

Q24621, Memorandum of Association, the Hebrew Sick Benefit Association of Winnipeg, January, 1907

Q24670, Declaration of Association, 23 December 1913

Alex Dworkin Canadian Jewish Archives (formerly the Canadian Jewish Congress National Archives)

ICA, Canada Collection, Box 3, File AB 2.

JIAS, Series C, Box 9, File 2042 and File 2194

City of Winnipeg Archives

Associated Charities of the City of Winnipeg

City Comptroller's Annual Reports

Civic Charities Endorsement Bureau

Minutes of City Council

Jewish Heritage Centre Archives, Winnipeg

JHC 7, File 17, Minute Book, Jewish Medical Society of Winnipeg

JHC File 9F8, Constitution of the Hebrew Sick Benefit Association, 1931?

JHC 10, File 1, Jewish Orphanage and Children's Aid of Western Canada

JHC 10, File 2, Sec. 4, Constitution of the Jewish Orphanage and Children's Aid of Western Canada

JHC 10, File 9, By-Laws of the United Hebrew Relief

JHC 10, File 10, H.E. Wilder, "Historical Sketch, the Jewish Orphanage and Children's Aid of Western Canada," n.d.

JHC 11, File 3, Jewish Old Folk's Home of Western Canada

JHC 115, File 11, Jewish Immigrant Aid Society

JHC 116, File 3, Jewish Immigrant Aid Society

JHC 123, File 3, Jewish Immigrant Aid Society

JHC 124, File 3, Jewish Immigrant Aid Society

JHC, uncatalogued file, Jewish Organizations, Letters Patent

JHC, uncatalogued file, Immigrant Aid and Relief of War Sufferers, 1918

JHC, uncatalogued file, Immigrant Aid and Relief, 1920

JHC, uncatalogued file, Immigration and Relief, 1921–23

JHC, uncatalogued file, Western Canada's Jewish Fund for the Relief of War Sufferers, 1919

Library and Archives Canada

MG 26, J 13, Diaries of Prime Minister William Lyon Mackenzie King

MG 28, V 83, Jewish Colonization Association

MG 28, V 86, Jewish Family Services of the Baron de Hirsch Institute

MG 28, V 114 Western Division of the Jewish Immigrant Aid Society

RG 76, Immigration, Passenger Lists, 1865–1922

Manitoba Historical Society

Historic Sites, http://www.mhs.mb.ca/docs/sites/

Memorable Manitobans, http://www.mhs.mb.ca/docs/people/

Manitoba Legislative Library

Acts of the Legislature of Manitoba, 1923, 17th Parliament, 1st Session, Vol. 2.

Acts of the Legislature of Manitoba, 1926, 17th Parliament, 5th Session, Vol. 2.

Government of Manitoba, Third and Final Report of the Public Welfare Commission of Manitoba (Winnipeg: Phillip Purcell, 1920).

Journals of the Legislative Assembly of Manitoba.

Manitoba, Legislative Assembly, "Financial Statement, Esther Robinson Jewish Orphanage," *Sessional Papers, 1917*, vol. 50.

Manitoba, Provincial Treasurer, Public Accounts of Manitoba, 1922–23.

Manitoba, Public Accounts of Manitoba, 1934–35.

Manitoba, "Report of Activities of Minimum Wage Board from November 30th, 1918 to November 30th, 1919," Public Works Department, Annual Report for 1919, *Sessional Papers, 1918–19*, vol. 52.

Manitoba, "Third Annual Report of the Manitoba Mothers' Allowance Commission," *Sessional Papers, 1918–19*, vol. 52.

Manitoba, Royal Commission on the Administration of the Child Welfare Division, *Report of the Royal Commission Appointed by Order-in-Council Number 747-28 to Inquire into the Administration of the Child Welfare Division of the Department of Health and Public Welfare* (Winnipeg: Department of Health and Welfare, 1929).

The Manitoba Museum, Winnipeg

Oral Histories, Master Tapes nos. 266, 292, and 429

The Peel Library, University of Alberta

Peel's Prairie Provinces, http://peel.library.ualberta.ca/index.html

United Church Archives, Toronto

Methodist Church of Canada

YIVO Archives

HIAS/HICEM, 245.4, MKM 15.22, xd-2, Western Division of the Jewish Immigrant Aid Society of Canada

Canadian Government Documents and Reports

An Act Respecting Immigration and Immigrants, 1869. SC 32–33, c .10.

An Act Respecting Immigration and Immigrants, 1906. SC 6, c. 19.

An Act Respecting Immigration, 1910. SC 9–10, c. 27.

An Act Respecting British Nationality, Naturalization, and Aliens, 1914. SC 4–5, c. 44.

An Act to Amend the Immigration Act, 1919. SC 9–10, c. 25.

1911 Census. http://www.bac-lac.gc.ca/eng/census/1911/Pages/about-census.aspx.

1916 Census (Prairie Provinces). http://www.bac-lac.gc.ca/eng/census/1916/Pages/about-census.aspx.

Canada. Parliament. House of Commons. *Report of the Select Committee on Agriculture and Colonization*. Ottawa: F.A. Acland, 1928.

Census of Canada, 1880–81. Recensement du Canada, 1880–81. Ottawa: Maclean, Roger, and Company, 1882.

Census of Canada, 1890–91. Recensement du Canada, 1890–91. Ottawa: S.E. Dawson, 1893.

Census of Manitoba, 1885–6. Recensement de Manitoba, 1885–6. Ottawa: Maclean, Roger, 1887.

Fourth Census of Canada, 1901. Ottawa: S.E. Dawson, Printer to the King, 1902.

Fifth Census of Canada, 1911. Ottawa: Printer to the King, 1912.

Sixth Census of Canada, 1921. Ottawa: F.A. Acland, King's Printer, 1924.

Seventh Census of Canada, 1931. Ottawa: Patenaude, 1933.

Department of Immigration and Colonization. "Report of the Department of Immigration and Colonization for the Fiscal Year Ended March 31, 1921." *Sessional Papers, 1922*, no. 18.

———. "Report of the Department of Immigration and Colonization for the Fiscal Year Ended March 31, 1922." *Sessional Papers, 1923*, no. 13.

———. "Report of the Department of Immigration and Colonization for the Fiscal Year Ended March 31, 1923." *Sessional Papers, 1924*, no. 13.

———. *Report of the Department of Immigration and Colonization for the Fiscal Year Ended March 31, 1925.* Ottawa: F.A. Acland, 1926.

———. *Report of the Department of Immigration and Colonization for the Fiscal Year Ended March 31, 1926.* Ottawa: F.A. Acland, 1927.

———. *Report of the Department of Immigration and Colonization for the Fiscal Year Ended March 31, 1929.* Ottawa: F.C. Acland, 1930.

———. *Report of the Department of Immigration and Colonization for the Fiscal Year Ended March 31, 1930.* Ottawa: F.A. Acland, 1931.

———. *Report of the Department of Immigration and Colonization for the Fiscal Year Ended March 31, 1931.* Ottawa: F.A. Acland, 1932.

Department of the Interior. "Report of the Department of the Interior for 1914." *Sessional Papers 1915*, no. 25,.

Department of Labour. *Report of the Board of Inquiry into the Cost of Living in Canada.* Ottawa: J. de Tache, 1915.

Privy Council Office. Guide to Ministries since Confederation. http://www.pco-bcp.gc.ca/mgm/.

Statistics Canada. Tables by Subject: Population and Demography. https://www.statcan.gc.ca/tables-tableaux/sum-som/l01/ind01/l2_3867-eng.htm.

Other Government Documents and Reports

Government of Manitoba. *Third and Final Report of the Public Welfare Commission of Manitoba.* Winnipeg: Phillip Purcell, 1920.

Great Britain. House of Commons. *Royal Commission on the Natural Resources, Trade, and Legislation of Certain Portions of His Majesty's Dominions*, vols. 15–16. London: HMSO, 1917.

Hall, Emmett M. *Royal Commission on Health Services.* Ottawa: R. Duhamel, Queen's Printer, 1964.

Legislative Assembly of Ontario. *The Report of the Registrar of Friendly Societies of Ontario.* Toronto: Clarkson W. James, 1923.

Manitoba. *The Revised Statutes of Manitoba: Being a Consolidation of the Consolidated Statutes of Manitoba, with the Subsequent Public General Acts of the Legislature of Manitoba, to and Including Those of 1891.* Winnipeg: D. Philip, 1892.

Manitoba, Legislative Assembly. *The Revised Statutes of Manitoba, 1913: Being a Consolidation of the Revised Statutes of Manitoba Enacted in the Year 1902, with the Subsequent Public General Acts of the Legislature of Manitoba to and Including Those of 1913.* Winnipeg: James Hooper, King's Printer, 1914.

———. *Revised Statutes of Manitoba, 1940: Being a Revision and Consolidation of the Revised Statutes of Manitoba, 1913, and the Subsequent Public General Acts of the Legislature of Manitoba up to and Including Those of 1939.* Winnipeg: J.L. Cowie, King's Printer, 1940.

Periodicals and Newspapers

Canadian Jewish Chronicle
Canadian Jewish Review
Canadian Jewish Times
Canadian Magazine
Christian Guardian
Israelite Press
Jewish Post
Manitoba Free Press
Railway and Shipping World
The Voice
Western Jewish News
Winnipeg Telegram
Winnipeg Tribune

Secondary Sources

Abella, Irving, and Harold Troper. *None Is Too Many: Canada and the Jews of Europe 1933–1948.* Toronto: Lester and Orpen Dennys, 1983.

Arnold, A.J. "The Earliest Jews in Winnipeg, 1874–1882." *Beaver Magazine* 54, no. 2 (1974): 4–11.

Artibise, Alan F.J. *Winnipeg: A Social History of Urban Growth, 1874–1914.* Montreal: McGill-Queen's University Press, 1975.

Avery, Donald. *"Dangerous Foreigners": European Immigrant Workers and Labour Relations in Canada, 1896–1932.* Toronto: McClelland and Stewart, 1979.

Avrutin, Eugene M. *Jews and the Imperial State: Identification Politics in Tsarist Russia.* Ithaca, NY: Cornell University Press, 2010.

Barber, Marilyn. "Nationalism, Nativism, and the Social Gospel: The Protestant Church Response to Foreign Immigrants in Western Canada, 1897–1914." In *The Social Gospel in Canada*, edited by Richard Allen, 186–226. Ottawa: National Museums of Canada, 1975.

Baron, Salo W. *The Russian Jew under Tsars and Soviets.* 2nd ed. New York: Macmillan, 1976.

Beizer, Michael. "The American Joint Distribution Committee." In *The YIVO Encyclopedia of Jews in Eastern Europe*, vol. 1, edited by Gershon David Hundert, 39–44. New Haven, CT: Yale University Press, 2009.

Belkin, Simon. *Through Narrow Gates: A Review of Jewish Immigration, Colonization, and Immigrant Aid Work in Canada (1840–1940).* Montreal: Eagle Publishing Company, 1966.

Bellan, R.C. "Relief in Winnipeg: The Economic Background." MA thesis, University of Toronto, 1941.

Bellan, Reuben. *Winnipeg's First Century: An Economic History.* Winnipeg: Queenston, 1978.

Berenbaum, Michael, and Fred S. Skolnik, eds. *Encyclopedia Judaica*. 2nd ed. Vol. 16. Detroit: Macmillan Reference USA, 2007.

Bertolone, Paola. "The Text of Goldfadn's *Di kishefmarkherin* and the Operetta Tradition." In *Yiddish Theater: New Approaches*, edited by Joel Berkowitz. Oxford: Littman Library of Jewish Civilization, 2003.

Blanchard, James. "Rodmond P. Roblin, 1900–1915." In *Manitoba Premiers of the 19th and 20th Centuries*, edited by Barry Ferguson and Robert Wardhaugh,118–138. Regina: Canadian Plains Research Center, 2010.

Blanchard, Jim. *Winnipeg 1912*. Winnipeg: University of Manitoba Press, 2005.

Blatman, Daniel. "Bund." In *The YIVO Encyclopedia of Jews in Eastern Europe*, vol. 1, edited by Gershon David Hundert, 274–280. New Haven, CT: Yale University Press, 2009.

Bryden, Kenneth. *Old Age Pensions and Policy-Making in Canada*. Montreal: McGill-Queen's University Press, 1974.

Burrows, Paul. "'Apostle of Anarchy': Emma Goldman's First Visit to Winnipeg in 1907." *Manitoba History* 57 (2008): 2–15.

Bush, Peter. *The Presbyterian Church in Canada's Mission on the Prairies and North, 1885–1925*. Winnipeg: Watson and Dwyer, 2000.

Canadian Club of Winnipeg. *Annual Report of the Canadian Club of Winnipeg, 1904–1906*. Winnipeg: Canadian Club of Winnipeg, 1906.

———. *Fourth Annual Report of the Canadian Club of Winnipeg, 1907–1908*. Winnipeg: Canadian Club of Winnipeg, 1908.

———. *Fifth Annual Report of the Canadian Club of Winnipeg, 1908–1909*. Winnipeg: Canadian Club of Winnipeg, 1909.

———. *Ninth Annual Report of the Canadian Club of Winnipeg, 1912–191*3. Winnipeg: Canadian Club of Winnipeg, 1913.

———. *Tenth Annual Report of the Canadian Club of Winnipeg, 1913–1914*. Winnipeg: Canadian Club of Winnipeg, 1914.

———. *Eleventh Annual Report of the Canadian Club of Winnipeg, 1914–1915*. Winnipeg: Canadian Club of Winnipeg, 1915.

Chiel, Arthur A. *The Jews in Manitoba: A Social History*. Toronto: University of Toronto Press, 1961.

Chipman, George Fisher. "The Refining Process." *Canadian Magazine* 33, no. 6 (1909): 548–54.

———. "Winnipeg: The Melting Pot," *Canadian Magazine* 33, no. 5 (1909): 413–14.

Chisvin, Sharon, ed. *Jewish Life and Times*. Vol. 7. Winnipeg: Jewish Historical Society of Western Canada, 1998.

Dalin, David G. "*Tzedakah* with Dignity: Jewish Charity and Self-Help in Rabbinic Tradition." *Conservative Judaism* 51, no. 3 (1999): 3–22.

Devine, Edward T. *Welfare Work in Winnipeg: A Social Audit of Those Welfare Institutions which Participate in the Funding of the Federated Budget Board of Winnipeg*. Winnipeg: Federated Budget Board of Winnipeg, 1925.

Donnelly, Murray. *Dafoe of the* Free Press. Toronto: University of Toronto Press, 1968.

Dubnow, S.M. *History of the Jews in Russia and Poland*. Vol. 2. Philadelphia: Jewish Publication Society of America, 1946.

Easterbrook, W.T., and Hugh G.J. Aitkin. *Canadian Economic History*. Toronto: University of Toronto Press, 1988.

Emery, G.N. "The Methodist Church and the 'European Foreigner' of Winnipeg: The All People's Mission, 1889–1914." *MHS Transactions* 3, no. 28 (1971–72). http://www.mhs.mb.ca/docs/transactions/3/allpeoplesmission.shtml.

Emery, George, and J.C. Herbert Emery. *A Young Man's Benefit: The IOOF and Sickness Insurance in the United States and Canada, 1860–1929*. Montreal: McGill-Queen's University Press, 1999.

Epstein, Lisa Rae, "Caring for the Soul's House: The Jews of Russia and Health Care 1860–1914." PhD diss., Yale University, 1995.

Etkes, Immanuel. "Haskalah." In *The YIVO Encyclopedia of Jews in Eastern Europe*, vol. 1, edited by Gershon David Hundert, 681–688. New Haven, CT: Yale University Press, 2009.

Evans, Mrs. Sandford. "A Message from Winnipeg." In *Addresses before the Canadian Club of Toronto*, vol. 8, 234. Toronto: Warwick Brothers and Rutter, 1911.

Ewart, J.S. "Inaugural Presidential Address." In *Report of the Canadian Club of Winnipeg, 1904–1906*, 11–32. Winnipeg: Winnipeg Telegram, 1906?.

Federated Budget Board of Winnipeg. *A Great Community Organization: An Outline of the History, Constitution, Objects, and Accomplishments of the Federated Budget Board of Winnipeg*. Winnipeg: Federated Budget Board of Winnipeg, 1926.

Fishman, David E. *The Rise of Modern Yiddish Culture*. Pittsburgh: University of Pittsburgh Press, 2005.

Frankel, Jonathan. *Prophecy and Politics: Socialism, Nationalism, and the Russian Jews, 1862–1917*. Cambridge, UK: Cambridge University Press, 1981.

Freeze, ChaeRan F. *Jewish Marriage and Divorce in Imperial Russia*. Hanover, NH: Brandeis University Press, 2002.

Friesen, Gerald. *The Canadian Prairies: A History*. Toronto: University of Toronto Press, 1984.

Gale, Harry. "The Jewish Labour Movement in Winnipeg." In *First Annual Publication: A Selection of Papers Presented in 1968–1969*, 1–14. Winnipeg: Jewish Historical Society of Western Canada, 1970.

Gassenschmidt, Christoph. *Jewish Liberal Politics in Tsarist Russia, 1900–1914: The Modernization of Russian Jewry*. New York: New York University Press, 1995.

Gitelman, Zvi. "A Century of Jewish Politics in Eastern Europe: The Legacy of the Bund and Zionist Movement." In *The Emergence of Modern Jewish Politics: Bundism and Zionism in Eastern Europe*, edited by Zvi Gitelman, 5–12. Pittsburgh: University of Pittsburgh Press, 2003.

Gower, David. "A Note on Canadian Unemployment since 1921." *Perspectives on Income and Labour* 4, no. 3, 1992. http://www.statcan.gc.ca/pub/75-001-x/1992003/87-eng.pdf.

Gray, Mavis E. "The Great Wheat Boom: The Winnipeg Construction Industry, 1896–1914." MA thesis, University of Manitoba, 1997.

Greenbaum, Avraham. "Newspapers and Periodicals." In *The YIVO Encyclopedia of Jews in Eastern Europe*, vol 1., edited by Gershon David Hundert, 1260–68. New Haven, CT: Yale University Press, 2009.

Greenberg, Annalee. *The Sharon Home: Building on a Tradition of Caring*. Winnipeg: Sharon Home, 1997.

Gutkin, Harry. *Journey into Our Heritage: The Story of the Jewish People in the Canadian West*. Toronto: Lester and Orpen Dennys, 1980.

Hart, Arthur Daniel, ed. *The Jew in Canada*. Toronto: Jewish Publications, 1926.

Henderson's Winnipeg Directory. Winnipeg: Henderson Directories, 1920.

Henry, Wade A. "W. Sanford Evans and the Canadian Club of Winnipeg, 1904–1919." *Manitoba History* 27 (1994): 2–8.

Herstein, Harvey H. "The Growth of the Winnipeg Jewish Community and the Evolution of Its Educational Institutions." MA thesis, University of Manitoba, 1964.

Hiebert, Daniel. "Class, Ethnicity, and Residential Structure: The Social Geography of Winnipeg, 1901–1921." *Journal of Historical Geography* 17, no. 1 (1991): 56–86.

Himmel, David. *A Camp Story: The History of Lake of the Woods and Greenwoods Camps*. Charleston, SC: History Press, 2012.

Horowitz, Brian. *Jewish Philanthropy and Enlightenment in Late-Tsarist Russia*. Seattle: University of Washington Press, 2009.

Jewish Foundation of Manitoba. *Annual Report*. Winnipeg: Jewish Foundation of Manitoba, 2014.

Jones, Esyllt W. *Influenza 1918: Disease, Death, and Struggle in Winnipeg*. Toronto: University of Toronto Press, 2007.

Kahan, Arcadius. "Impact of Industrialization on the Jews in Tsarist Russia." In *Essays in Jewish Social and Economic History*, edited by Roger Weiss, 1–69. Chicago: University of Chicago Press, 1986.

Kelley, Ninette, and Michael Trebilcock. *The Making of the Mosaic: A History of Canadian Immigration Policy*. 2nd ed. Toronto: University of Toronto Press, 2010.

Klier, John D. "Russian Jewry on the Eve of the Pogroms." In *Pogroms: Anti-Jewish Violence in Modern Jewish History*, edited by John D. Klier and Shlomo Lambroza, 3–12. Cambridge, UK: Cambridge University Press, 1992.

Kramer, Reinhold, and Tom Mitchell. *When the State Trembled: How A.J. Andrews and the Citizens' Committee Broke the Winnipeg General Strike*. Toronto: University of Toronto Press, 2010.

Kuznets, Simon. "Immigration of Russian Jews to the United States: Background and Structure." *Perspectives in American History* 9 (1975): 35–127.

Lederhendler, Eli. "Classless: On the Social Status of Jews in Russia and Eastern Europe in the Late Nineteenth Century." *Contemporary Studies in Society and History* 50, no. 2 (2008): 509–34.

———. *The Road to Modern Jewish Politics: Political Tradition and Political Reconstruction in the Jewish Community of Tsarist Russia*. New York: Oxford University Press, 1989.

Levin, Vladimir. "The Jewish Socialist Parties in Russia in the Period of Reaction." In *The Revolution of 1905 and Russia's Jews*, edited by Stefani Hoffman and Ezra Mendelsohn, 111–127. Philadelphia: University of Pennsylvania Press, 2008.

———. "Orthodox Jewry and the Russian Government: An Attempt at Rapprochement, 1907–1914." *East European Jewish Affairs* 29, no. 2 (2009): 187–204.

Levine, Allan. *Coming of Age: A History of the Jewish People of Manitoba*. Winnipeg: Heartland Associates, 2009.

———. *The Exchange: 100 Years of Trading Grain in Winnipeg*. Winnipeg: Peguis, 1987.

Levitats, Isaac. *The Jewish Community in Russia, 1844–1917*. Jerusalem: Posner and Sons, 1981.

Lindenmeyr, Adele. *Poverty Is Not a Vice: Charity, Society, and State in Imperial Russia*. Princeton, NJ: Princeton University Press, 1996.

Lohr, Eric. "The Russian Army and the Jews: Mass Deportation, Hostages, and Violence during World War I." *Russian Review* 60, no. 3 (2001): 404–19.

Lowe, Heinz-Dietrich. *The Tsars and the Jews: Reform, Reaction, and Anti-Semitism in Imperial Russia, 1772–1917*. Chur, Switzerland: Harwood Academic Publications, 1993.

———. "From Charity to Social Policy: The Emergence of Jewish 'Self-Help' Organizations in Russia, 1800–1914." *East European Jewish Affairs* 27, no. 2 (1997): 53–75.

Magrath, C.A. *Canada's Growth and Some Problems Affecting It*. Ottawa: Mortimer Press, 1910.

Martynowych, Orest T. "Ukrainian Section of the Socialist Party of Canada/Social Democratic Party of Canada." Centre for Ukrainian Canadian Studies, University of Manitoba. http://umanitoba.ca/faculties/arts/departments/ukrainian_canadian_studies/media/12_The_Ukrainian_Section_of_the_SPC_and_SDPC.pdf.

McCormack, A. Ross. "Networks among British Immigrants and Accommodation to Canadian Society: Winnipeg, 1900–1914." In *Immigration in Canada: Historical Perspectives,* edited by Gerald Tulchinsky, 203–222. Toronto: Copp Clark Longman, 1994.

———. *Reformers, Rebels, and Revolutionaries: The Western Canadian Radical Movement, 1899–1919*. Toronto: University of Toronto Press, 1977.

McKinnon, Mary. "Trade Unions and Employment Stability at the Canadian Pacific Railway, 1903–1929." In *Origins of the Modern Career*, edited by David Mitch, John Brown, and Marco D.H. van Leeuve, 126–124. Aldershot, UK: Ashgate, 2004.

McLaren, Angus. *Our Own Master Race: Eugenics in Canada, 1885–1945*. Toronto: McClelland and Stewart, 1990.

Medovy, Harry. "The Early Jewish Physicians in Manitoba" *MHS Transactions* 3, no. 29 (1972–1973): n.p. http://www.mhs.mb.ca/docs/transactions/3/jewishphysicians.shtml.

Meir, Natan. "From Communal Charity to National Welfare: Jewish Orphanages in Eastern Europe before and after World War I." *East European Jewish Affairs* 39, no. 1 (2009): 19–34.

———. *Kiev, Jewish Metropolis: A History, 1859–1914*. Bloomington: Indiana University Press, 2010.

Mendelsohn, Ezra. *Class Struggle in the Pale: The Formative Years of the Jewish Workers' Movement in Tsarist Russia*. Cambridge, UK: Cambridge University Press, 1970.

———, ed. *The Revolution of 1905 and Russia's Jews*. Philadelphia: University of Pennsylvania Press, 2008.

Metcalfe, Alan. *Canada Learns to Play: The Emergence of Organized Sport, 1807–1914*. Toronto: McClelland and Stewart, 1987.

Miller, Tamara. "'All Our Friends and Patients Know Us': The Margaret Scott Nursing Mission." In *Prairie Metropolis: New Essays in Winnipeg Social History*, edited by Esyllt W. Jones and Gerald Friesen, 82–100. Winnipeg: University of Manitoba Press, 2009.

Morozov, Boris. "Out of the Soviet Union: The Exiles and Pompolit." In *Exiled to Palestine: The Emigration of Zionist Convicts from the Soviet Union, 1924–1934*, edited by Ziva Galili and Boris Morozov, 14–40. London: Routledge, 2006.

Moss, Kenneth. "Printing and Publishing after 1800." In *The YIVO Encyclopedia of Jews in Eastern Europe*, vol. 2, edited by Gershon David Hundert, 1459–1468. New Haven, CT: Yale University Press, 2009.

Murray, S.C. *The Challenge of Our Prairie Provinces*. Toronto: Committee of the Forward Movement, Presbyterian Church, 1920.

Nadav, Mordechai. *The Jews of Pinsk, 1506–1880*. Edited by Mark Jay Mirsky and Moshe Rosman. Stanford, CA: Stanford University Press, 2008.

Narvey, Fred. "Personal Perspective on the Leftist Theatre of the 1930s." In *Jewish Radicalism in Winnipeg, 1905–1960*, edited by Daniel Stone, 82–86. Winnipeg: Jewish Heritage Centre of Western Canada, 2002.

Nathans, Benjamin. *Beyond the Pale: The Jewish Encounter with Late Imperial Russia*. Berkeley: University of California Press, 2002.

Nerbas, Don. "Wealth and Privilege: An Analysis of Winnipeg's Early Business Elite." *Manitoba History* 47 (2004): 42–64. http://www.mhs.mb.ca/docs/mb_history/47/index.shtml.

Norman, Theodore. *An Outstretched Arm: A History of the Jewish Colonization Association*. London: Routledge and Kegan Paul, 1985.

Orbach, Alexander. "The Jewish People's Group and Jewish Politics in Tsarist Russia, 1906–1914." *Modern Judaism* 10, no. 1 (1990): 1–15.

Peled, Yoav. *Class and Ethnicity in the Pale: The Political Economy of Jewish Workers' Nationalism in Late Imperial Russia*. New York: St. Martin's Press, 1989.

Penslar, Derek J. *Shylock's Children: Economics and Jewish Identity in Modern Europe*. Berkeley: University of California Press, 2001.

Petrovsky-Shtern, Yohanan. *Jews in the Russian Army, 1827–1917*. Oxford: Oxford University Press, 2009.

Pioneer Winnipeg Women's Work, 1883–1907. Winnipeg: Winnipeg Telegram, 1907.

Polonsky, Antony. *The Jews in Poland and Russia, Volume I, 1350–1881*. Oxford: Littman Library of Jewish Civilization, 2010.

———. "Warsaw." In *The YIVO Encyclopedia of Jews in Eastern Europe*, vol. 2, edited by Gershon David Hundert, 1993–2004. New Haven, CT: Yale University Press, 2009.

Portnoy, Samuel A. *Vladimir Medem: The Life and Soul of a Legendary Jewish Socialist*. New York: Ktav Publishing House, 1979.

Rizzo, Dee Dee. "A History of the Mount Carmel Clinic: An Ethnic and Socio-Economic Perspective." Major paper, Department of Foundations/Administration, University of Manitoba, 1980.

Roberts, Barbara. *Whence They Came: Deportation from Canada, 1900–1935*. Ottawa: University of Ottawa Press, 1988.

Rohold, S.B. *The Jews in Canada*. 2nd ed. Toronto: Board of Home Missions, Presbyterian Church, 1913.

Rome, David. *Clouds in the Thirties: On Anti-Semitism in Canada, 1929–1939.* Montreal: Canadian Jewish Congress, 1979.

———. *Early Documents on the Canadian Jewish Congress: 1914–1921.* Canadian Jewish Archives: New Series, No. 1. Montreal: National Archives, Canadian Jewish Congress, 1974.

Rosenberg, Louis. *A Population Study of Winnipeg's Jewish Community.* Montreal: Canadian Jewish Congress, 1946.

Rosenberg, Louis, and M. Weinfeld. *Canada's Jews: A Social and Economic Study of Jews in Canada in the 1930s.* Montreal: McGill-Queen's University Press, 1993.

Rosenthal, Henry. "Agricultural Colonies in Present Day Russia." In *The Jewish Encyclopedia: A Descriptive Record of the Earliest Times to the Present Day*, vol 1., edited by Isadore Singer, 252–256. New York: Funk and Wagnalls, 1901.

Rubinow, Isaac M. *Economic Condition of the Jews in Russia.* New York: Arno Press, 1975.

Russin, Geraldine Carol. "The Ukrainian United Church in Winnipeg, Manitoba, 1903–1961: A History of a Unique Religious Experience." MA thesis, University of Manitoba, 1999.

Scott, W.D. "Immigration and Population." In *Canada and Its Provinces: A History of the Canadian People and Their Institutions*, vol. 7, edited by Adam Shortt and Arthur G. Doughty, 517–590. Toronto: Publishers Association of Canada, 1914.

Silber, Marcos. "Credit." In *The YIVO Encyclopedia of Jews in Eastern Europe*, vol. 1, edited by Gershon David Hundert, 361–363. New Haven, CT: Yale University Press, 2009.

Skolnik, Fred, and Michael Berenbaum, eds. *Encyclopaedia Judaica.* Vol. 17. Detroit: Macmillan Reference USA in association with the Keter Publishing House, 2007.

Slonim, Reubin. *Grand to Be an Orphan.* Toronto: Clarke, Irwin and Company, 1983.

Smith, Allan. "The Myth of the Self-Made Man in English Canada." *Canadian Historical Review* 59, no. 2 (1978): 189–219.

Smith, Doug. *Let Us Rise! An Illustrated History of the Manitoba Labour Movement.* Vancouver: New Star Books, 1985.

———. *The Winnipeg Labour Council, 1894–1994: A Century of Labour Education, Organization, and Agitation.* Winnipeg: Manitoba Labour Education Centre, 1994.

Soyer, Daniel. *Jewish Immigrant Associations and American Identity in New York, 1880–1939.* Cambridge, MA: Harvard University Press, 1997.

Srebrnik, Henry. *Creating the Chupah: The Zionist Movement and the Drive for Jewish Communal Unity in Canada, 1898–1921.* Boston: Academic Studies Press, 2011.

Stampfer, Shaul. "Heder Study, Knowledge of Torah, and the Maintenance of Social Stratification." *Studies in Jewish Education* 3 (1988): 271–89.

———. "Scientific Welfare and Lonely Old People: The Development of Old-Age Homes." In *Families, Rabbis, and Education: Traditional Jewish Society in Nineteenth-Century Eastern Europe*, edited by Shaul Stampfer, 86–101. Oxford: Littman Library of Jewish Civilization, 2010.

Stanislowski, Michael. "Russian Jewry, the Russian State, and the Dynamics of Russian Emancipation." In *Paths of Emancipation: Jews, States, and Citizenship*, edited by Pierre Birnbaum and Ira Katznelson, 262–284. Princeton, NJ: Princeton University Press, 1995.

Stein, Sarah Abrevaya. *Making Jews Modern: The Yiddish and Ladino Press in the Russian and Ottoman Empires*. Bloomington: Indiana University Press, 2004.

Stone, Daniel. "Moving South: The Other Jewish Winnipeg before the Second World War." *Manitoba History* 76 (2014): 2–11.

Strong-Boag, Victoria. "'Wages for Housework': Mothers' Allowances and the Beginnings of Social Security in Canada." *Journal of Canadian Studies* 14, no. 1 (1979): 24–34.

Szajkowski, Zosa. "Private and Organized American Jewish Overseas Relief (1914–1938)." *American Jewish Historical Quarterly* 57, no. 1 (1967): 52–53, 55–106.

Tapper, Lawrence F., ed. *A Biographical Dictionary of Canadian Jewry, 1909–1914: From the* Canadian Jewish Times. Teaneck, N.J.: Avotaynu, 1992.

Tillotson, Shirley. "A New Taxpayer for a New State: Charitable Fundraising and the Origins of the Welfare State." In *Social Fabric or Patchwork Quilt: The Development of Social Policy in Canada*, edited by Raymond B. Blake and Jeffrey A. Keshen, 138–155. Peterborough, ON: Broadview Press, 2006.

Tobias, Henry J. *The Jewish Bund in Russia: From Its Origins to 1905*. Stanford, CA: Stanford University Press, 1972.

Trachtenberg, Henry. "Ethnic Politics on the Urban Frontier: 'Fighting Joe' Martin and the Jews of Winnipeg, 1893–1896." *Manitoba History* 35 (1998): 2–14.

———. "'The Old Clo' Move': Anti-Semitism, Politics, and the Jews of Winnipeg, 1882–1921." PhD diss., York University, 1984.

———. "Peddling, Politics, and Winnipeg's Jews, 1891–1895: The Political Acculturation of an Urban Immigrant Community." *Histoire sociale/Social History* 57, no. 29 (1996): 159–86.

———. "The Winnipeg Jewish Community and Politics: The Inter-War Years, 1919–1939." *Transactions of the Historical and Scientific Society of Manitoba*, Series III, 34 and 35 (1977–78 and 1978–79): 115–53.

Tulchinsky, Gerald. *Branching Out: The Transformation of the Canadian Jewish Community*. Toronto: Stoddart, 1998.

———. *Canada's Jews: A People's Journey*. Toronto: University of Toronto Press, 2008.

Turnbull, Aleda Winnifred. "Progressive Social Policy in Manitoba, 1915–1939." MA thesis, University of Manitoba, 1980.

Urquhart, M.C., and Kenneth A.H. Buckley. *Historical Statistics of Canada*. Toronto: Macmillan, 1965.

Ury, Scott. "Der Fraynd." In *The YIVO Encyclopedia of Jews in Eastern Europe*, vol. 2, edited by Gershon David Hundert, 547–8. New Haven, CT: Yale University Press, 2009.

Usiskin, Roz. "'The Alien and the Bolshevik in Our Midst': The 1919 Winnipeg General Strike." *Jewish Life and Times* 5 (1988): 28–49.

———. "Toward a Theoretical Reformulation between Political Ideology, Social Class, and Ethnicity: A Case Study of the Winnipeg Jewish Radical Community." MA thesis, University of Manitoba, 1978.

———. "The Winnipeg Jewish Community: Its Radical Elements, 1905–1918." *MHS Transactions* 3, no. 33 (1976–77): 1–26.

———. "Winnipeg's Jewish Women of the Left: Traditional and Radical." In *Jewish Radicalism in Winnipeg, 1905–1960*, edited by Daniel Stone, 106–121. Winnipeg: Jewish Heritage Centre of Western Canada, 2002.

Veidlinger, Jeffrey. *Jewish Public Culture in the Late Russian Empire*. Bloomington: Indiana University Press, 2009.

Vineberg, Robert. "Welcoming Immigrants at the Gateway to Canada's West: Immigration Halls in Winnipeg, 1872–1975." *Manitoba History* 65 (2011): 14–22.

Virginia Commonwealth University Social Welfare History Project. http://www.socialwelfarehistory.com/people/devine-edward-t-3/.

Vital, David. *A People Apart: The Jews in Europe, 1789–1939*. Oxford: Oxford University Press, 1999.

Wahl, Robert. *The Generation of 1914*. Cambridge, MA: Harvard University Press, 1979.

Weinberg, David H. *Between Tradition and Modernity*. New York: Holmes and Meier, 1996.

Weinberg, Robert. "The Russian Right Responds to 1905: Visual Depictions of Jews in Postrevolutionary Russia." In *The Revolution of 1905 and Russia's Jews*, edited by Stefani Hoffman and Ezra Mendelsohn, 55–69. Philadelphia: University of Pennsylvania Press, 2008.

Wilder, H.E., ed. *The Hundredth Anniversary Souvenir of Jewish Emancipation in Canada and the 50th Anniversary of the Jew in the West*. Winnipeg: Israelite Press, 1932.

"Winnipeg Canadian Pacific Railway Station." *Canada's Historic Places*. http://www.historicplaces.ca/en/rep-reg/place-lieu.aspx?id=6345&pid=13321&h=Winnipeg,CPR,Station.

"Winnipeg Development and Industrial Bureau." In *Gateway City: Documents on the City of Winnipeg, 1873–1913*, edited by Alan F.J. Artibise, 141–178. Winnipeg: Manitoba Records Society Publications and University of Manitoba, 1979.

Winnipeg Labour Council. *1894–1994: A Century of Labour Education, Organization, and Agitation*. http://www.winnipeglabour.ca/pdf/WLC%20History.pdf.

Wischnitzer, Mark. *To Dwell in Safety: The Story of Jewish Migration since 1800*. Philadelphia: Jewish Publication Society of America, 1948.

Wolitz, Seth L. "Forging a Hero for the Jewish Stage: Goldfadn's *Bar Kokhba*." *Shofar* 20, no. 3 (2002): 53–65.

Woodsworth, J.S. "The Immigrant Invasion after the War—Are We Ready for It?" In *Eleventh Annual Report of the Canadian Club of Winnipeg, 1914–1915*, 28–33. Winnipeg: Canadian Club of Winnipeg, 1916.

———. *My Neighbour*. Toronto: University of Toronto Press, 1972.

———. *Strangers within Our Gates: Or, Becoming Canadians*. Toronto: F.C. Stephenson, 1909; reprinted, Toronto: University of Toronto Press, 1971.

Wortman, Richard. "Nicholas II and the Revolution." In *The Revolution of 1905 and Russia's Jews*, edited by Stefani Hoffman and Ezra Mendelsohn. Philadelphia: University of Pennsylvania Press, 2008.

Wright, C.P., and J.S. Davis. "Canada as a Producer and Exporter of Wheat." *Wheat Studies* 1, no. 8 (1925): 217–87.

Zalkin, Mordechai. "Charity." In *The YIVO Encyclopedia of Jews in Eastern Europe*, vol. 1, edited by Gershon David Hundert. New Haven, CT: Yale University Press, 2009.

Zolf, Falek. *Di leste fun a dor: Heymishe geshtaltn*. Winnipeg: Israelite Press, 1952.

ILLUSTRATION CREDITS

1. Courtesy of University of Alberta Library, Peel's Prairie Provinces, PC001219. **2.** Archives of Manitoba, N21668. **3.** Map design by Weldon Hiebert. Contains information licensed under the Open Government Licence – Canada. **4–7.** Courtesy of Jewish Heritage Centre of Western Canada (JHCWC). **8.** *Jewish Post*, 21 January 1927. **9.** JHCWC. **10.** *Report of the Jewish People's Relief Committee Convention*, April 1918, JDC Archives, AR191418-2-3-60. **11–13.** JHCWC. **14.** *Winnipeg Tribune*, 11 August 1919. **15.** Courtesy of Manitoba Historical Society. **16–23.** JHCWC. **24.** Archives of Manitoba, Towne Studio Fonds, Box Q8761, detail from Mount Carmel Board of Directors 1929 photo. **25.** Courtesy of the Sheps family. **26–27.** Courtesy of Alex Dworkin Canadian Jewish Archives. **28.** JHCWC.

INDEX